TEDDY

TEDDY

LAURENCE LUCKINBILL

ADAPTED BY ERYCK TAIT

DEAD RECKONING

Annapolis, Maryland

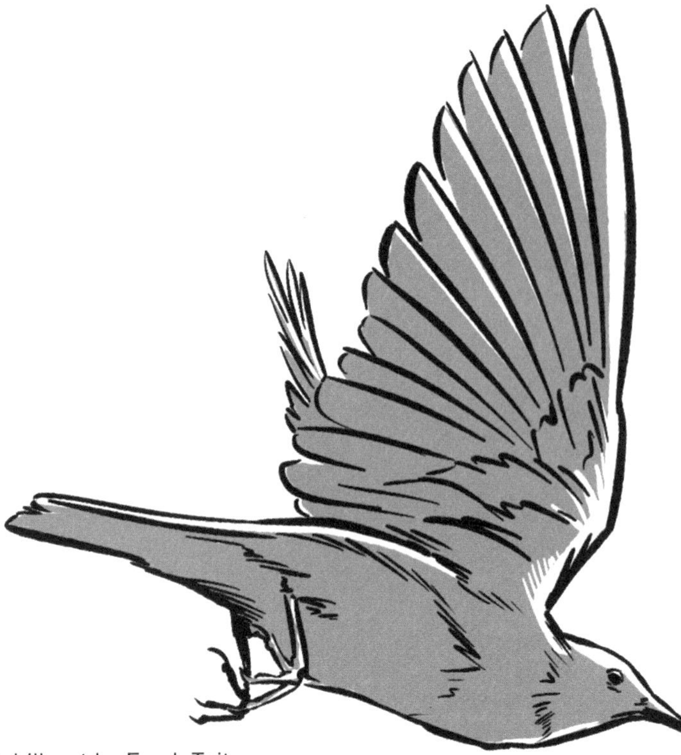

Published by Dead Reckoning
291 Wood Road
Annapolis, MD 21402

Library of Congress Cataloging-in-Publication Data
Names: Luckinbill, Laurence, author. | Tait, Eryck, illustrator.
Title: Teddy / Laurence Luckinbill ; adapted by Eryck Tait.
Description: Annapolis, Maryland : Dead Reckoning, 2021.
Identifiers: LCCN 2020027592 (print) | LCCN 2020027593 (ebook) | ISBN 9781682474877 (paperback) | ISBN 9781682475621 (epub) | ISBN 9781682475621 (pdf)
Subjects: LCSH: Roosevelt, Theodore, 1858–1919—Juvenile literature. | Roosevelt, Theodore, 1858–1919—Comic books, strips, etc. | Roosevelt, Theodore, 1858–1919—Family—Juvenile literature. | Roosevelt, Theodore, 1858–1919—Family—Comic books, strips, etc. | Roosevelt family—Juvenile literature. | Roosevelt family—Comic books, strips, etc. | Presidents—United States—Biography—Juvenile literature. | Presidents—United States—Biography—Comic books, strips, etc. | LCGFT: Graphic novels.
Classification: LCC E757 .L94 2021 (print) | LCC E757 (ebook) | DDC 973.91/1092 [B]—dc23
LC record available at https://lccn.loc.gov/2020027592
LC ebook record available at https://lccn.loc.gov/2020027593

∞ Print editions meet the requirements of ANSI/NISO z39.48-1992 (Permanence of Paper).
Printed in the United States of America.

29 28 27 26 25 24 23 22 21 9 8 7 6 5 4 3 2 1
First printing

I dedicate this story to **THEODORE ROOSEVELT**,
who dreamed of a kind, just, and honest America—
and, like the man in the arena he wrote about,
"dared greatly" to make it real.

And to my family, Lucie, Nicholas, Benjamin,
Simon, Joseph, and Kate.

—LAURENCE "LARRY" LUCKINBILL

This book would not have been possible
without the endless support and encouragement
from my friends and family.
I remain humbled to be so fortunate.
All my love to my wife, Rachel,
and a special thanks to the generous
and tireless staff at Sagamore Hill.

—ERYCK TAIT

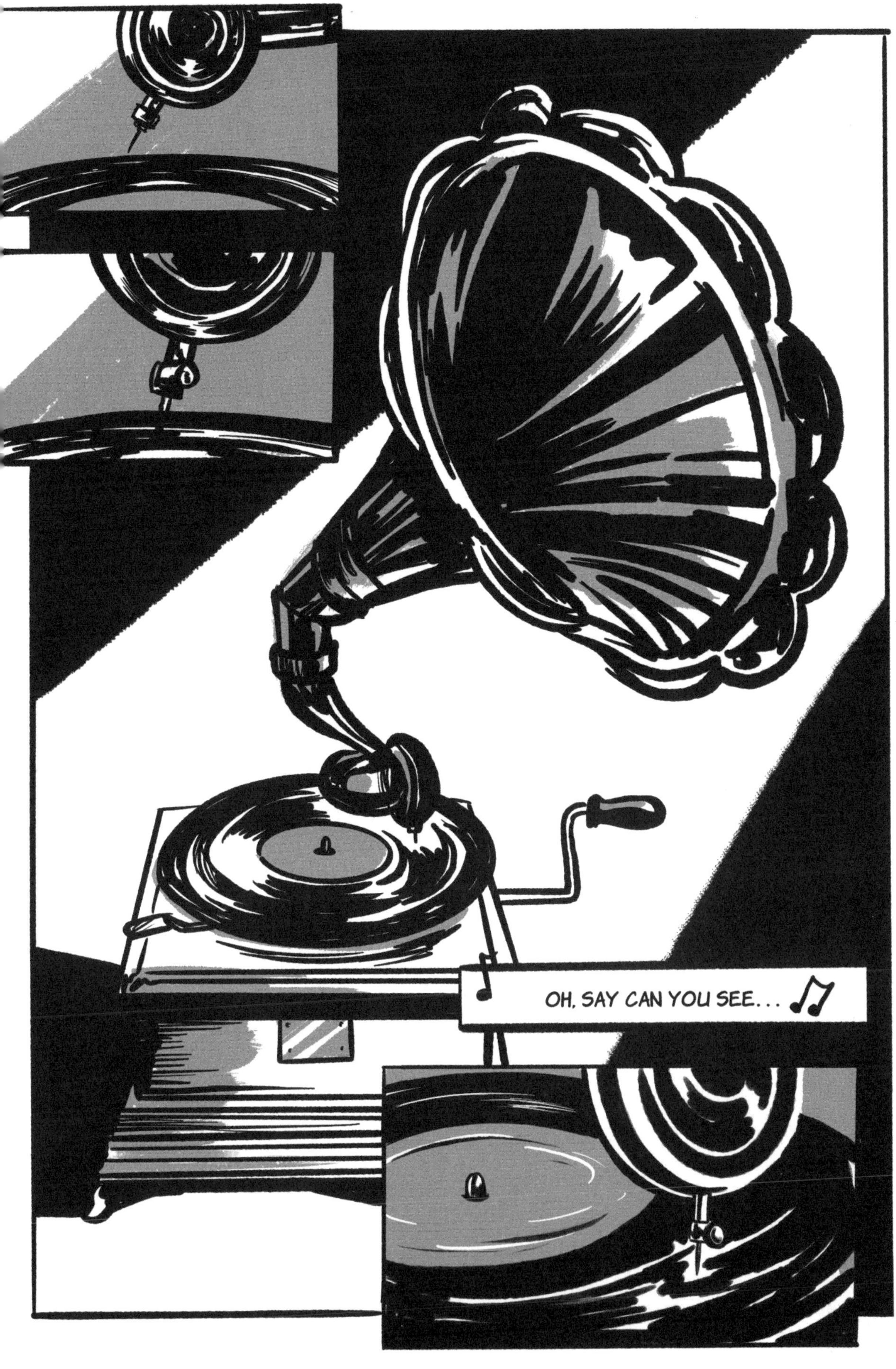
OH, SAY CAN YOU SEE...

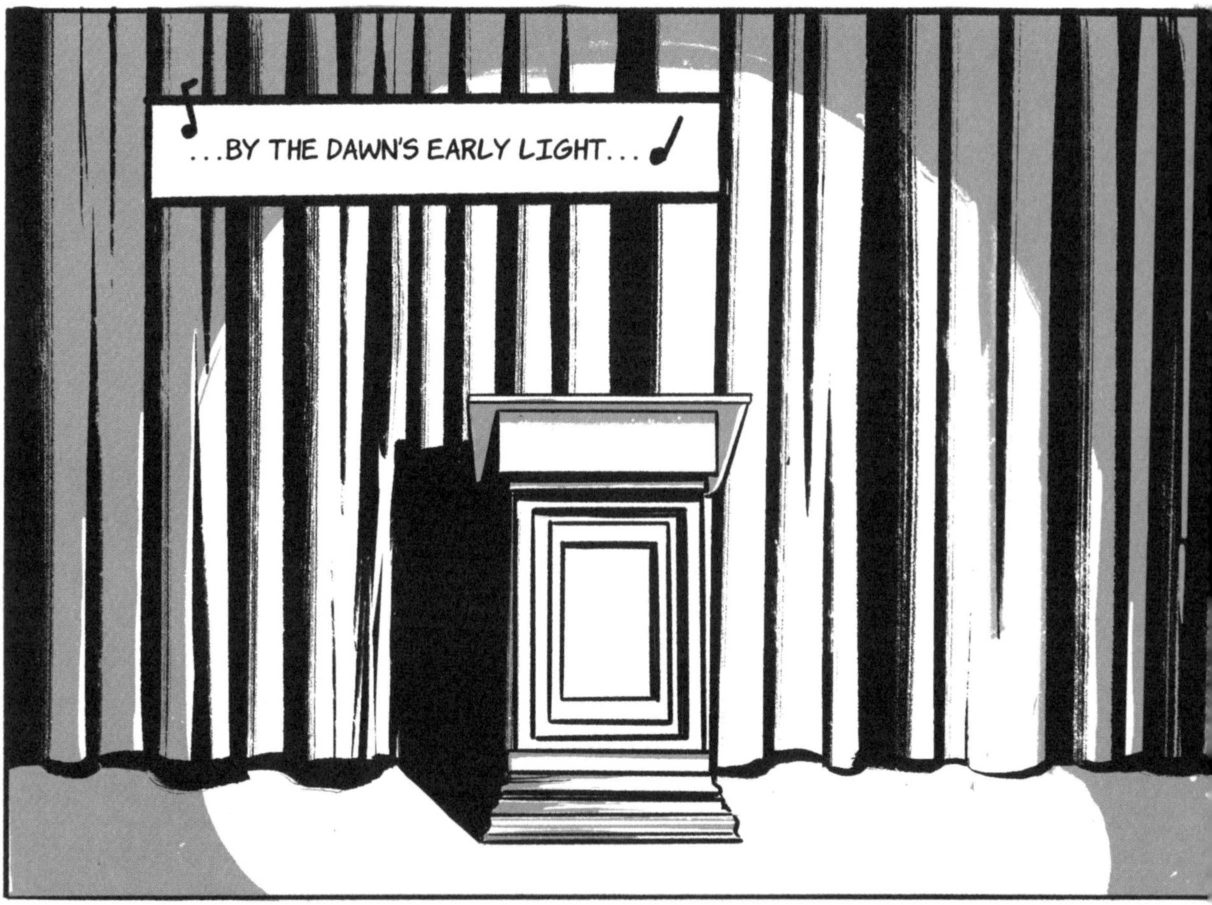
...BY THE DAWN'S EARLY LIGHT...

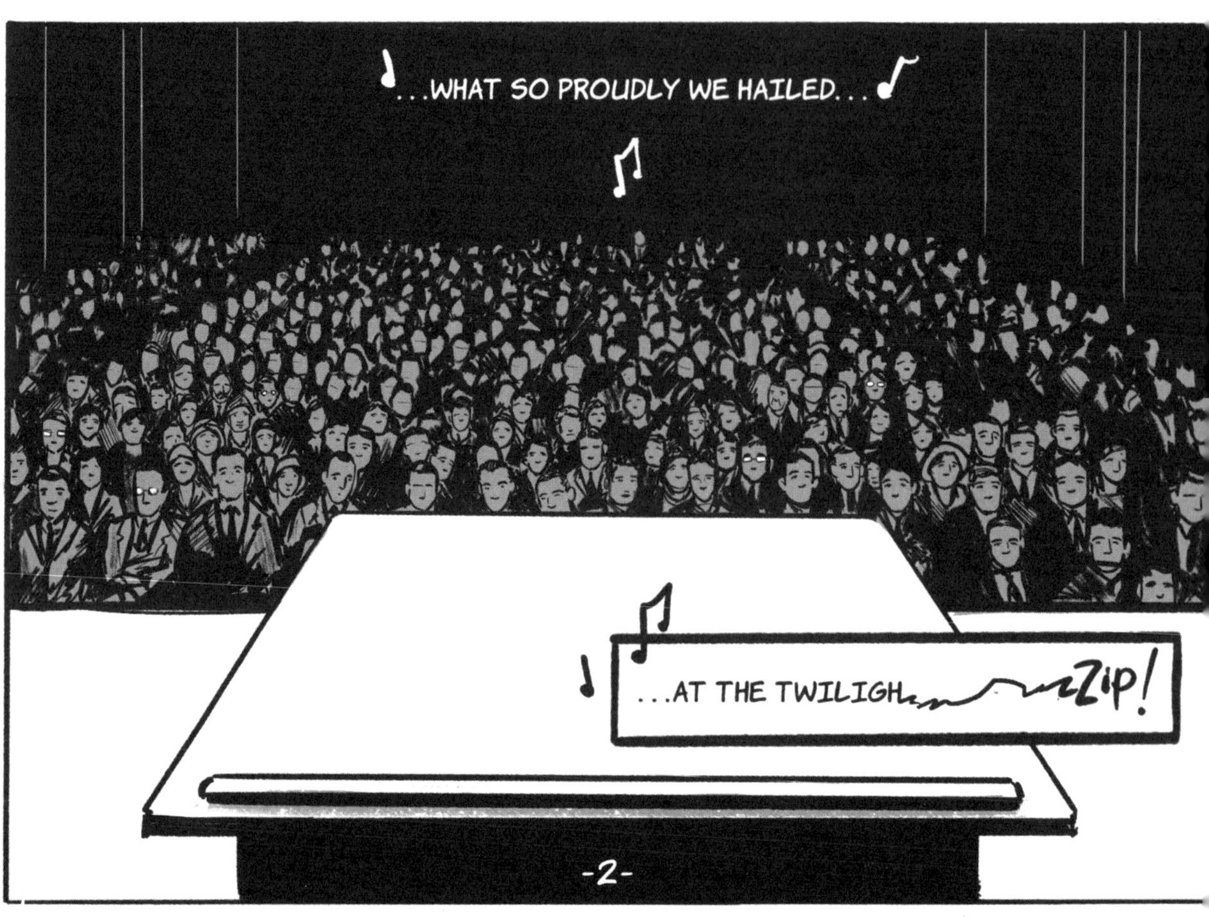
...WHAT SO PROUDLY WE HAILED...
...AT THE TWILIGH
ZIP!

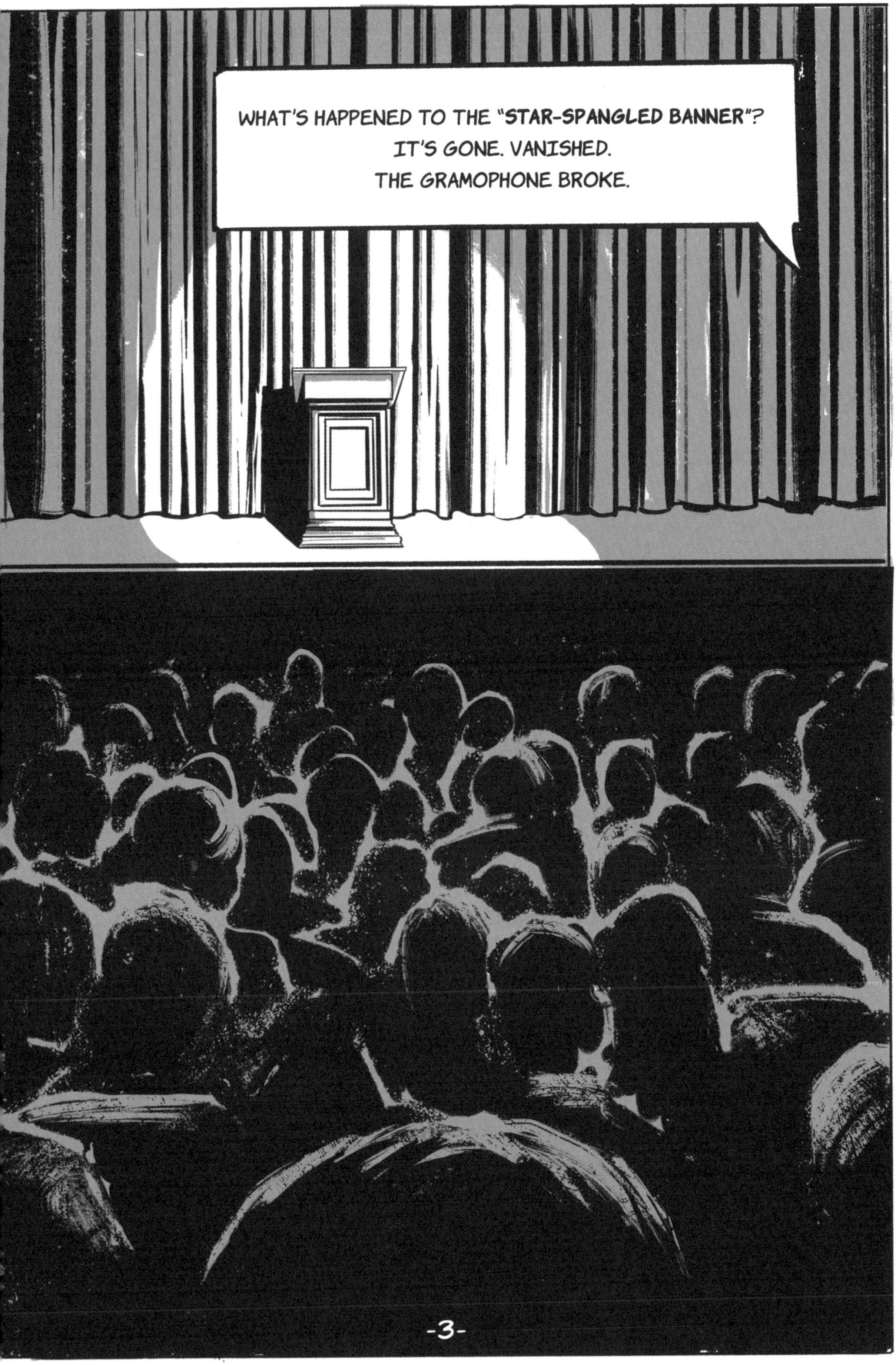
WHAT'S HAPPENED TO THE "STAR-SPANGLED BANNER"? IT'S GONE. VANISHED. THE GRAMOPHONE BROKE.

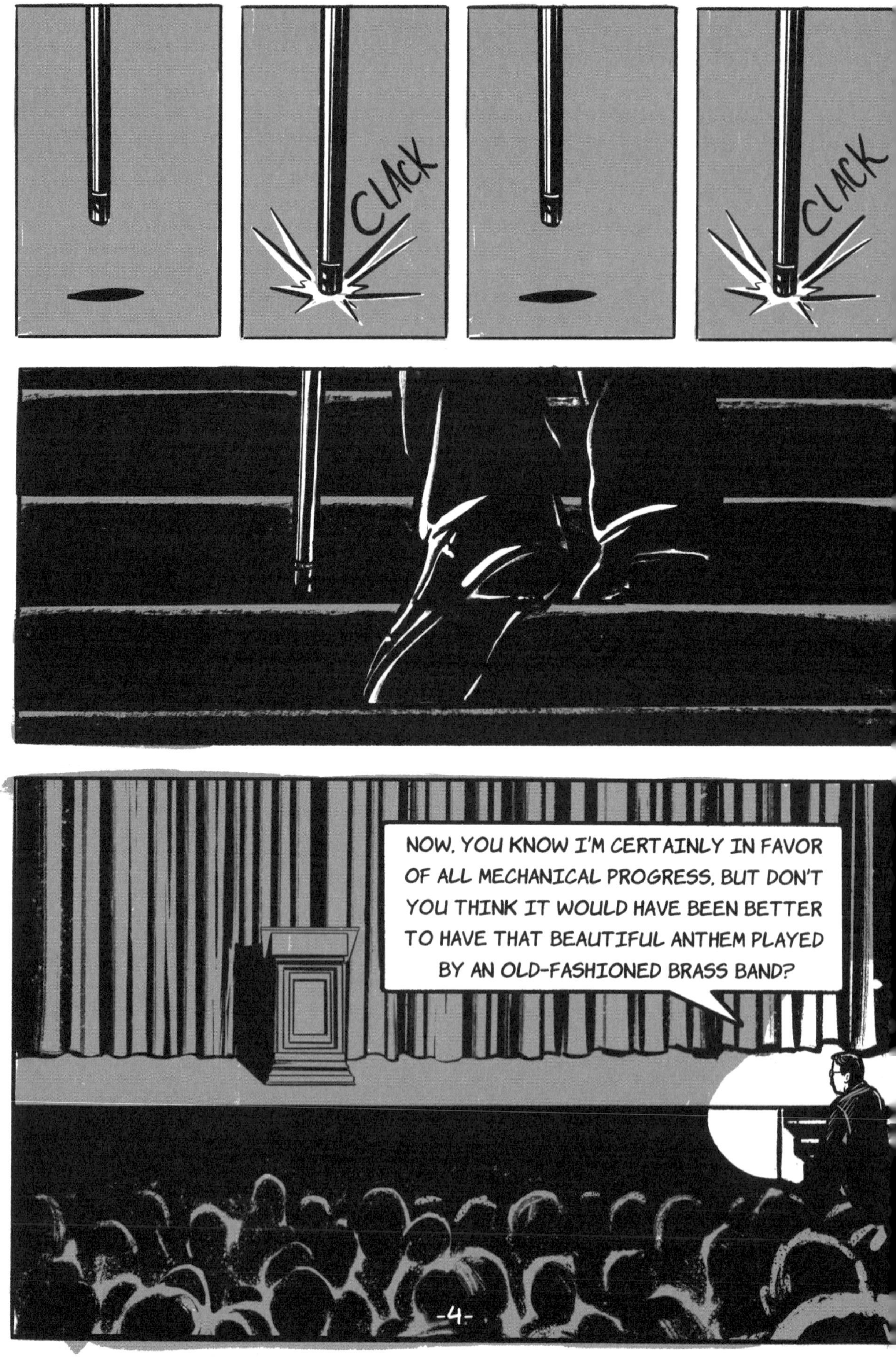
CLACK
CLACK
NOW, YOU KNOW I'M CERTAINLY IN FAVOR OF ALL MECHANICAL PROGRESS, BUT DON'T YOU THINK IT WOULD HAVE BEEN BETTER TO HAVE THAT BEAUTIFUL ANTHEM PLAYED BY AN OLD-FASHIONED BRASS BAND?

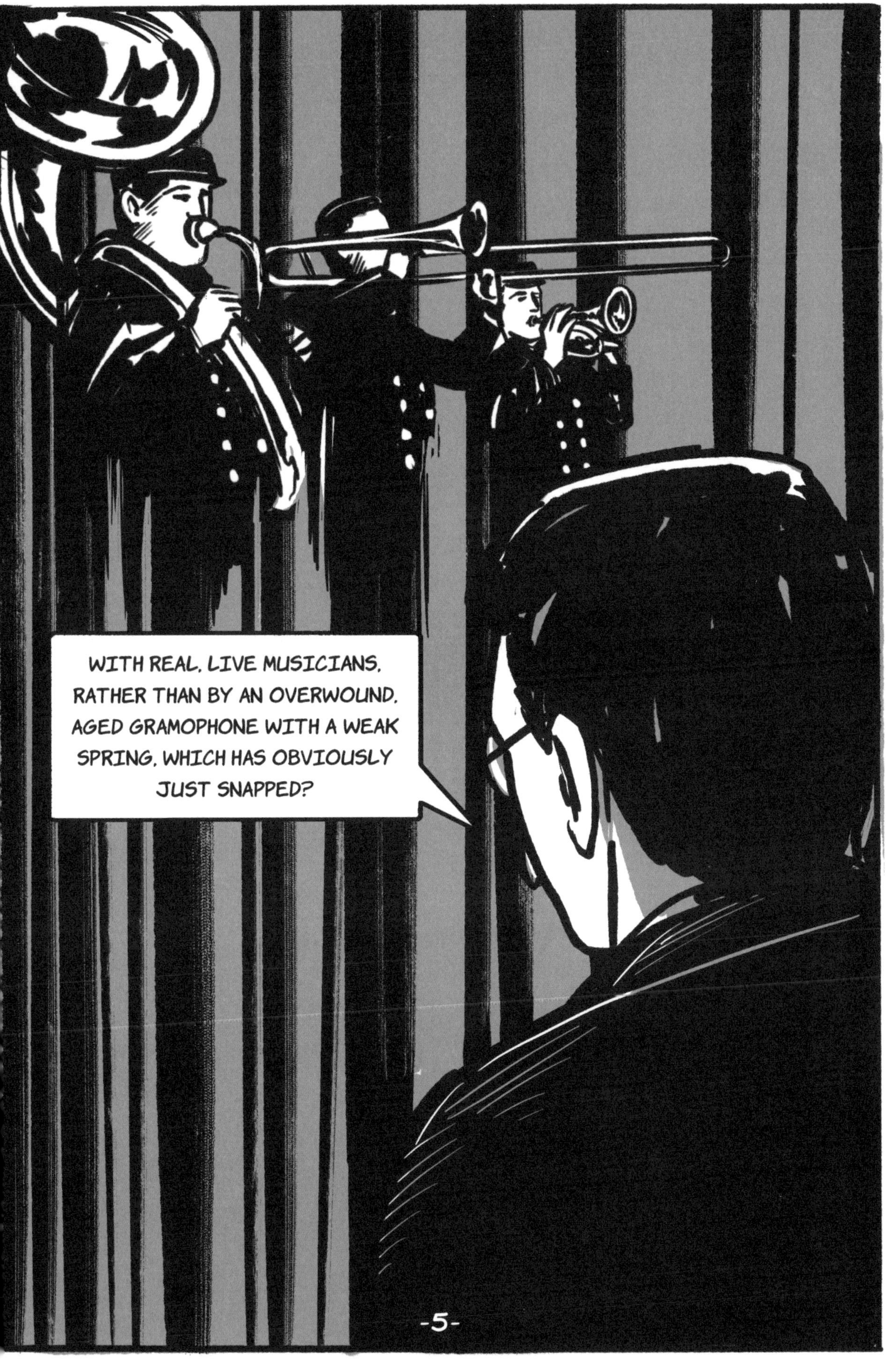
WITH REAL, LIVE MUSICIANS, RATHER THAN BY AN OVERWOUND, AGED GRAMOPHONE WITH A WEAK SPRING, WHICH HAS OBVIOUSLY JUST SNAPPED?

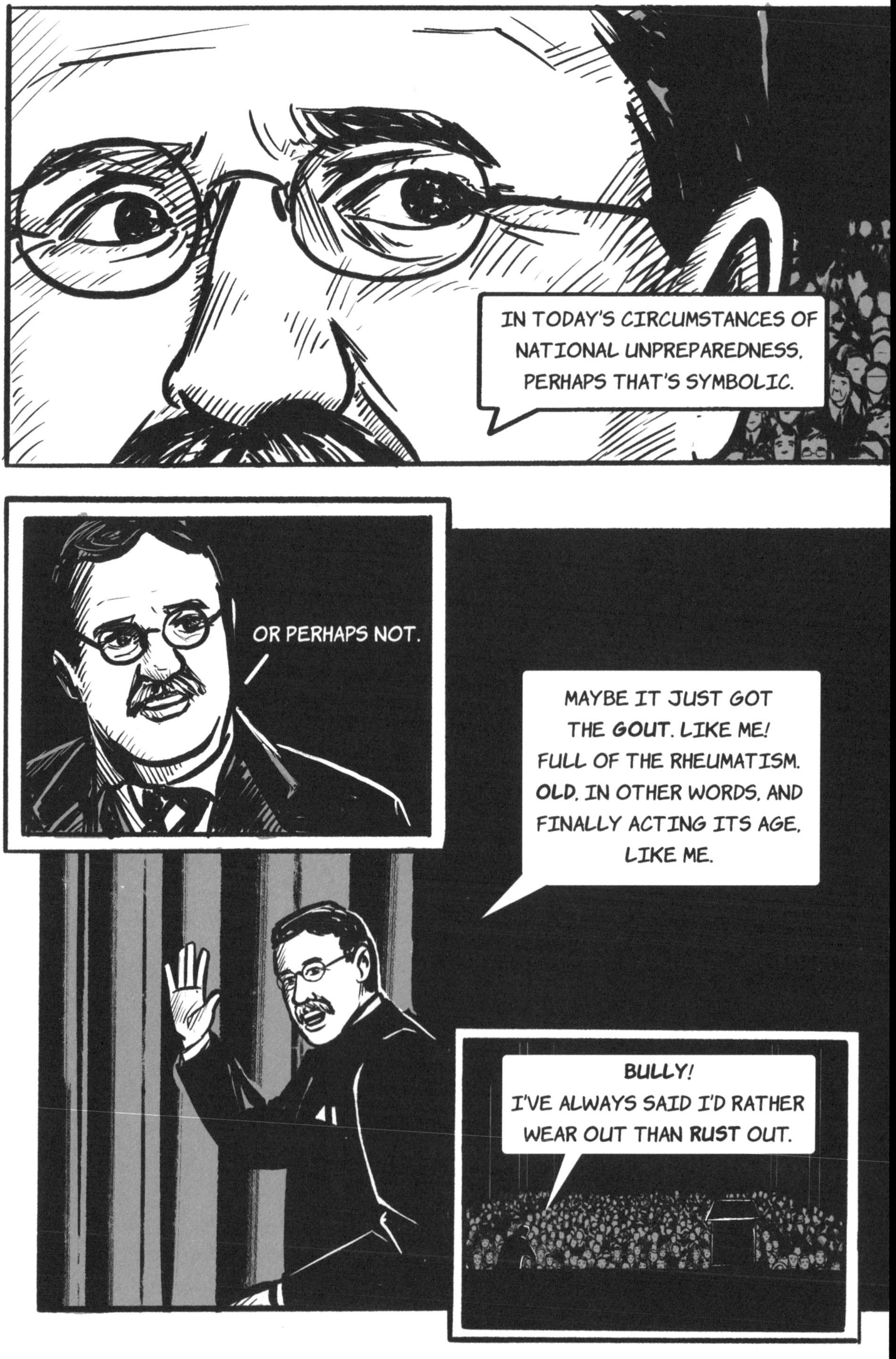
IN TODAY'S CIRCUMSTANCES OF NATIONAL UNPREPAREDNESS, PERHAPS THAT'S SYMBOLIC.
OR PERHAPS NOT.
MAYBE IT JUST GOT THE GOUT. LIKE ME! FULL OF THE RHEUMATISM. OLD, IN OTHER WORDS, AND FINALLY ACTING ITS AGE. LIKE ME.
BULLY! I'VE ALWAYS SAID I'D RATHER WEAR OUT THAN RUST OUT.

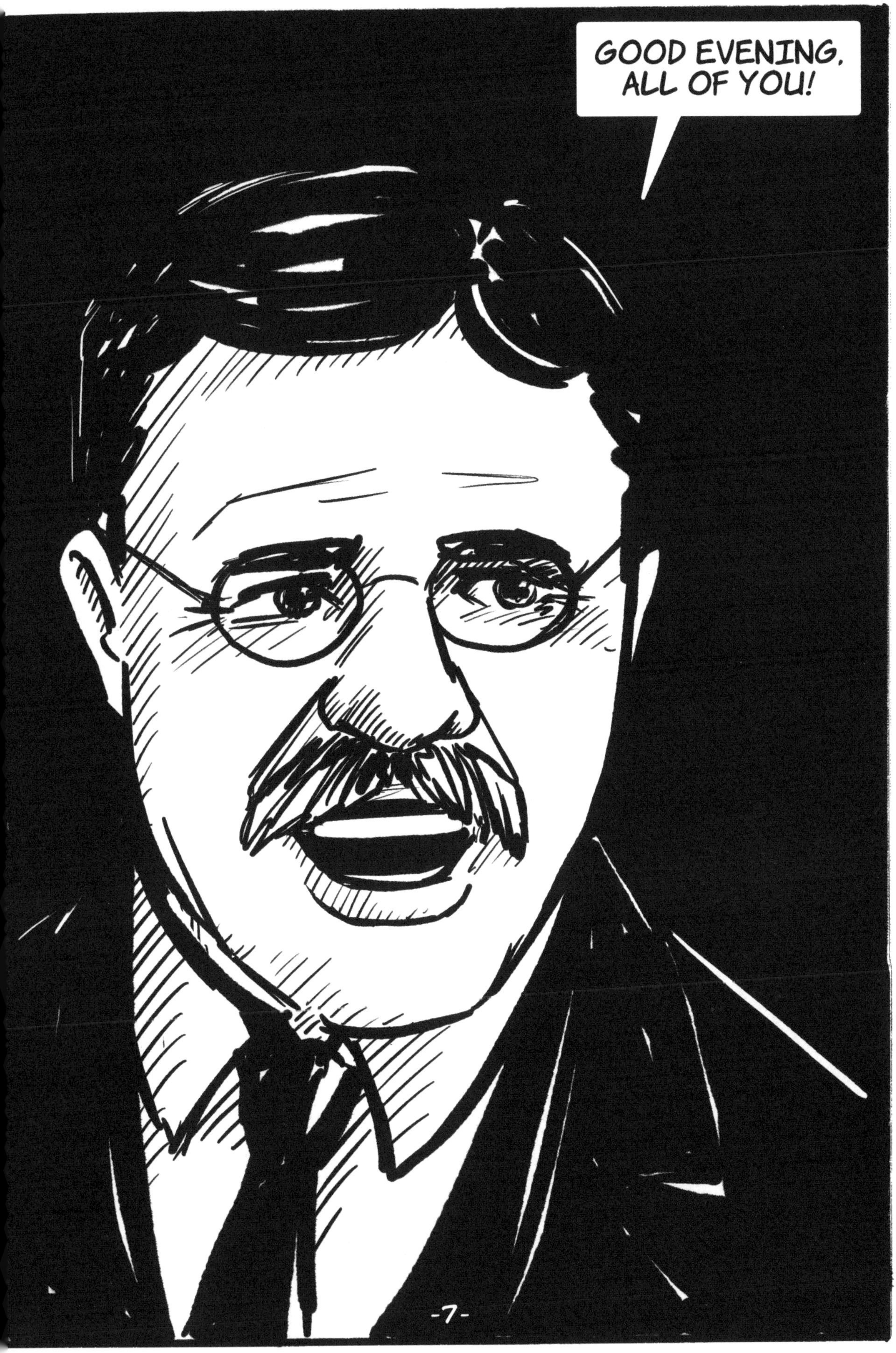
GOOD EVENING, ALL OF YOU!

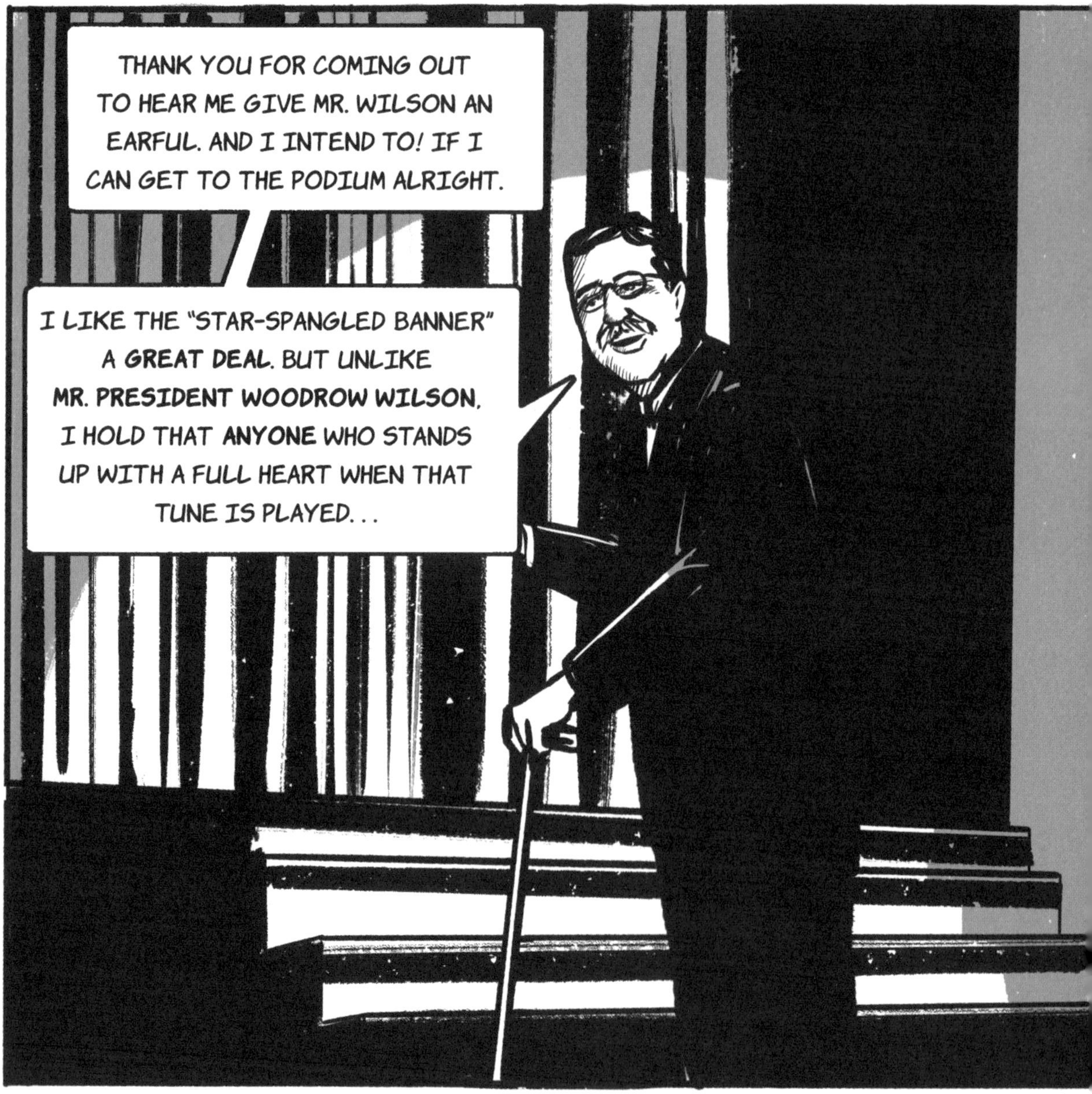
THANK YOU FOR COMING OUT TO HEAR ME GIVE MR. WILSON AN EARFUL. AND I INTEND TO! IF I CAN GET TO THE PODIUM ALRIGHT.
I LIKE THE "STAR-SPANGLED BANNER" A **GREAT DEAL**. BUT UNLIKE **MR. PRESIDENT WOODROW WILSON**, I HOLD THAT **ANYONE** WHO STANDS UP WITH A FULL HEART WHEN THAT TUNE IS PLAYED...

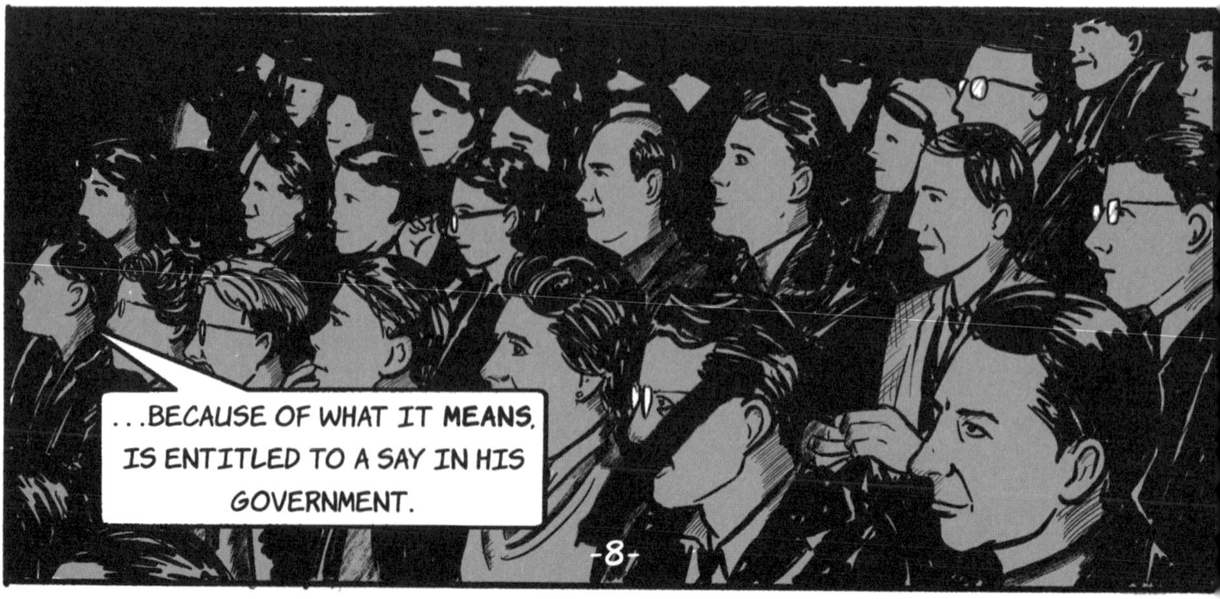
...BECAUSE OF WHAT IT **MEANS**, IS ENTITLED TO A SAY IN HIS GOVERNMENT.

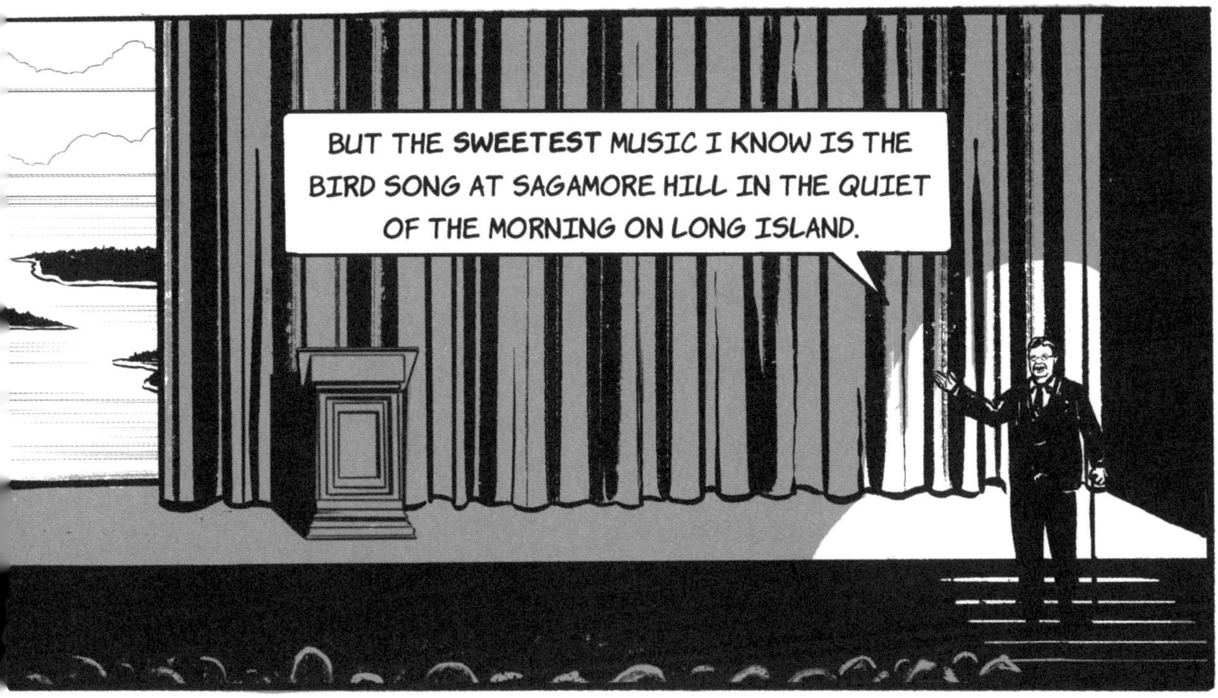
BUT THE SWEETEST MUSIC I KNOW IS THE BIRD SONG AT SAGAMORE HILL IN THE QUIET OF THE MORNING ON LONG ISLAND.

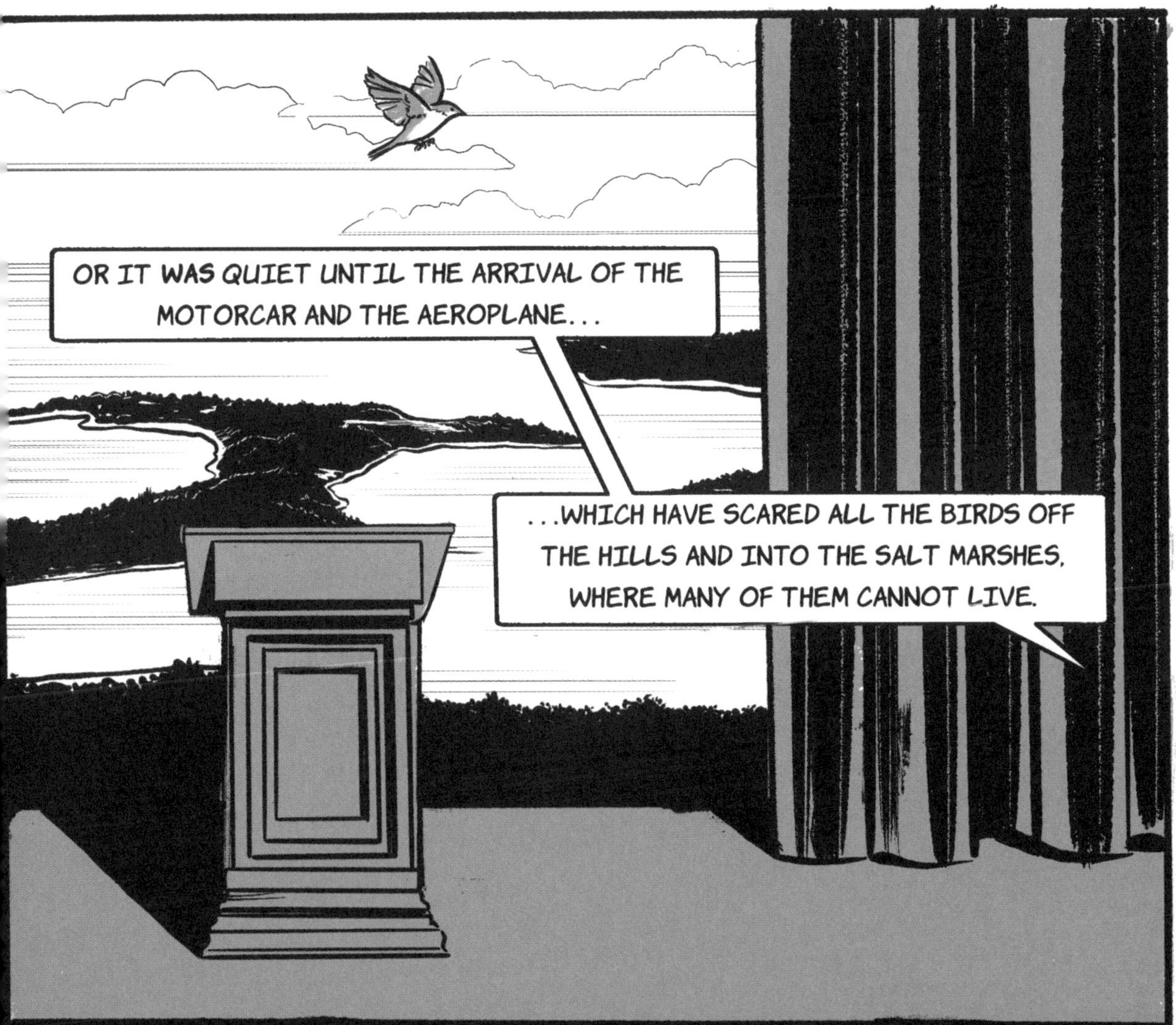
OR IT WAS QUIET UNTIL THE ARRIVAL OF THE MOTORCAR AND THE AEROPLANE...
...WHICH HAVE SCARED ALL THE BIRDS OFF THE HILLS AND INTO THE SALT MARSHES, WHERE MANY OF THEM CANNOT LIVE.

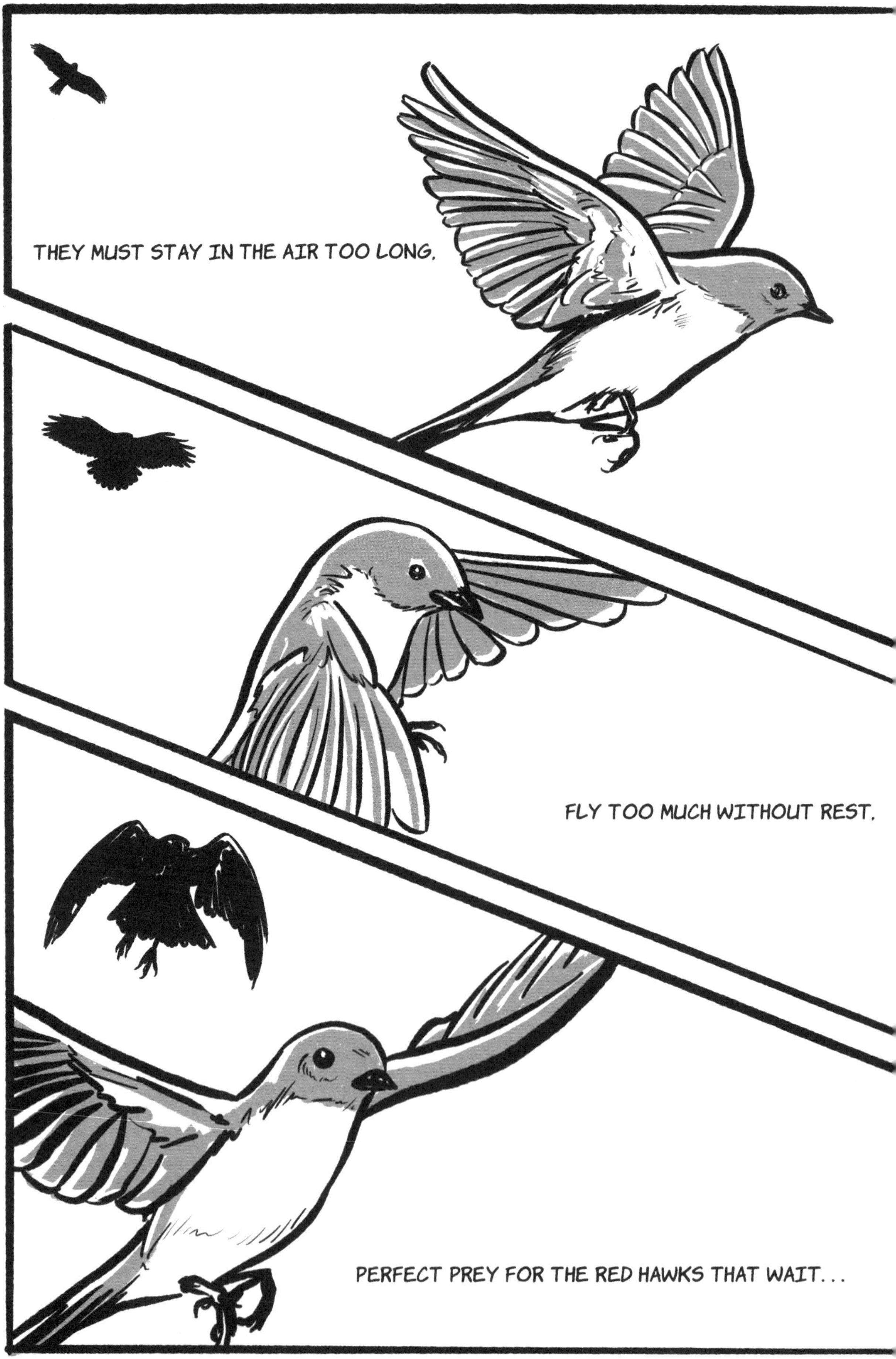
THEY MUST STAY IN THE AIR TOO LONG.
FLY TOO MUCH WITHOUT REST.
PERFECT PREY FOR THE RED HAWKS THAT WAIT...

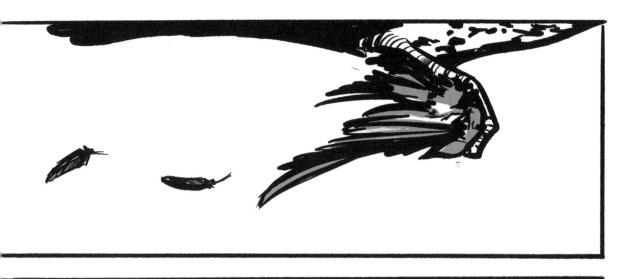

I CAN DO THIS.

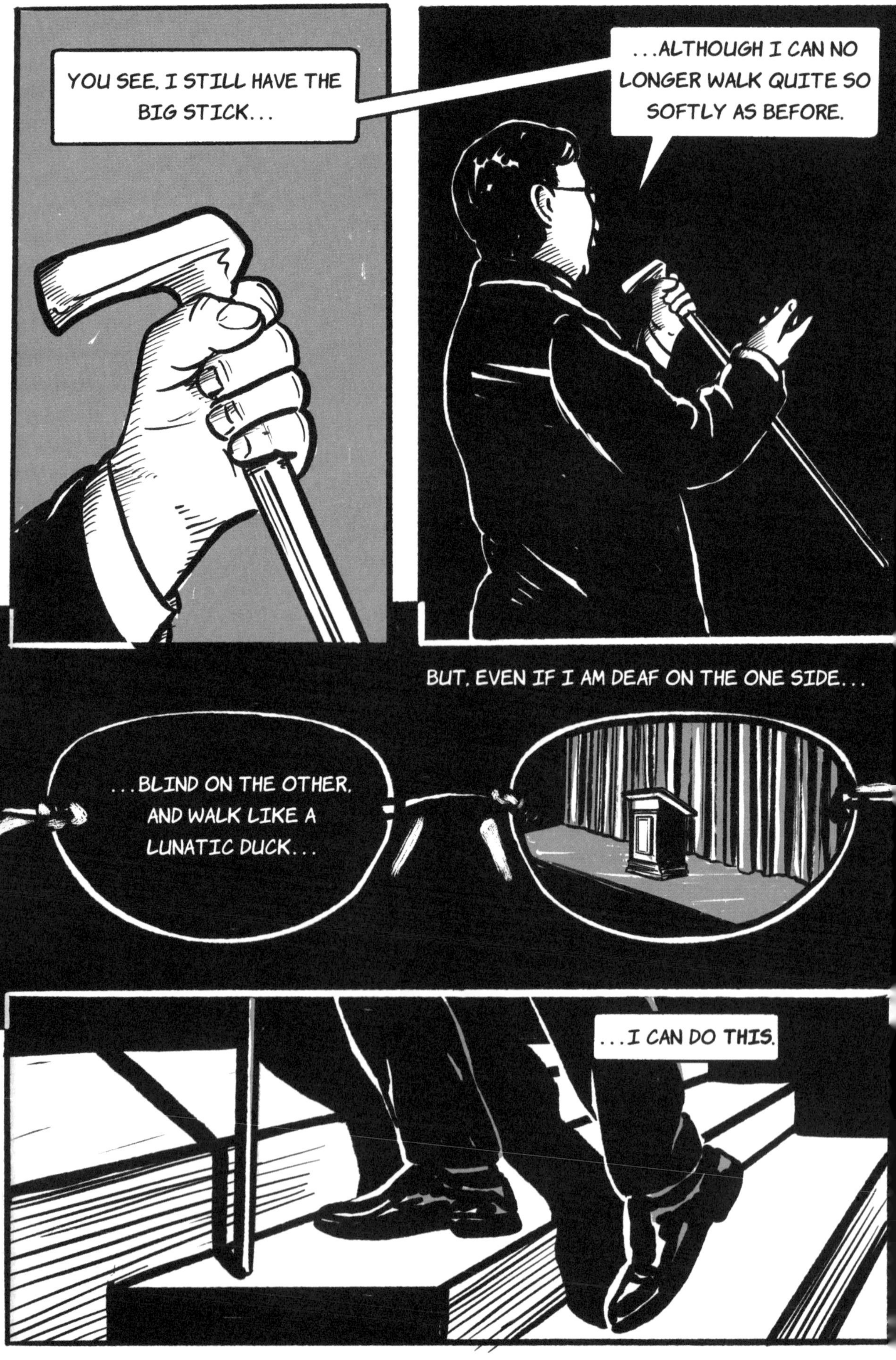
YOU SEE, I STILL HAVE THE BIG STICK...
...ALTHOUGH I CAN NO LONGER WALK QUITE SO SOFTLY AS BEFORE.
BUT, EVEN IF I AM DEAF ON THE ONE SIDE...
...BLIND ON THE OTHER, AND WALK LIKE A LUNATIC DUCK...
...I CAN DO THIS.

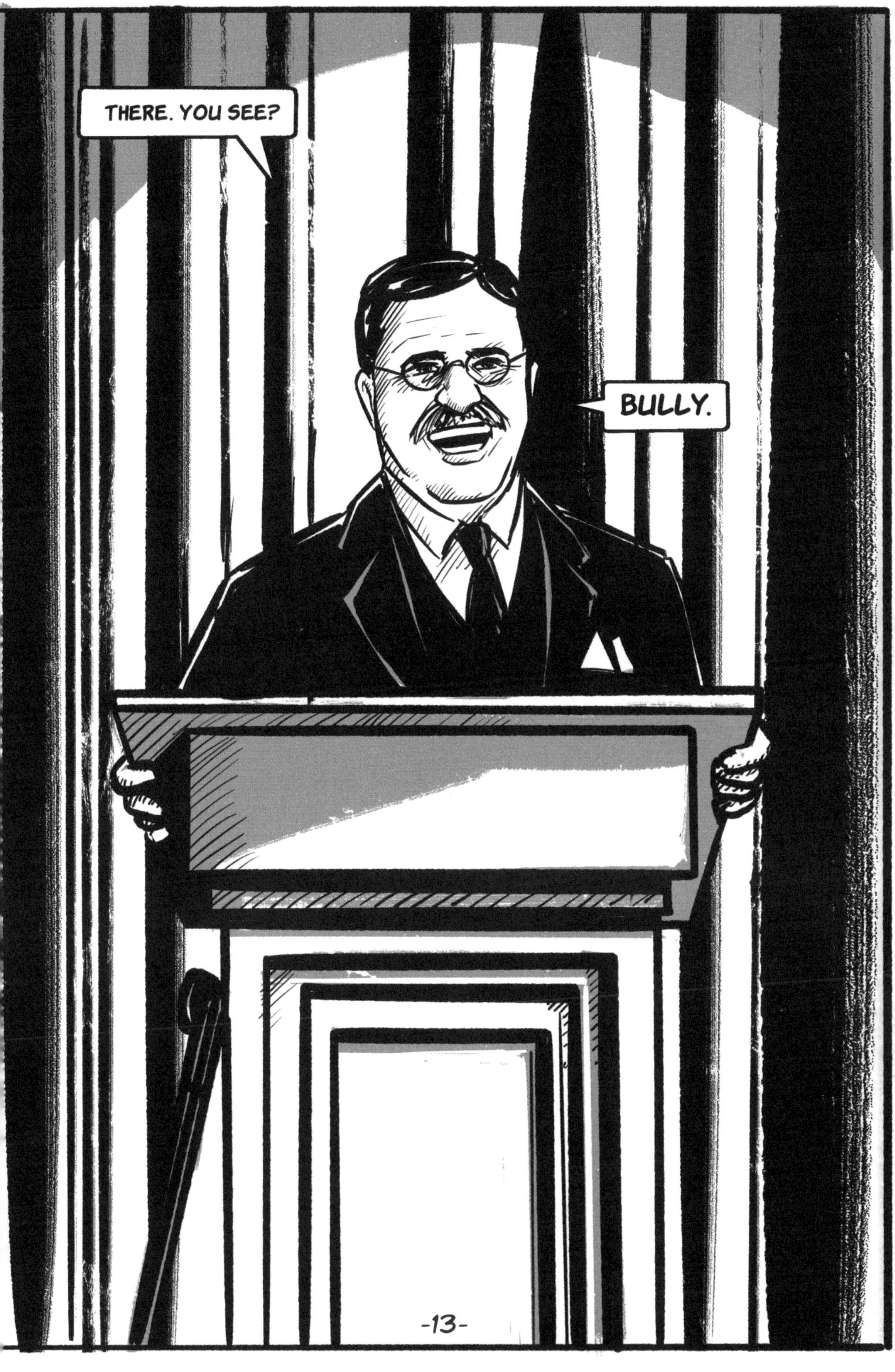
THERE. YOU SEE?
BULLY.

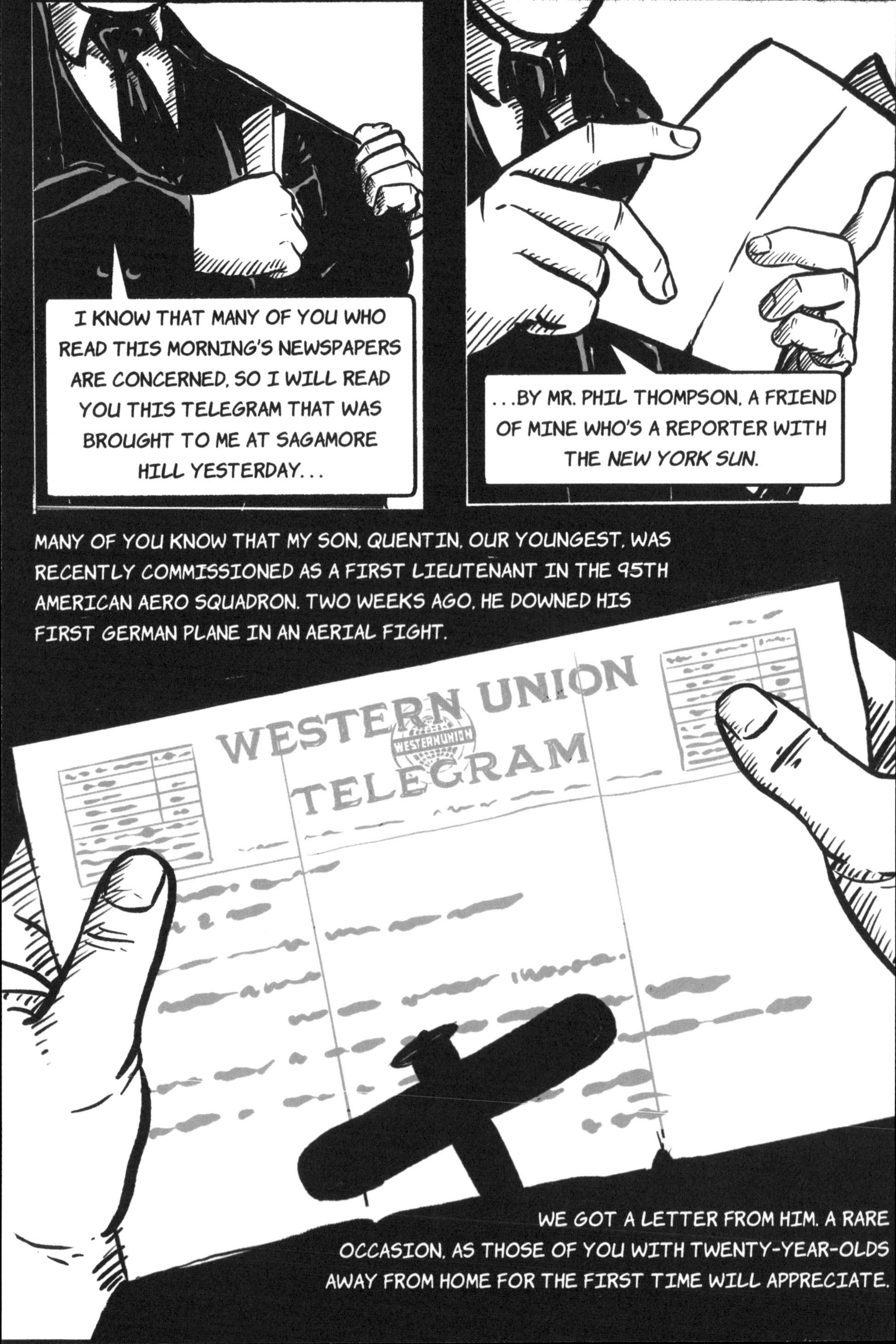

I KNOW THAT MANY OF YOU WHO READ THIS MORNING'S NEWSPAPERS ARE CONCERNED, SO I WILL READ YOU THIS TELEGRAM THAT WAS BROUGHT TO ME AT SAGAMORE HILL YESTERDAY...
...BY MR. PHIL THOMPSON, A FRIEND OF MINE WHO'S A REPORTER WITH THE *NEW YORK SUN.*
MANY OF YOU KNOW THAT MY SON, QUENTIN, OUR YOUNGEST, WAS RECENTLY COMMISSIONED AS A FIRST LIEUTENANT IN THE 95TH AMERICAN AERO SQUADRON. TWO WEEKS AGO, HE DOWNED HIS FIRST GERMAN PLANE IN AN AERIAL FIGHT.
WESTERN UNION TELEGRAM
WESTERN UNION
WE GOT A LETTER FROM HIM. A RARE OCCASION, AS THOSE OF YOU WITH TWENTY-YEAR-OLDS AWAY FROM HOME FOR THE FIRST TIME WILL APPRECIATE.

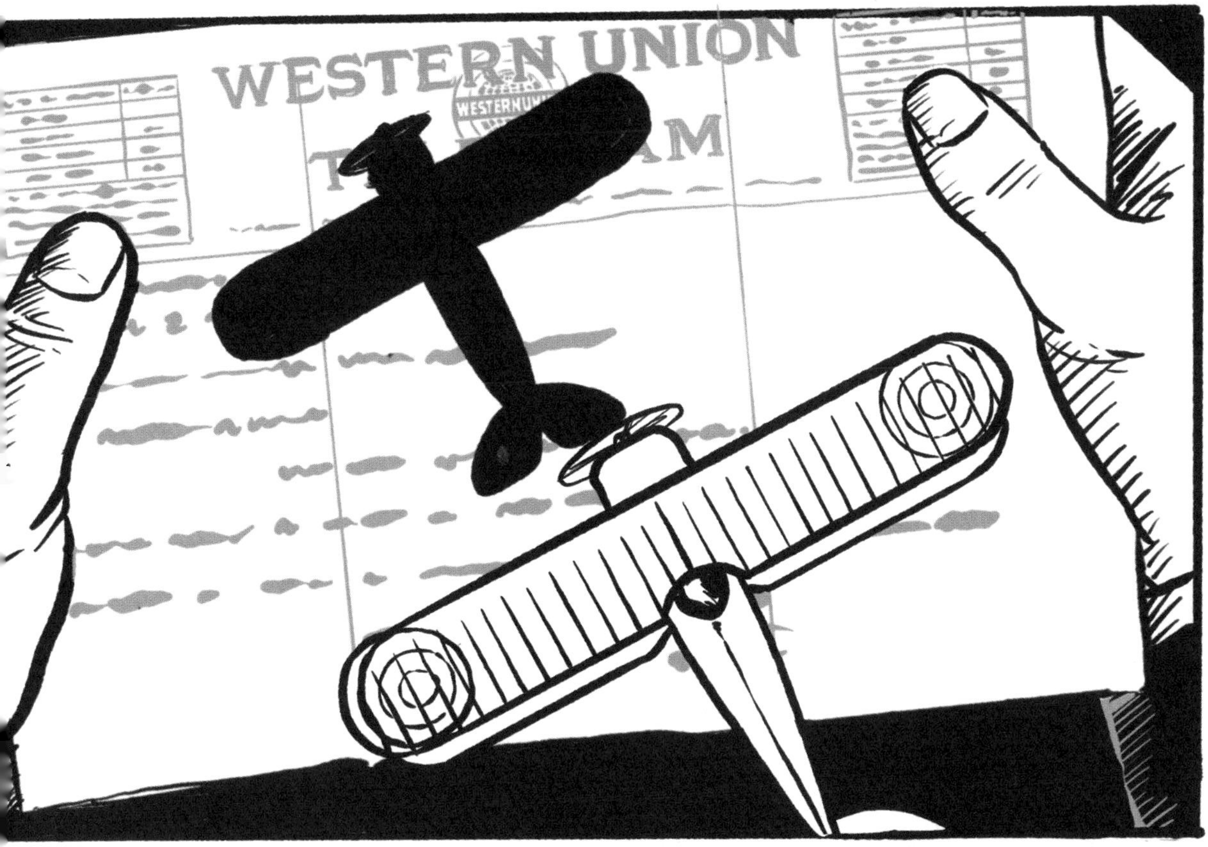
WESTERN UNION
WESTERNUNION

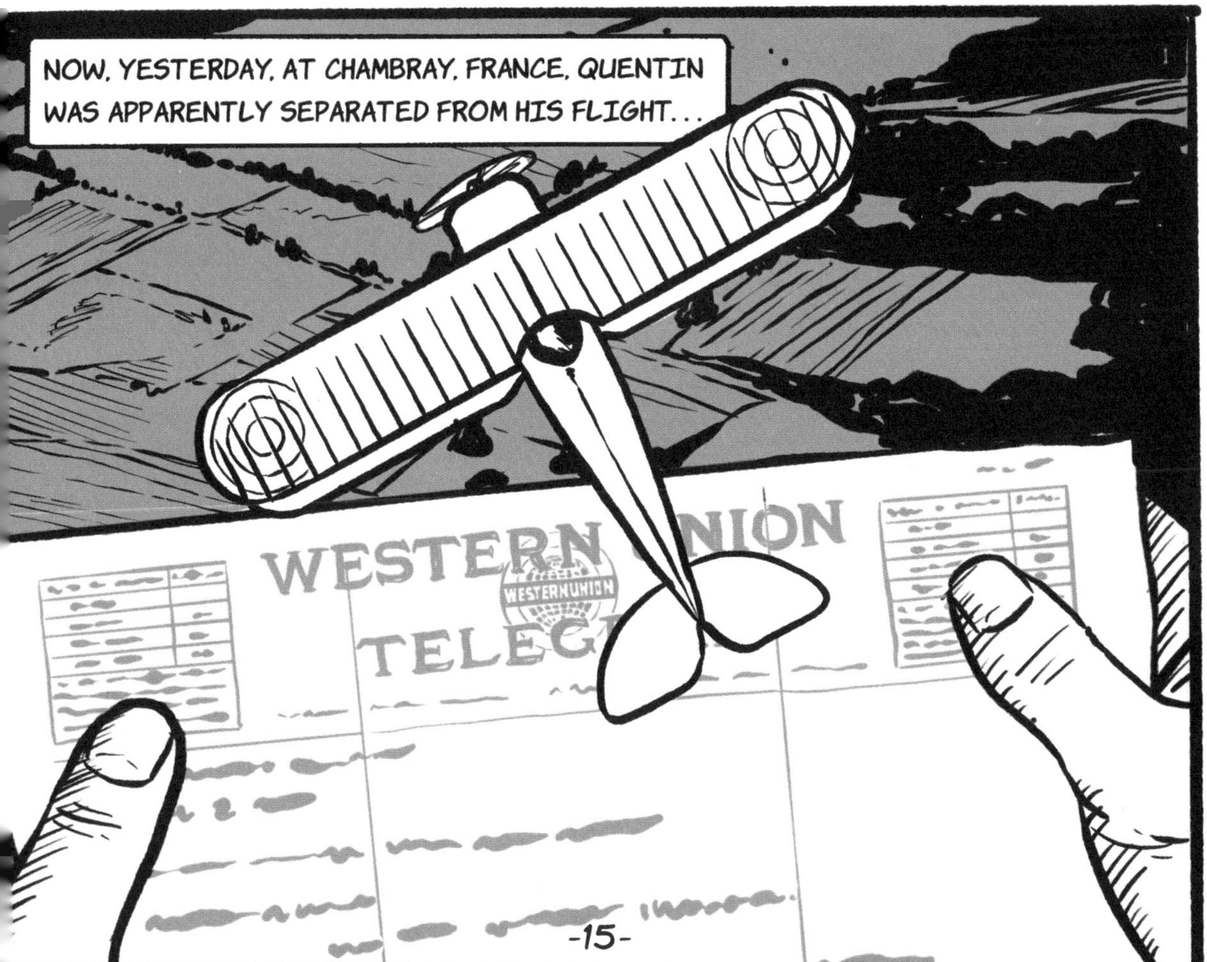
NOW, YESTERDAY, AT CHAMBRAY, FRANCE, QUENTIN WAS APPARENTLY SEPARATED FROM HIS FLIGHT...
WESTERNUNION

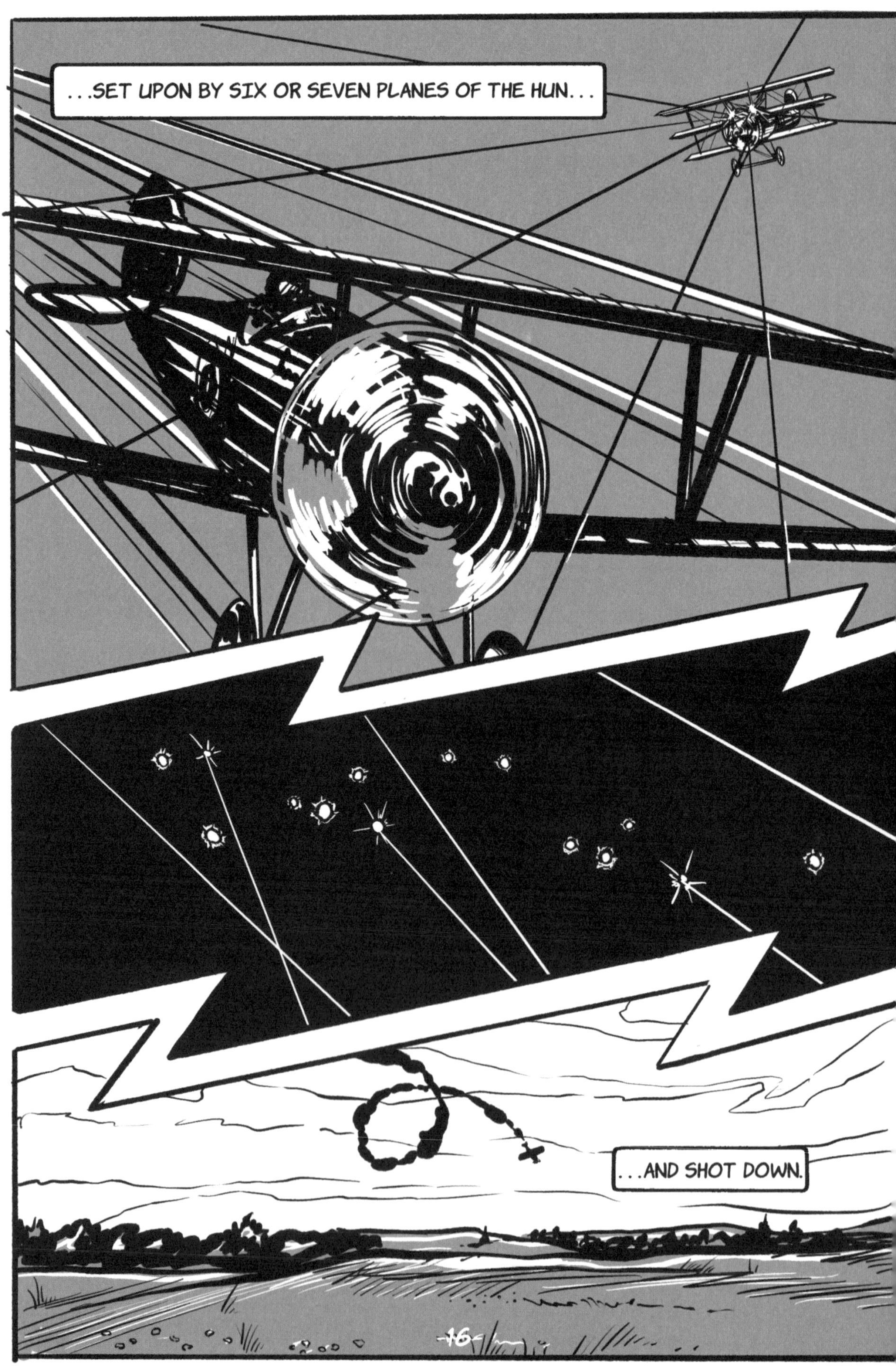
...SET UPON BY SIX OR SEVEN PLANES OF THE HUN...
...AND SHOT DOWN.

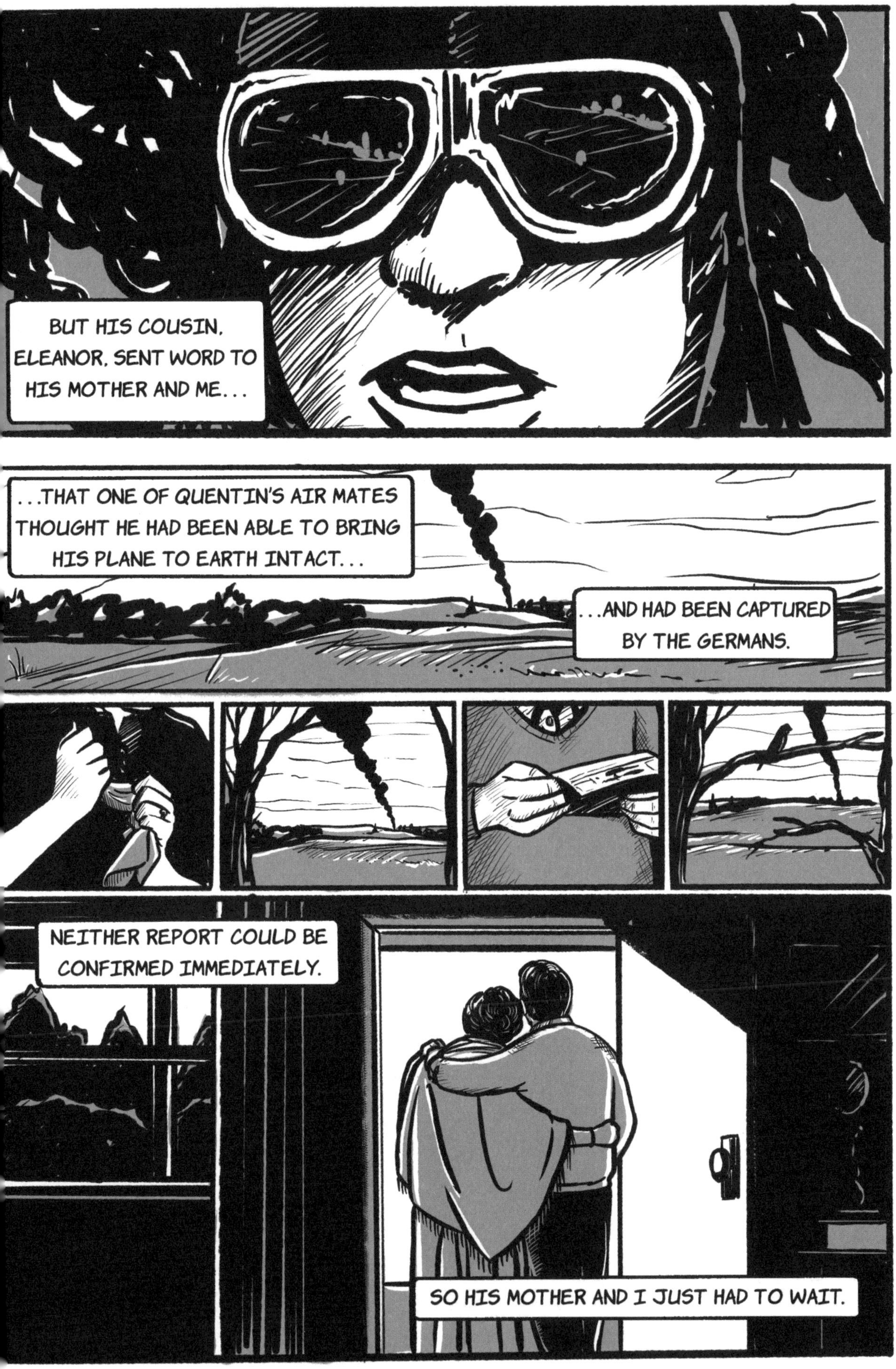

BUT HIS COUSIN, ELEANOR, SENT WORD TO HIS MOTHER AND ME...
...THAT ONE OF QUENTIN'S AIR MATES THOUGHT HE HAD BEEN ABLE TO BRING HIS PLANE TO EARTH INTACT...
...AND HAD BEEN CAPTURED BY THE GERMANS.
NEITHER REPORT COULD BE CONFIRMED IMMEDIATELY.
SO HIS MOTHER AND I JUST HAD TO WAIT.

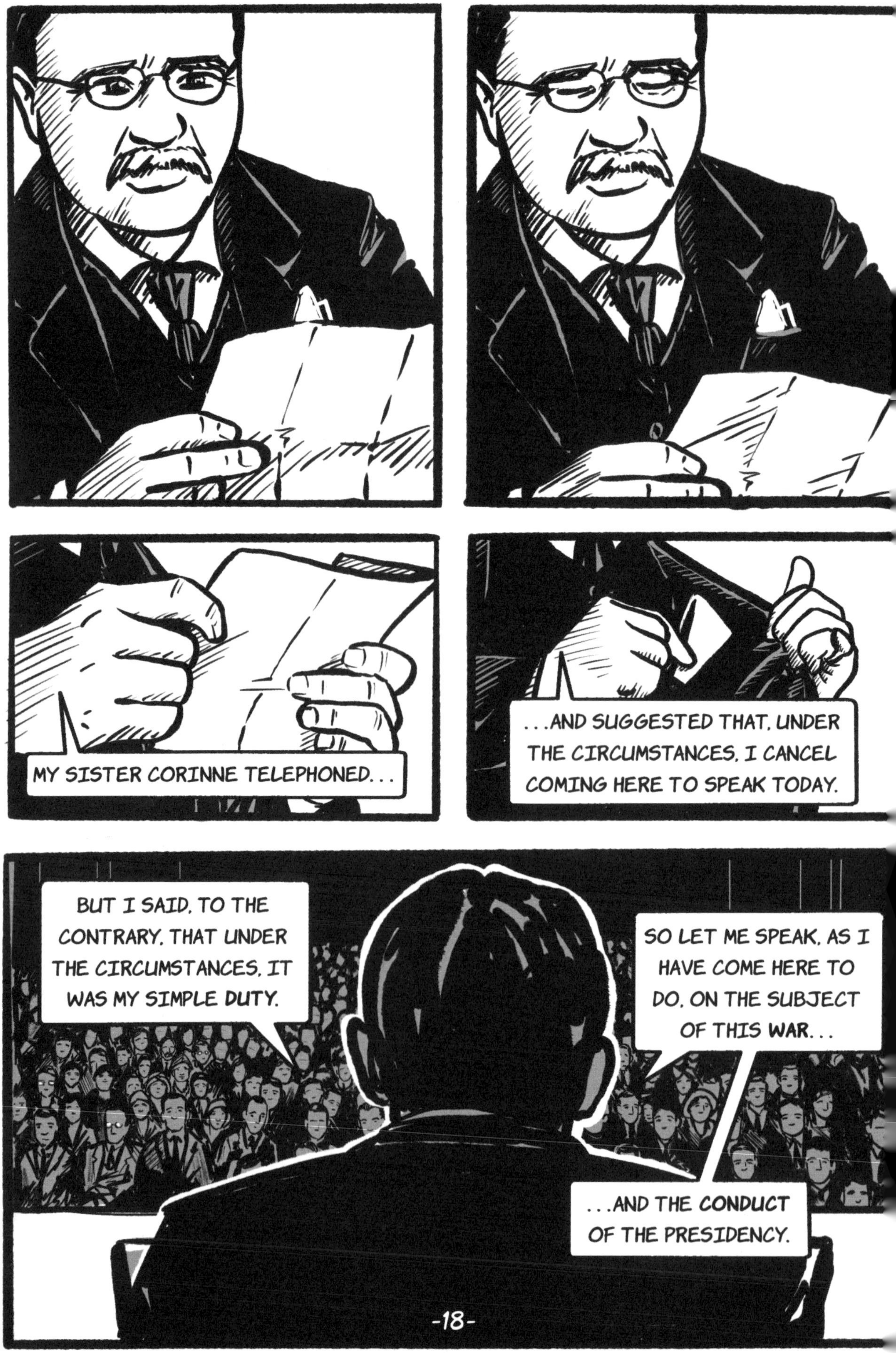
MY SISTER CORINNE TELEPHONED...
...AND SUGGESTED THAT, UNDER THE CIRCUMSTANCES, I CANCEL COMING HERE TO SPEAK TODAY.
BUT I SAID, TO THE CONTRARY, THAT UNDER THE CIRCUMSTANCES, IT WAS MY SIMPLE DUTY.
SO LET ME SPEAK, AS I HAVE COME HERE TO DO, ON THE SUBJECT OF THIS WAR...
...AND THE CONDUCT OF THE PRESIDENCY.

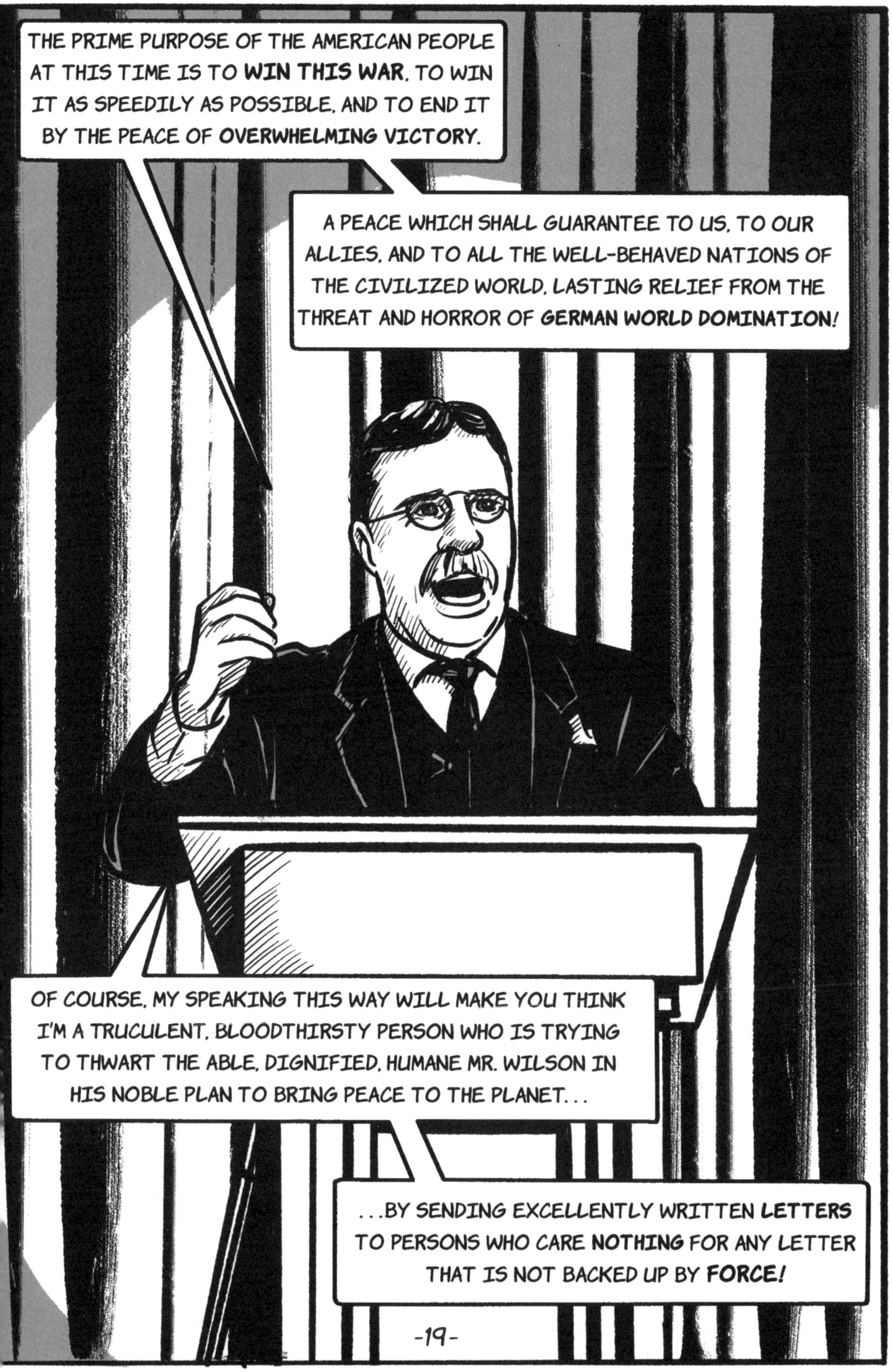

THE PRIME PURPOSE OF THE AMERICAN PEOPLE AT THIS TIME IS TO **WIN THIS WAR**, TO WIN IT AS SPEEDILY AS POSSIBLE, AND TO END IT BY THE PEACE OF **OVERWHELMING VICTORY**.
A PEACE WHICH SHALL GUARANTEE TO US, TO OUR ALLIES, AND TO ALL THE WELL-BEHAVED NATIONS OF THE CIVILIZED WORLD, LASTING RELIEF FROM THE THREAT AND HORROR OF **GERMAN WORLD DOMINATION**!
OF COURSE, MY SPEAKING THIS WAY WILL MAKE YOU THINK I'M A TRUCULENT, BLOODTHIRSTY PERSON WHO IS TRYING TO THWART THE ABLE, DIGNIFIED, HUMANE MR. WILSON IN HIS NOBLE PLAN TO BRING PEACE TO THE PLANET...
...BY SENDING EXCELLENTLY WRITTEN **LETTERS** TO PERSONS WHO CARE **NOTHING** FOR ANY LETTER THAT IS NOT BACKED UP BY **FORCE**!

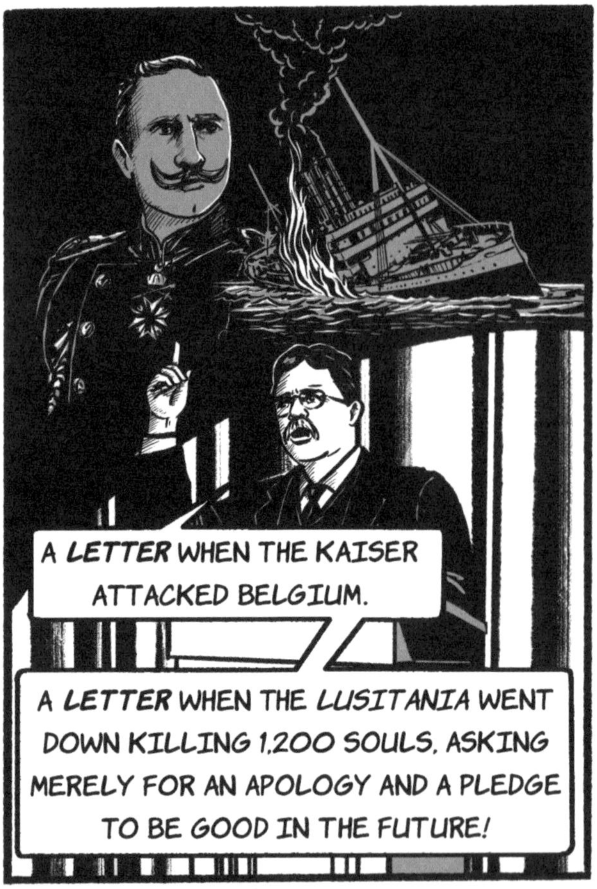
A *LETTER* WHEN THE KAISER ATTACKED BELGIUM.
A *LETTER* WHEN THE *LUSITANIA* WENT DOWN KILLING 1,200 SOULS, ASKING MERELY FOR AN APOLOGY AND A PLEDGE TO BE GOOD IN THE FUTURE!

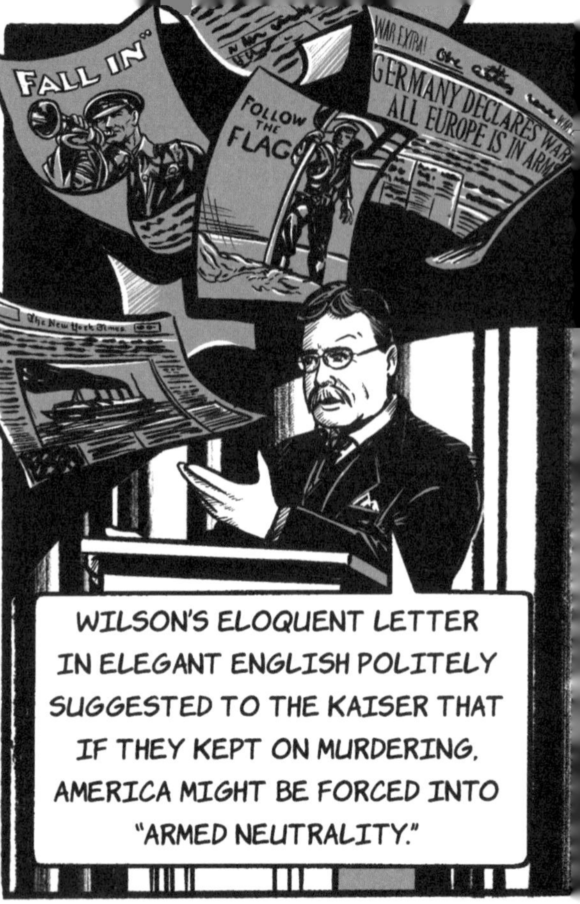
FALL IN
FOLLOW THE FLAG
WAR EXTRA!
GERMANY DECLARES WAR
The New York Times
WILSON'S ELOQUENT LETTER IN ELEGANT ENGLISH POLITELY SUGGESTED TO THE KAISER THAT IF THEY KEPT ON MURDERING, AMERICA MIGHT BE FORCED INTO "ARMED NEUTRALITY."

FINALLY, THE TERRIFIED HUN RESPONDED.
HOW? BY **SUBMARINE TORPEDOING THREE MORE OF OUR SHIPS**, KILLING ALMOST EVERYONE IN THEM. COWARDLY, UNSCRUPULOUS, COLDBLOODED, HYPOCRITICAL. AND THAT'S THE **PRESIDENT**. A PRESIDENT WHO PROCLAIMS THAT AMERICANS ARE "TOO PROUD TO FIGHT."

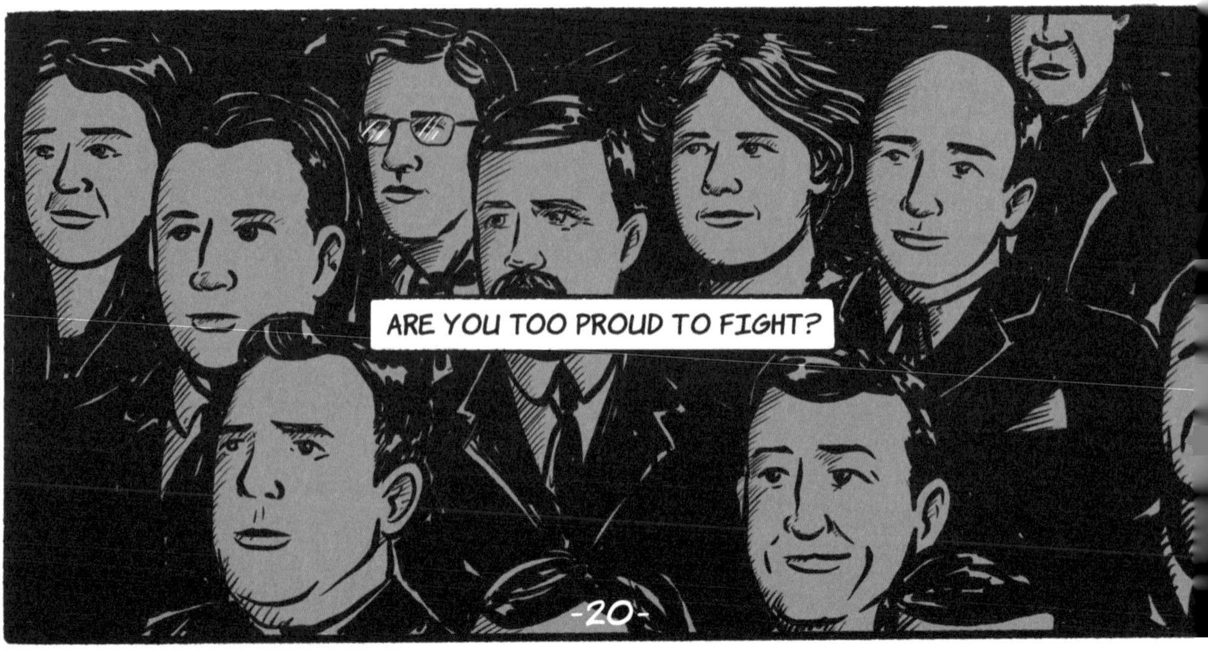
ARE YOU TOO PROUD TO FIGHT?

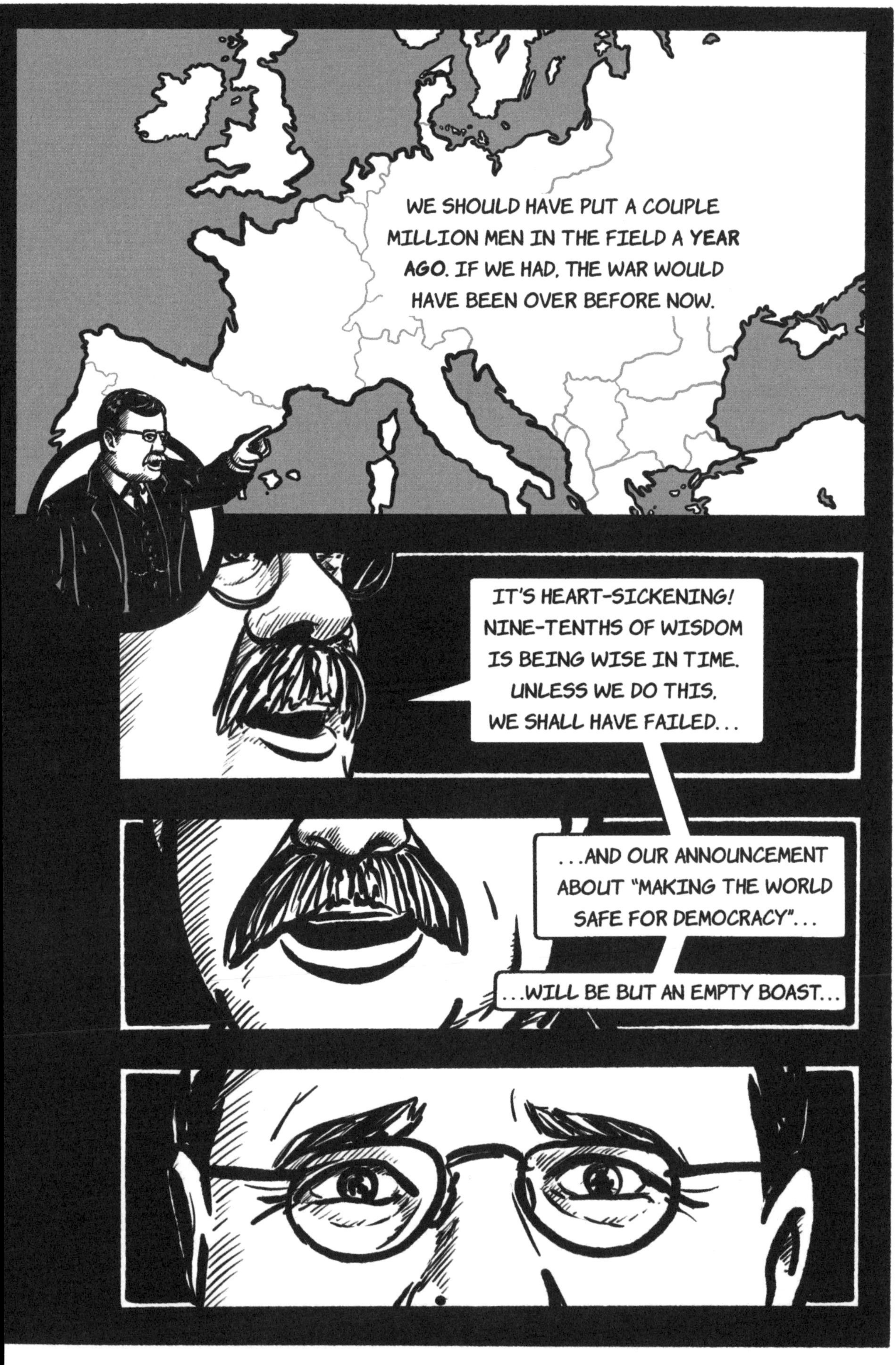
WE SHOULD HAVE PUT A COUPLE MILLION MEN IN THE FIELD A YEAR AGO. IF WE HAD, THE WAR WOULD HAVE BEEN OVER BEFORE NOW.
IT'S HEART-SICKENING! NINE-TENTHS OF WISDOM IS BEING WISE IN TIME. UNLESS WE DO THIS, WE SHALL HAVE FAILED...
...AND OUR ANNOUNCEMENT ABOUT "MAKING THE WORLD SAFE FOR DEMOCRACY"...
...WILL BE BUT AN EMPTY BOAST...

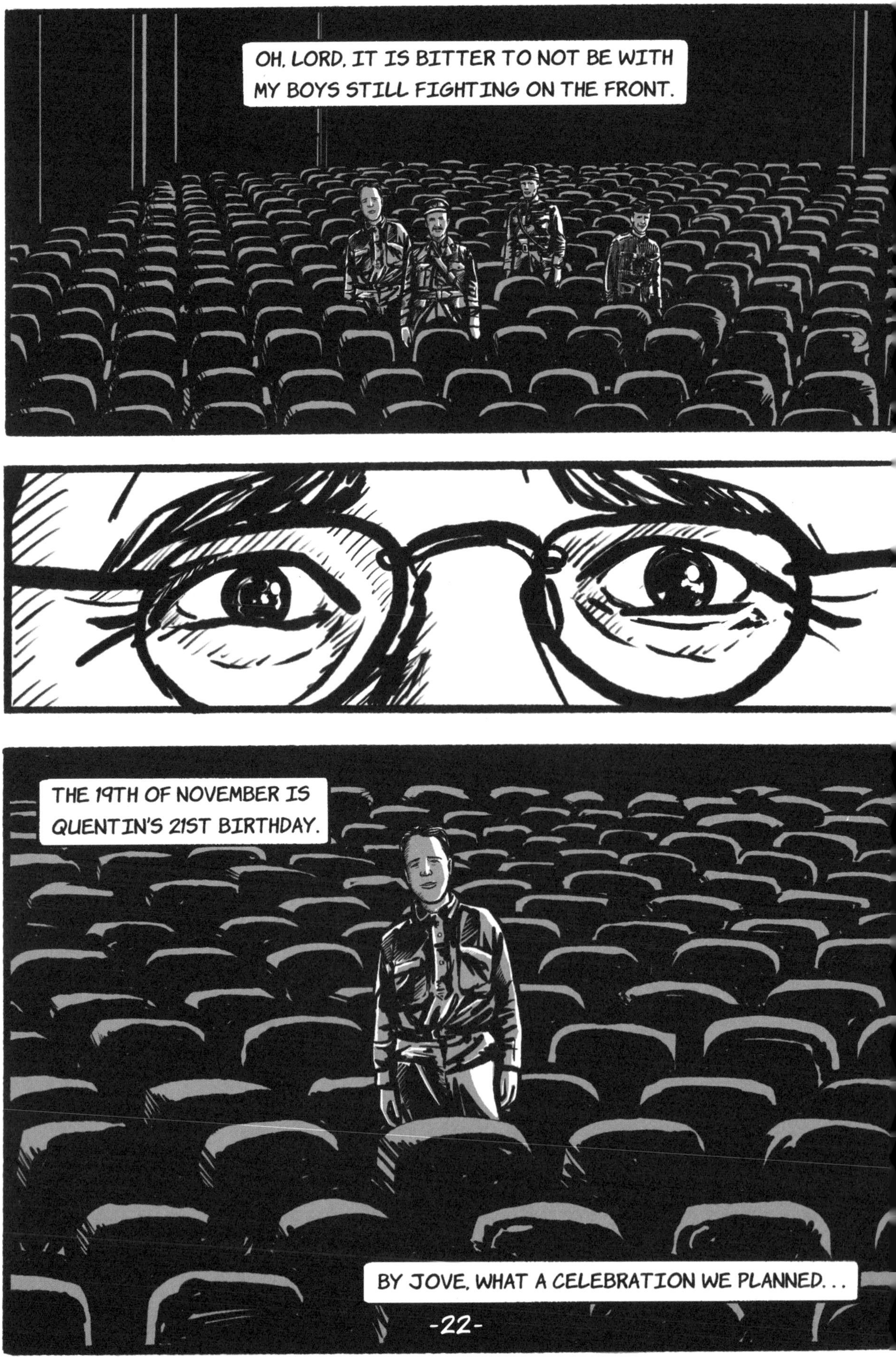
OH, LORD, IT IS BITTER TO NOT BE WITH MY BOYS STILL FIGHTING ON THE FRONT.
THE 19TH OF NOVEMBER IS QUENTIN'S 21ST BIRTHDAY.
BY JOVE, WHAT A CELEBRATION WE PLANNED. . .

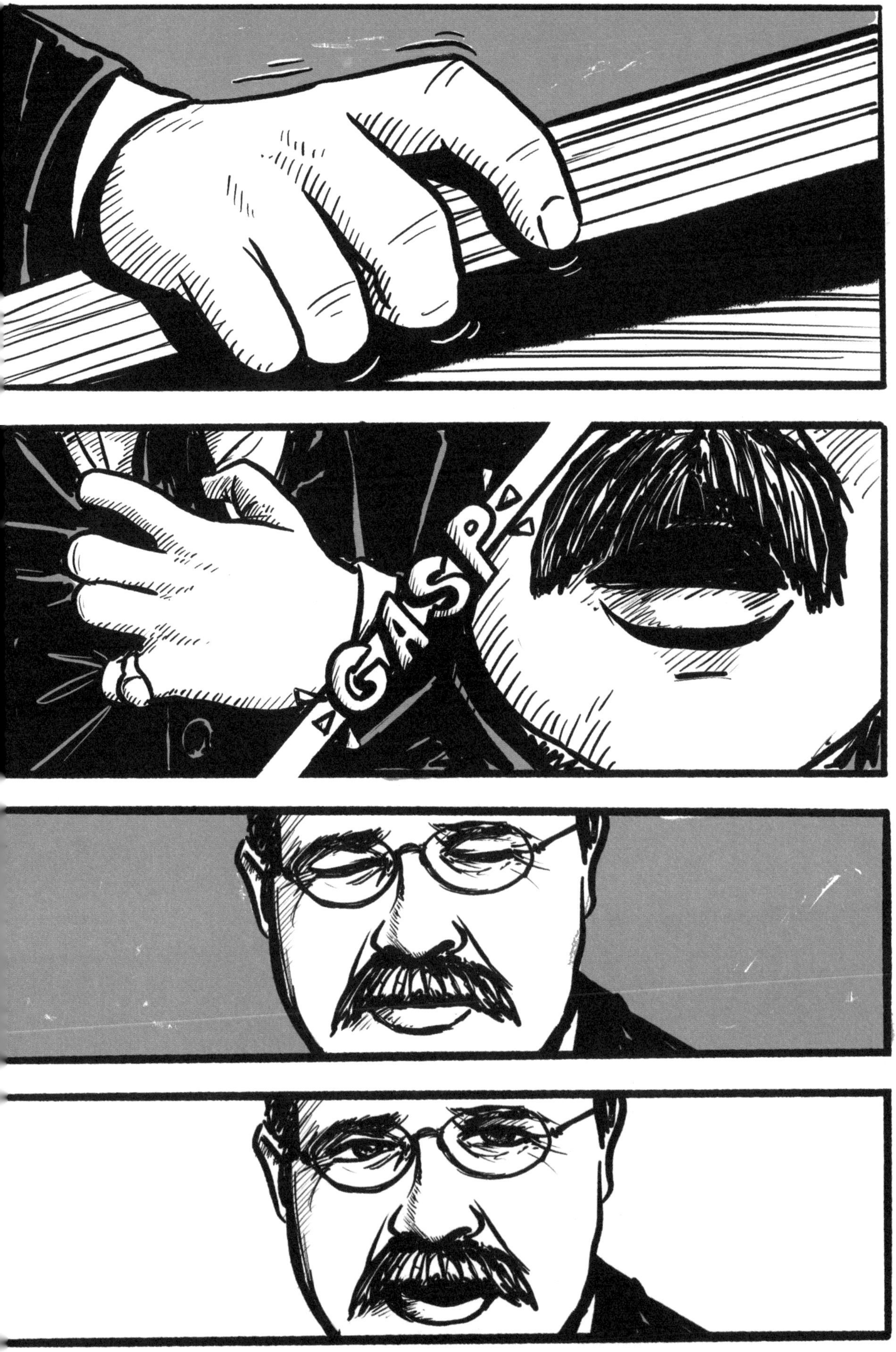
GASP

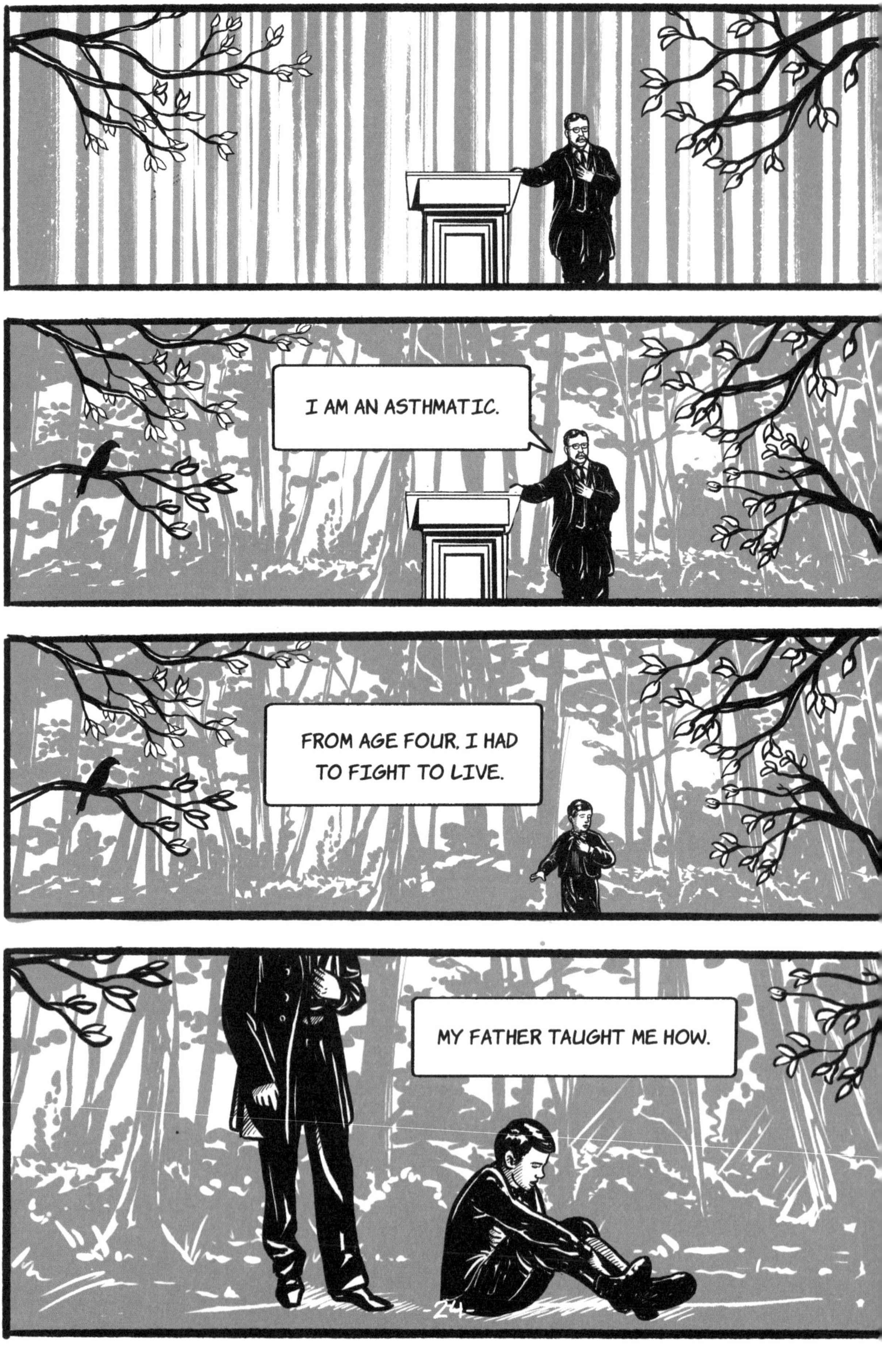
I AM AN ASTHMATIC.
FROM AGE FOUR, I HAD TO FIGHT TO LIVE.
MY FATHER TAUGHT ME HOW.

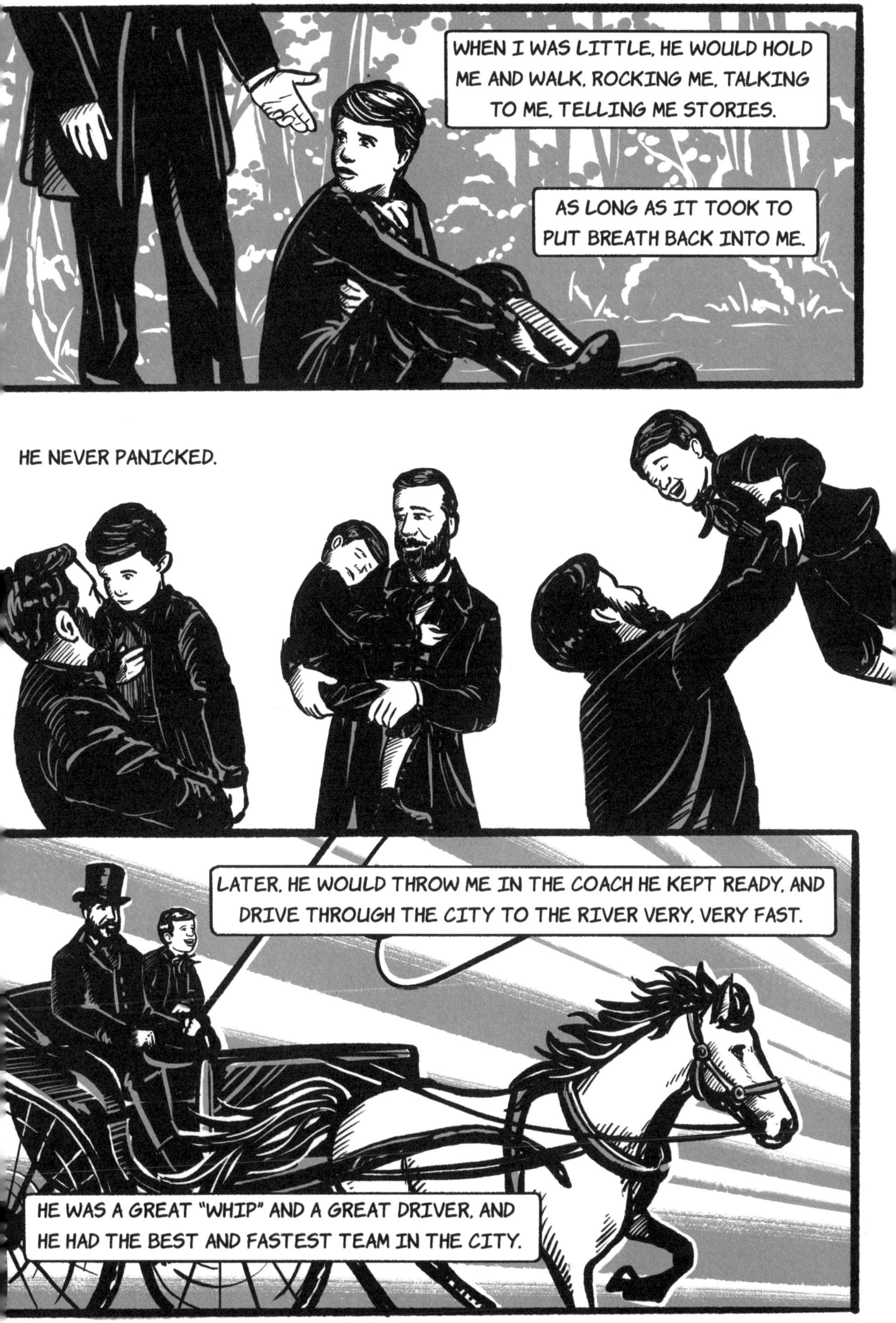
WHEN I WAS LITTLE, HE WOULD HOLD ME AND WALK, ROCKING ME, TALKING TO ME, TELLING ME STORIES.
AS LONG AS IT TOOK TO PUT BREATH BACK INTO ME.
HE NEVER PANICKED.
LATER, HE WOULD THROW ME IN THE COACH HE KEPT READY, AND DRIVE THROUGH THE CITY TO THE RIVER VERY, VERY FAST.
HE WAS A GREAT "WHIP" AND A GREAT DRIVER, AND HE HAD THE BEST AND FASTEST TEAM IN THE CITY.

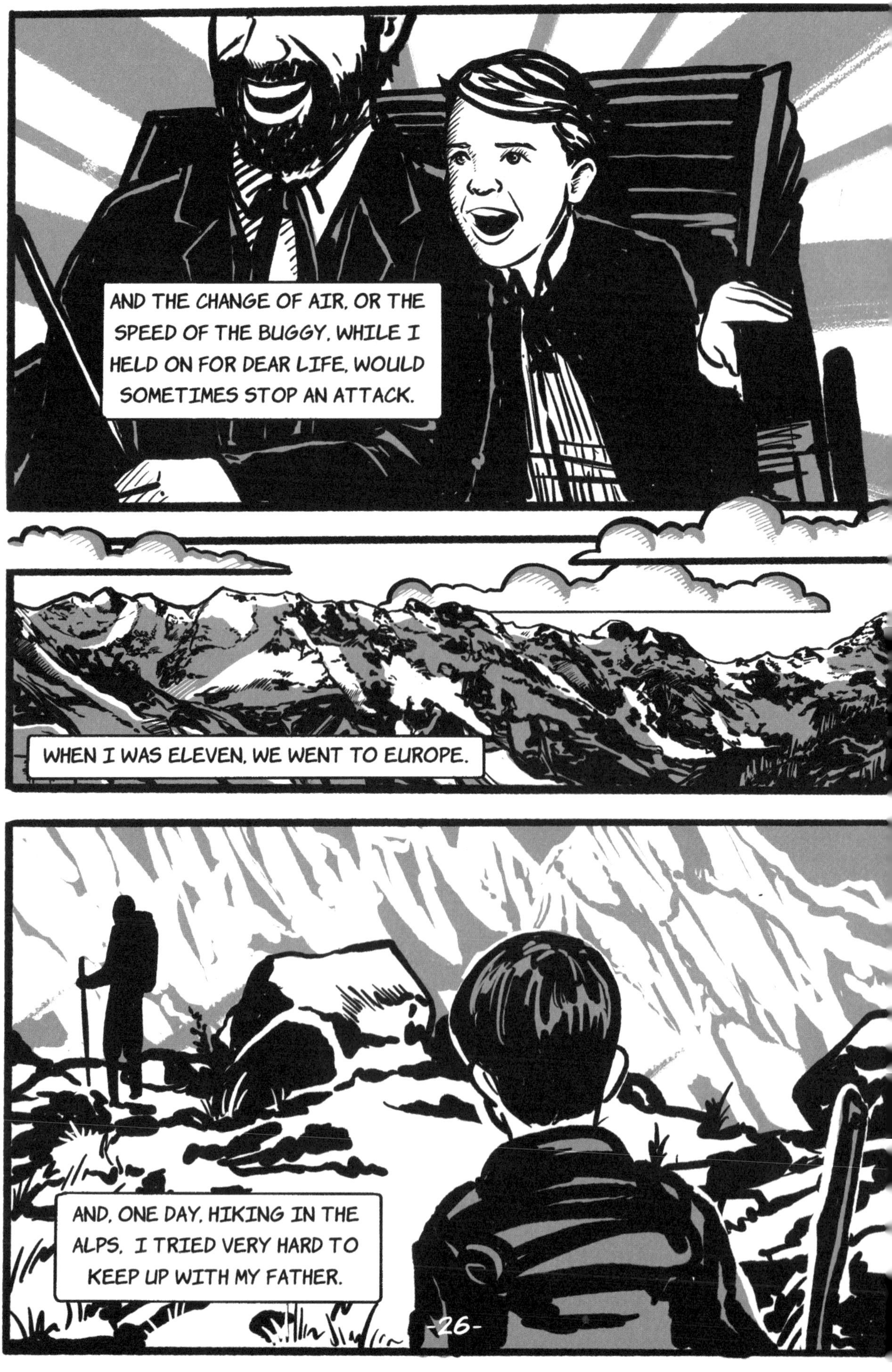
AND THE CHANGE OF AIR, OR THE SPEED OF THE BUGGY, WHILE I HELD ON FOR DEAR LIFE, WOULD SOMETIMES STOP AN ATTACK.
WHEN I WAS ELEVEN, WE WENT TO EUROPE.
AND, ONE DAY, HIKING IN THE ALPS, I TRIED VERY HARD TO KEEP UP WITH MY FATHER.

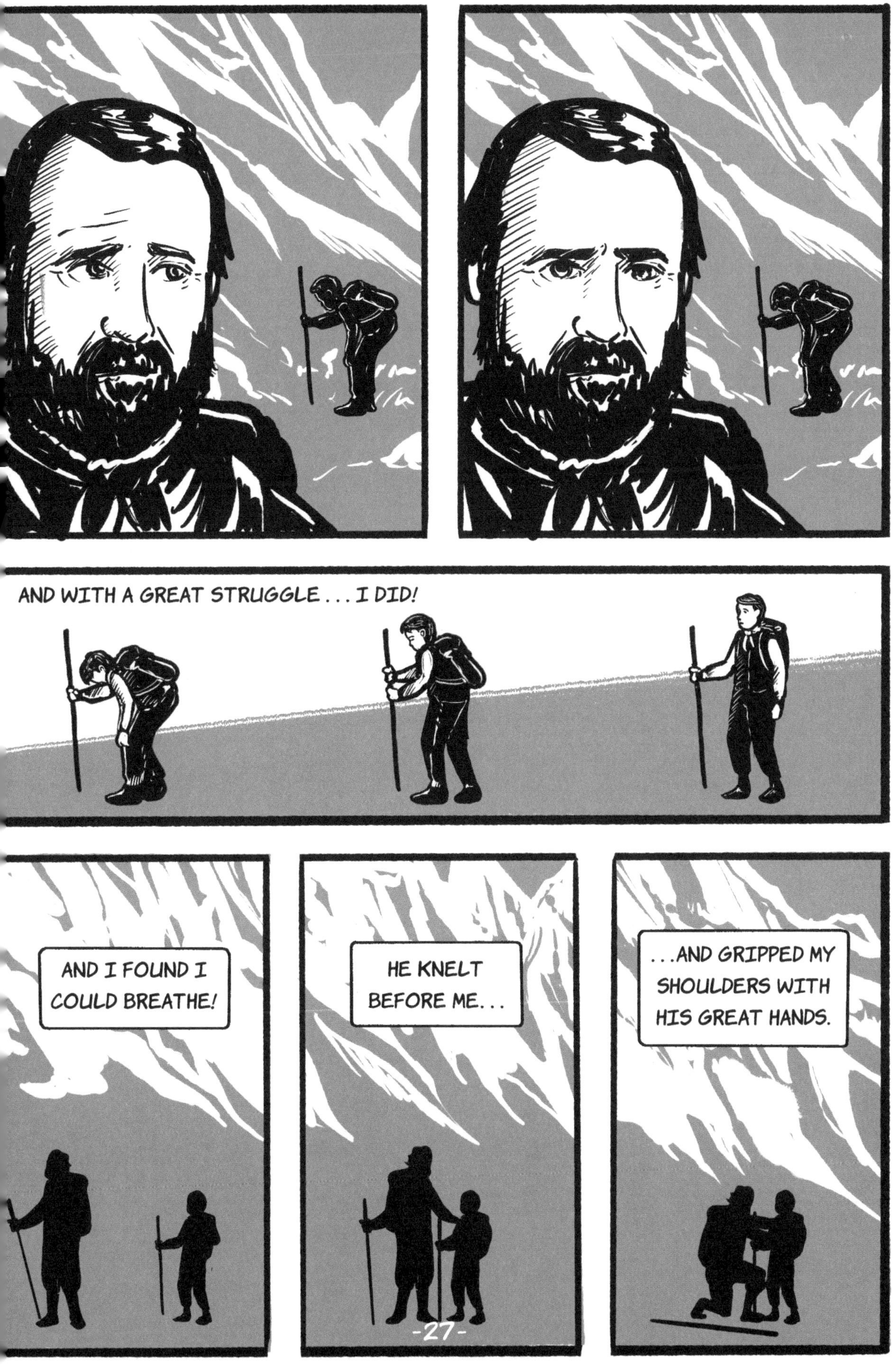

AND WITH A GREAT STRUGGLE . . . I DID!
AND I FOUND I COULD BREATHE!
HE KNELT BEFORE ME. . .
. . .AND GRIPPED MY SHOULDERS WITH HIS GREAT HANDS.

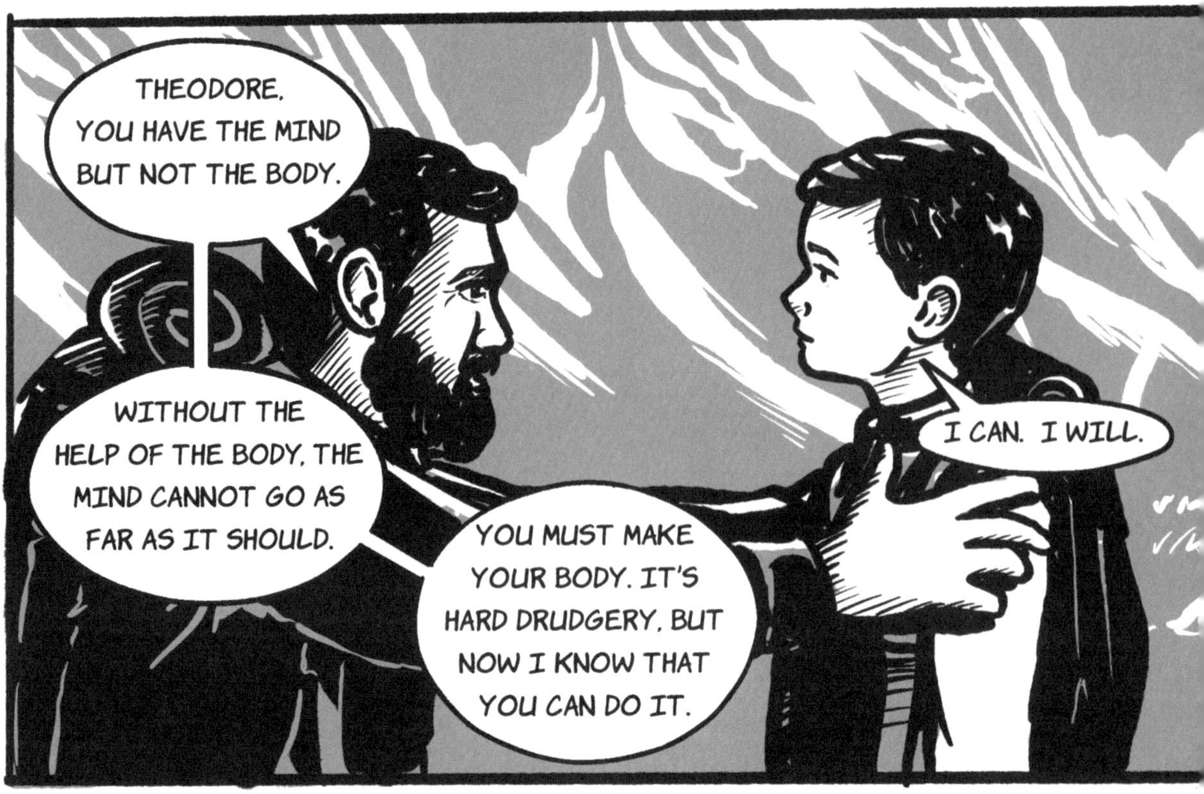
THEODORE, YOU HAVE THE MIND BUT NOT THE BODY.
WITHOUT THE HELP OF THE BODY, THE MIND CANNOT GO AS FAR AS IT SHOULD.
YOU MUST MAKE YOUR BODY. IT'S HARD DRUDGERY, BUT NOW I KNOW THAT YOU CAN DO IT.
I CAN. I WILL.

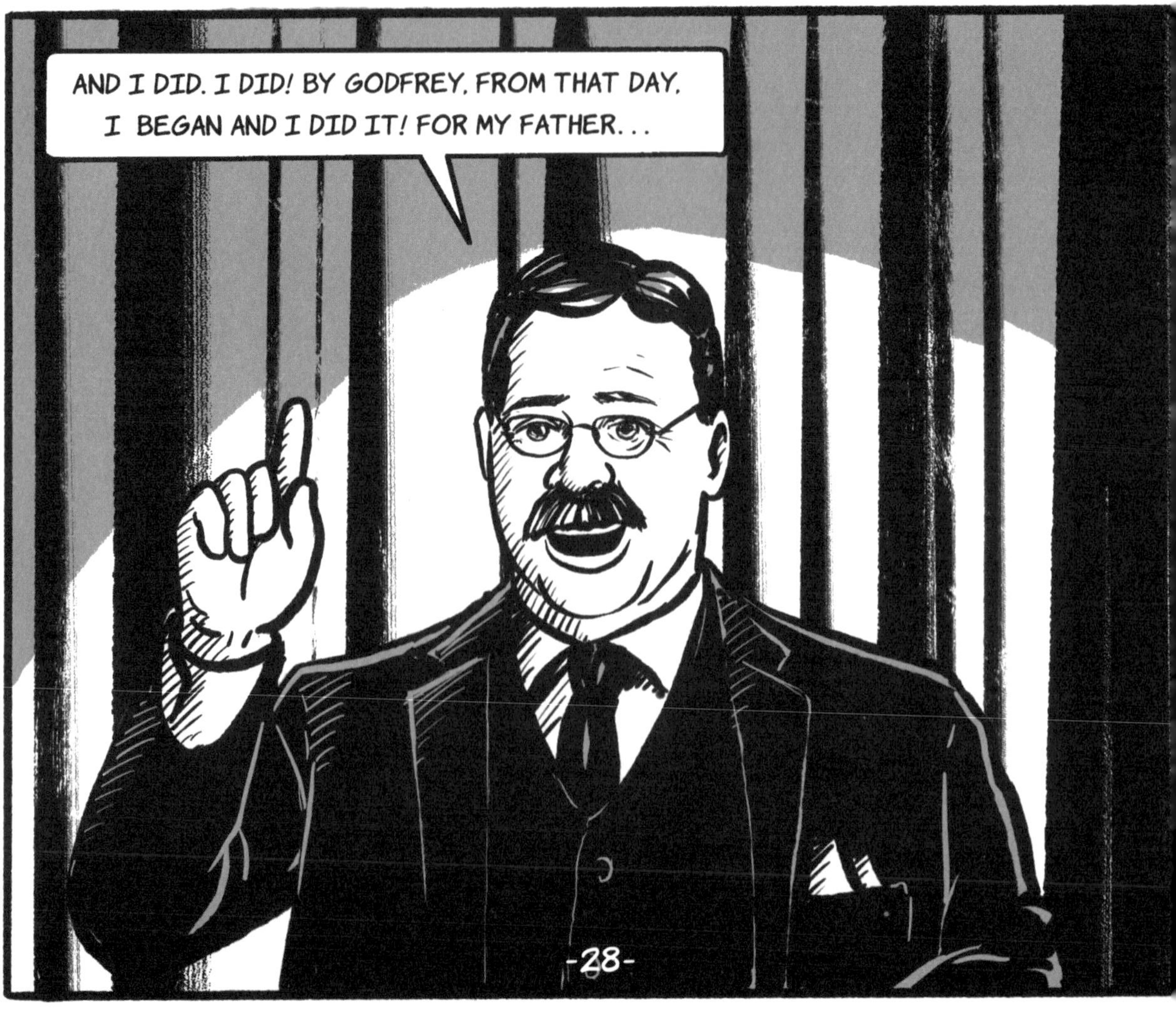
AND I DID. I DID! BY GODFREY, FROM THAT DAY, I BEGAN AND I DID IT! FOR MY FATHER. . .

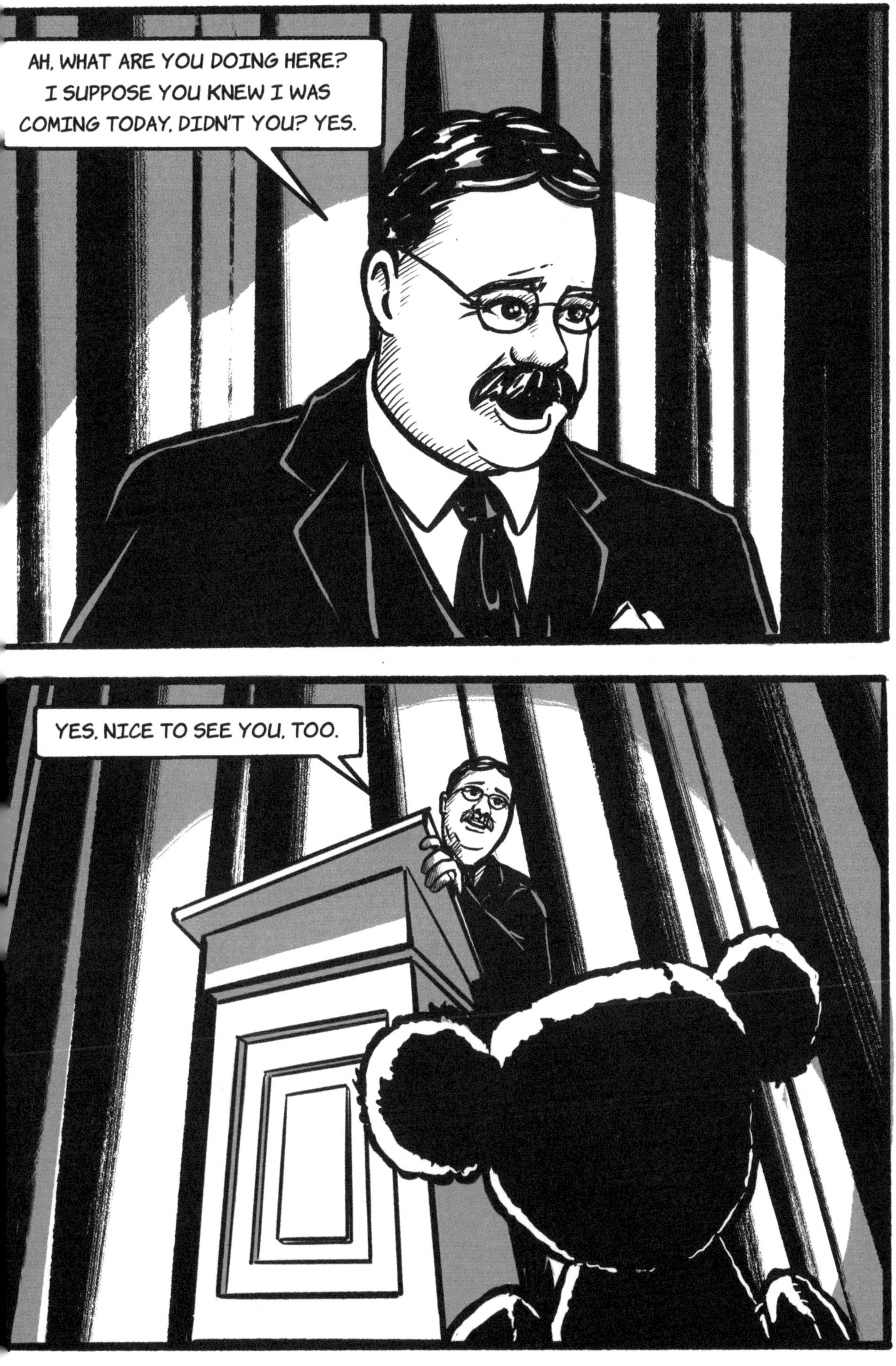
AH, WHAT ARE YOU DOING HERE? I SUPPOSE YOU KNEW I WAS COMING TODAY, DIDN'T YOU? YES.
YES, NICE TO SEE YOU, TOO.

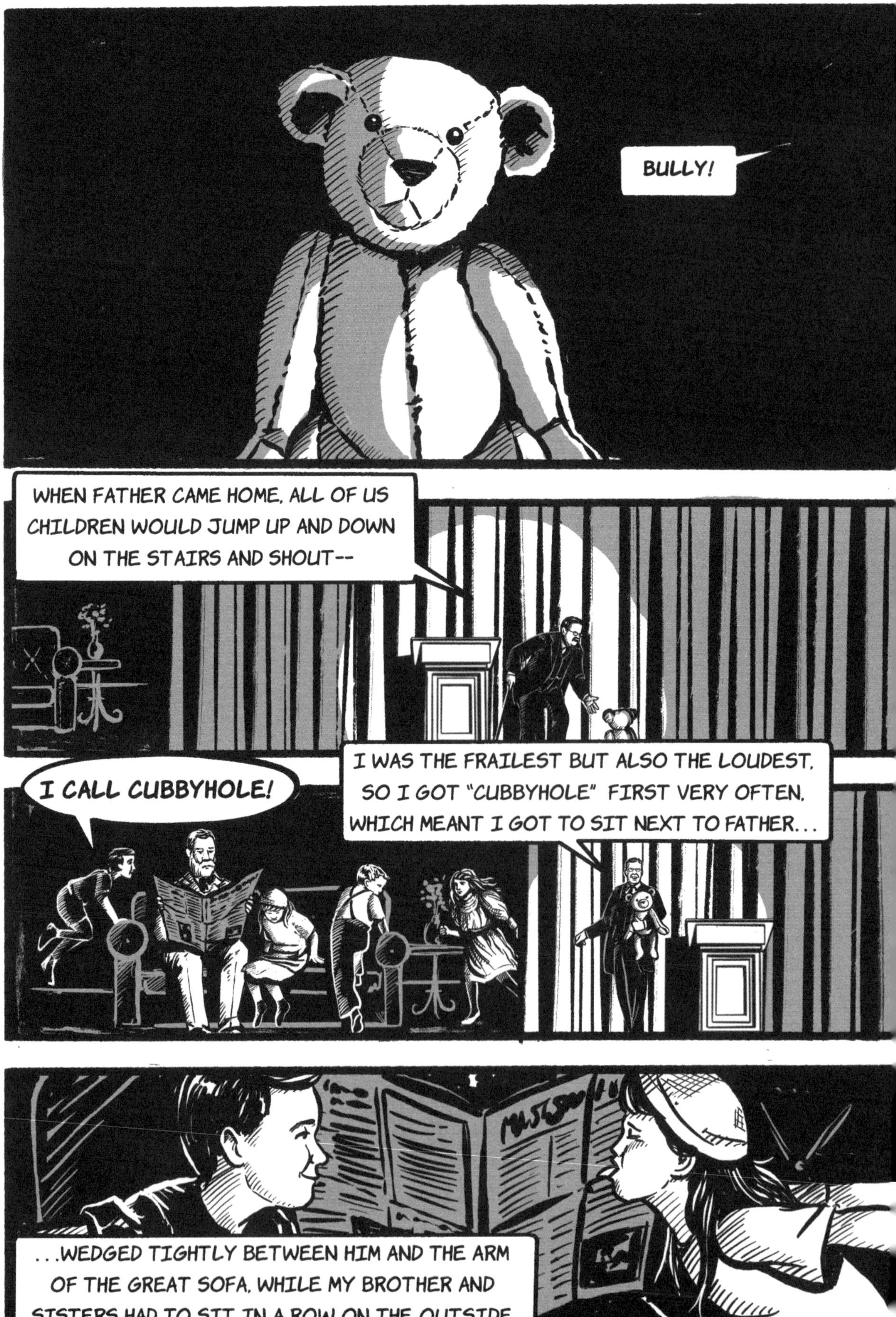
BULLY!
WHEN FATHER CAME HOME, ALL OF US CHILDREN WOULD JUMP UP AND DOWN ON THE STAIRS AND SHOUT--
I CALL CUBBYHOLE!
I WAS THE FRAILEST BUT ALSO THE LOUDEST, SO I GOT "CUBBYHOLE" FIRST VERY OFTEN, WHICH MEANT I GOT TO SIT NEXT TO FATHER...
...WEDGED TIGHTLY BETWEEN HIM AND THE ARM OF THE GREAT SOFA, WHILE MY BROTHER AND SISTERS HAD TO SIT IN A ROW ON THE OUTSIDE.

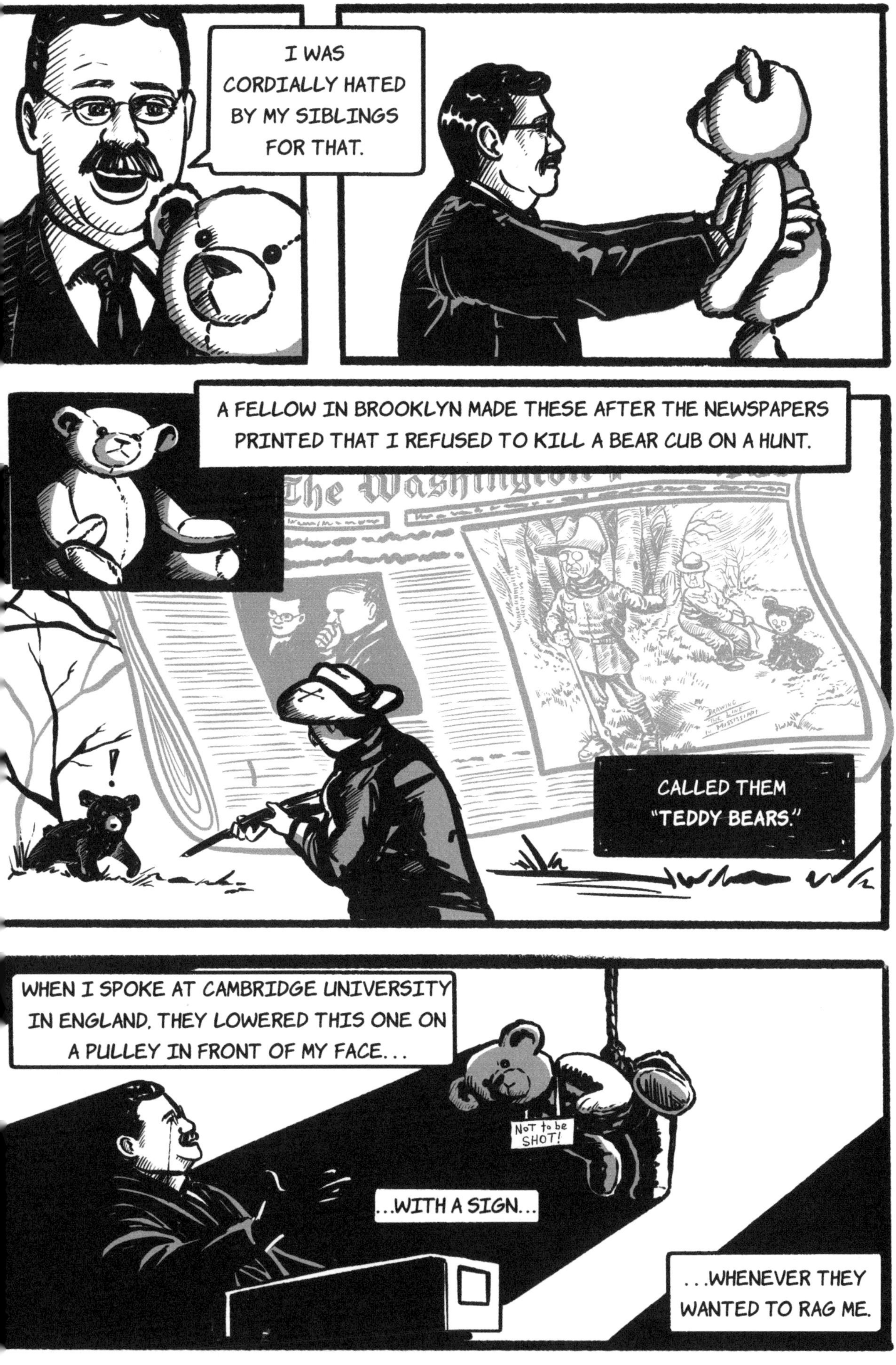

I WAS CORDIALLY HATED BY MY SIBLINGS FOR THAT.
A FELLOW IN BROOKLYN MADE THESE AFTER THE NEWSPAPERS PRINTED THAT I REFUSED TO KILL A BEAR CUB ON A HUNT.
DRAWING THE LINE IN MISSISSIPPI
CALLED THEM "TEDDY BEARS."
WHEN I SPOKE AT CAMBRIDGE UNIVERSITY IN ENGLAND, THEY LOWERED THIS ONE ON A PULLEY IN FRONT OF MY FACE...
Not to be SHOT!
...WITH A SIGN...
...WHENEVER THEY WANTED TO RAG ME.

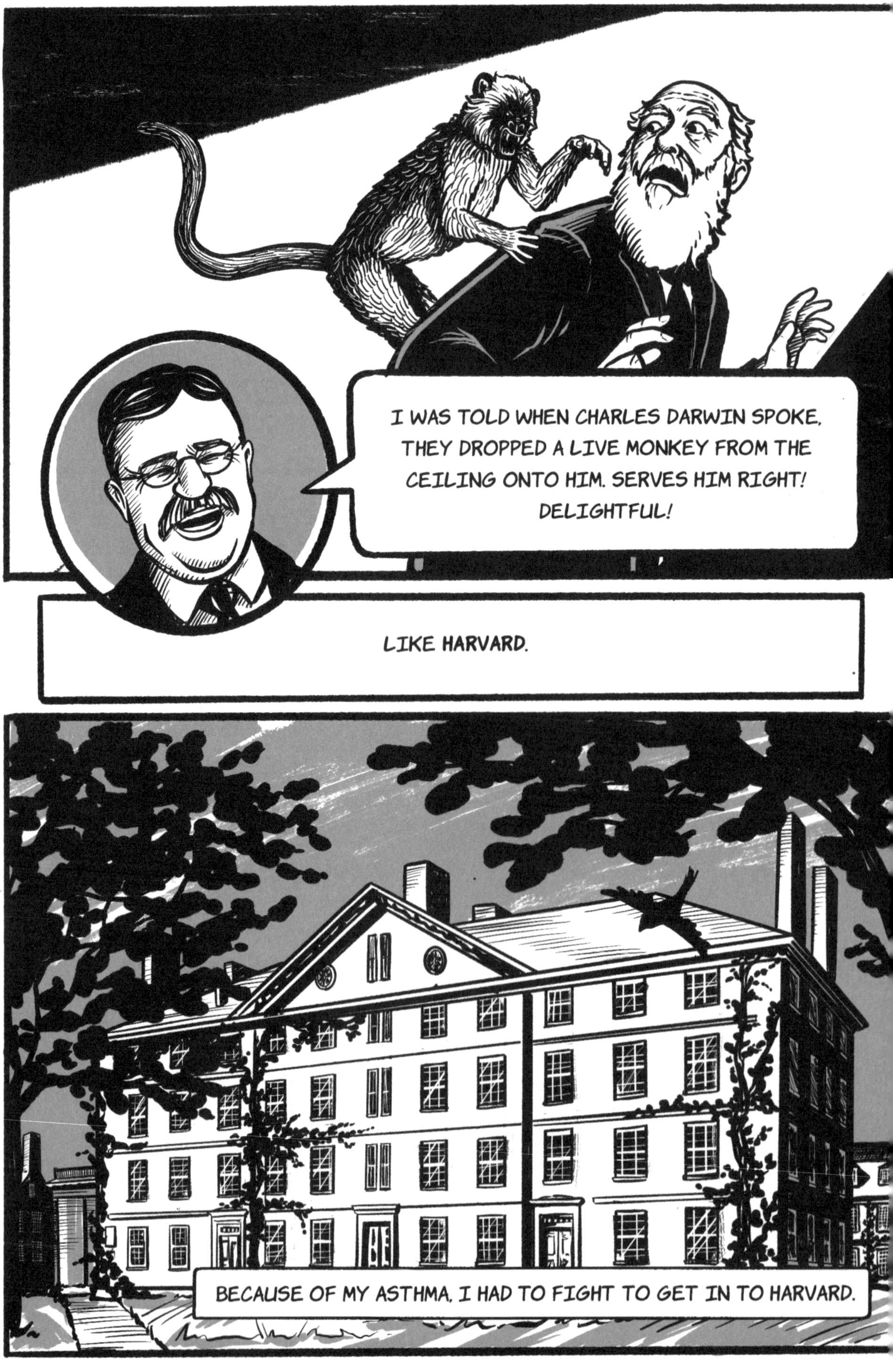

I WAS TOLD WHEN CHARLES DARWIN SPOKE, THEY DROPPED A LIVE MONKEY FROM THE CEILING ONTO HIM. SERVES HIM RIGHT! DELIGHTFUL!
LIKE HARVARD.
BECAUSE OF MY ASTHMA, I HAD TO FIGHT TO GET IN TO HARVARD.

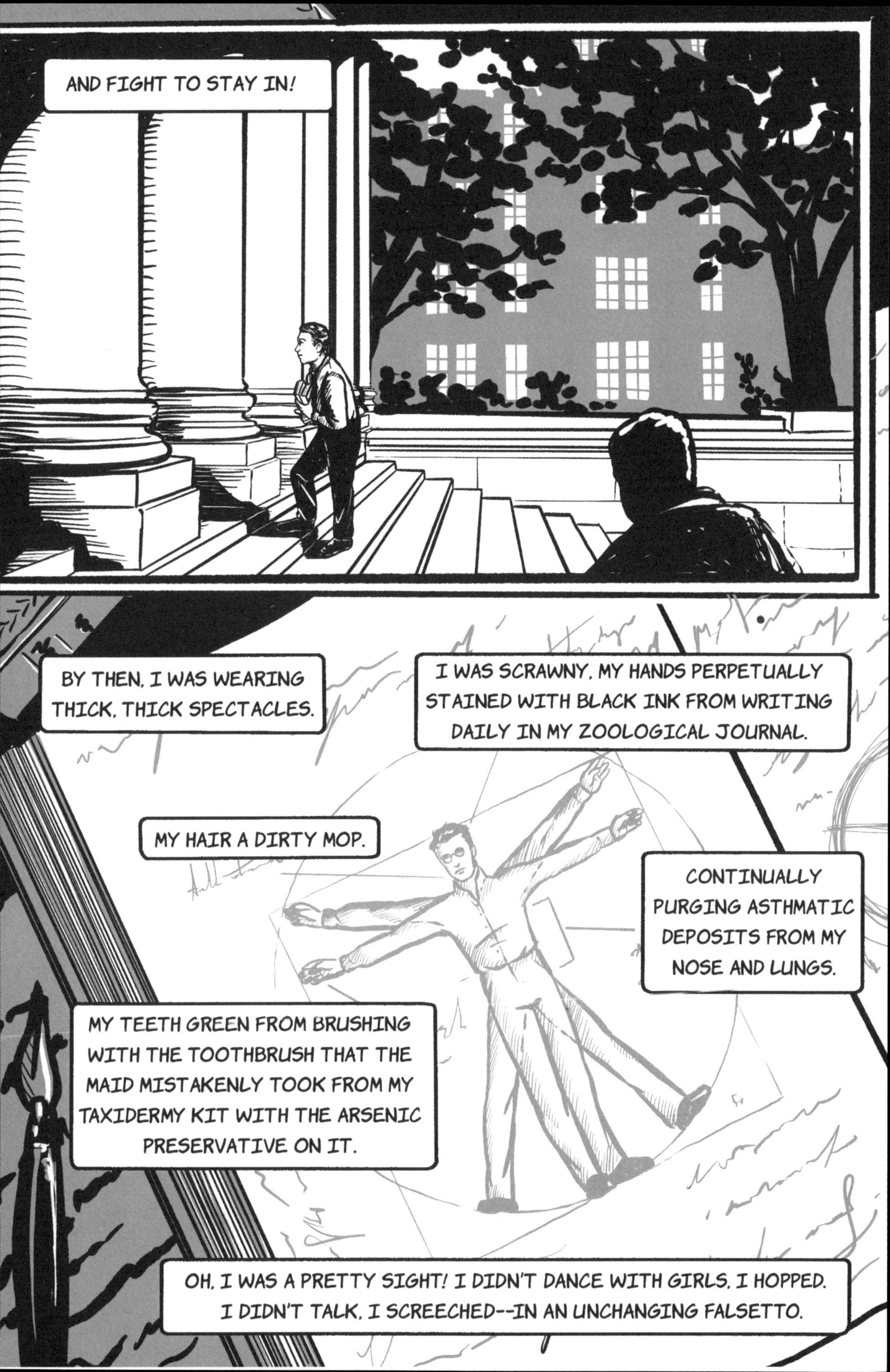
AND FIGHT TO STAY IN!
BY THEN, I WAS WEARING THICK, THICK SPECTACLES.
I WAS SCRAWNY, MY HANDS PERPETUALLY STAINED WITH BLACK INK FROM WRITING DAILY IN MY ZOOLOGICAL JOURNAL.
MY HAIR A DIRTY MOP.
CONTINUALLY PURGING ASTHMATIC DEPOSITS FROM MY NOSE AND LUNGS.
MY TEETH GREEN FROM BRUSHING WITH THE TOOTHBRUSH THAT THE MAID MISTAKENLY TOOK FROM MY TAXIDERMY KIT WITH THE ARSENIC PRESERVATIVE ON IT.
OH, I WAS A PRETTY SIGHT! I DIDN'T DANCE WITH GIRLS, I HOPPED. I DIDN'T TALK, I SCREECHED--IN AN UNCHANGING FALSETTO.

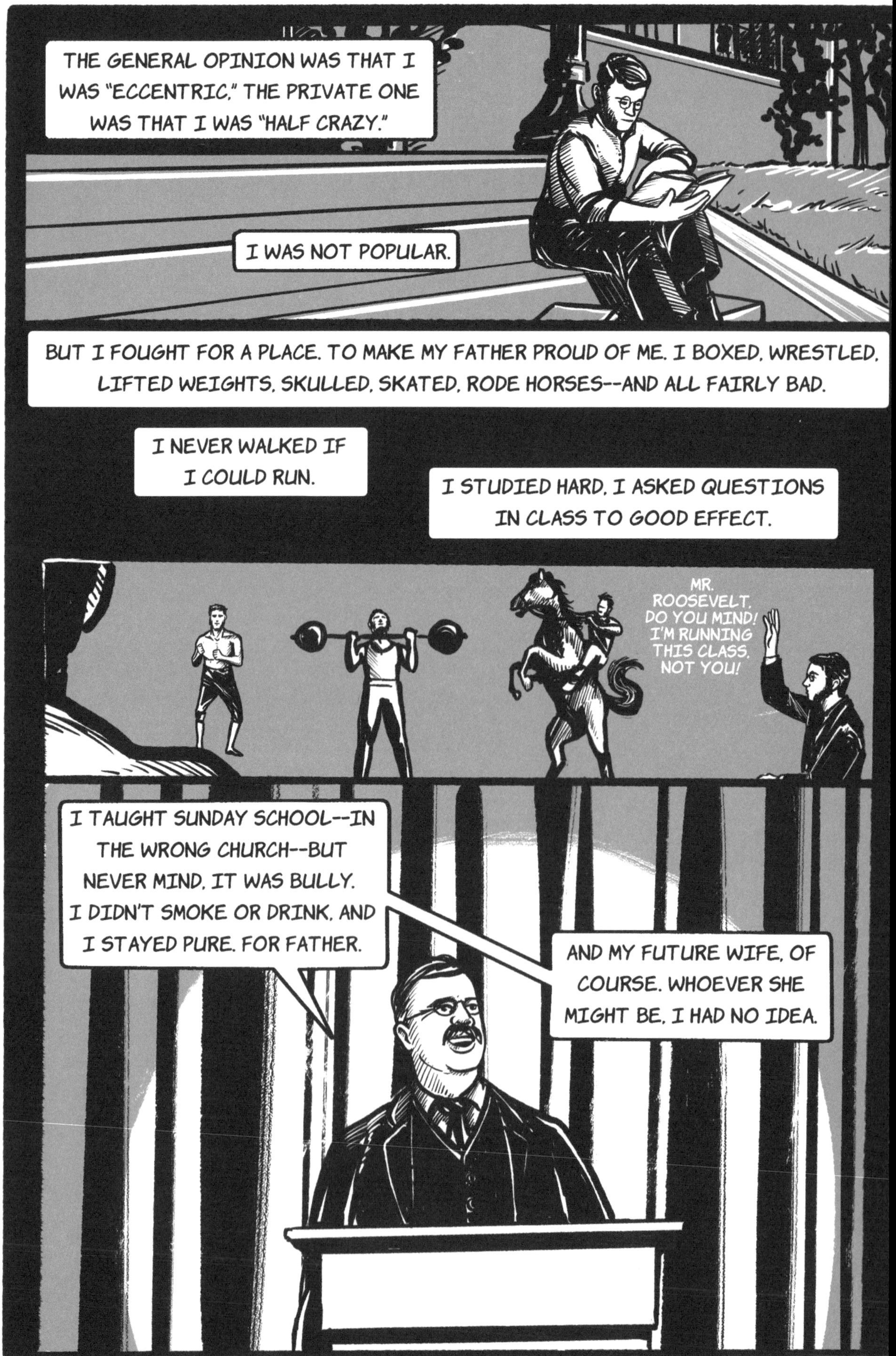
THE GENERAL OPINION WAS THAT I WAS "ECCENTRIC," THE PRIVATE ONE WAS THAT I WAS "HALF CRAZY."
I WAS NOT POPULAR.
BUT I FOUGHT FOR A PLACE. TO MAKE MY FATHER PROUD OF ME. I BOXED, WRESTLED, LIFTED WEIGHTS, SKULLED, SKATED, RODE HORSES--AND ALL FAIRLY BAD.
I NEVER WALKED IF I COULD RUN.
I STUDIED HARD, I ASKED QUESTIONS IN CLASS TO GOOD EFFECT.
MR. ROOSEVELT, DO YOU MIND! I'M RUNNING THIS CLASS, NOT YOU!
I TAUGHT SUNDAY SCHOOL--IN THE WRONG CHURCH--BUT NEVER MIND, IT WAS BULLY. I DIDN'T SMOKE OR DRINK, AND I STAYED PURE. FOR FATHER.
AND MY FUTURE WIFE, OF COURSE. WHOEVER SHE MIGHT BE, I HAD NO IDEA.

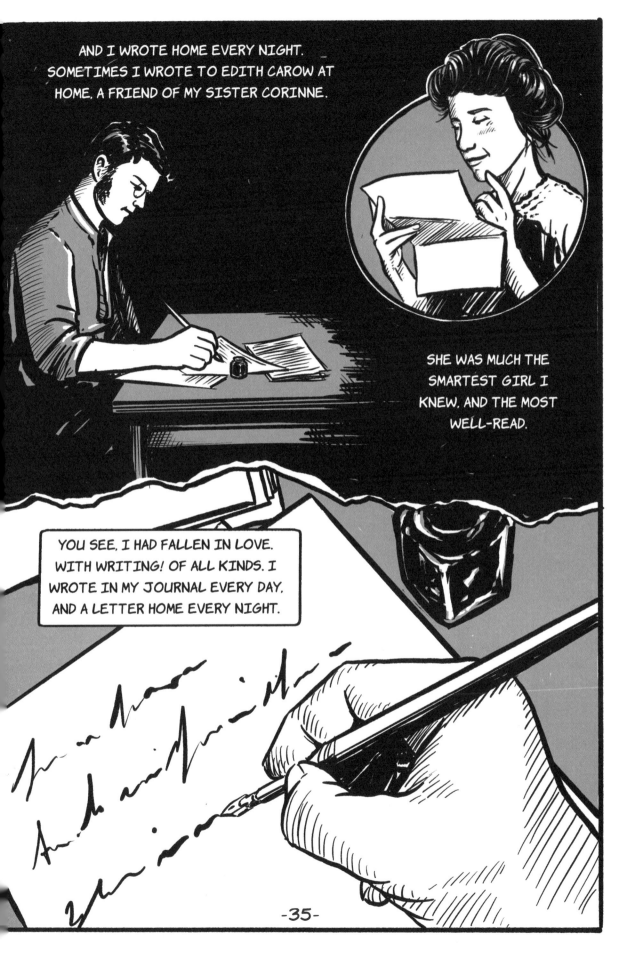

AND I WROTE HOME EVERY NIGHT. SOMETIMES I WROTE TO EDITH CAROW AT HOME, A FRIEND OF MY SISTER CORINNE.

SHE WAS MUCH THE SMARTEST GIRL I KNEW, AND THE MOST WELL-READ.

YOU SEE, I HAD FALLEN IN LOVE. WITH WRITING! OF ALL KINDS. I WROTE IN MY JOURNAL EVERY DAY, AND A LETTER HOME EVERY NIGHT.

I WAS HAPPY.

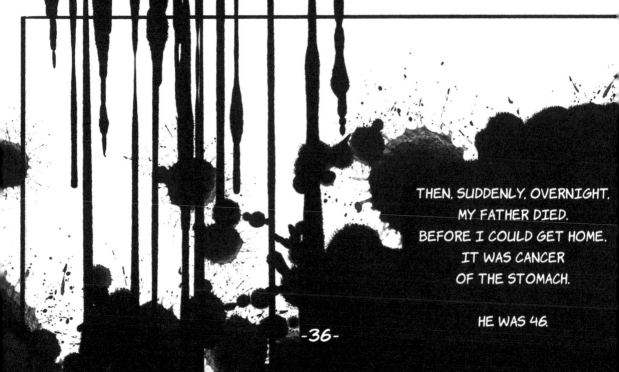

THEN, SUDDENLY, OVERNIGHT,
MY FATHER DIED.
BEFORE I COULD GET HOME.
IT WAS CANCER
OF THE STOMACH.

HE WAS 46.

I ADORED MY FATHER. HE WAS THE BEST MAN I EVER KNEW.

THE ONLY MAN I WAS EVER AFRAID OF,
BECAUSE I WANTED HIS GOOD OPINION SO MUCH.

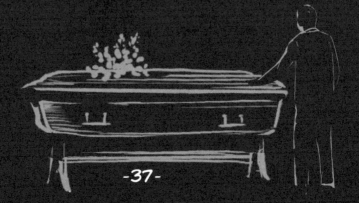

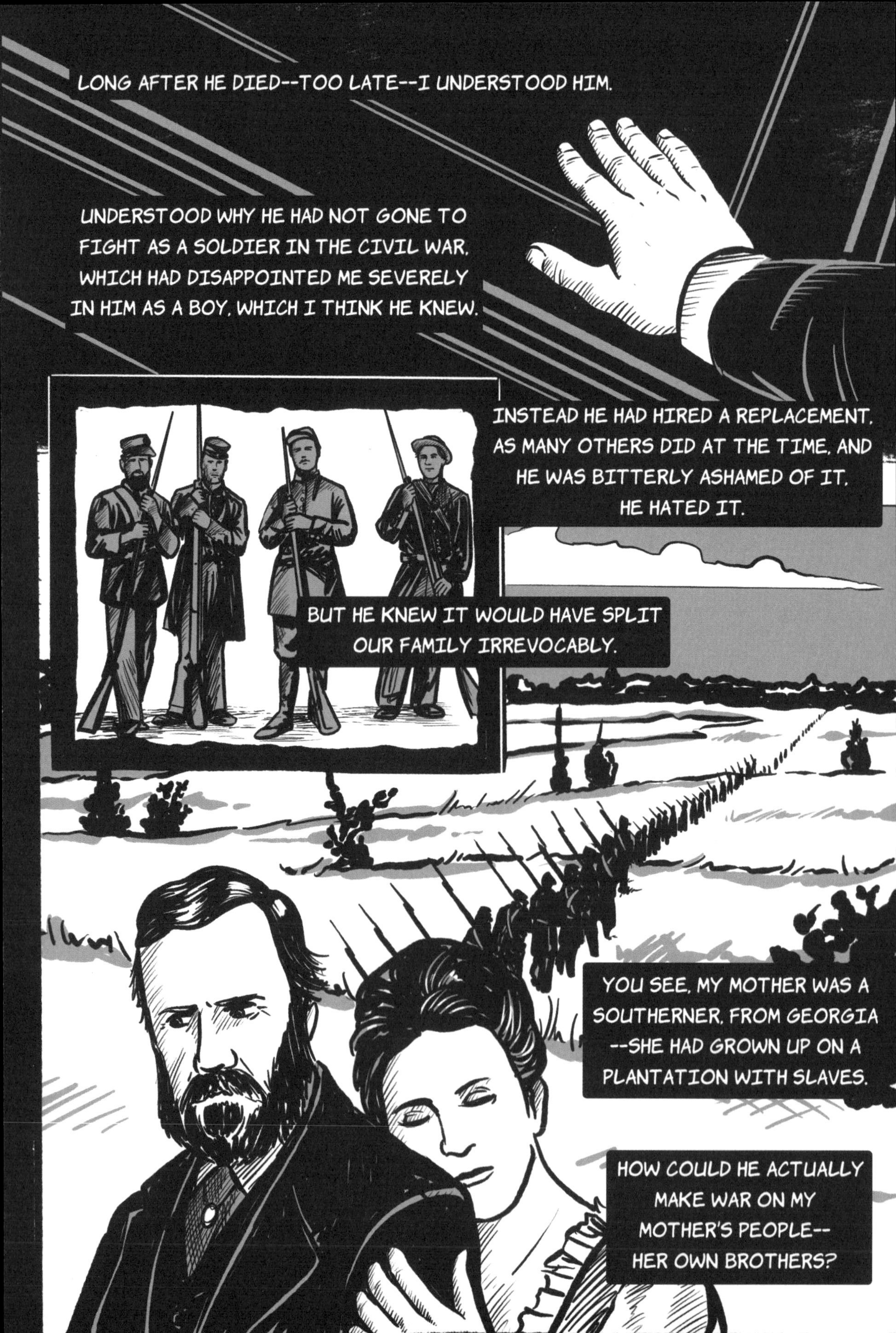
LONG AFTER HE DIED--TOO LATE--I UNDERSTOOD HIM.
UNDERSTOOD WHY HE HAD NOT GONE TO FIGHT AS A SOLDIER IN THE CIVIL WAR, WHICH HAD DISAPPOINTED ME SEVERELY IN HIM AS A BOY, WHICH I THINK HE KNEW.
INSTEAD HE HAD HIRED A REPLACEMENT, AS MANY OTHERS DID AT THE TIME, AND HE WAS BITTERLY ASHAMED OF IT. HE HATED IT.
BUT HE KNEW IT WOULD HAVE SPLIT OUR FAMILY IRREVOCABLY.
YOU SEE, MY MOTHER WAS A SOUTHERNER, FROM GEORGIA --SHE HAD GROWN UP ON A PLANTATION WITH SLAVES.
HOW COULD HE ACTUALLY MAKE WAR ON MY MOTHER'S PEOPLE-- HER OWN BROTHERS?

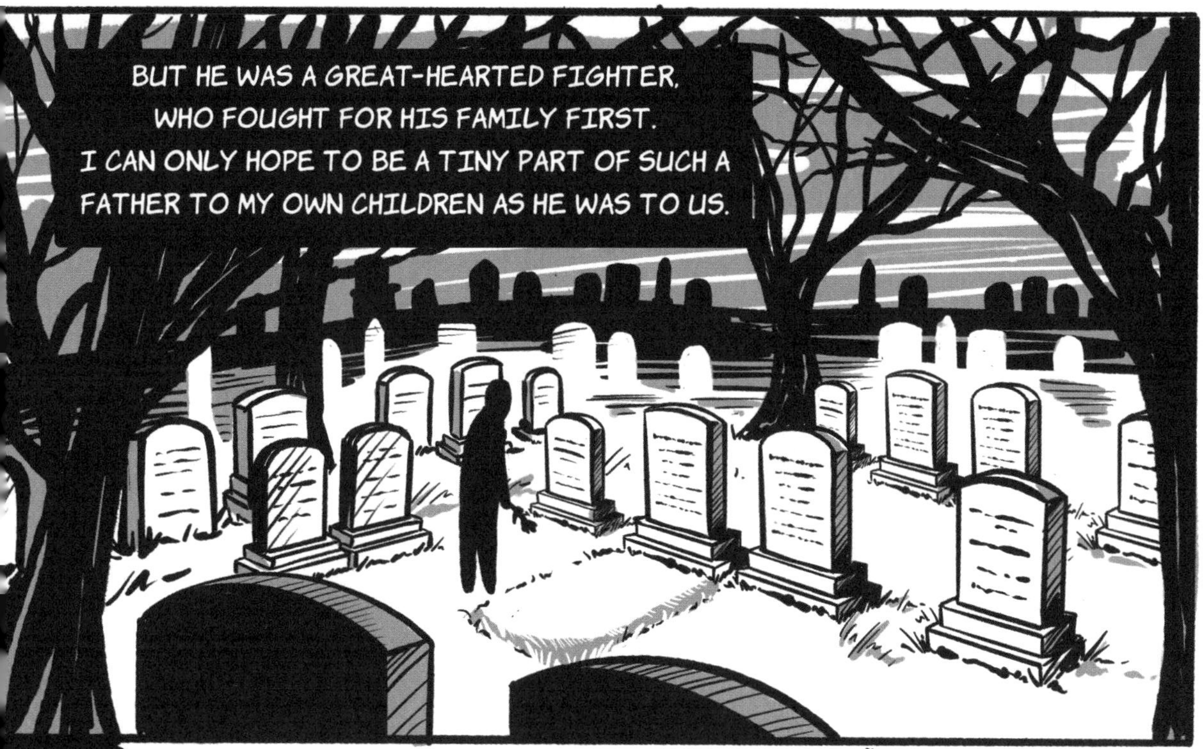
BUT HE WAS A GREAT-HEARTED FIGHTER, WHO FOUGHT FOR HIS FAMILY FIRST. I CAN ONLY HOPE TO BE A TINY PART OF SUCH A FATHER TO MY OWN CHILDREN AS HE WAS TO US.

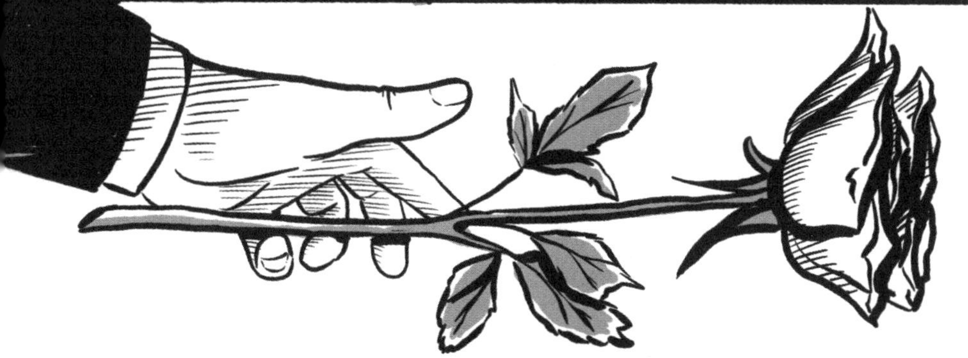

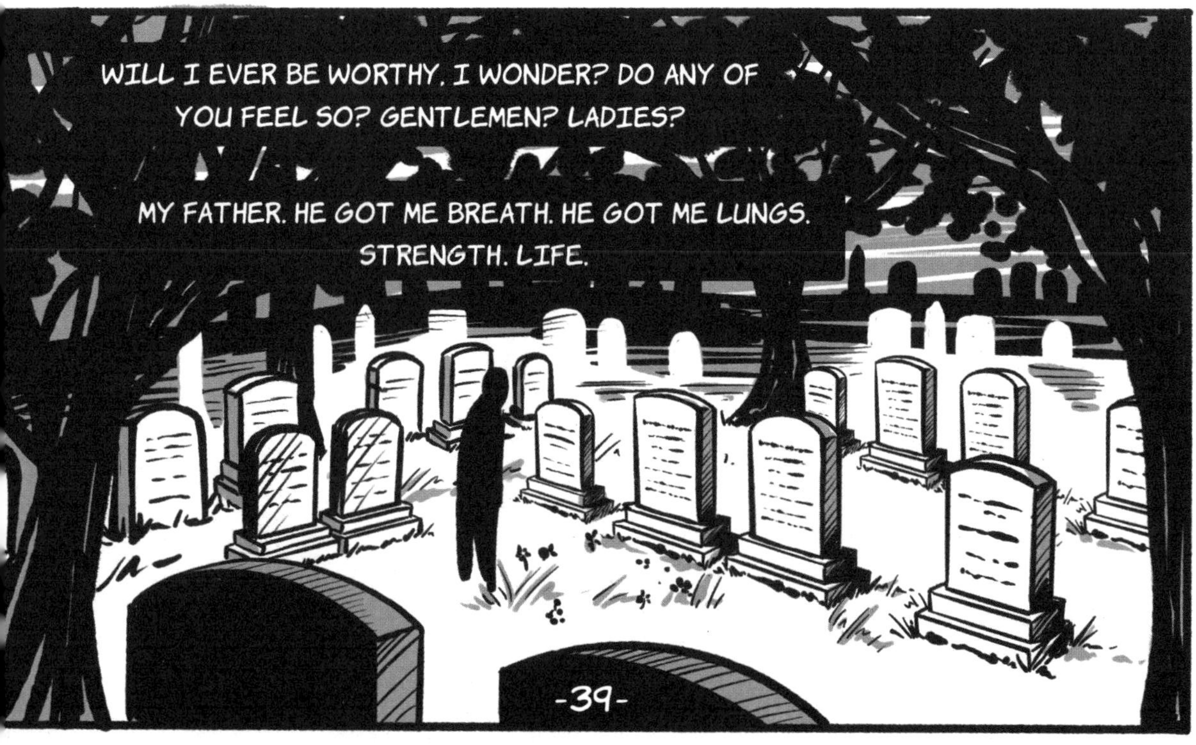
WILL I EVER BE WORTHY, I WONDER? DO ANY OF YOU FEEL SO? GENTLEMEN? LADIES?
MY FATHER. HE GOT ME BREATH. HE GOT ME LUNGS. STRENGTH. LIFE.

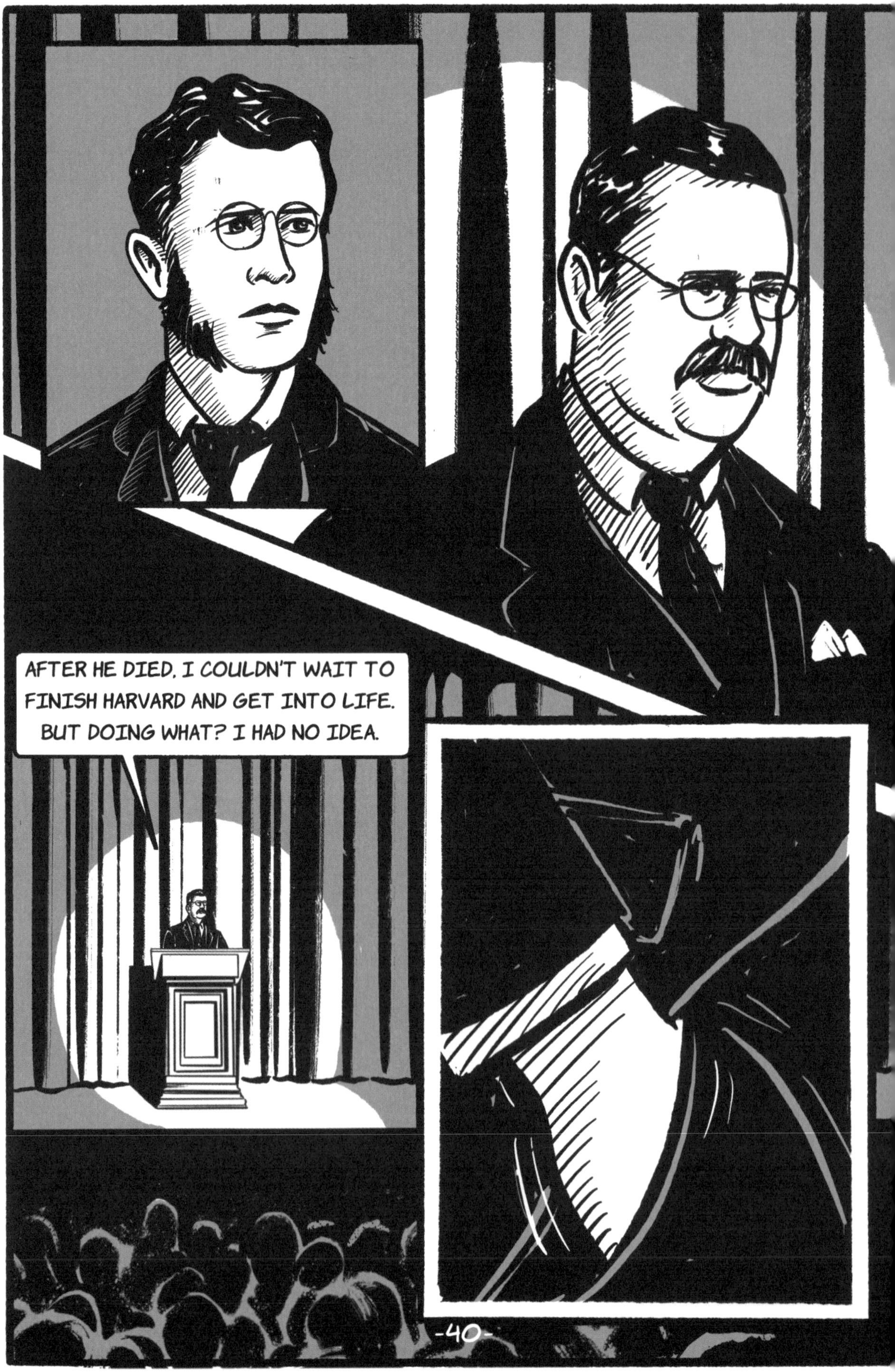
AFTER HE DIED, I COULDN'T WAIT TO FINISH HARVARD AND GET INTO LIFE. BUT DOING WHAT? I HAD NO IDEA.

WELL, WELL, WELL...

I PICKED THIS UP THIS MORNING IN SAGAMORE HILL.

A FOX SPARROW... A FLEDGLING... PROBABLY KILLED BY A HAWK.

I SUPPOSED MYSELF A NATURALIST, AN OUTDOORSMAN, HAVING COLLECTED AND CLASSIFIED HUNDREDS OF SPECIMENS FROM BIRDS TO SNAKES TO SEALS ALL MY LIFE.

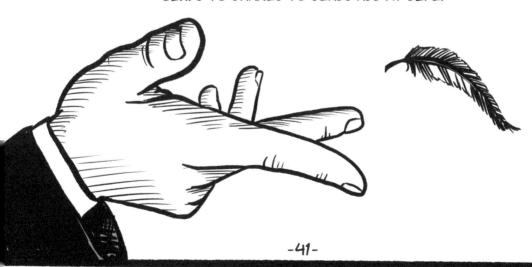

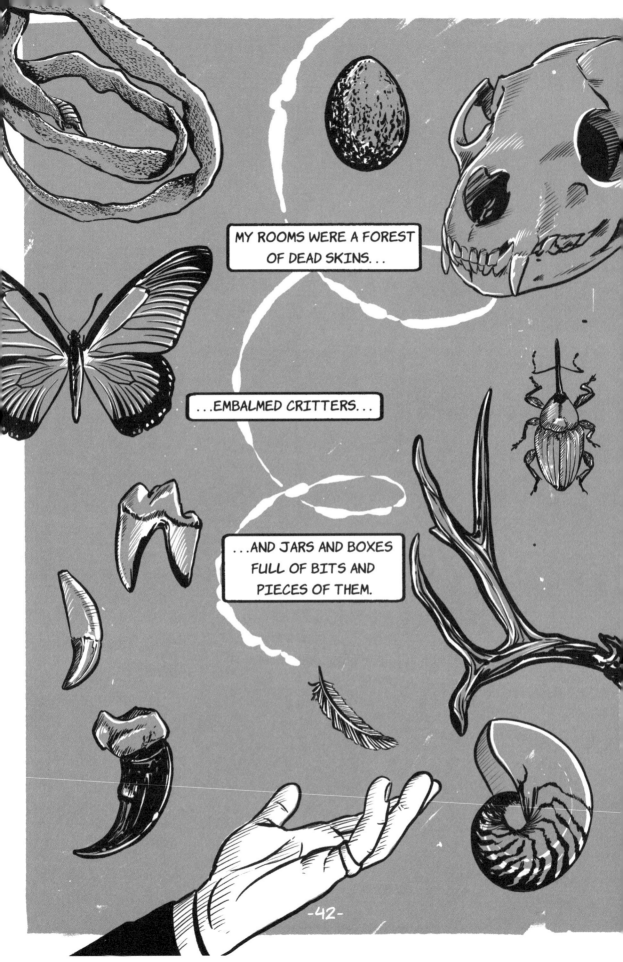

MY ROOMS WERE A FOREST OF DEAD SKINS...

...EMBALMED CRITTERS...

...AND JARS AND BOXES FULL OF BITS AND PIECES OF THEM.

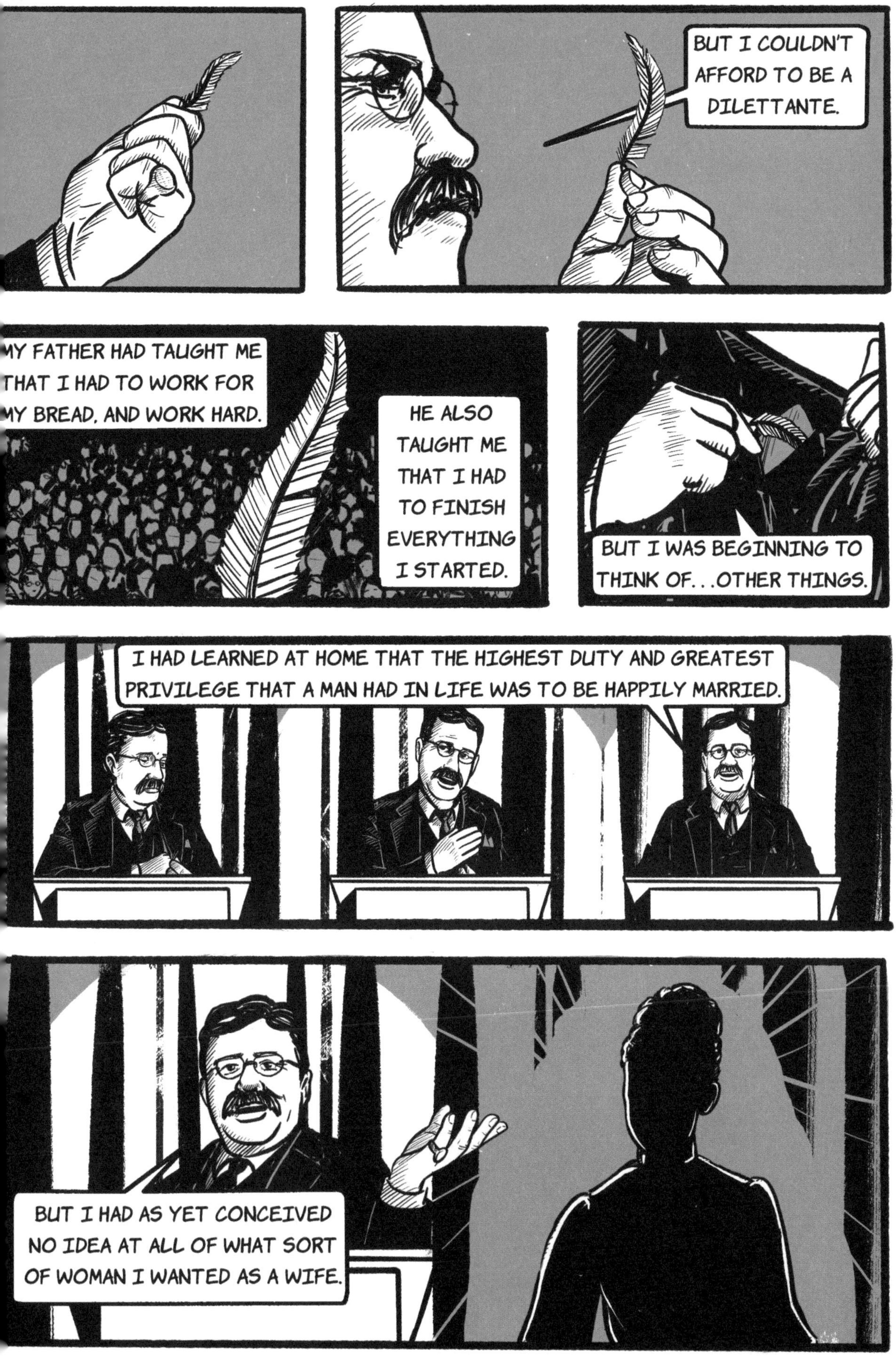
BUT I COULDN'T AFFORD TO BE A DILETTANTE.
MY FATHER HAD TAUGHT ME THAT I HAD TO WORK FOR MY BREAD, AND WORK HARD.
HE ALSO TAUGHT ME THAT I HAD TO FINISH EVERYTHING I STARTED.
BUT I WAS BEGINNING TO THINK OF. . .OTHER THINGS.
I HAD LEARNED AT HOME THAT THE HIGHEST DUTY AND GREATEST PRIVILEGE THAT A MAN HAD IN LIFE WAS TO BE HAPPILY MARRIED.
BUT I HAD AS YET CONCEIVED NO IDEA AT ALL OF WHAT SORT OF WOMAN I WANTED AS A WIFE.

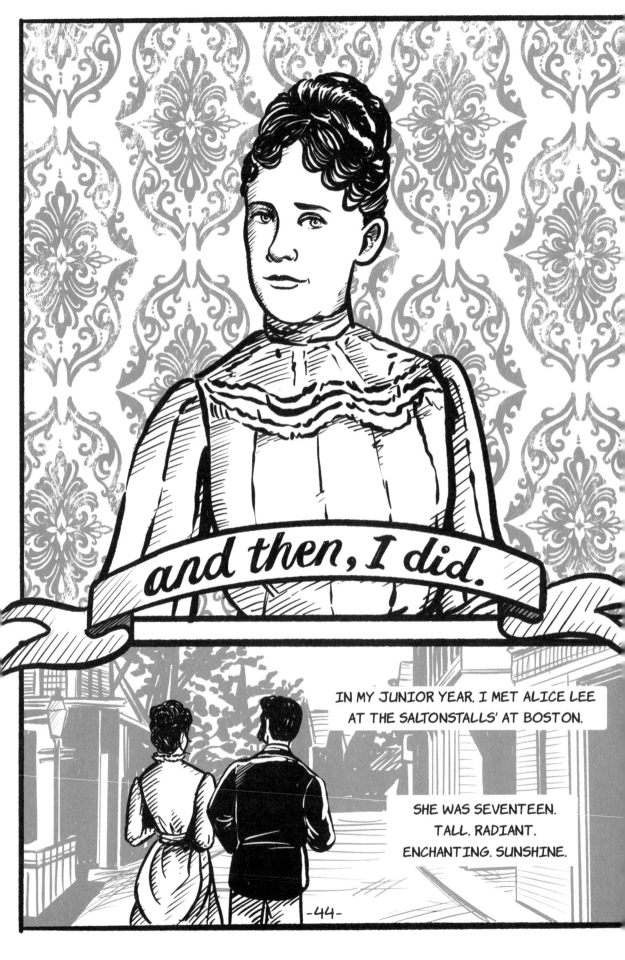

and then, I did.

IN MY JUNIOR YEAR, I MET ALICE LEE AT THE SALTONSTALLS' AT BOSTON.

SHE WAS SEVENTEEN.
TALL. RADIANT.
ENCHANTING. SUNSHINE.

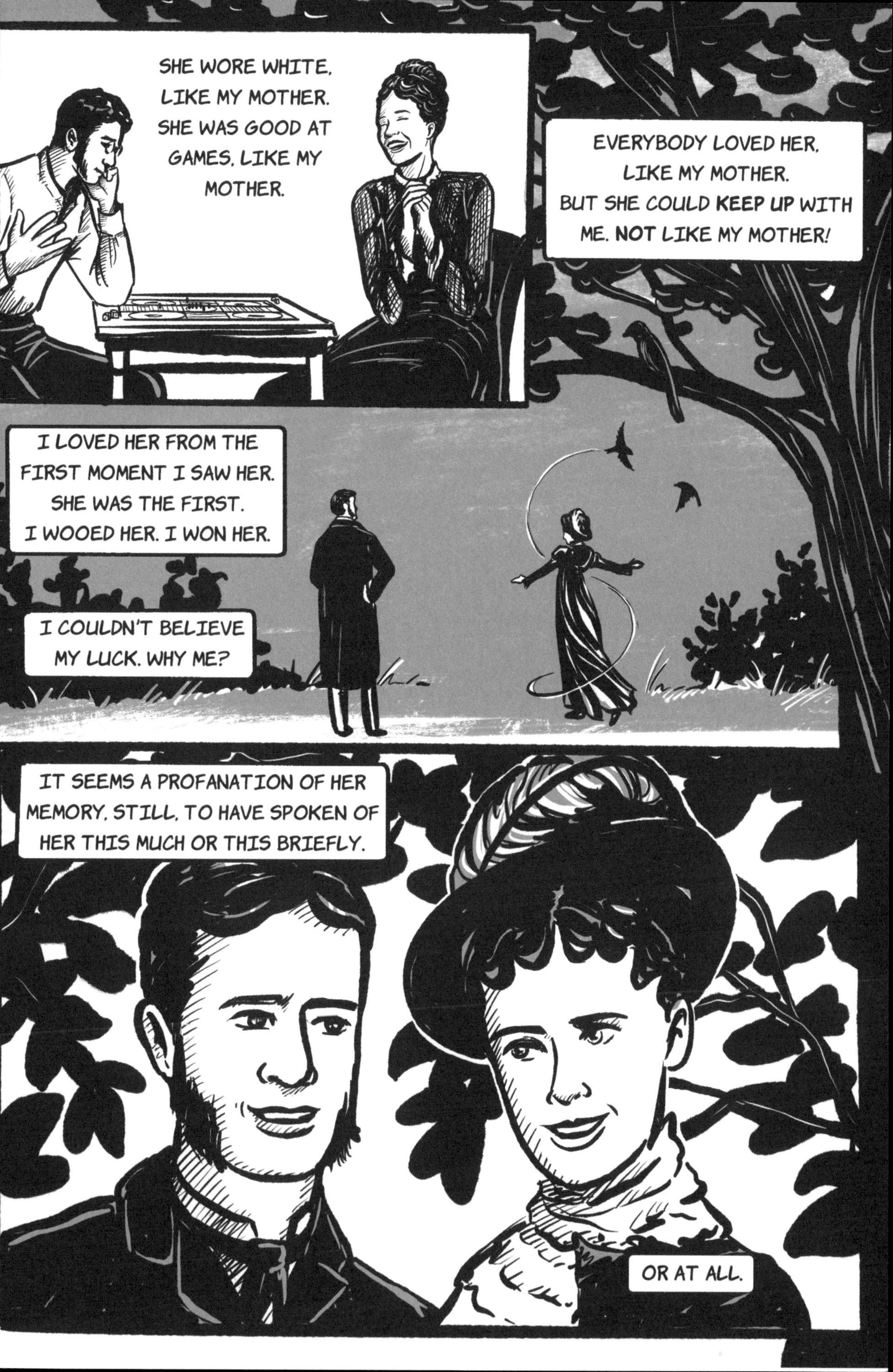
SHE WORE WHITE, LIKE MY MOTHER. SHE WAS GOOD AT GAMES, LIKE MY MOTHER.
EVERYBODY LOVED HER, LIKE MY MOTHER. BUT SHE COULD KEEP UP WITH ME. NOT LIKE MY MOTHER!
I LOVED HER FROM THE FIRST MOMENT I SAW HER. SHE WAS THE FIRST. I WOOED HER. I WON HER.
I COULDN'T BELIEVE MY LUCK. WHY ME?
IT SEEMS A PROFANATION OF HER MEMORY, STILL, TO HAVE SPOKEN OF HER THIS MUCH OR THIS BRIEFLY.
OR AT ALL.

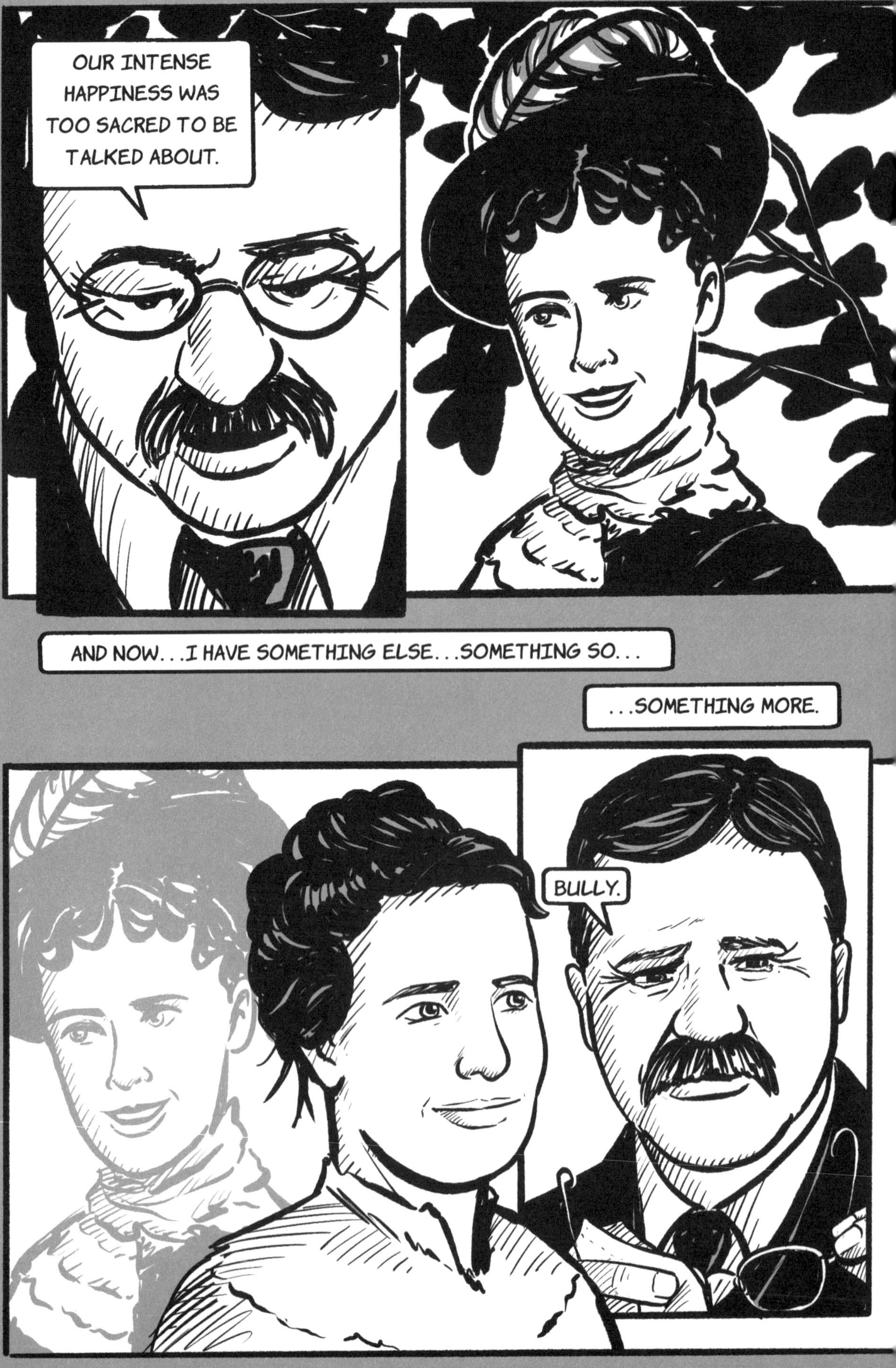
OUR INTENSE HAPPINESS WAS TOO SACRED TO BE TALKED ABOUT.
AND NOW...I HAVE SOMETHING ELSE...SOMETHING SO...
...SOMETHING MORE.
BULLY.

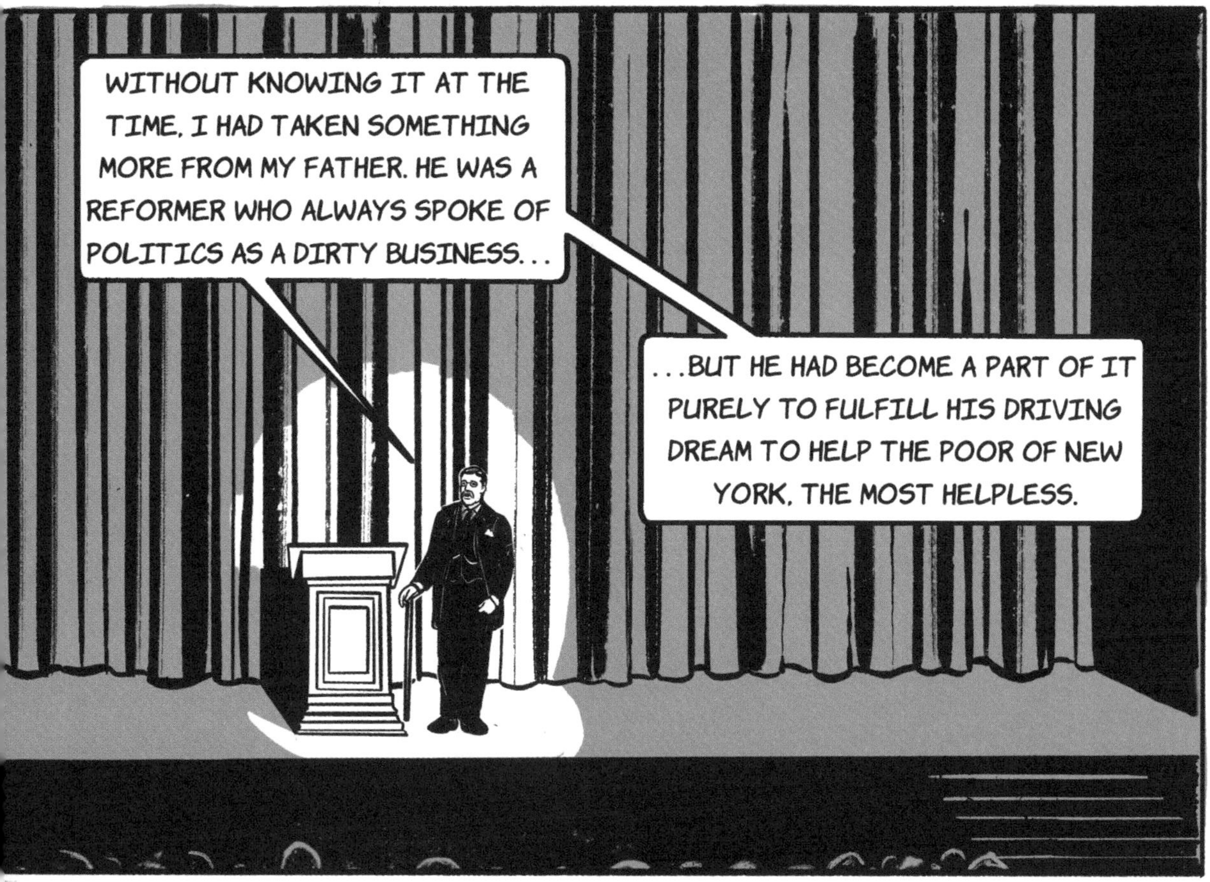
WITHOUT KNOWING IT AT THE TIME, I HAD TAKEN SOMETHING MORE FROM MY FATHER. HE WAS A REFORMER WHO ALWAYS SPOKE OF POLITICS AS A DIRTY BUSINESS...
...BUT HE HAD BECOME A PART OF IT PURELY TO FULFILL HIS DRIVING DREAM TO HELP THE POOR OF NEW YORK, THE MOST HELPLESS.

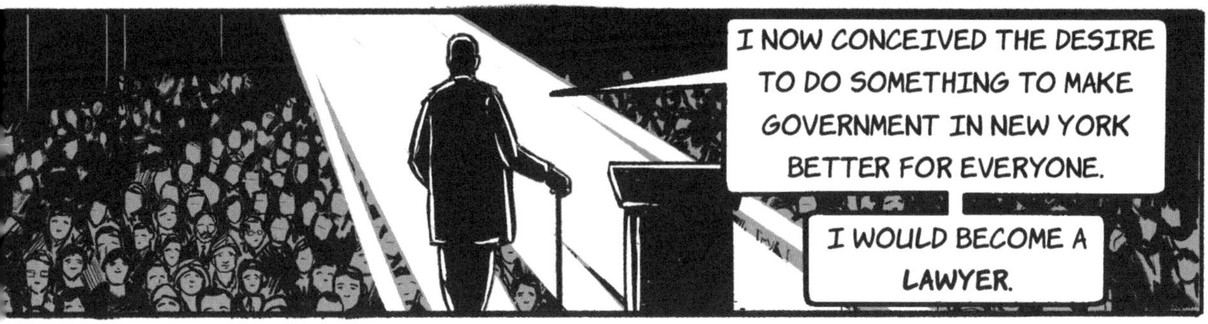
I NOW CONCEIVED THE DESIRE TO DO SOMETHING TO MAKE GOVERNMENT IN NEW YORK BETTER FOR EVERYONE.
I WOULD BECOME A LAWYER.

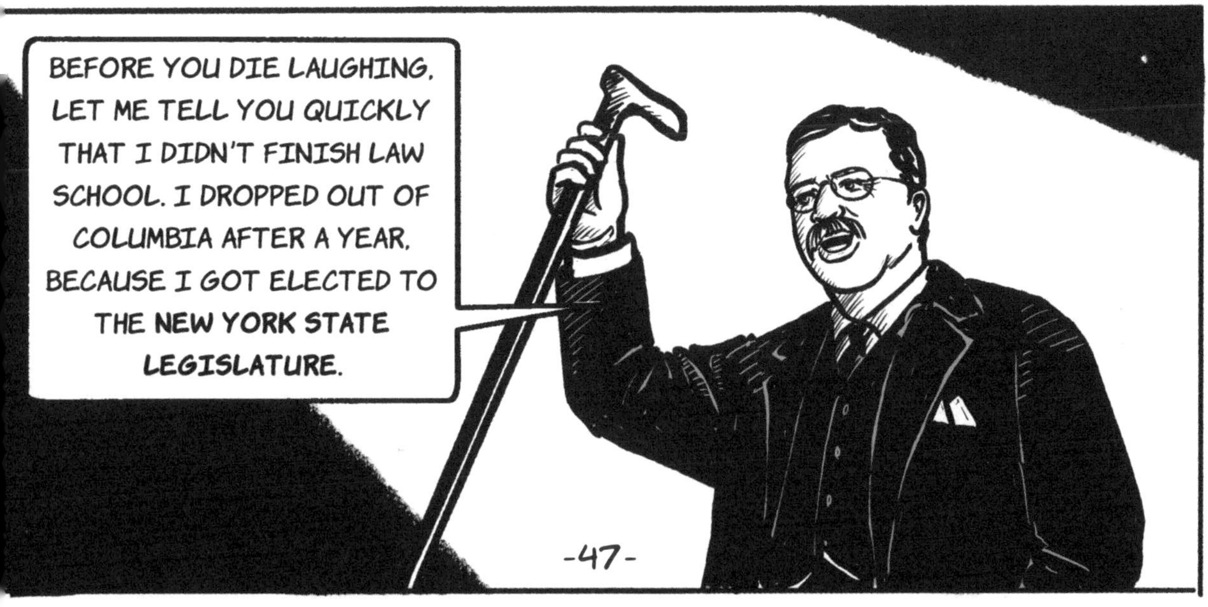
BEFORE YOU DIE LAUGHING, LET ME TELL YOU QUICKLY THAT I DIDN'T FINISH LAW SCHOOL. I DROPPED OUT OF COLUMBIA AFTER A YEAR, BECAUSE I GOT ELECTED TO THE NEW YORK STATE LEGISLATURE.

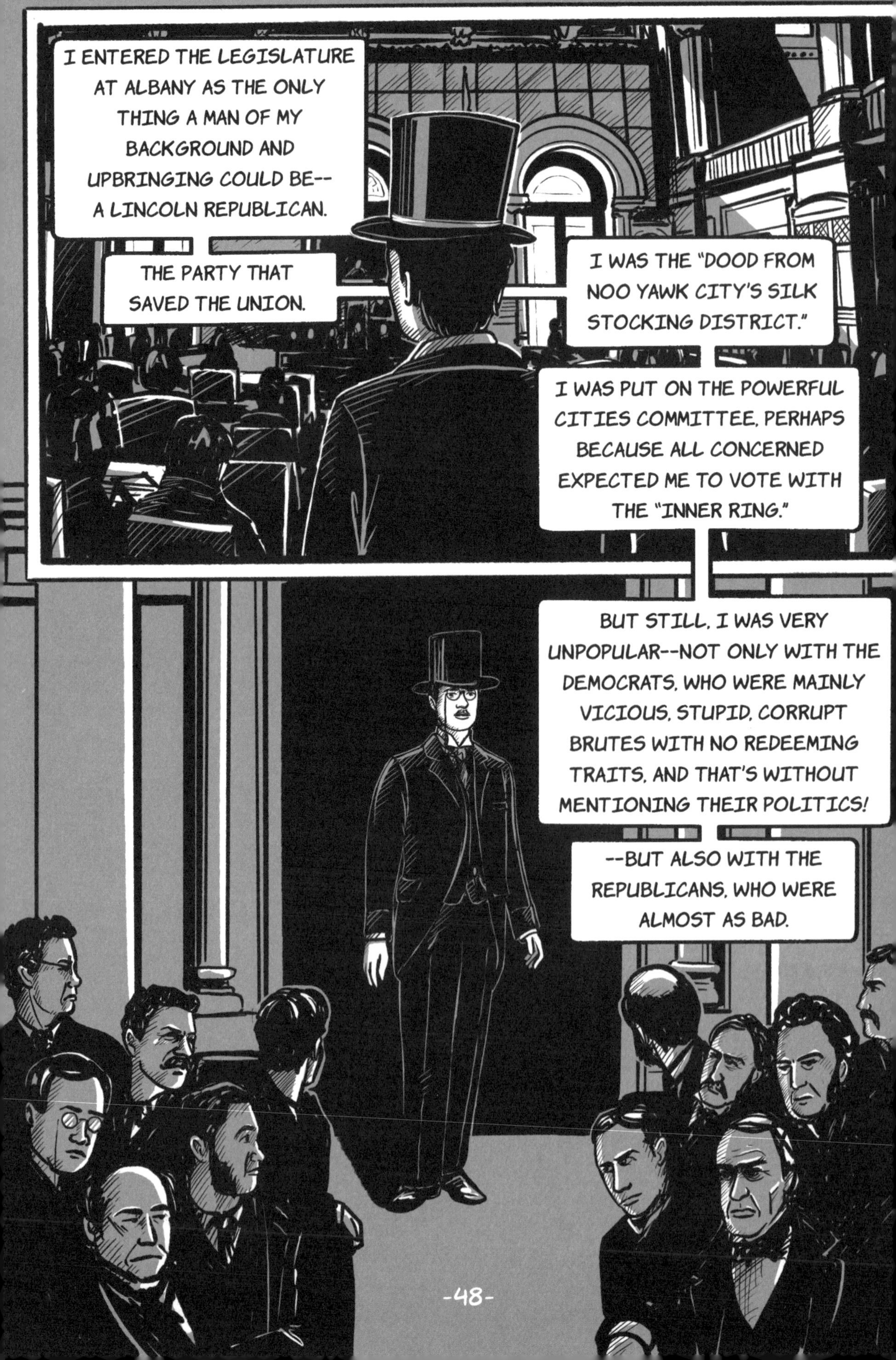
I ENTERED THE LEGISLATURE AT ALBANY AS THE ONLY THING A MAN OF MY BACKGROUND AND UPBRINGING COULD BE-- A LINCOLN REPUBLICAN.
THE PARTY THAT SAVED THE UNION.
I WAS THE "DOOD FROM NOO YAWK CITY'S SILK STOCKING DISTRICT."
I WAS PUT ON THE POWERFUL CITIES COMMITTEE, PERHAPS BECAUSE ALL CONCERNED EXPECTED ME TO VOTE WITH THE "INNER RING."
BUT STILL, I WAS VERY UNPOPULAR--NOT ONLY WITH THE DEMOCRATS, WHO WERE MAINLY VICIOUS, STUPID, CORRUPT BRUTES WITH NO REDEEMING TRAITS, AND THAT'S WITHOUT MENTIONING THEIR POLITICS!
--BUT ALSO WITH THE REPUBLICANS, WHO WERE ALMOST AS BAD.

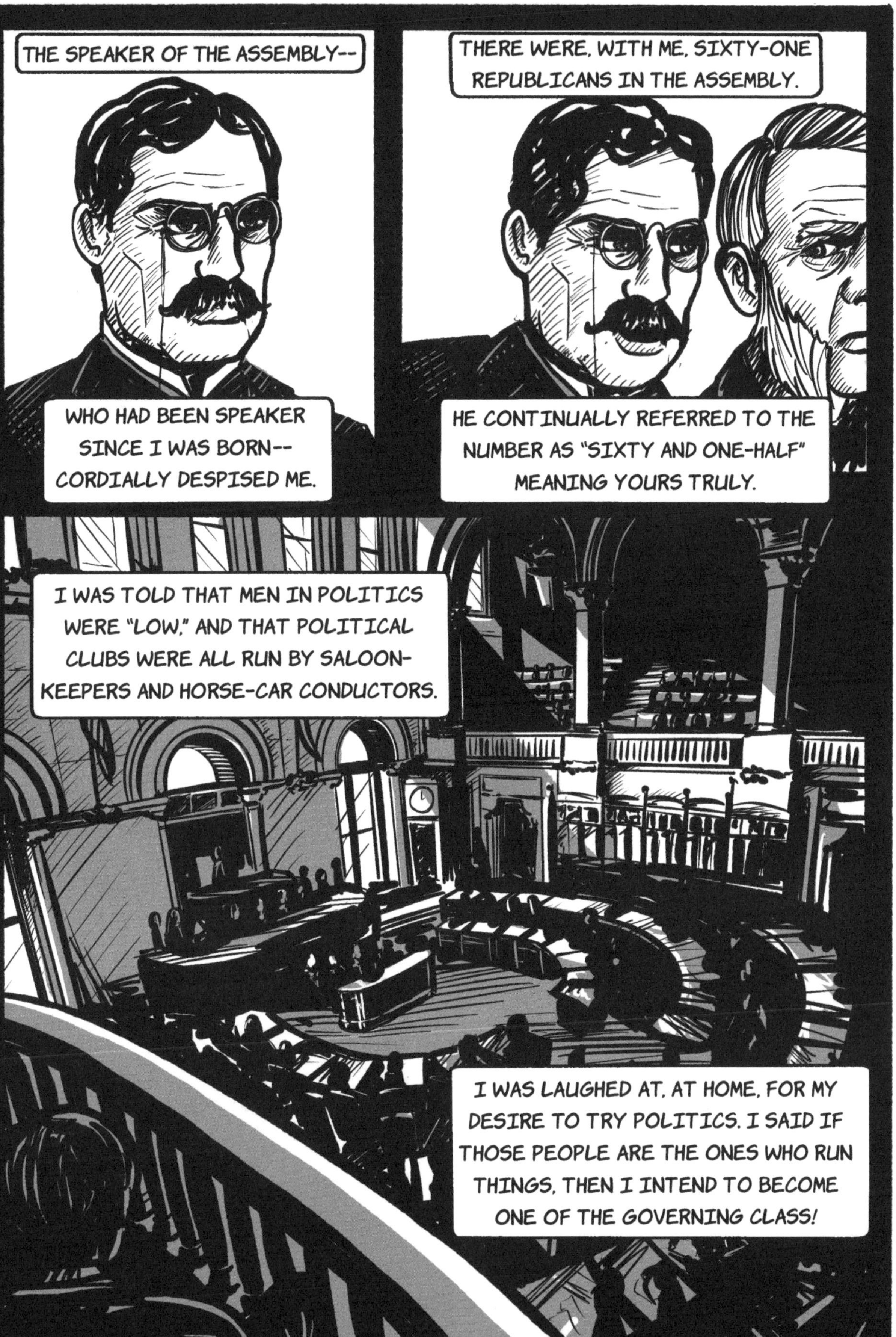
THE SPEAKER OF THE ASSEMBLY--
WHO HAD BEEN SPEAKER SINCE I WAS BORN-- CORDIALLY DESPISED ME.
THERE WERE, WITH ME, SIXTY-ONE REPUBLICANS IN THE ASSEMBLY.
HE CONTINUALLY REFERRED TO THE NUMBER AS "SIXTY AND ONE-HALF" MEANING YOURS TRULY.
I WAS TOLD THAT MEN IN POLITICS WERE "LOW," AND THAT POLITICAL CLUBS WERE ALL RUN BY SALOON-KEEPERS AND HORSE-CAR CONDUCTORS.
I WAS LAUGHED AT, AT HOME, FOR MY DESIRE TO TRY POLITICS. I SAID IF THOSE PEOPLE ARE THE ONES WHO RUN THINGS, THEN I INTEND TO BECOME ONE OF THE GOVERNING CLASS!

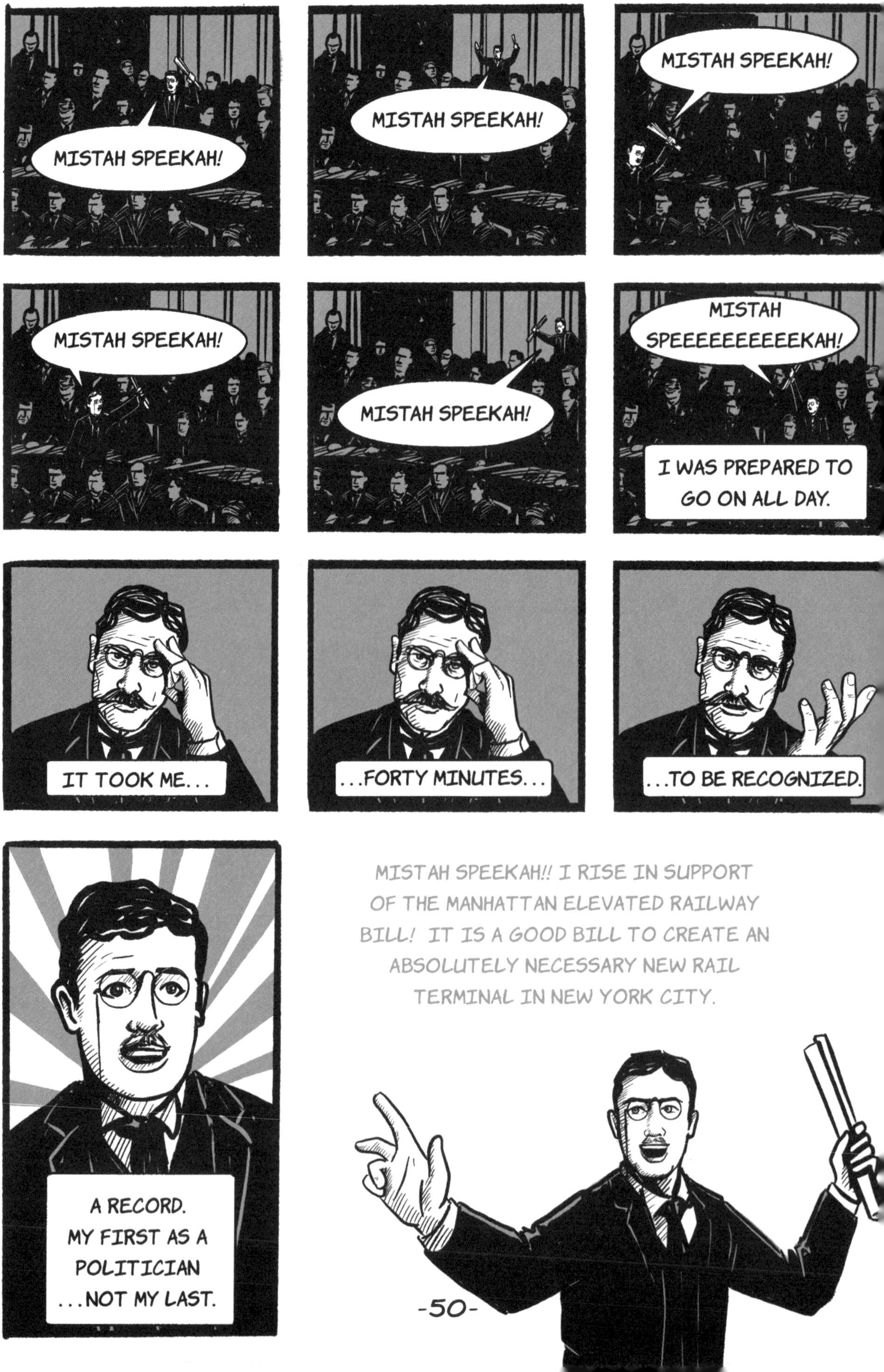
MISTAH SPEEKAH!
MISTAH SPEEKAH!
MISTAH SPEEKAH!
MISTAH SPEEKAH!
MISTAH SPEEKAH!
MISTAH SPEEEEEEEEEEEKAH!
I WAS PREPARED TO GO ON ALL DAY.
IT TOOK ME...
...FORTY MINUTES...
...TO BE RECOGNIZED.
A RECORD. MY FIRST AS A POLITICIAN ...NOT MY LAST.
MISTAH SPEEKAH!! I RISE IN SUPPORT OF THE MANHATTAN ELEVATED RAILWAY BILL! IT IS A GOOD BILL TO CREATE AN ABSOLUTELY NECESSARY NEW RAIL TERMINAL IN NEW YORK CITY.

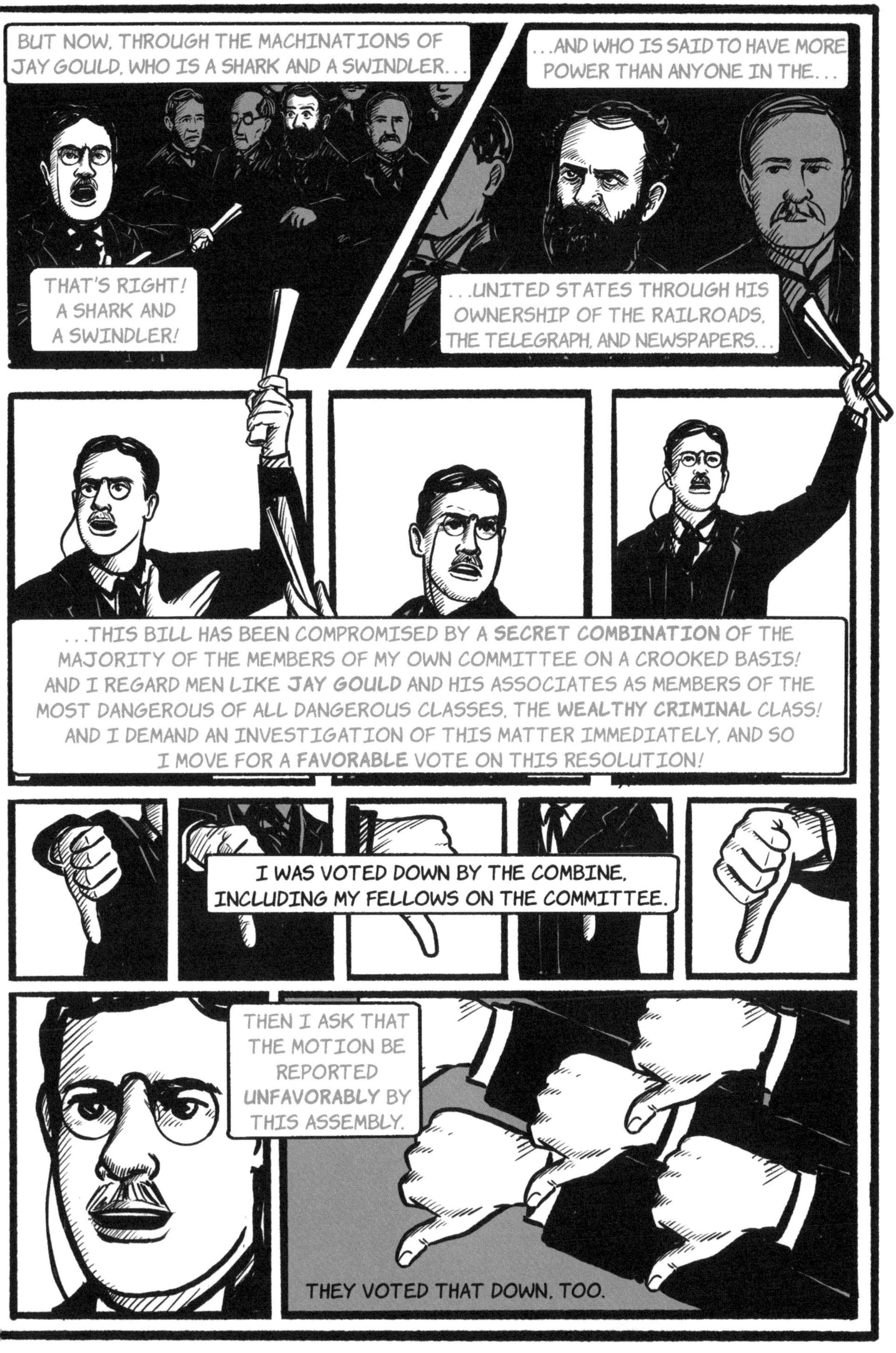
BUT NOW, THROUGH THE MACHINATIONS OF JAY GOULD, WHO IS A SHARK AND A SWINDLER...
THAT'S RIGHT! A SHARK AND A SWINDLER!
...AND WHO IS SAID TO HAVE MORE POWER THAN ANYONE IN THE...
...UNITED STATES THROUGH HIS OWNERSHIP OF THE RAILROADS, THE TELEGRAPH, AND NEWSPAPERS...
...THIS BILL HAS BEEN COMPROMISED BY A SECRET COMBINATION OF THE MAJORITY OF THE MEMBERS OF MY OWN COMMITTEE ON A CROOKED BASIS! AND I REGARD MEN LIKE JAY GOULD AND HIS ASSOCIATES AS MEMBERS OF THE MOST DANGEROUS OF ALL DANGEROUS CLASSES, THE WEALTHY CRIMINAL CLASS! AND I DEMAND AN INVESTIGATION OF THIS MATTER IMMEDIATELY, AND SO I MOVE FOR A FAVORABLE VOTE ON THIS RESOLUTION!
I WAS VOTED DOWN BY THE COMBINE, INCLUDING MY FELLOWS ON THE COMMITTEE.
THEN I ASK THAT THE MOTION BE REPORTED UNFAVORABLY BY THIS ASSEMBLY.
THEY VOTED THAT DOWN, TOO.

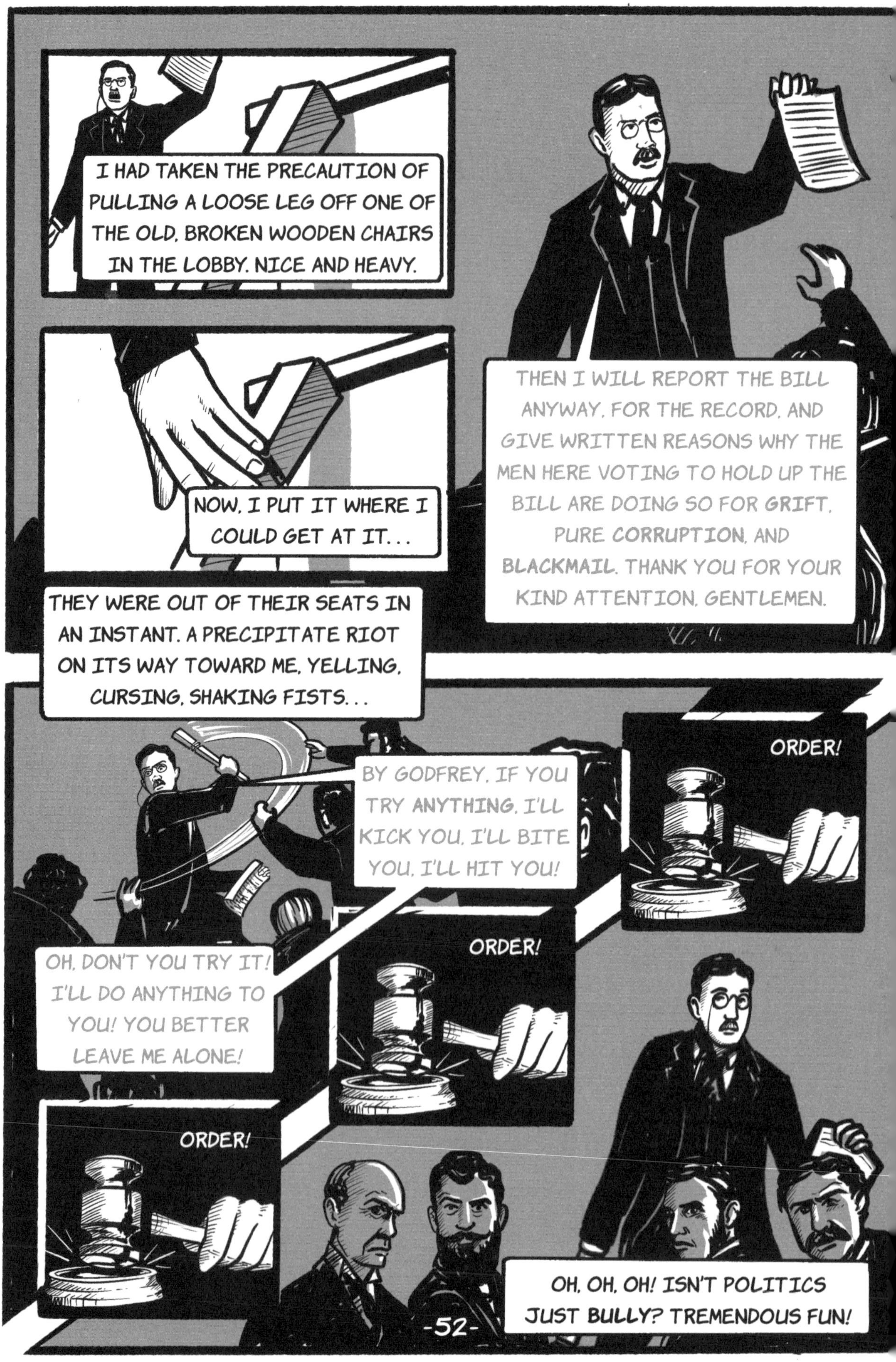
I HAD TAKEN THE PRECAUTION OF PULLING A LOOSE LEG OFF ONE OF THE OLD, BROKEN WOODEN CHAIRS IN THE LOBBY. NICE AND HEAVY.
THEN I WILL REPORT THE BILL ANYWAY, FOR THE RECORD, AND GIVE WRITTEN REASONS WHY THE MEN HERE VOTING TO HOLD UP THE BILL ARE DOING SO FOR GRIFT, PURE CORRUPTION, AND BLACKMAIL. THANK YOU FOR YOUR KIND ATTENTION, GENTLEMEN.
NOW, I PUT IT WHERE I COULD GET AT IT...
THEY WERE OUT OF THEIR SEATS IN AN INSTANT. A PRECIPITATE RIOT ON ITS WAY TOWARD ME, YELLING, CURSING, SHAKING FISTS...
BY GODFREY, IF YOU TRY ANYTHING, I'LL KICK YOU, I'LL BITE YOU, I'LL HIT YOU!
ORDER!
OH, DON'T YOU TRY IT! I'LL DO ANYTHING TO YOU! YOU BETTER LEAVE ME ALONE!
ORDER!
ORDER!
OH, OH, OH! ISN'T POLITICS JUST BULLY? TREMENDOUS FUN!

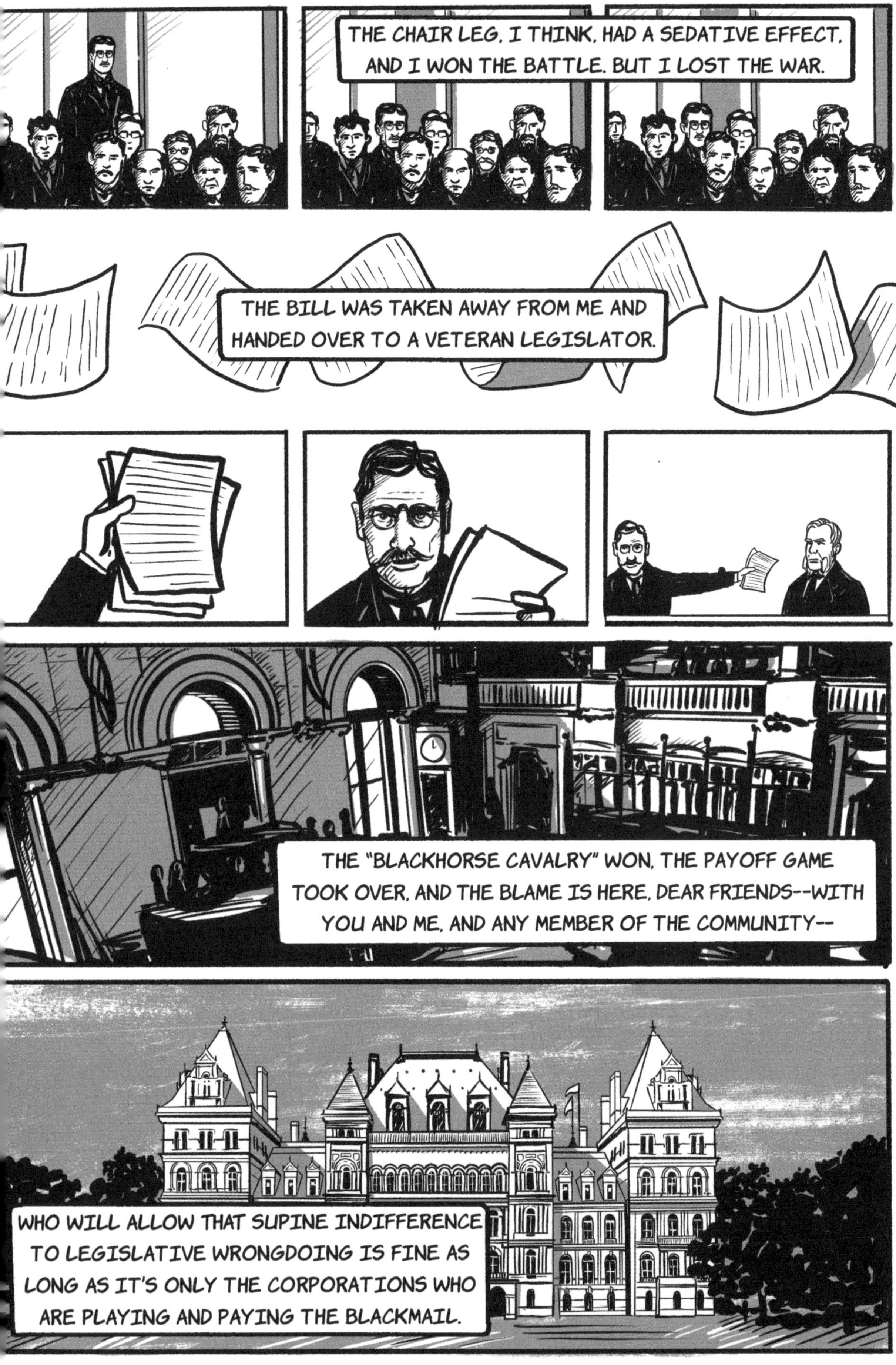
THE CHAIR LEG, I THINK, HAD A SEDATIVE EFFECT, AND I WON THE BATTLE. BUT I LOST THE WAR.
THE BILL WAS TAKEN AWAY FROM ME AND HANDED OVER TO A VETERAN LEGISLATOR.
THE "BLACKHORSE CAVALRY" WON, THE PAYOFF GAME TOOK OVER, AND THE BLAME IS HERE, DEAR FRIENDS--WITH YOU AND ME, AND ANY MEMBER OF THE COMMUNITY--
WHO WILL ALLOW THAT SUPINE INDIFFERENCE TO LEGISLATIVE WRONGDOING IS FINE AS LONG AS IT'S ONLY THE CORPORATIONS WHO ARE PLAYING AND PAYING THE BLACKMAIL.

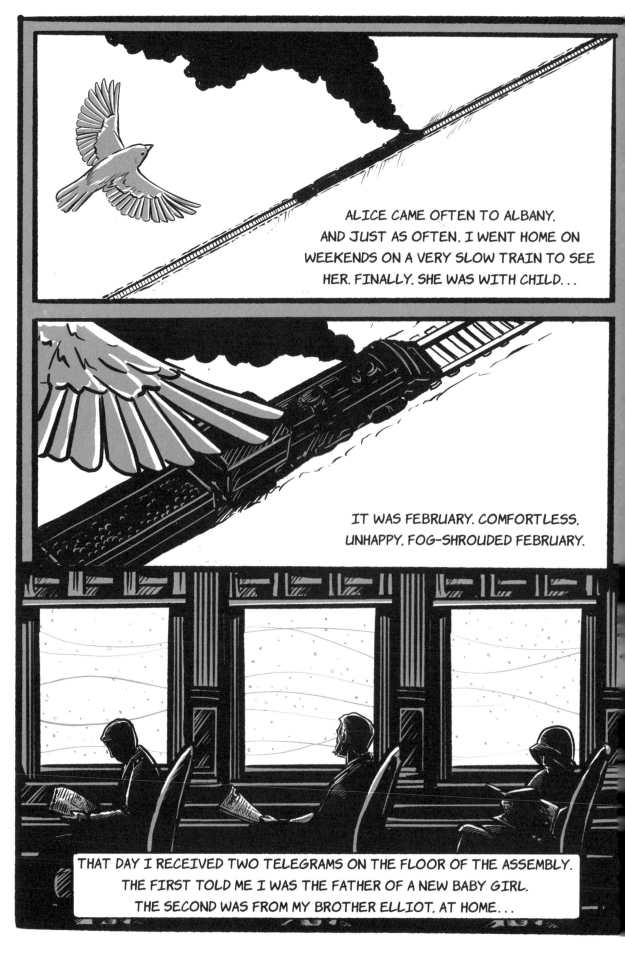

ALICE CAME OFTEN TO ALBANY, AND JUST AS OFTEN, I WENT HOME ON WEEKENDS ON A VERY SLOW TRAIN TO SEE HER. FINALLY, SHE WAS WITH CHILD...

IT WAS FEBRUARY. COMFORTLESS, UNHAPPY, FOG-SHROUDED FEBRUARY.

THAT DAY I RECEIVED TWO TELEGRAMS ON THE FLOOR OF THE ASSEMBLY. THE FIRST TOLD ME I WAS THE FATHER OF A NEW BABY GIRL. THE SECOND WAS FROM MY BROTHER ELLIOT, AT HOME...

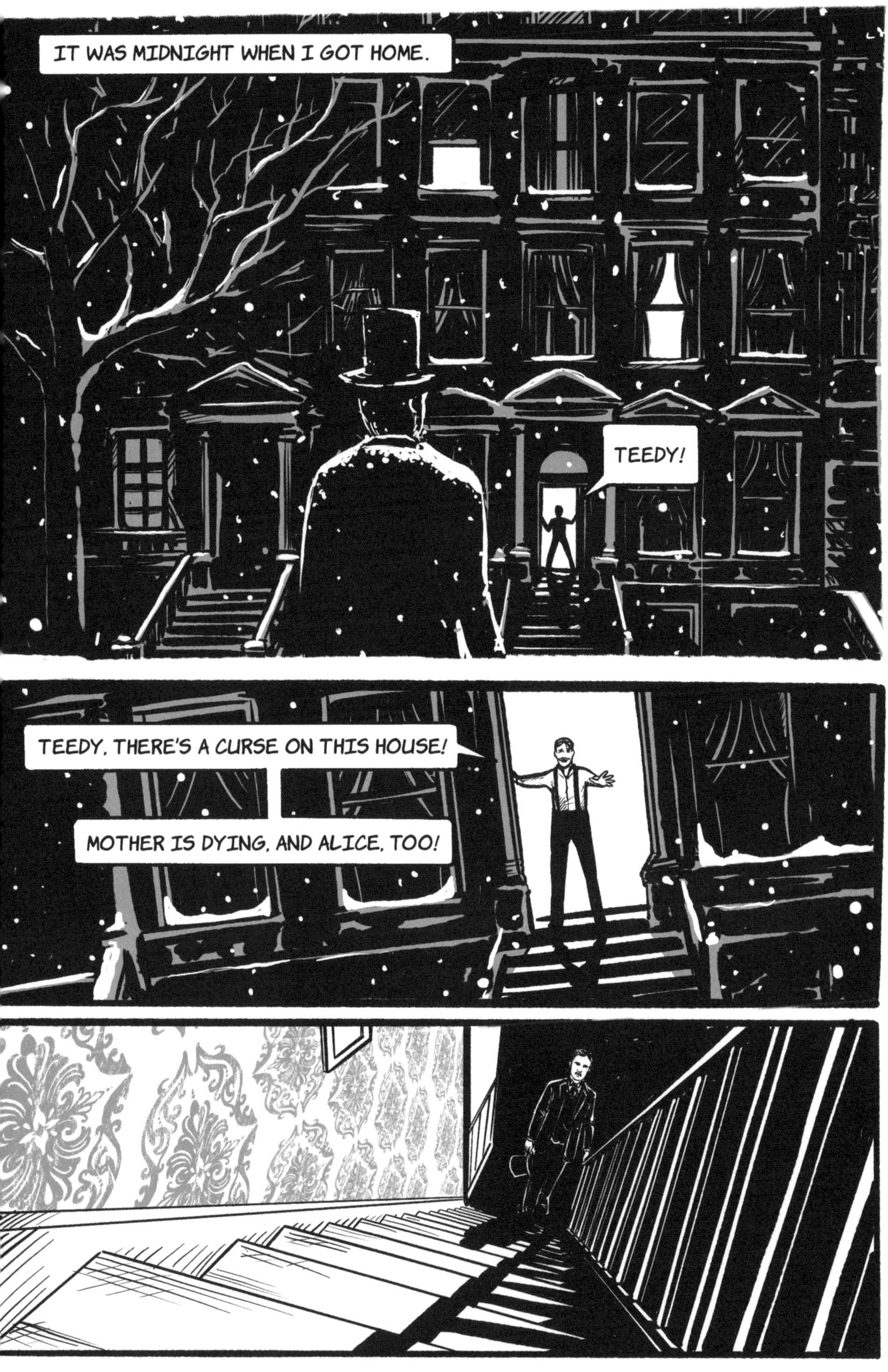
IT WAS MIDNIGHT WHEN I GOT HOME.
TEEDY!
TEEDY, THERE'S A CURSE ON THIS HOUSE!
MOTHER IS DYING, AND ALICE, TOO!

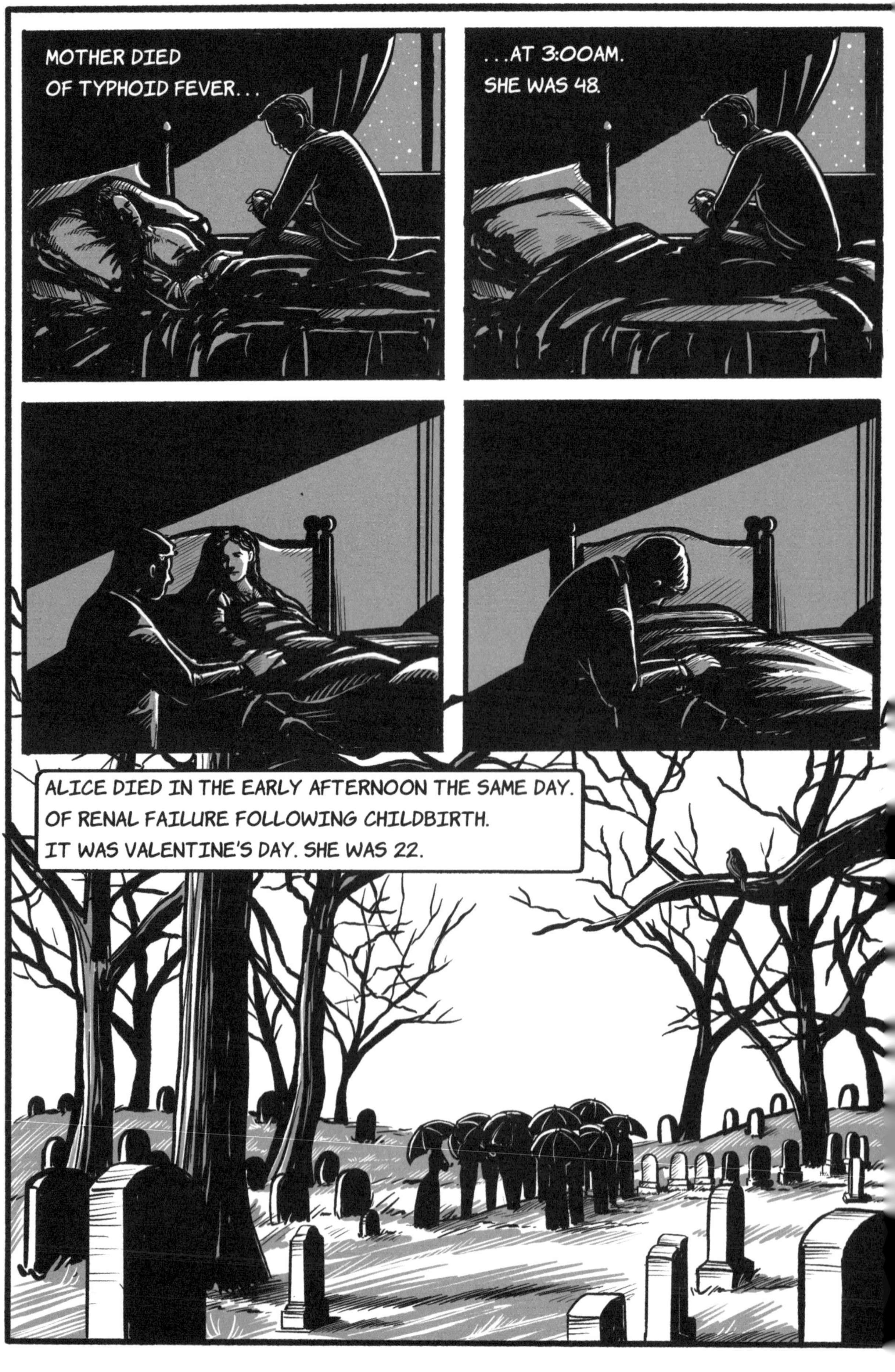
MOTHER DIED
OF TYPHOID FEVER...
...AT 3:00AM.
SHE WAS 48.
ALICE DIED IN THE EARLY AFTERNOON THE SAME DAY.
OF RENAL FAILURE FOLLOWING CHILDBIRTH.
IT WAS VALENTINE'S DAY. SHE WAS 22.

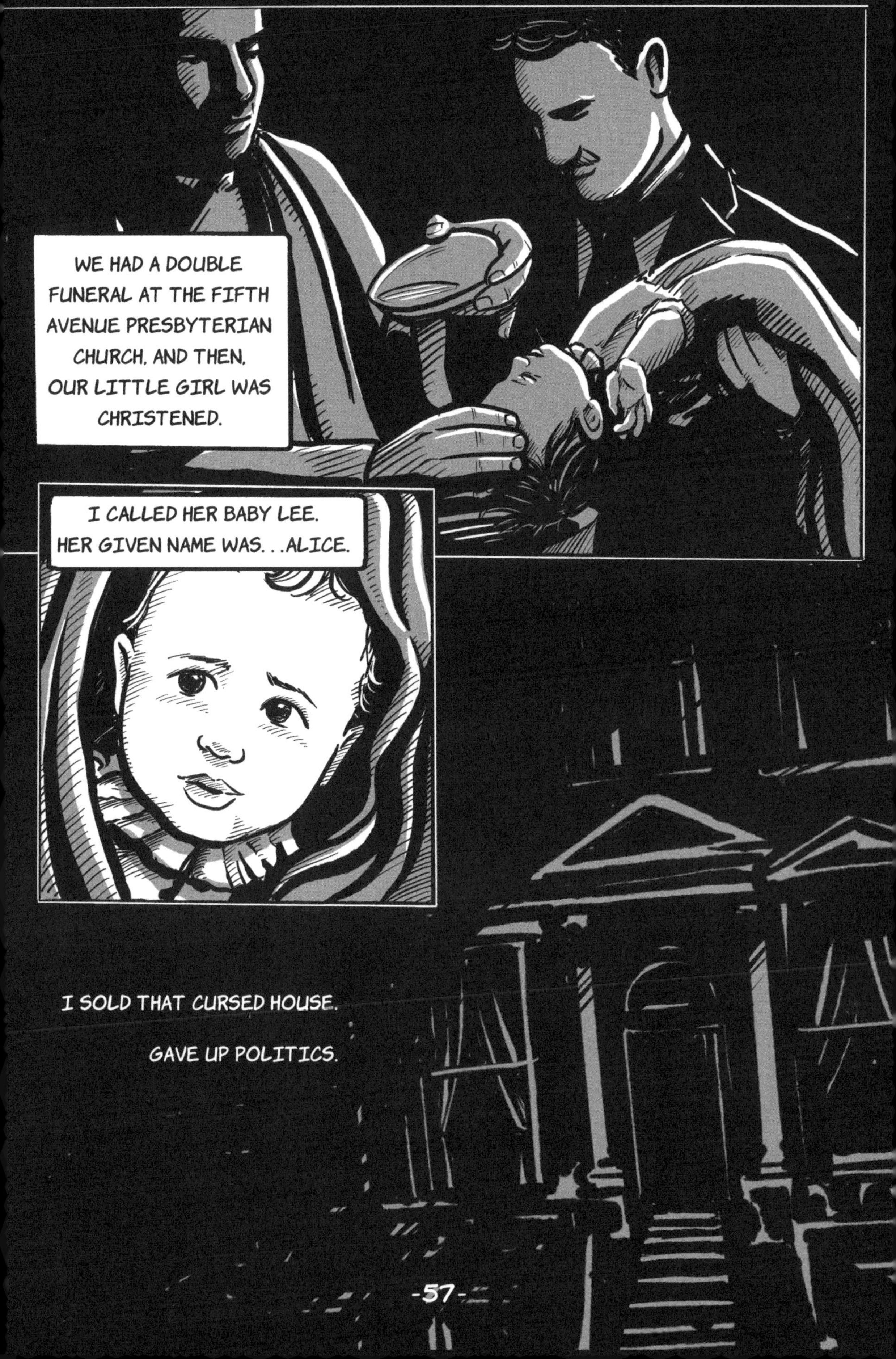
WE HAD A DOUBLE FUNERAL AT THE FIFTH AVENUE PRESBYTERIAN CHURCH, AND THEN, OUR LITTLE GIRL WAS CHRISTENED.
I CALLED HER BABY LEE. HER GIVEN NAME WAS. . .ALICE.
I SOLD THAT CURSED HOUSE.
GAVE UP POLITICS.

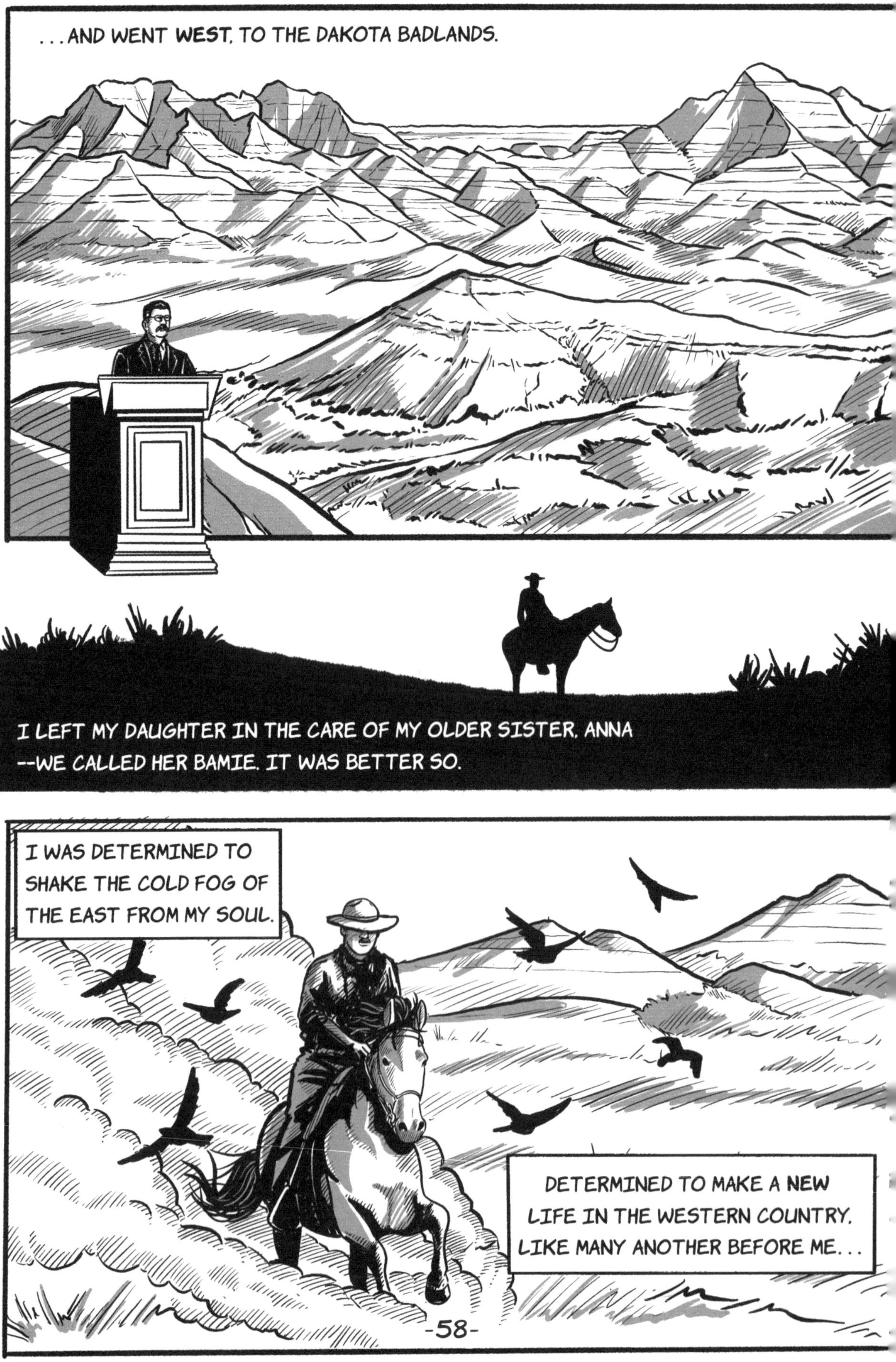
. . . AND WENT WEST, TO THE DAKOTA BADLANDS.
I LEFT MY DAUGHTER IN THE CARE OF MY OLDER SISTER, ANNA --WE CALLED HER BAMIE. IT WAS BETTER SO.
I WAS DETERMINED TO SHAKE THE COLD FOG OF THE EAST FROM MY SOUL.
DETERMINED TO MAKE A NEW LIFE IN THE WESTERN COUNTRY, LIKE MANY ANOTHER BEFORE ME. . .

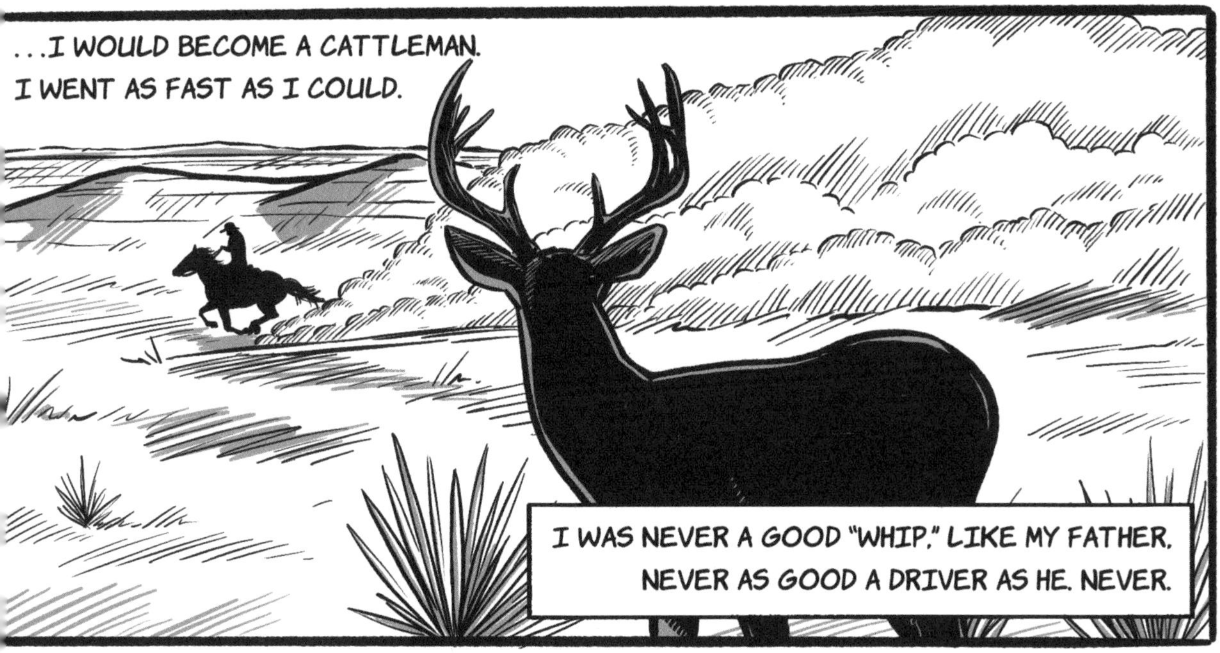
. . .I WOULD BECOME A CATTLEMAN.
I WENT AS FAST AS I COULD.
I WAS NEVER A GOOD "WHIP," LIKE MY FATHER. NEVER AS GOOD A DRIVER AS HE. NEVER.

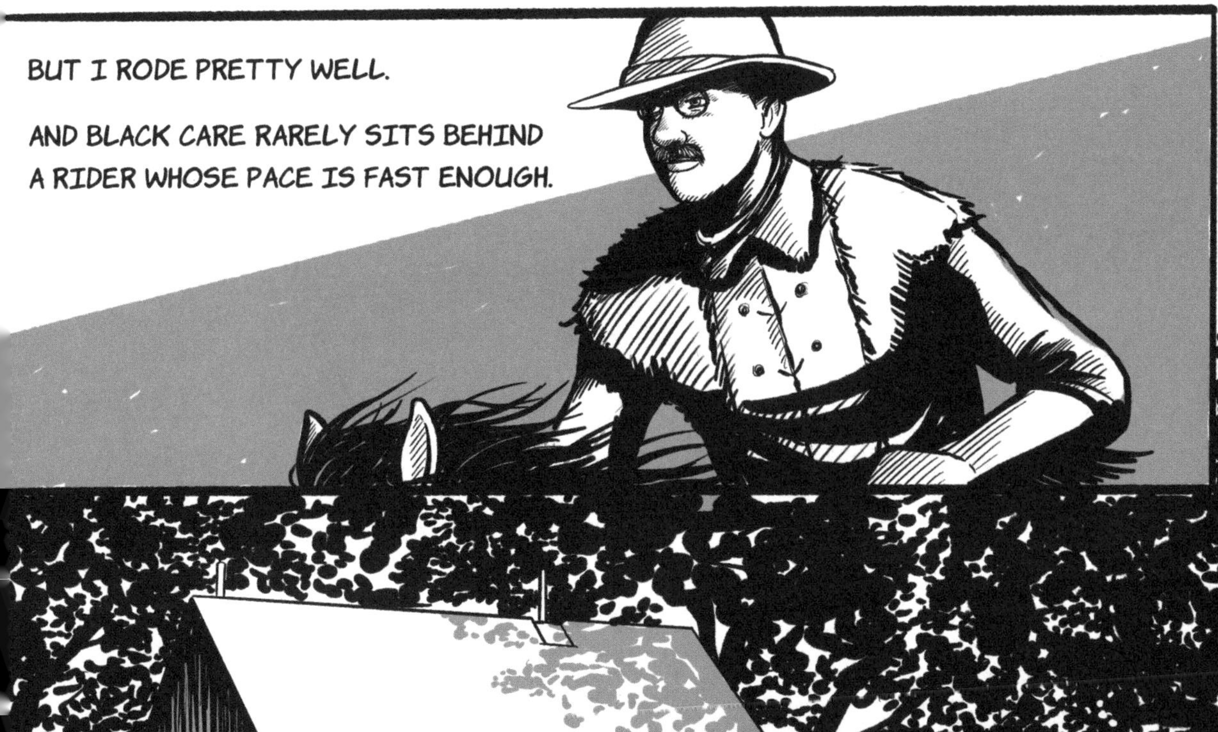
BUT I RODE PRETTY WELL.
AND BLACK CARE RARELY SITS BEHIND A RIDER WHOSE PACE IS FAST ENOUGH.

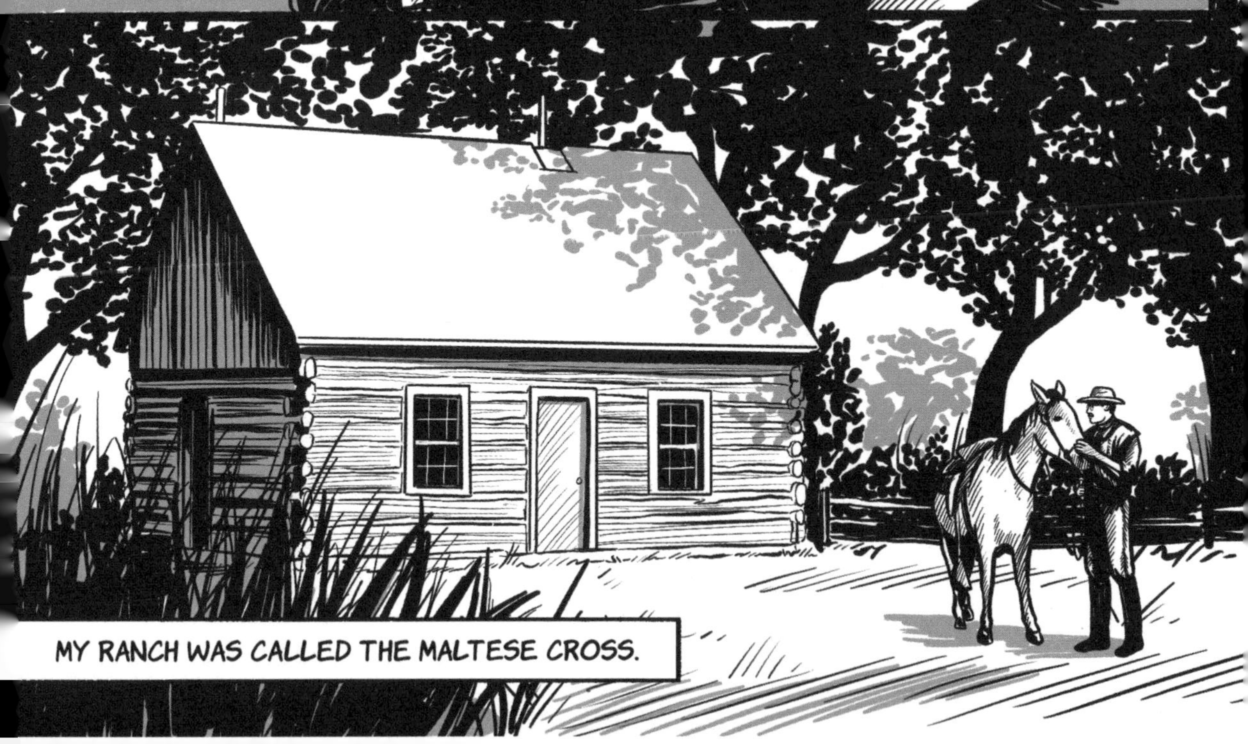
MY RANCH WAS CALLED THE MALTESE CROSS.

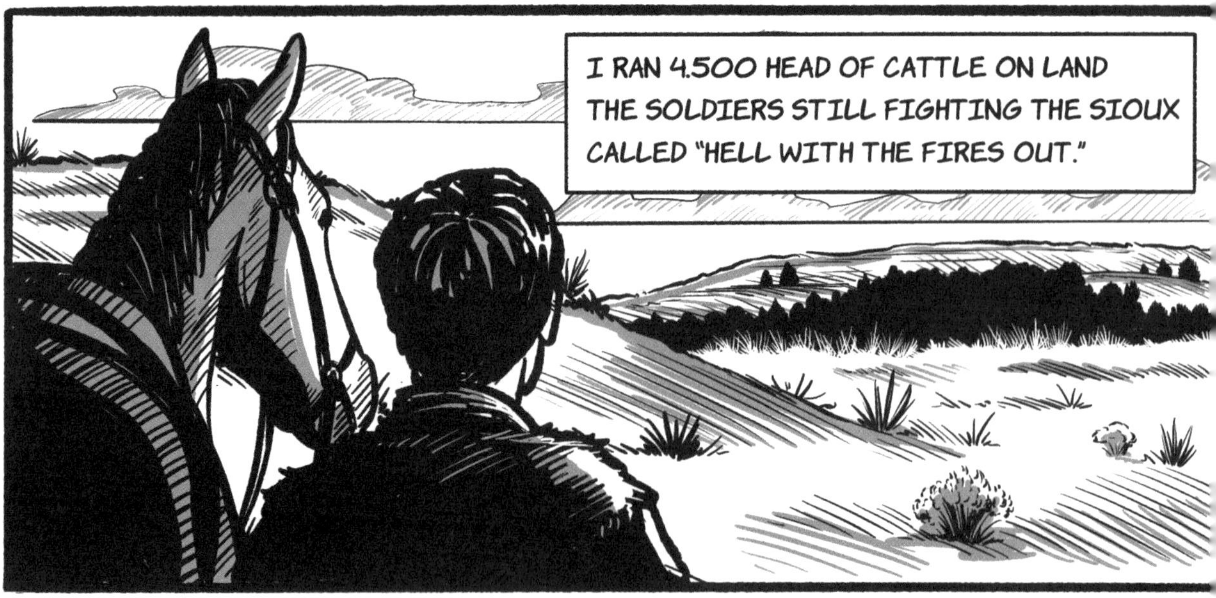
I RAN 4.500 HEAD OF CATTLE ON LAND THE SOLDIERS STILL FIGHTING THE SIOUX CALLED "HELL WITH THE FIRES OUT."

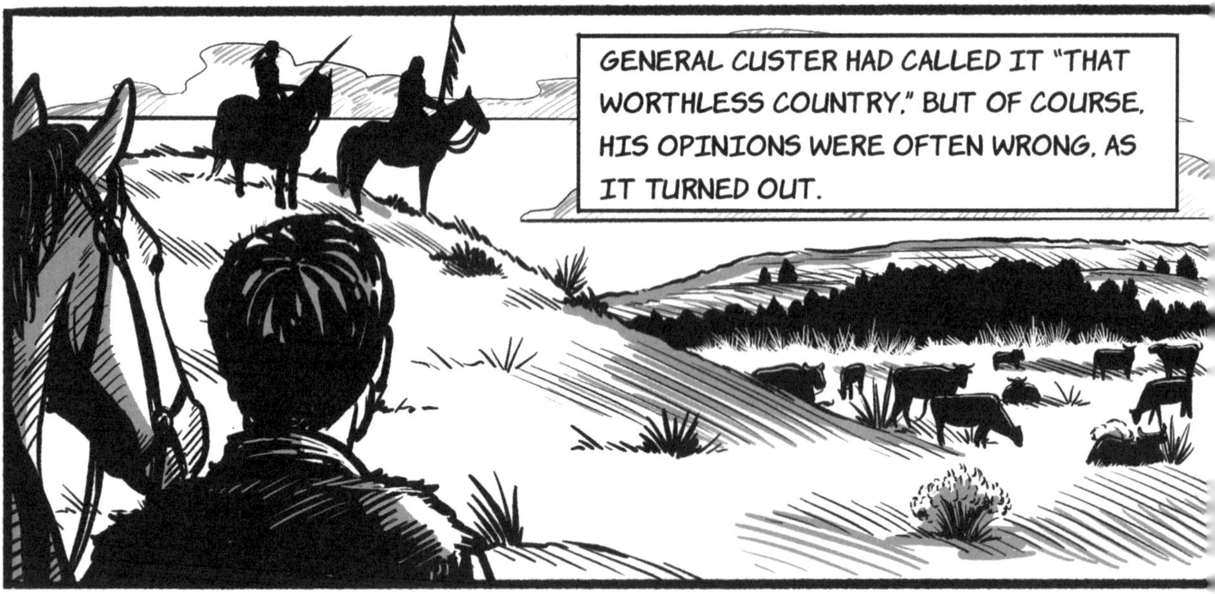
GENERAL CUSTER HAD CALLED IT "THAT WORTHLESS COUNTRY." BUT OF COURSE, HIS OPINIONS WERE OFTEN WRONG, AS IT TURNED OUT.

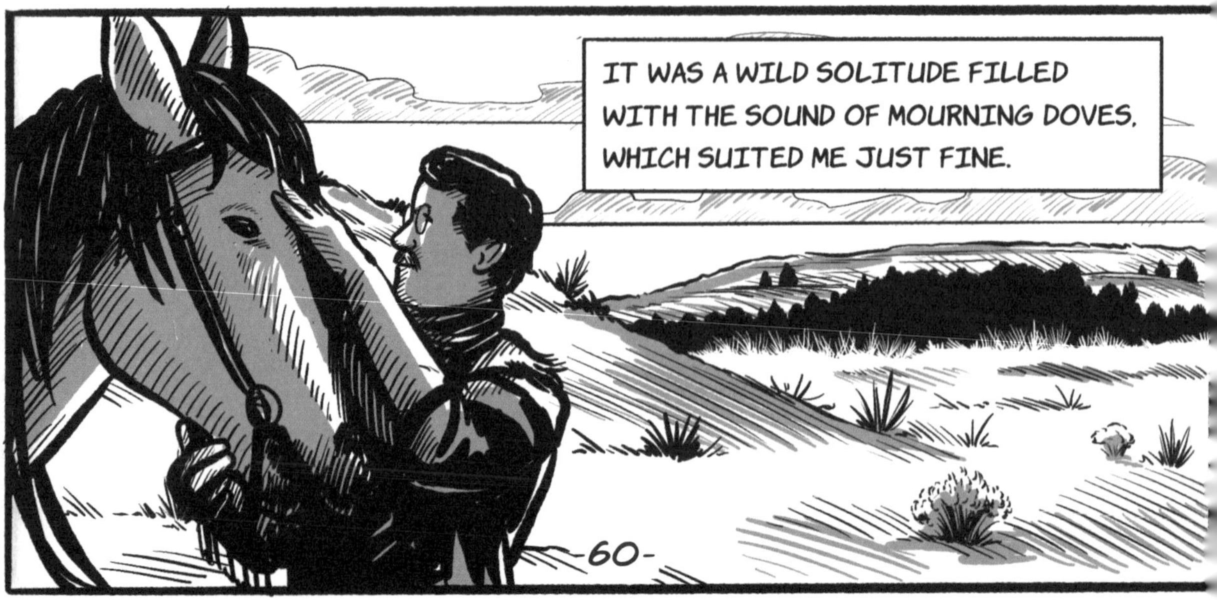
IT WAS A WILD SOLITUDE FILLED WITH THE SOUND OF MOURNING DOVES, WHICH SUITED ME JUST FINE.

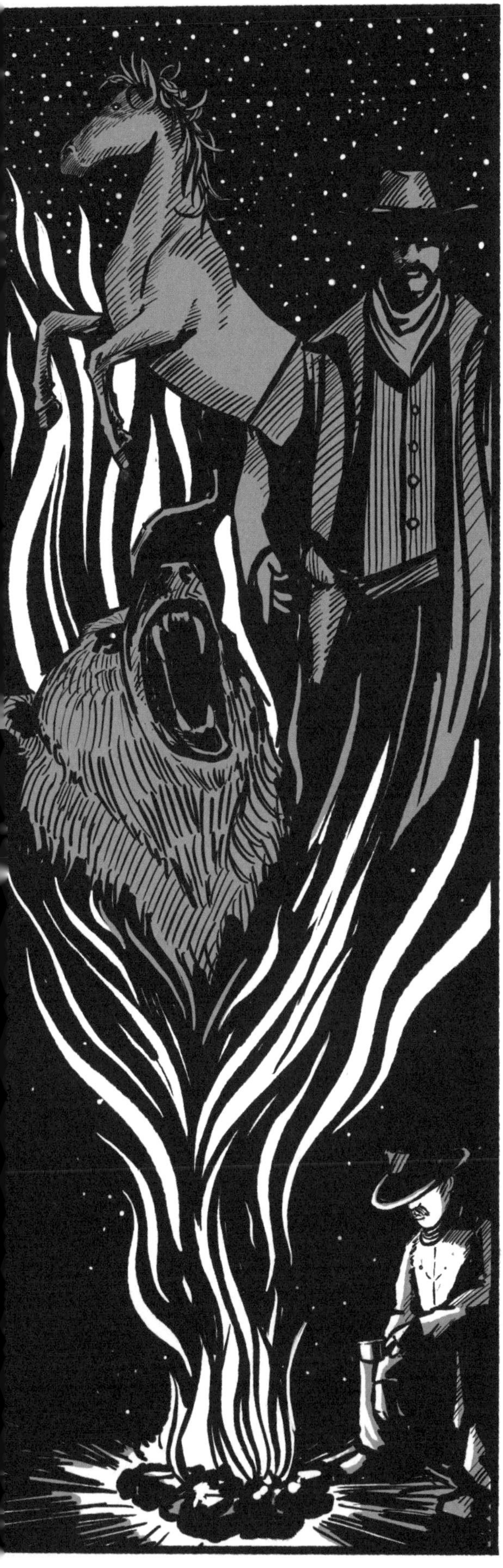

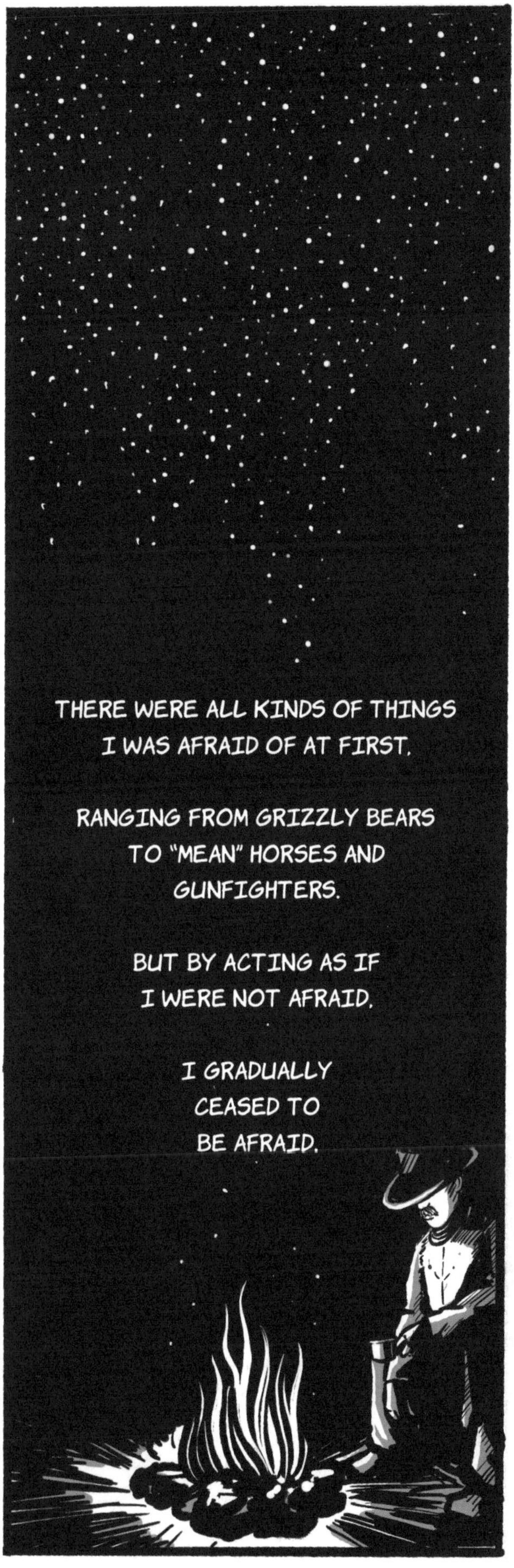
THERE WERE ALL KINDS OF THINGS
I WAS AFRAID OF AT FIRST.
RANGING FROM GRIZZLY BEARS
TO "MEAN" HORSES AND
GUNFIGHTERS.
BUT BY ACTING AS IF
I WERE NOT AFRAID.
I GRADUALLY
CEASED TO
BE AFRAID.

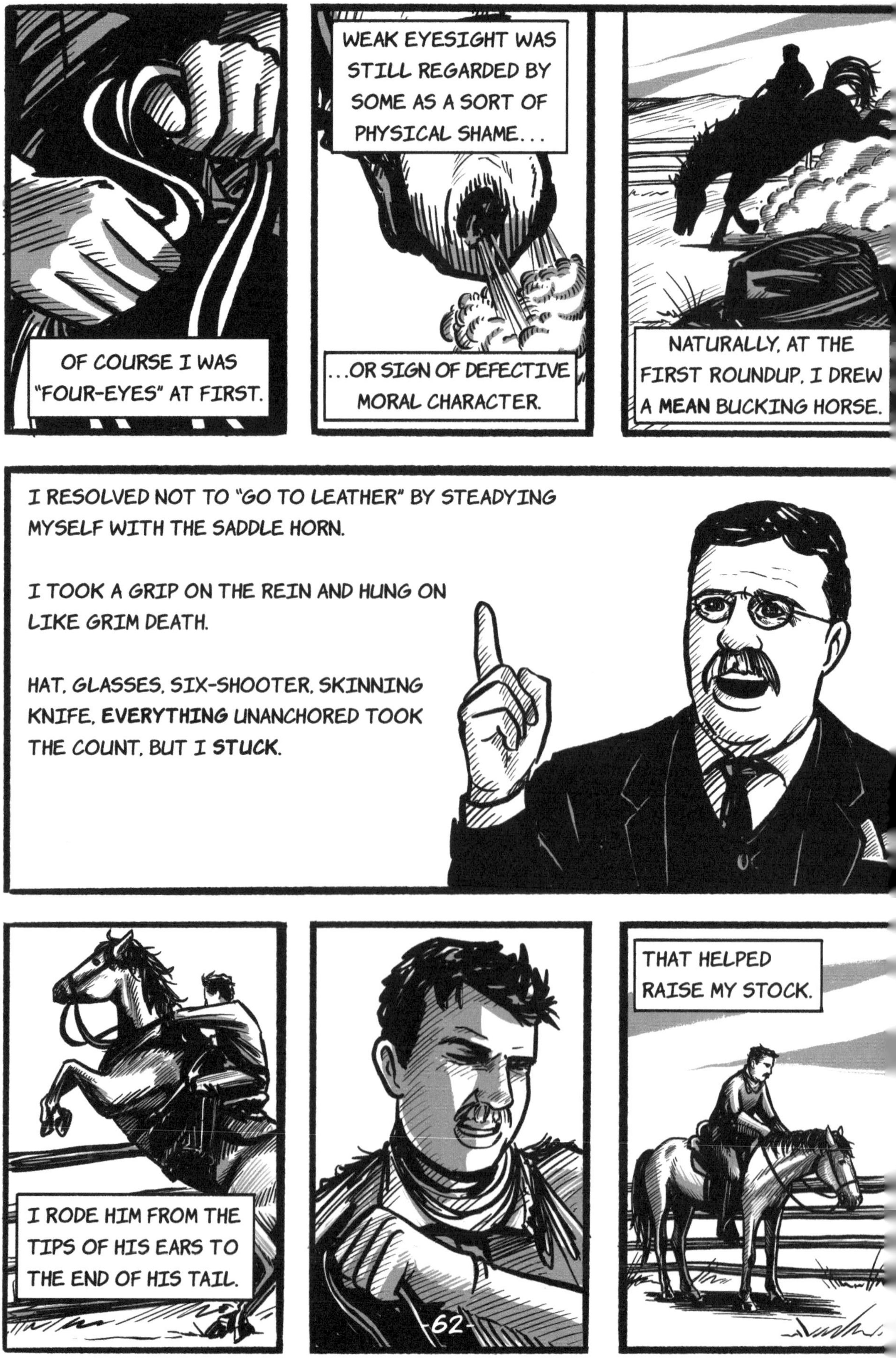
OF COURSE I WAS "FOUR-EYES" AT FIRST.
WEAK EYESIGHT WAS STILL REGARDED BY SOME AS A SORT OF PHYSICAL SHAME...
...OR SIGN OF DEFECTIVE MORAL CHARACTER.
NATURALLY, AT THE FIRST ROUNDUP, I DREW A **MEAN** BUCKING HORSE.
I RESOLVED NOT TO "GO TO LEATHER" BY STEADYING MYSELF WITH THE SADDLE HORN.
I TOOK A GRIP ON THE REIN AND HUNG ON LIKE GRIM DEATH.
HAT, GLASSES, SIX-SHOOTER, SKINNING KNIFE, **EVERYTHING** UNANCHORED TOOK THE COUNT, BUT I **STUCK**.
I RODE HIM FROM THE TIPS OF HIS EARS TO THE END OF HIS TAIL.
THAT HELPED RAISE MY STOCK.

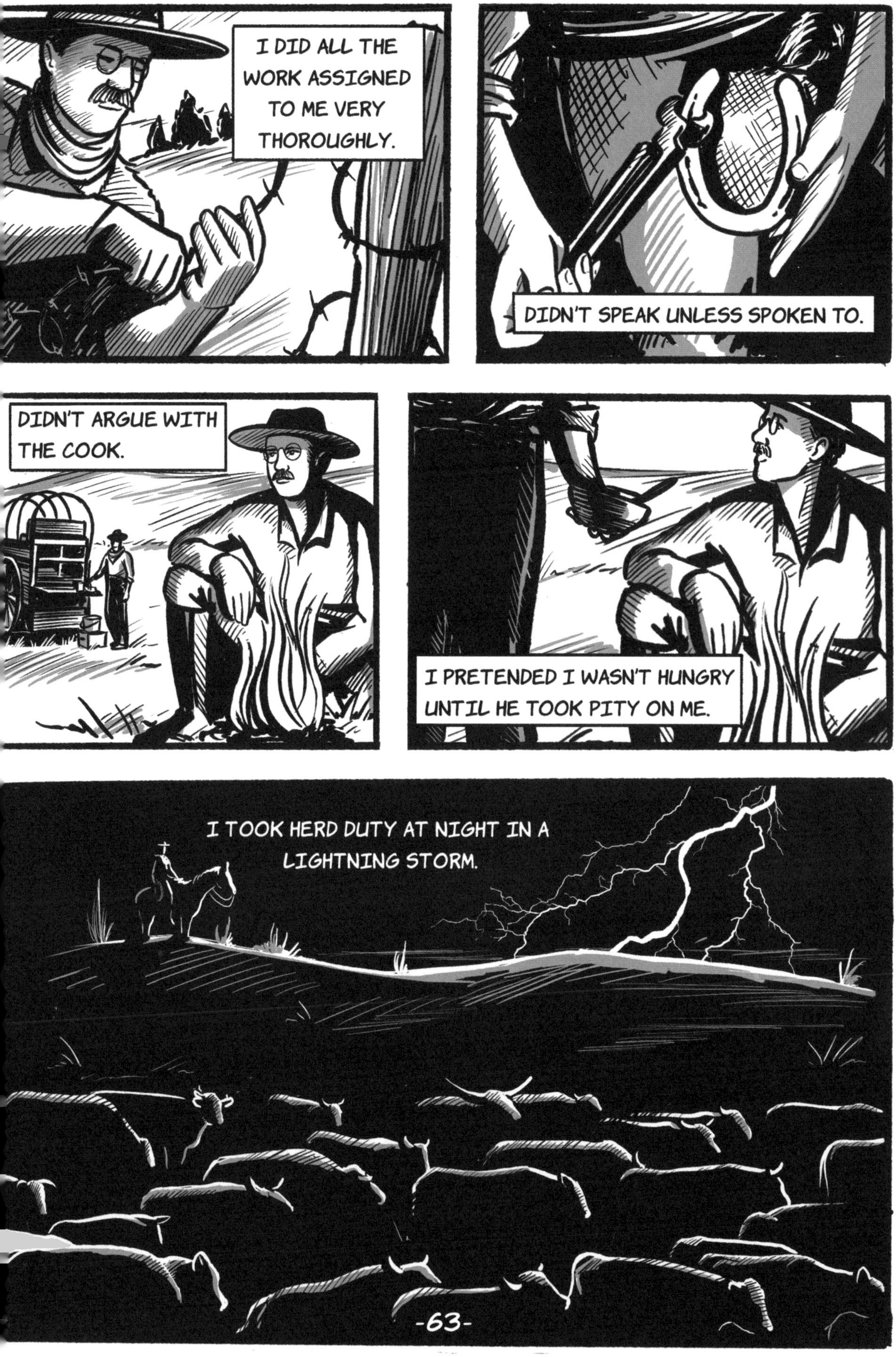
I DID ALL THE WORK ASSIGNED TO ME VERY THOROUGHLY.
DIDN'T SPEAK UNLESS SPOKEN TO.
DIDN'T ARGUE WITH THE COOK.
I PRETENDED I WASN'T HUNGRY UNTIL HE TOOK PITY ON ME.
I TOOK HERD DUTY AT NIGHT IN A LIGHTNING STORM.

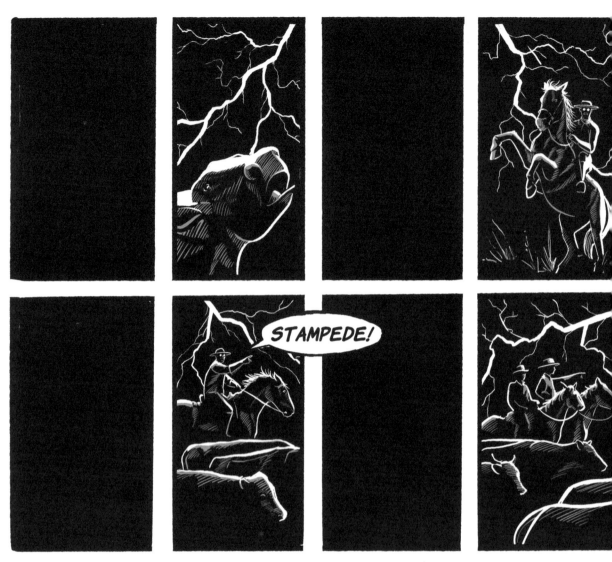

STAMPEDE!

THANK FATHER FOR RIDING LESSONS.

RODE FOR FORTY STRAIGHT HOURS AND WORE OUT FIVE HORSES TRYING TO GET THEM BACK.

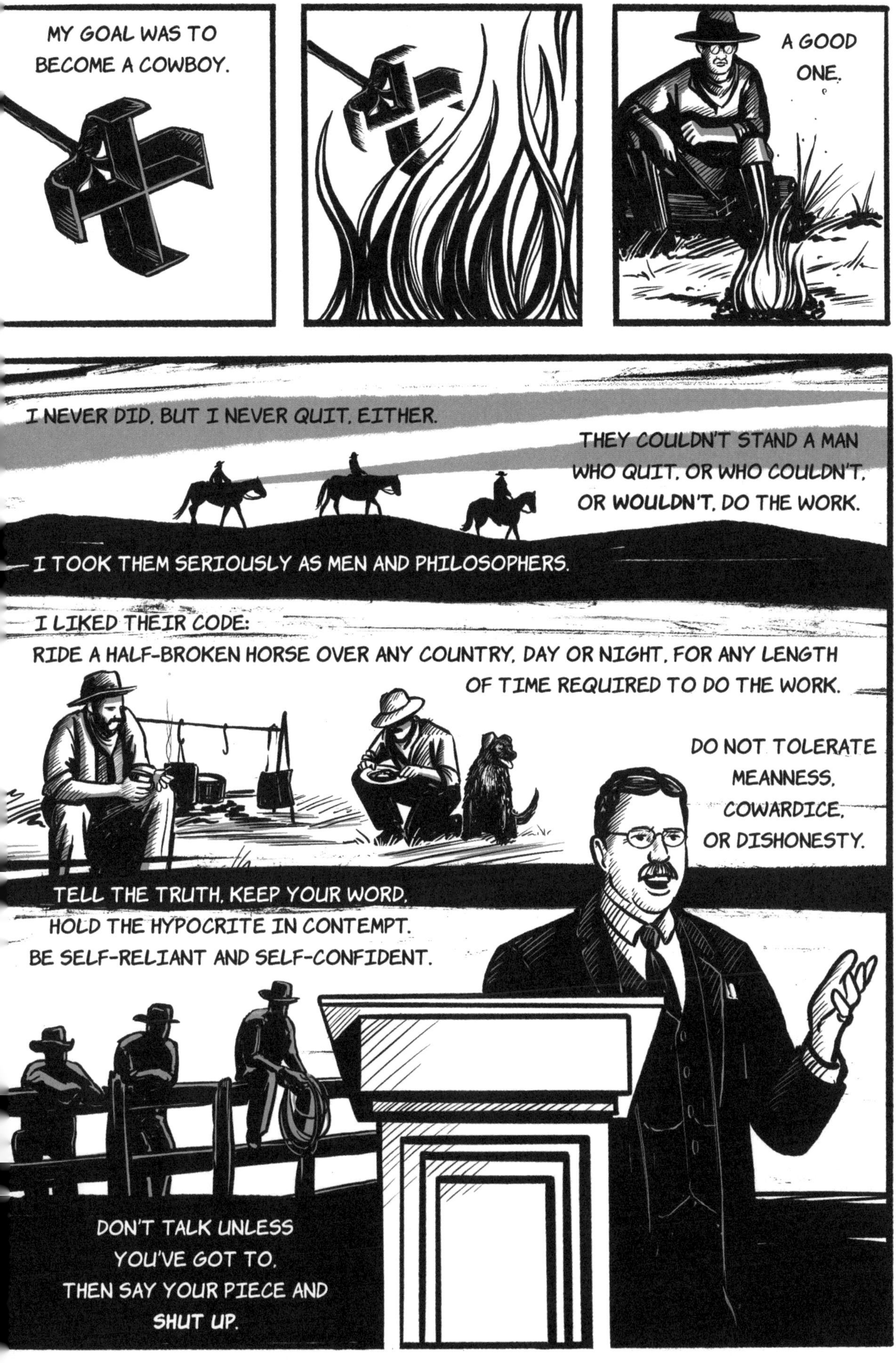
MY GOAL WAS TO BECOME A COWBOY.
A GOOD ONE.
I NEVER DID, BUT I NEVER QUIT, EITHER.
THEY COULDN'T STAND A MAN WHO QUIT, OR WHO COULDN'T, OR WOULDN'T, DO THE WORK.
I TOOK THEM SERIOUSLY AS MEN AND PHILOSOPHERS.
I LIKED THEIR CODE:
RIDE A HALF-BROKEN HORSE OVER ANY COUNTRY, DAY OR NIGHT, FOR ANY LENGTH OF TIME REQUIRED TO DO THE WORK.
DO NOT TOLERATE MEANNESS, COWARDICE, OR DISHONESTY.
TELL THE TRUTH, KEEP YOUR WORD,
HOLD THE HYPOCRITE IN CONTEMPT.
BE SELF-RELIANT AND SELF-CONFIDENT.
DON'T TALK UNLESS YOU'VE GOT TO.
THEN SAY YOUR PIECE AND SHUT UP.

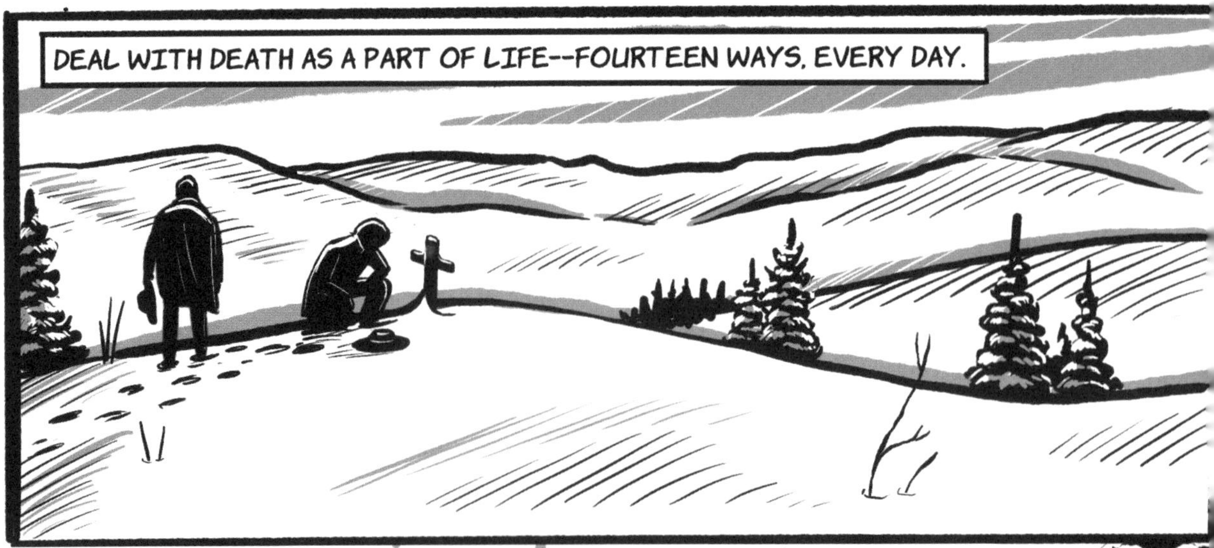
DEAL WITH DEATH AS A PART OF LIFE--FOURTEEN WAYS, EVERY DAY.

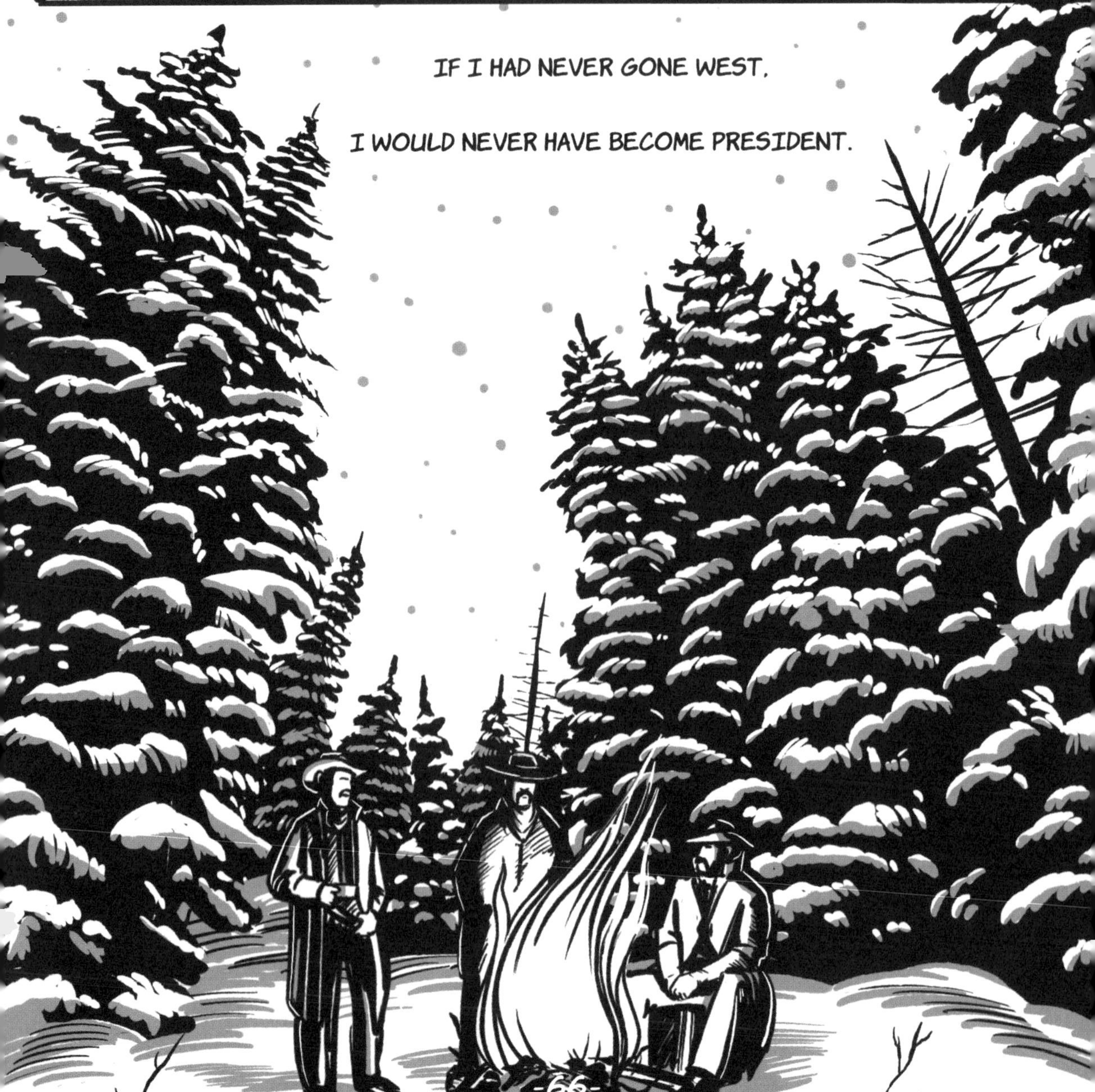
IF I HAD NEVER GONE WEST,
I WOULD NEVER HAVE BECOME PRESIDENT.

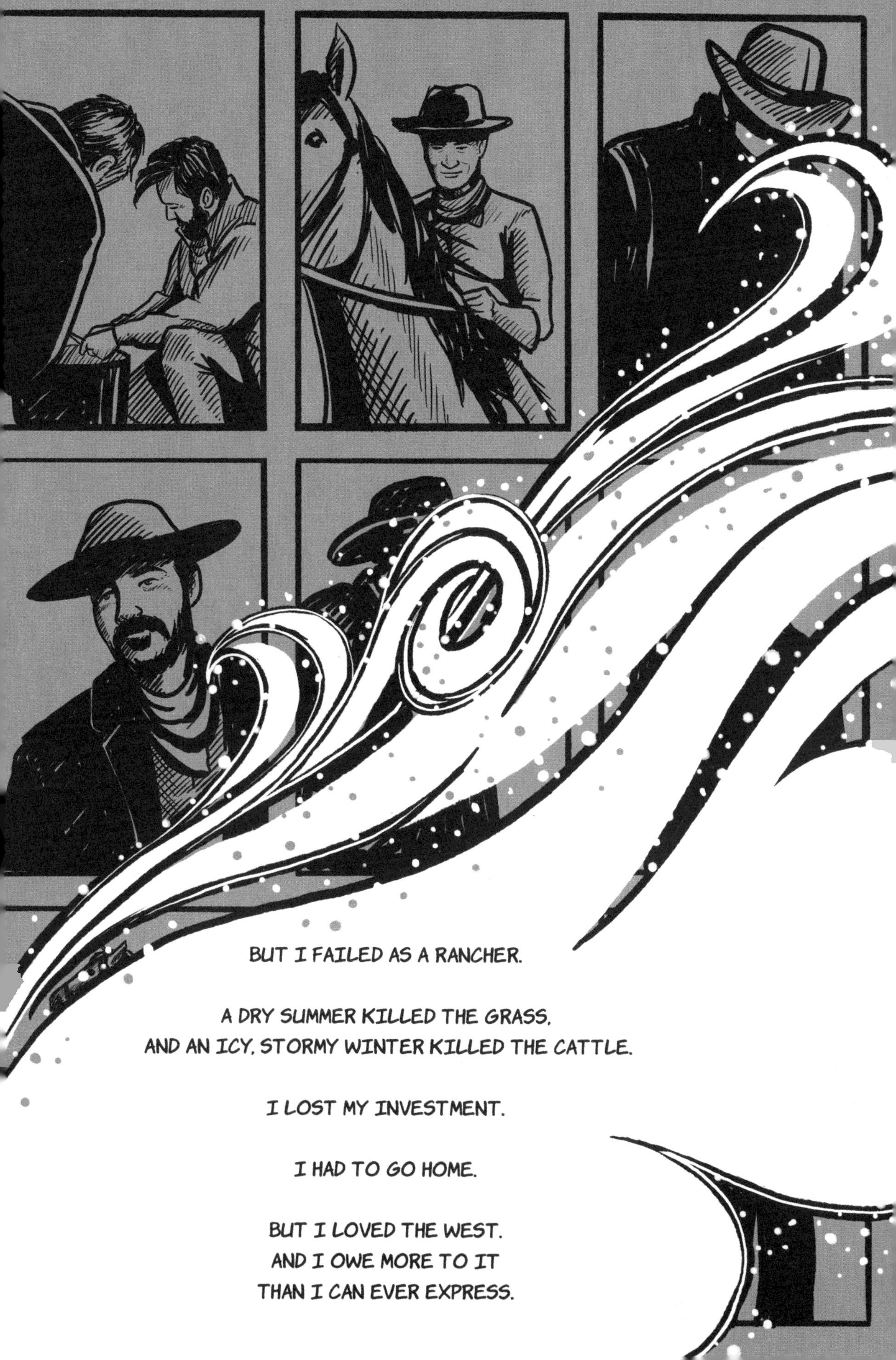
BUT I FAILED AS A RANCHER.
A DRY SUMMER KILLED THE GRASS,
AND AN ICY, STORMY WINTER KILLED THE CATTLE.
I LOST MY INVESTMENT.
I HAD TO GO HOME.
BUT I LOVED THE WEST.
AND I OWE MORE TO IT
THAN I CAN EVER EXPRESS.

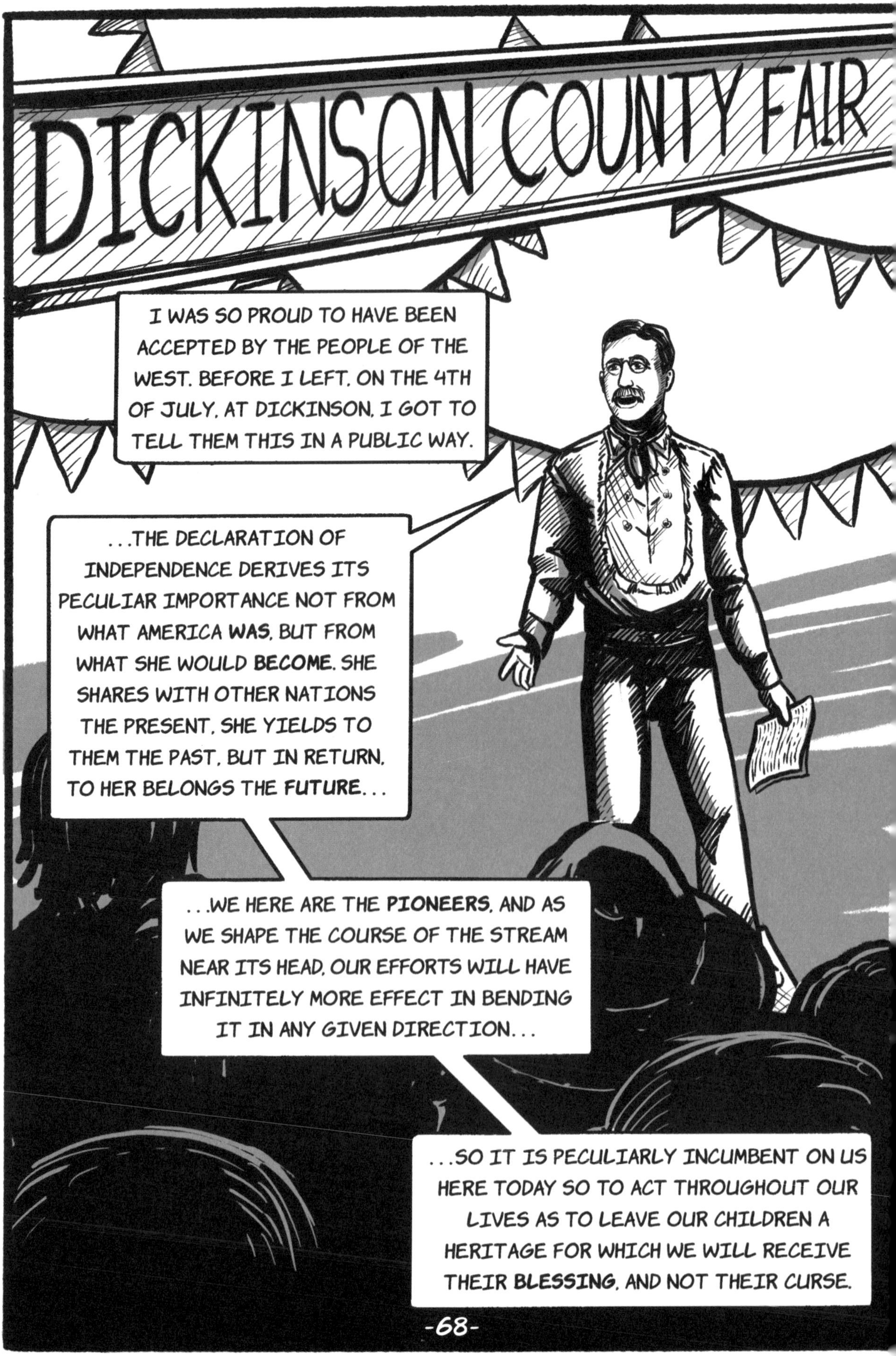
DICKINSON COUNTY FAIR
I WAS SO PROUD TO HAVE BEEN ACCEPTED BY THE PEOPLE OF THE WEST. BEFORE I LEFT, ON THE 4TH OF JULY, AT DICKINSON, I GOT TO TELL THEM THIS IN A PUBLIC WAY.
...THE DECLARATION OF INDEPENDENCE DERIVES ITS PECULIAR IMPORTANCE NOT FROM WHAT AMERICA WAS, BUT FROM WHAT SHE WOULD BECOME. SHE SHARES WITH OTHER NATIONS THE PRESENT, SHE YIELDS TO THEM THE PAST, BUT IN RETURN, TO HER BELONGS THE FUTURE...
...WE HERE ARE THE PIONEERS, AND AS WE SHAPE THE COURSE OF THE STREAM NEAR ITS HEAD, OUR EFFORTS WILL HAVE INFINITELY MORE EFFECT IN BENDING IT IN ANY GIVEN DIRECTION...
...SO IT IS PECULIARLY INCUMBENT ON US HERE TODAY SO TO ACT THROUGHOUT OUR LIVES AS TO LEAVE OUR CHILDREN A HERITAGE FOR WHICH WE WILL RECEIVE THEIR BLESSING, AND NOT THEIR CURSE.

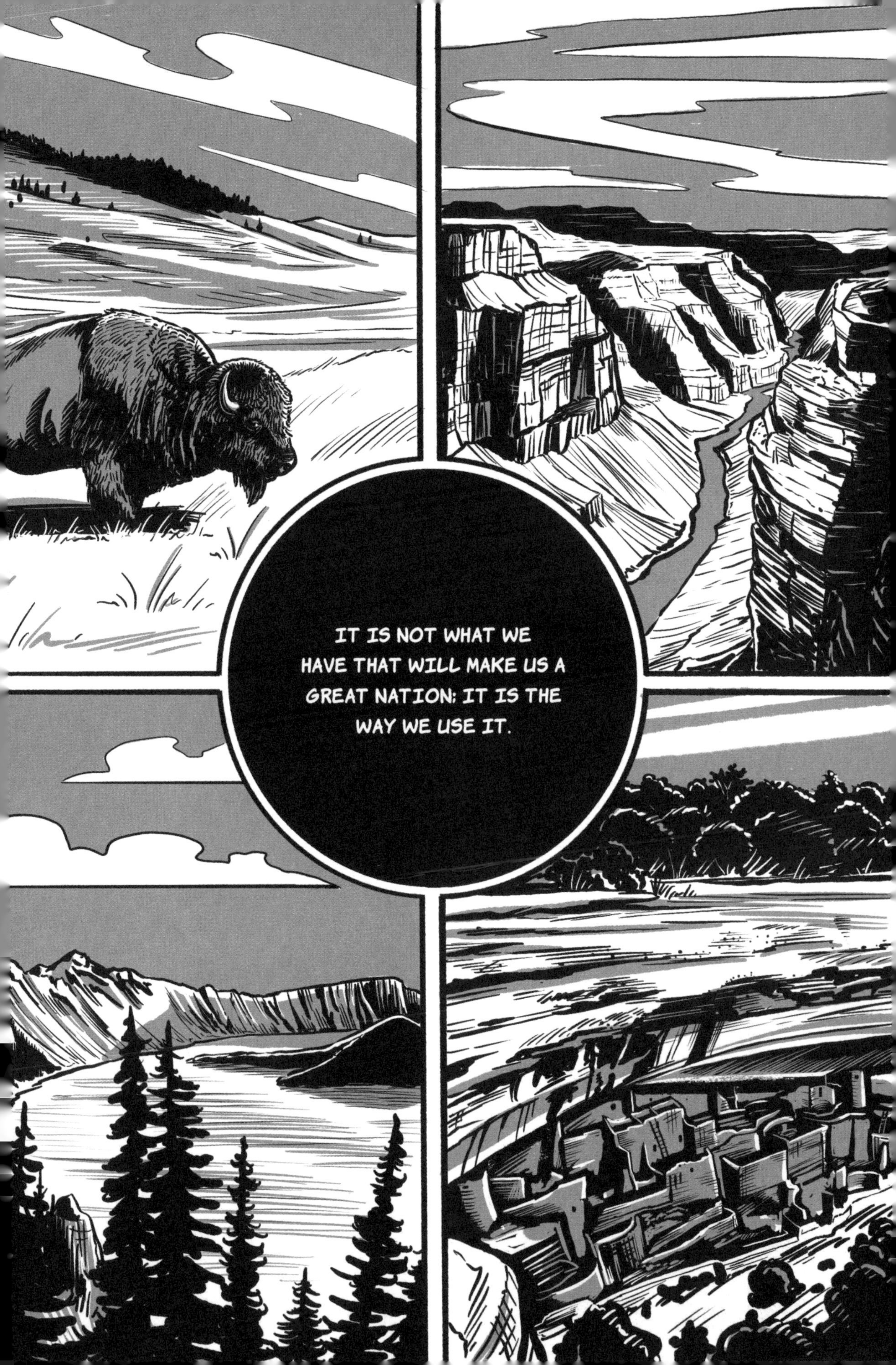
IT IS NOT WHAT WE HAVE THAT WILL MAKE US A GREAT NATION; IT IS THE WAY WE USE IT.

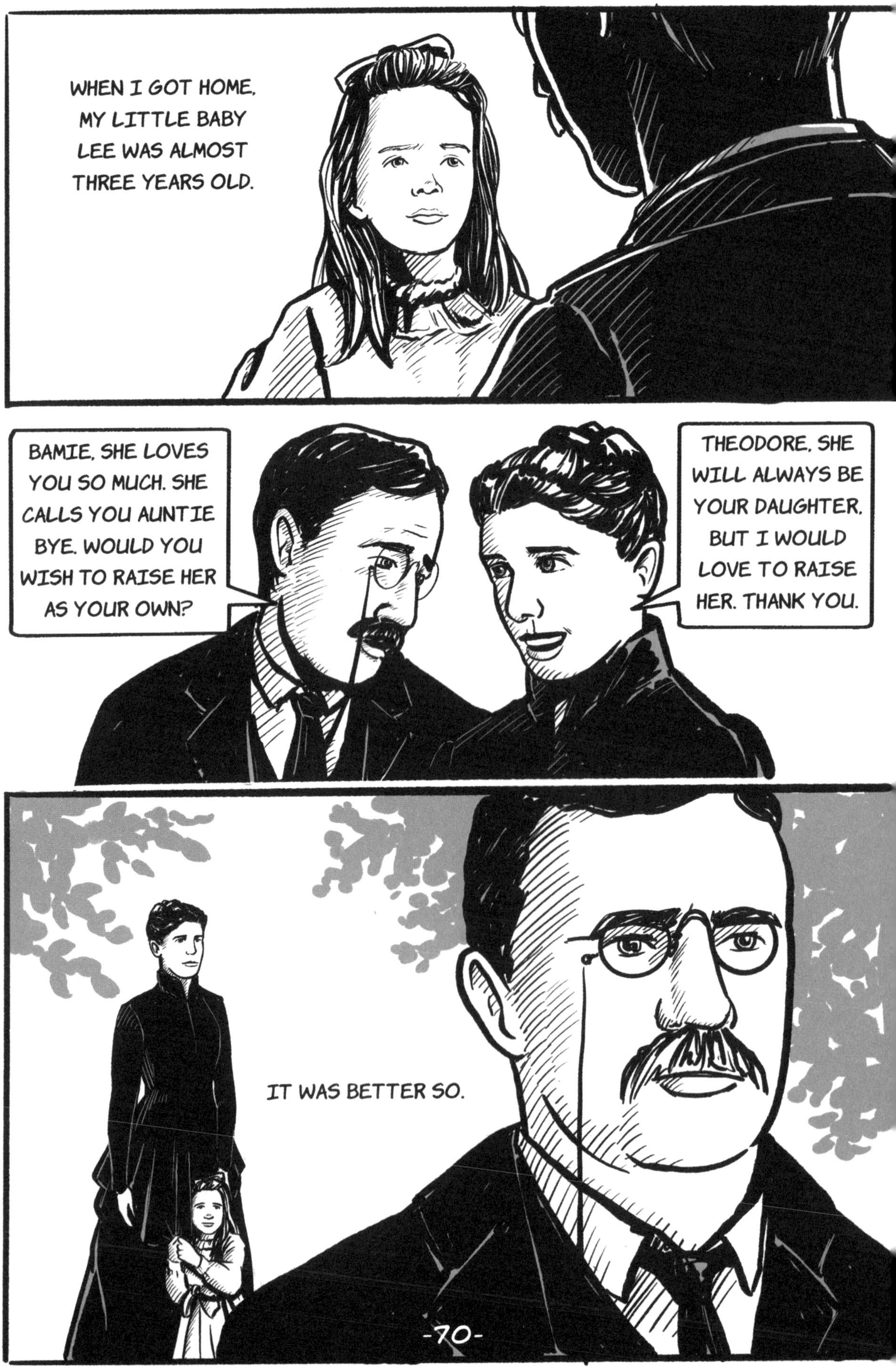
WHEN I GOT HOME, MY LITTLE BABY LEE WAS ALMOST THREE YEARS OLD.
BAMIE, SHE LOVES YOU SO MUCH. SHE CALLS YOU AUNTIE BYE. WOULD YOU WISH TO RAISE HER AS YOUR OWN?
THEODORE, SHE WILL ALWAYS BE YOUR DAUGHTER, BUT I WOULD LOVE TO RAISE HER. THANK YOU.
IT WAS BETTER SO.

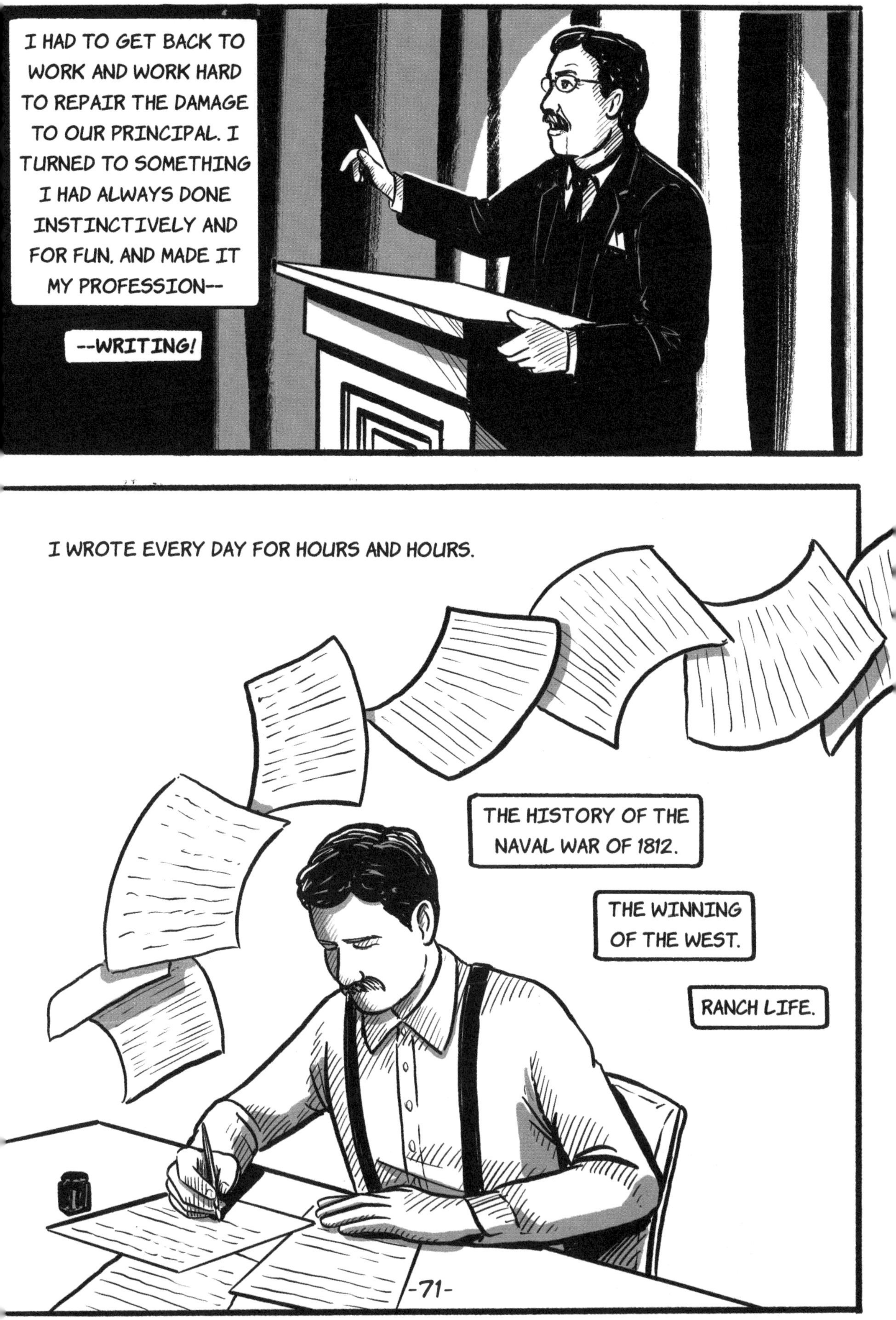
I HAD TO GET BACK TO WORK AND WORK HARD TO REPAIR THE DAMAGE TO OUR PRINCIPAL. I TURNED TO SOMETHING I HAD ALWAYS DONE INSTINCTIVELY AND FOR FUN, AND MADE IT MY PROFESSION--
--WRITING!
I WROTE EVERY DAY FOR HOURS AND HOURS.
THE HISTORY OF THE NAVAL WAR OF 1812.
THE WINNING OF THE WEST.
RANCH LIFE.

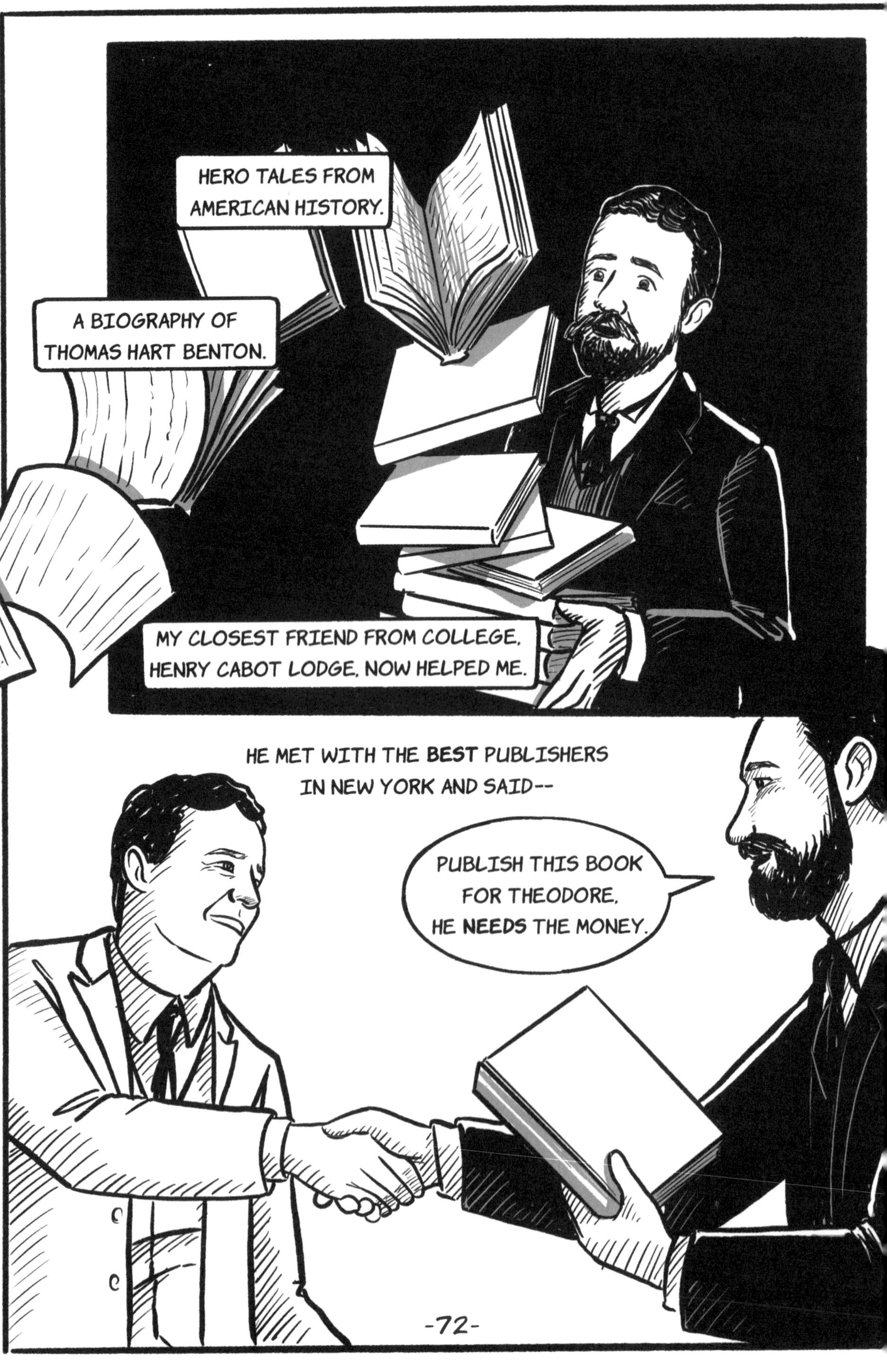
HERO TALES FROM AMERICAN HISTORY.
A BIOGRAPHY OF THOMAS HART BENTON.
MY CLOSEST FRIEND FROM COLLEGE, HENRY CABOT LODGE, NOW HELPED ME.
HE MET WITH THE **BEST** PUBLISHERS IN NEW YORK AND SAID--
PUBLISH THIS BOOK FOR THEODORE, HE **NEEDS** THE MONEY.

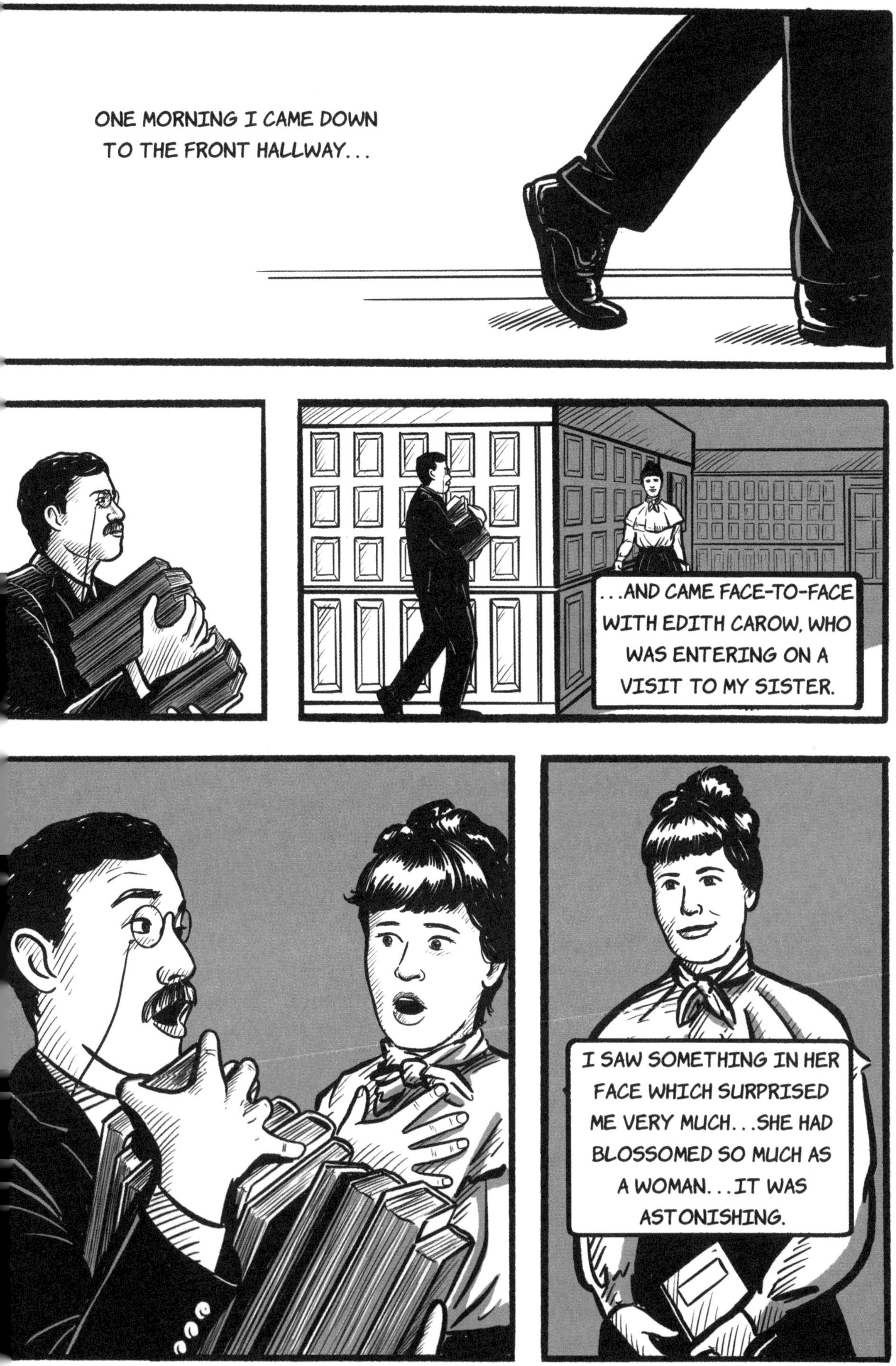
ONE MORNING I CAME DOWN TO THE FRONT HALLWAY...
...AND CAME FACE-TO-FACE WITH EDITH CAROW, WHO WAS ENTERING ON A VISIT TO MY SISTER.
I SAW SOMETHING IN HER FACE WHICH SURPRISED ME VERY MUCH...SHE HAD BLOSSOMED SO MUCH AS A WOMAN...IT WAS ASTONISHING.

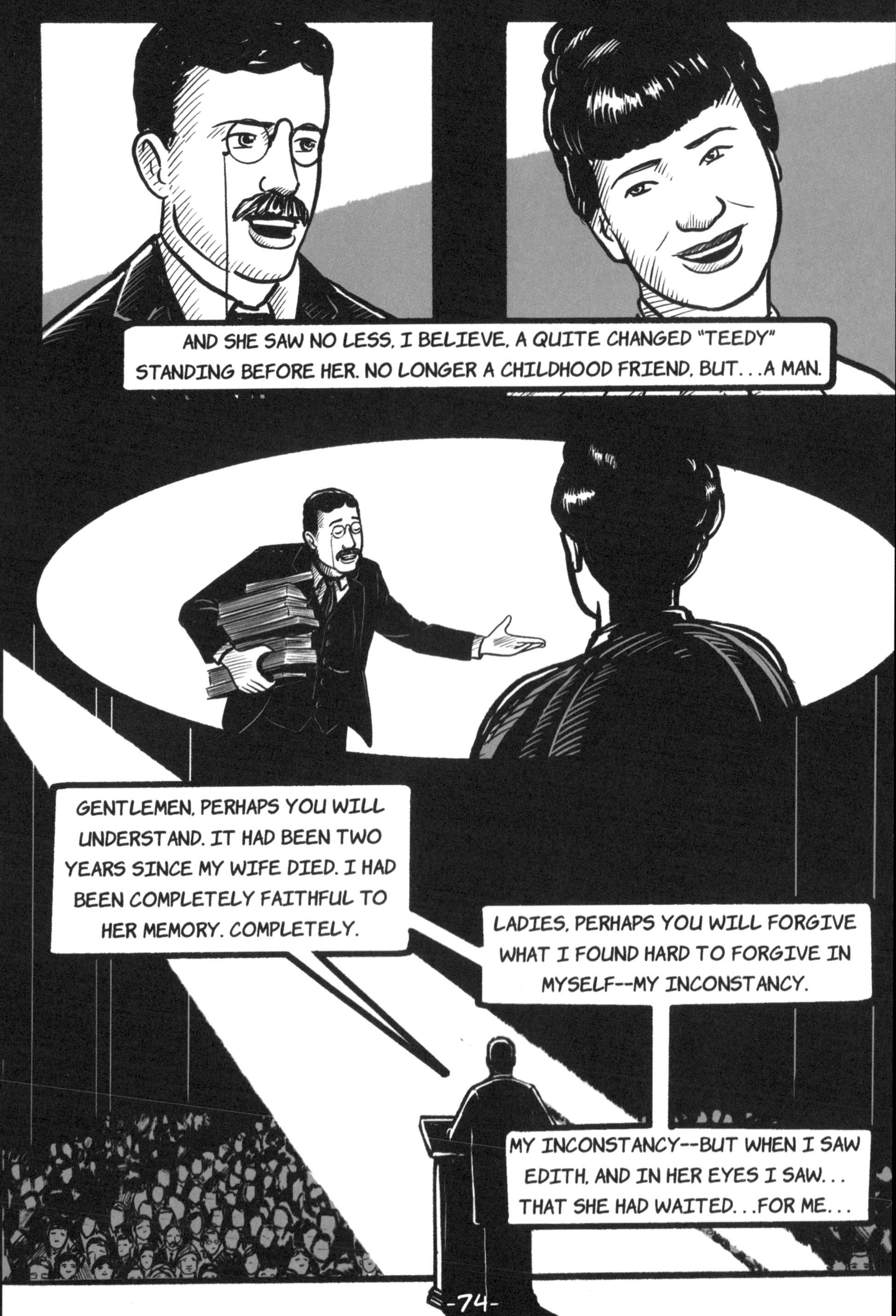
AND SHE SAW NO LESS, I BELIEVE, A QUITE CHANGED "TEEDY" STANDING BEFORE HER. NO LONGER A CHILDHOOD FRIEND, BUT. . .A MAN.
GENTLEMEN, PERHAPS YOU WILL UNDERSTAND. IT HAD BEEN TWO YEARS SINCE MY WIFE DIED. I HAD BEEN COMPLETELY FAITHFUL TO HER MEMORY. COMPLETELY.
LADIES, PERHAPS YOU WILL FORGIVE WHAT I FOUND HARD TO FORGIVE IN MYSELF--MY INCONSTANCY.
MY INCONSTANCY--BUT WHEN I SAW EDITH, AND IN HER EYES I SAW. . . THAT SHE HAD WAITED. . .FOR ME. . .

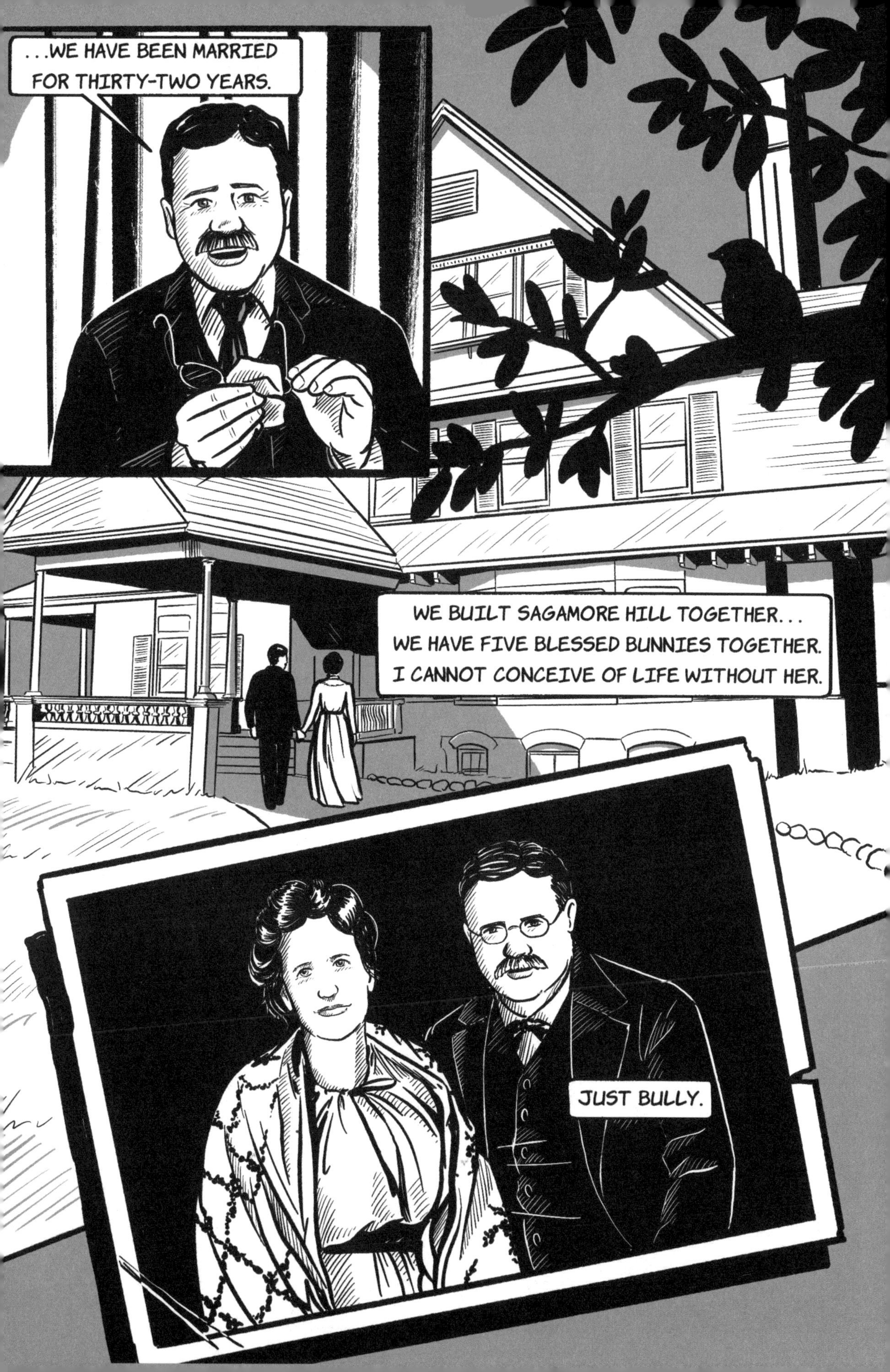
. . .WE HAVE BEEN MARRIED FOR THIRTY-TWO YEARS.
WE BUILT SAGAMORE HILL TOGETHER. . . WE HAVE FIVE BLESSED BUNNIES TOGETHER. I CANNOT CONCEIVE OF LIFE WITHOUT HER.
JUST BULLY.

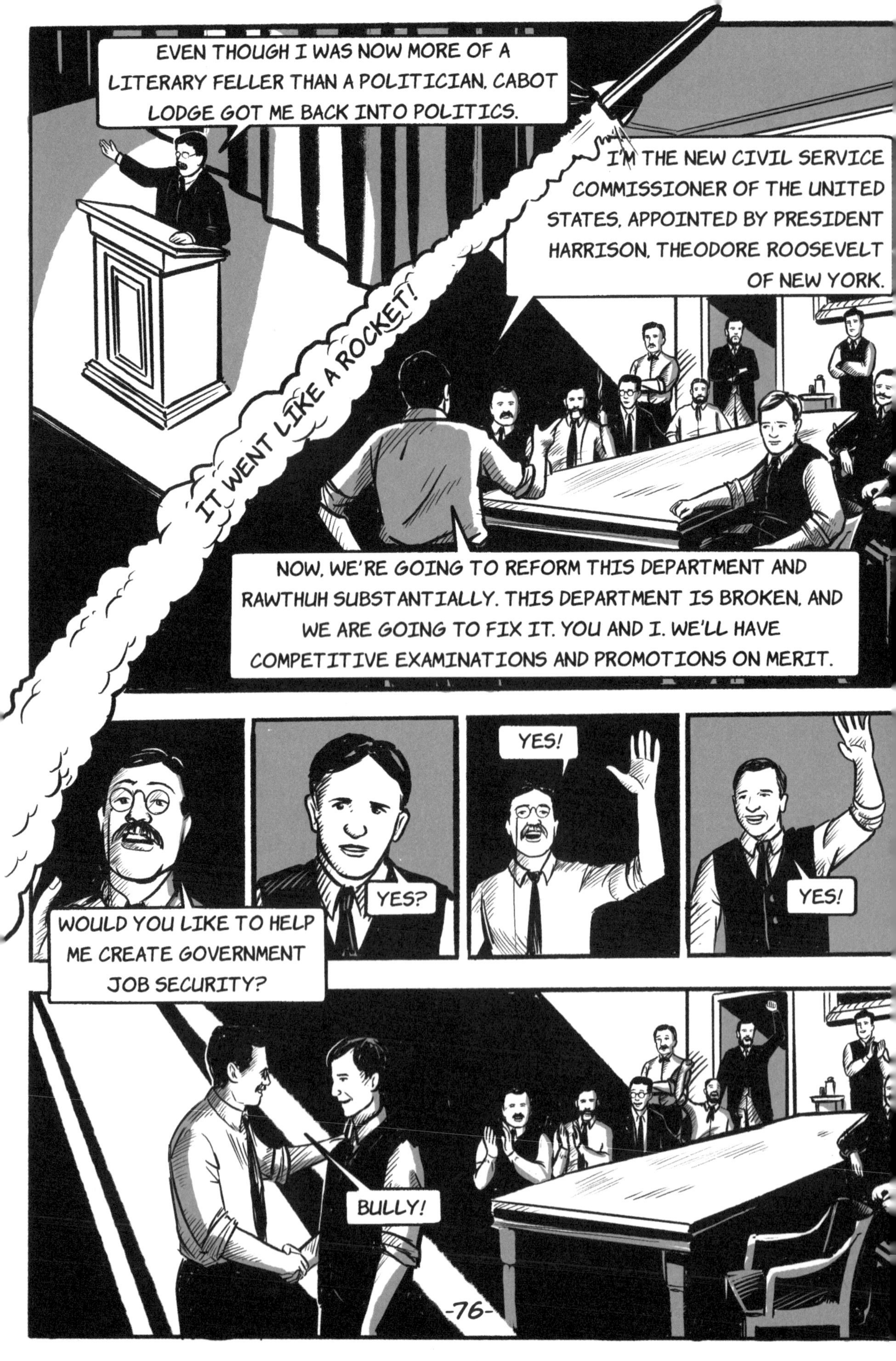
EVEN THOUGH I WAS NOW MORE OF A LITERARY FELLER THAN A POLITICIAN, CABOT LODGE GOT ME BACK INTO POLITICS.
IT WENT LIKE A ROCKET!
I'M THE NEW CIVIL SERVICE COMMISSIONER OF THE UNITED STATES, APPOINTED BY PRESIDENT HARRISON, THEODORE ROOSEVELT OF NEW YORK.
NOW, WE'RE GOING TO REFORM THIS DEPARTMENT AND RAWTHUH SUBSTANTIALLY. THIS DEPARTMENT IS BROKEN, AND WE ARE GOING TO FIX IT. YOU AND I. WE'LL HAVE COMPETITIVE EXAMINATIONS AND PROMOTIONS ON MERIT.
WOULD YOU LIKE TO HELP ME CREATE GOVERNMENT JOB SECURITY?
YES?
YES!
YES!
BULLY!

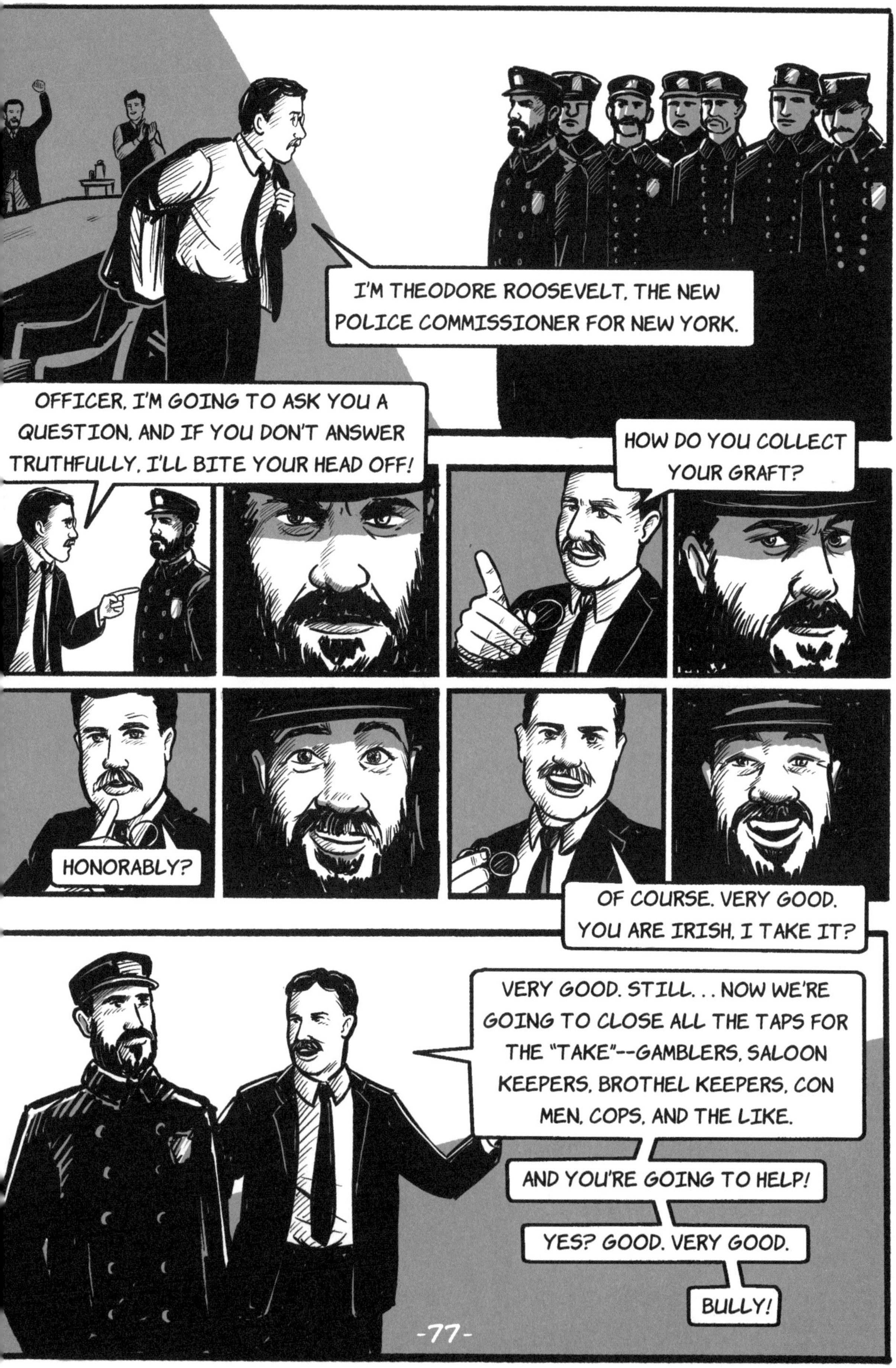
I'M THEODORE ROOSEVELT, THE NEW POLICE COMMISSIONER FOR NEW YORK.
OFFICER, I'M GOING TO ASK YOU A QUESTION, AND IF YOU DON'T ANSWER TRUTHFULLY, I'LL BITE YOUR HEAD OFF!
HOW DO YOU COLLECT YOUR GRAFT?
HONORABLY?
OF COURSE. VERY GOOD. YOU ARE IRISH, I TAKE IT?
VERY GOOD. STILL. . . NOW WE'RE GOING TO CLOSE ALL THE TAPS FOR THE "TAKE"--GAMBLERS, SALOON KEEPERS, BROTHEL KEEPERS, CON MEN, COPS, AND THE LIKE.
AND YOU'RE GOING TO HELP!
YES? GOOD. VERY GOOD.
BULLY!

ALL OF YOU WHO WOULD LIKE TO HELP ME MAKE THIS CITY A BETTER PLACE TO **LIVE** AND **WORK** IN FOR ALL THOSE WHO HAVE THE HARDEST TIME **LIVING** AND **WORKING**, SAY YES!

YES!!!

AND NOW YOU KNOW WHAT ELSE TO SAY!

BULLY!!!

SO LET'S OPEN THE DEPARTMENT TO JEWS!

I CALLED MY NEW JEWISH COPS MY "MACCABEES." AN ANTI-SEMITE CAM[E] TO NEW YORK FROM BERLIN TO PREACH A CRUSADE AGAINST JEWS.

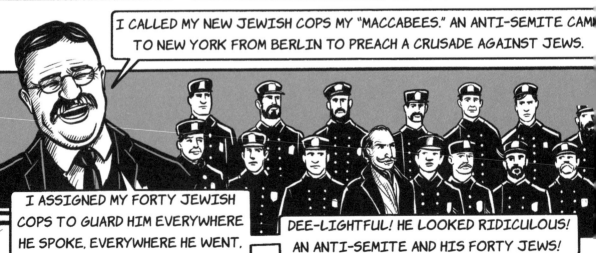

I ASSIGNED MY FORTY JEWISH COPS TO GUARD HIM EVERYWHERE HE SPOKE, EVERYWHERE HE WENT, EVEN TO THE BATHROOM.

DEE-LIGHTFUL! HE LOOKED RIDICULOUS! AN ANTI-SEMITE AND HIS FORTY JEWS!

-78-

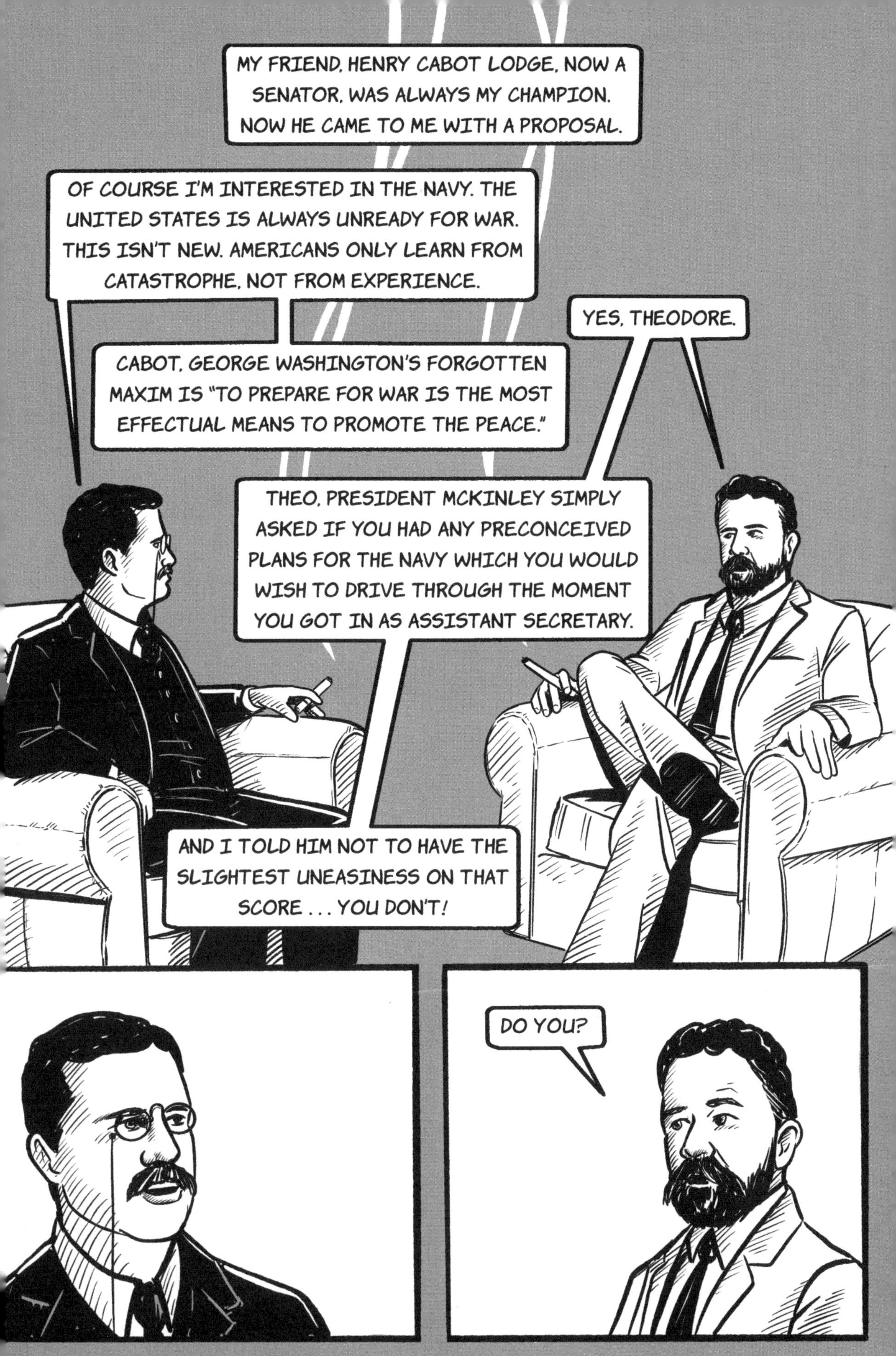
MY FRIEND, HENRY CABOT LODGE, NOW A SENATOR, WAS ALWAYS MY CHAMPION. NOW HE CAME TO ME WITH A PROPOSAL.
OF COURSE I'M INTERESTED IN THE NAVY. THE UNITED STATES IS ALWAYS UNREADY FOR WAR. THIS ISN'T NEW. AMERICANS ONLY LEARN FROM CATASTROPHE, NOT FROM EXPERIENCE.
CABOT, GEORGE WASHINGTON'S FORGOTTEN MAXIM IS "TO PREPARE FOR WAR IS THE MOST EFFECTUAL MEANS TO PROMOTE THE PEACE."
YES, THEODORE.
THEO, PRESIDENT MCKINLEY SIMPLY ASKED IF YOU HAD ANY PRECONCEIVED PLANS FOR THE NAVY WHICH YOU WOULD WISH TO DRIVE THROUGH THE MOMENT YOU GOT IN AS ASSISTANT SECRETARY.
AND I TOLD HIM NOT TO HAVE THE SLIGHTEST UNEASINESS ON THAT SCORE . . . YOU DON'T!
DO YOU?

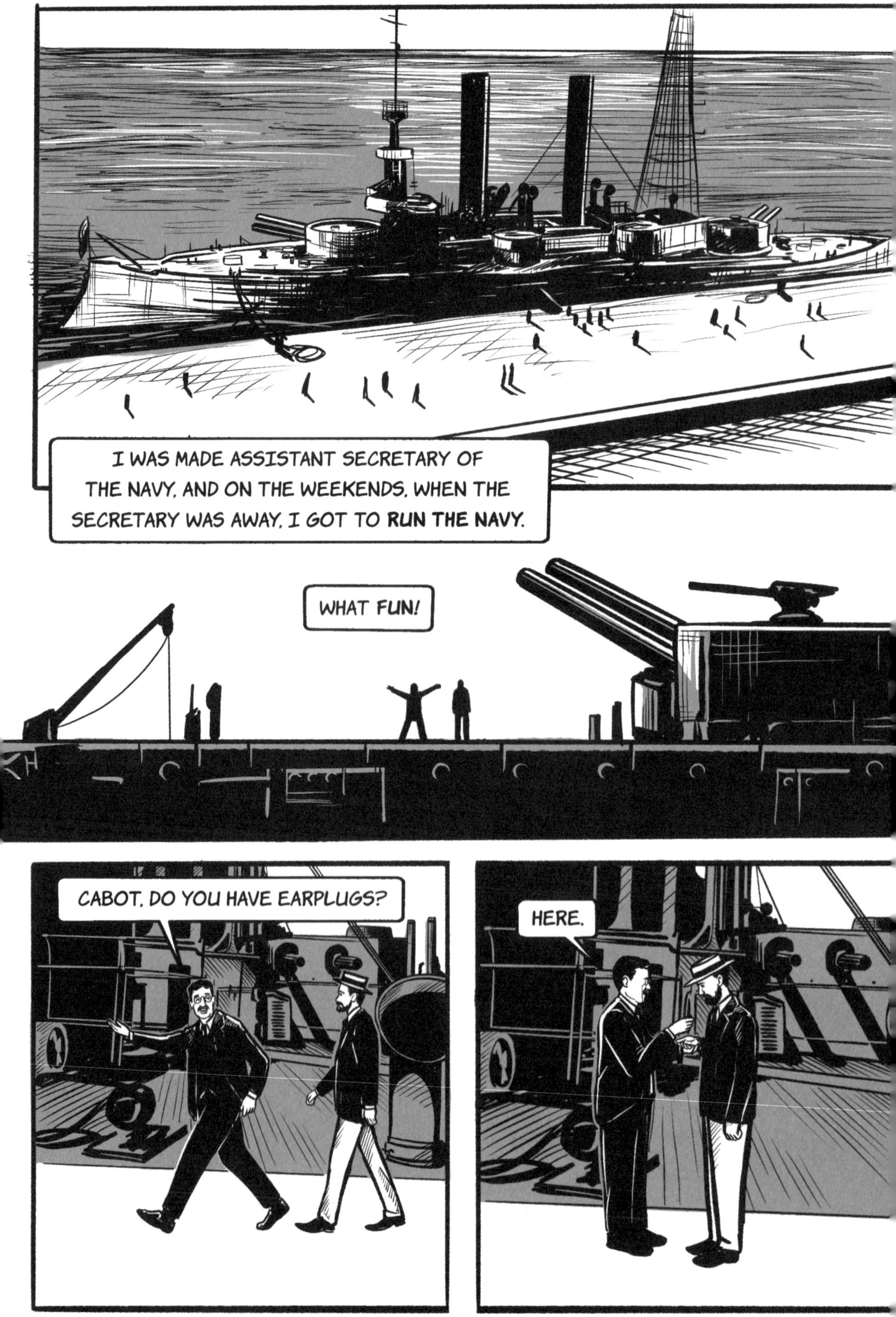
I WAS MADE ASSISTANT SECRETARY OF THE NAVY, AND ON THE WEEKENDS, WHEN THE SECRETARY WAS AWAY, I GOT TO **RUN THE NAVY**.
WHAT FUN!
CABOT, DO YOU HAVE EARPLUGS?
HERE.

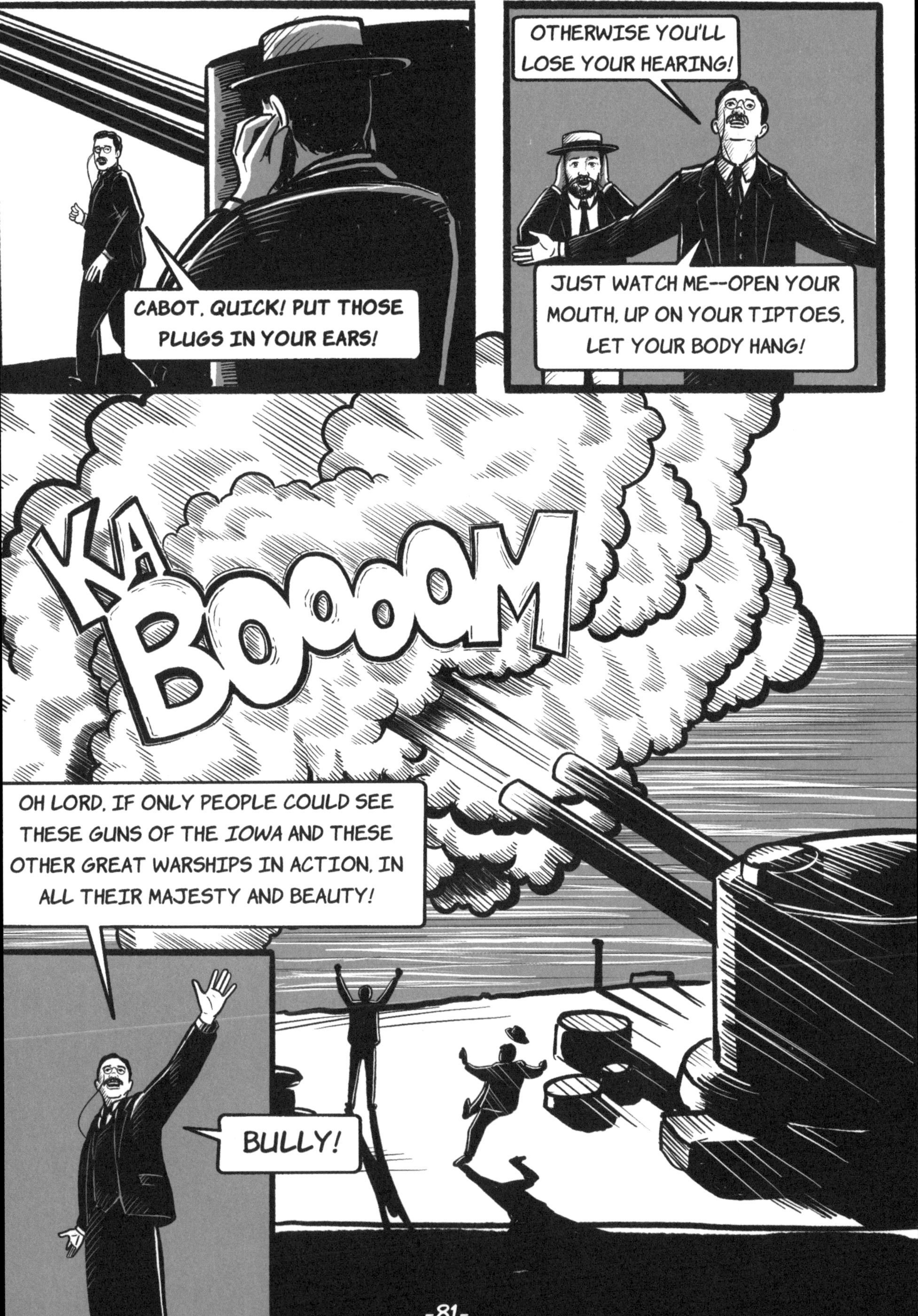
CABOT. QUICK! PUT THOSE PLUGS IN YOUR EARS!
OTHERWISE YOU'LL LOSE YOUR HEARING!
JUST WATCH ME--OPEN YOUR MOUTH, UP ON YOUR TIPTOES, LET YOUR BODY HANG!
KA BOOOOM
OH LORD, IF ONLY PEOPLE COULD SEE THESE GUNS OF THE *IOWA* AND THESE OTHER GREAT WARSHIPS IN ACTION, IN ALL THEIR MAJESTY AND BEAUTY!
BULLY!

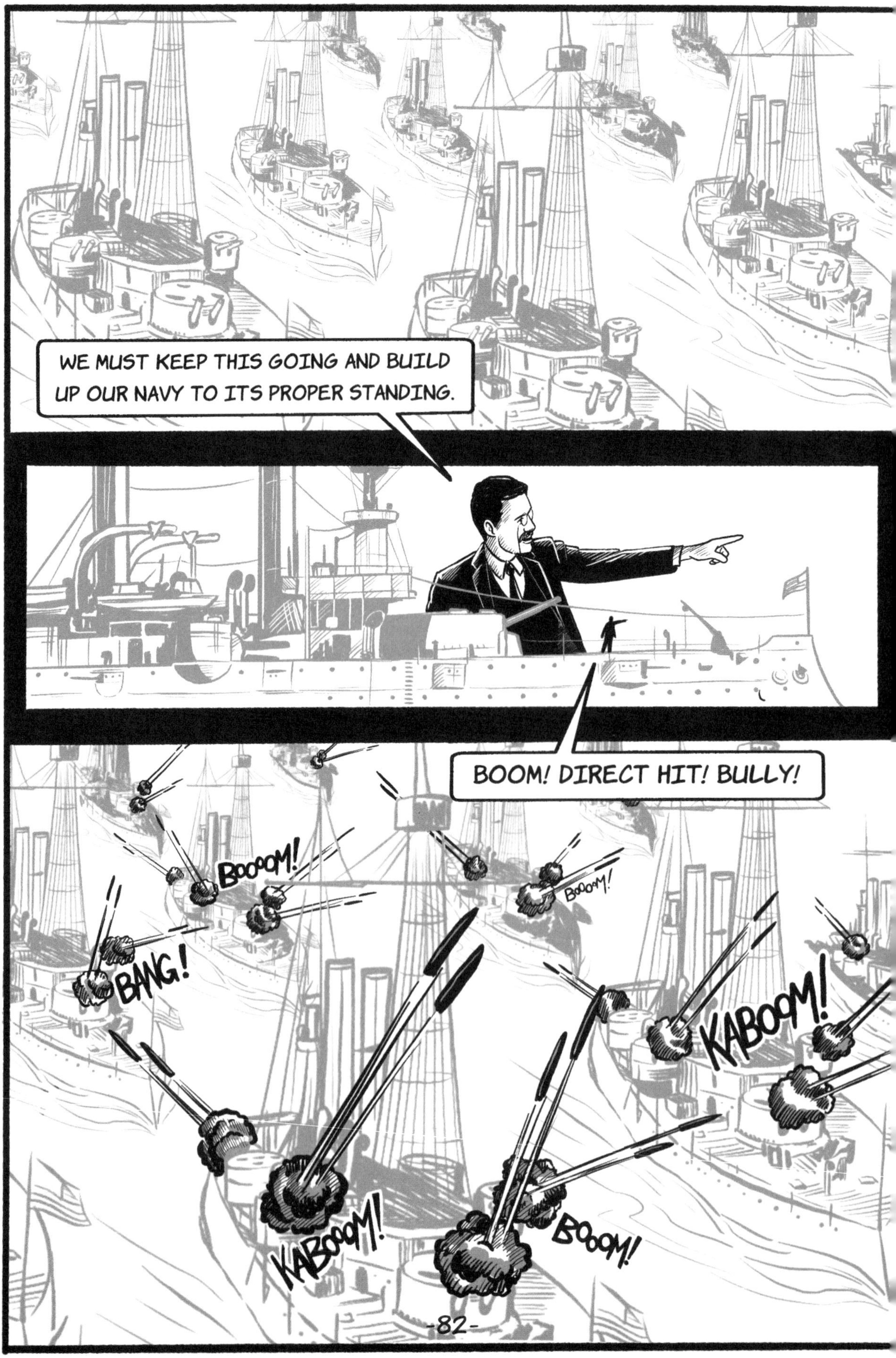
WE MUST KEEP THIS GOING AND BUILD UP OUR NAVY TO ITS PROPER STANDING.
BOOM! DIRECT HIT! BULLY!
BOOOOM!
BOOOOM!
BANG!
KABOOOM!
KABOOOM!
BOOOOM!

CABOT? CABOT? WHERE ARE YOU?

OH, DEAR.

OH, ENSIGN?

I'M ASSISTANT SECRETARY OF THE NAVY, THEODORE ROOSEVELT--

--YES, THEODORE ROOSEVELT. HERE'S THE HYPOTHETICAL PROBLEM. MAKE PLANS TO DEAL WITH IT.

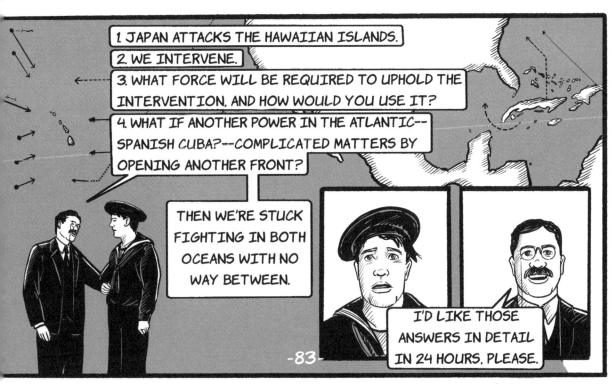

1. JAPAN ATTACKS THE HAWAIIAN ISLANDS.

2. WE INTERVENE.

3. WHAT FORCE WILL BE REQUIRED TO UPHOLD THE INTERVENTION, AND HOW WOULD YOU USE IT?

4. WHAT IF ANOTHER POWER IN THE ATLANTIC-- SPANISH CUBA?--COMPLICATED MATTERS BY OPENING ANOTHER FRONT?

THEN WE'RE STUCK FIGHTING IN BOTH OCEANS WITH NO WAY BETWEEN.

I'D LIKE THOSE ANSWERS IN DETAIL IN 24 HOURS, PLEASE.

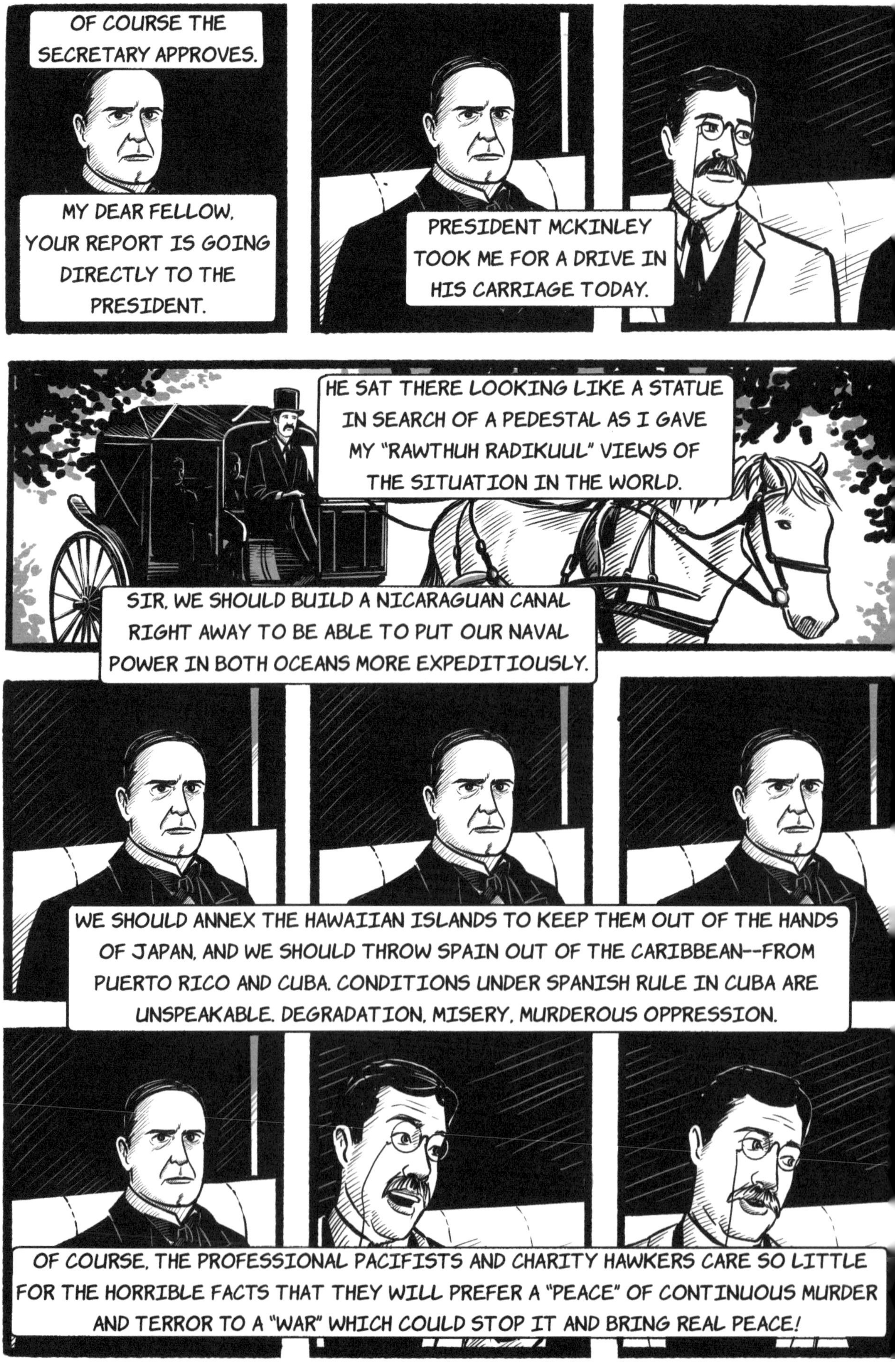

OF COURSE THE SECRETARY APPROVES.
MY DEAR FELLOW, YOUR REPORT IS GOING DIRECTLY TO THE PRESIDENT.
PRESIDENT MCKINLEY TOOK ME FOR A DRIVE IN HIS CARRIAGE TODAY.
HE SAT THERE LOOKING LIKE A STATUE IN SEARCH OF A PEDESTAL AS I GAVE MY "RAWTHUH RADIKUUL" VIEWS OF THE SITUATION IN THE WORLD.
SIR, WE SHOULD BUILD A NICARAGUAN CANAL RIGHT AWAY TO BE ABLE TO PUT OUR NAVAL POWER IN BOTH OCEANS MORE EXPEDITIOUSLY.
WE SHOULD ANNEX THE HAWAIIAN ISLANDS TO KEEP THEM OUT OF THE HANDS OF JAPAN, AND WE SHOULD THROW SPAIN OUT OF THE CARIBBEAN--FROM PUERTO RICO AND CUBA. CONDITIONS UNDER SPANISH RULE IN CUBA ARE UNSPEAKABLE. DEGRADATION, MISERY, MURDEROUS OPPRESSION.
OF COURSE, THE PROFESSIONAL PACIFISTS AND CHARITY HAWKERS CARE SO LITTLE FOR THE HORRIBLE FACTS THAT THEY WILL PREFER A "PEACE" OF CONTINUOUS MURDER AND TERROR TO A "WAR" WHICH COULD STOP IT AND BRING REAL PEACE!

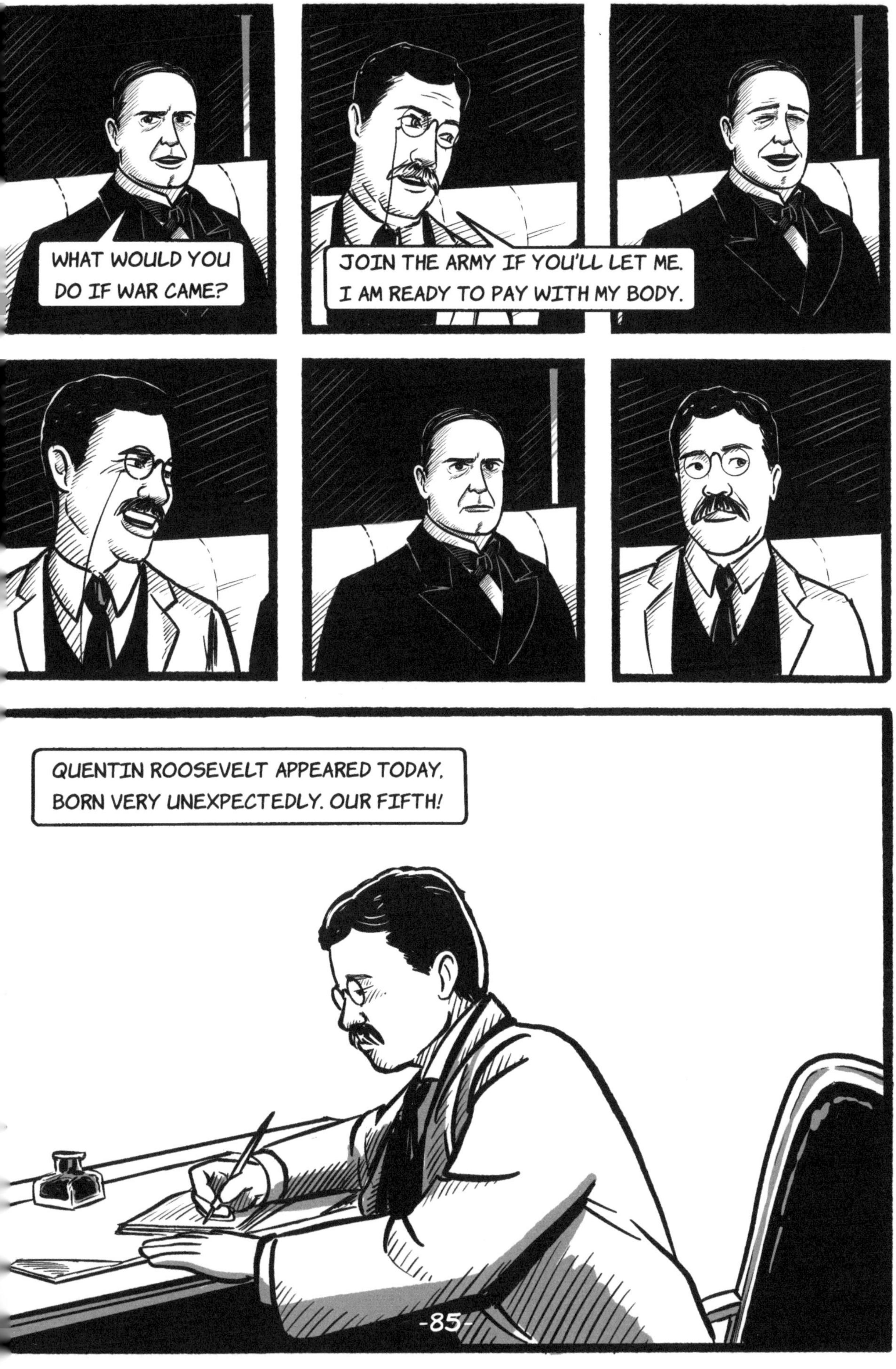
WHAT WOULD YOU DO IF WAR CAME?
JOIN THE ARMY IF YOU'LL LET ME. I AM READY TO PAY WITH MY BODY.
QUENTIN ROOSEVELT APPEARED TODAY. BORN VERY UNEXPECTEDLY. OUR FIFTH!

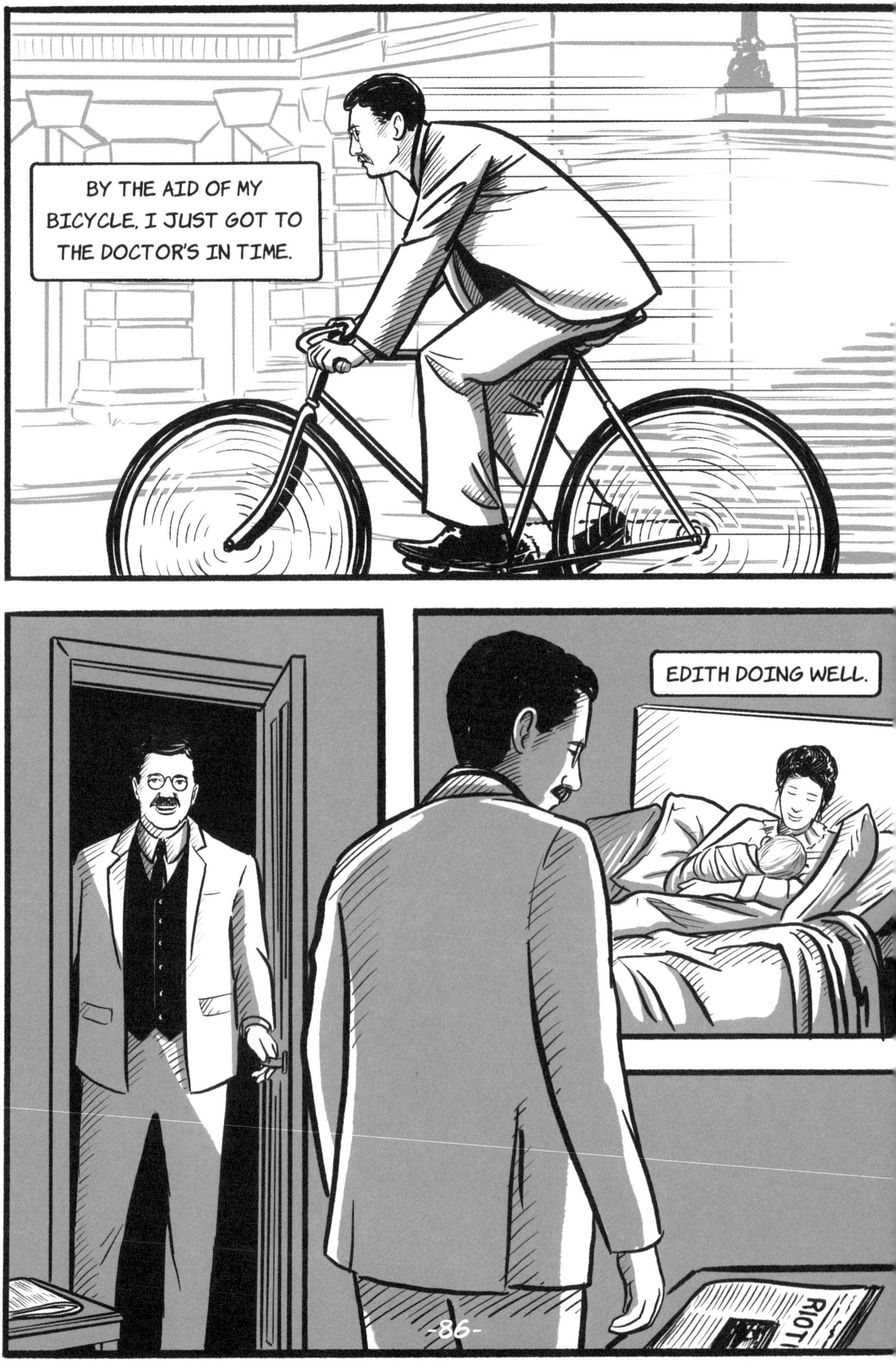
BY THE AID OF MY BICYCLE, I JUST GOT TO THE DOCTOR'S IN TIME.
EDITH DOING WELL.

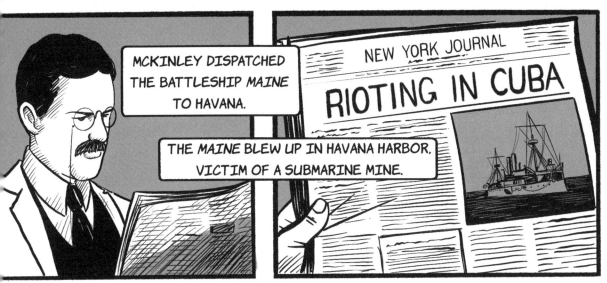

MCKINLEY DISPATCHED THE BATTLESHIP MAINE TO HAVANA.

NEW YORK JOURNAL

RIOTING IN CUBA

THE *MAINE* BLEW UP IN HAVANA HARBOR, VICTIM OF A SUBMARINE MINE.

WHETHER ACCIDENTAL OR INTENTIONAL, IT IS WAR, WITH SPAIN.

MY FATHER HAD NOT FOUGHT IN THE CIVIL WAR FOR MANY GOOD REASONS.

I WAS NOW THE FATHER OF SIX, WITH A WIFE WHO WAS RECUPERATING NOT ONLY FROM CHILDBIRTH, BUT FROM A DIFFICULT SURGERY. I WAS 40 YEARS OLD, NOT IN THE BEST CONDITION, BUT FOLLOWING MY INSTINCT AND NOT MY REASON,

I WENT TO DO MY DUTY.

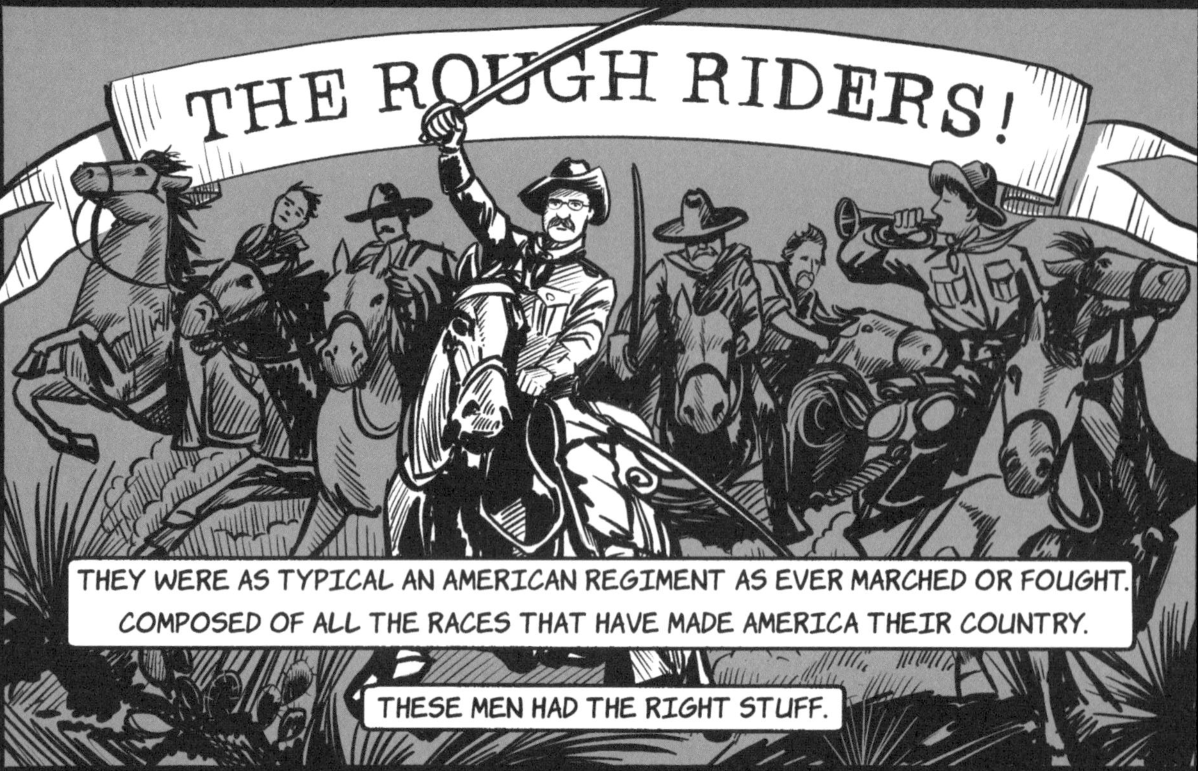
THE ROUGH RIDERS!
THEY WERE AS TYPICAL AN AMERICAN REGIMENT AS EVER MARCHED OR FOUGHT. COMPOSED OF ALL THE RACES THAT HAVE MADE AMERICA THEIR COUNTRY.
THESE MEN HAD THE RIGHT STUFF.

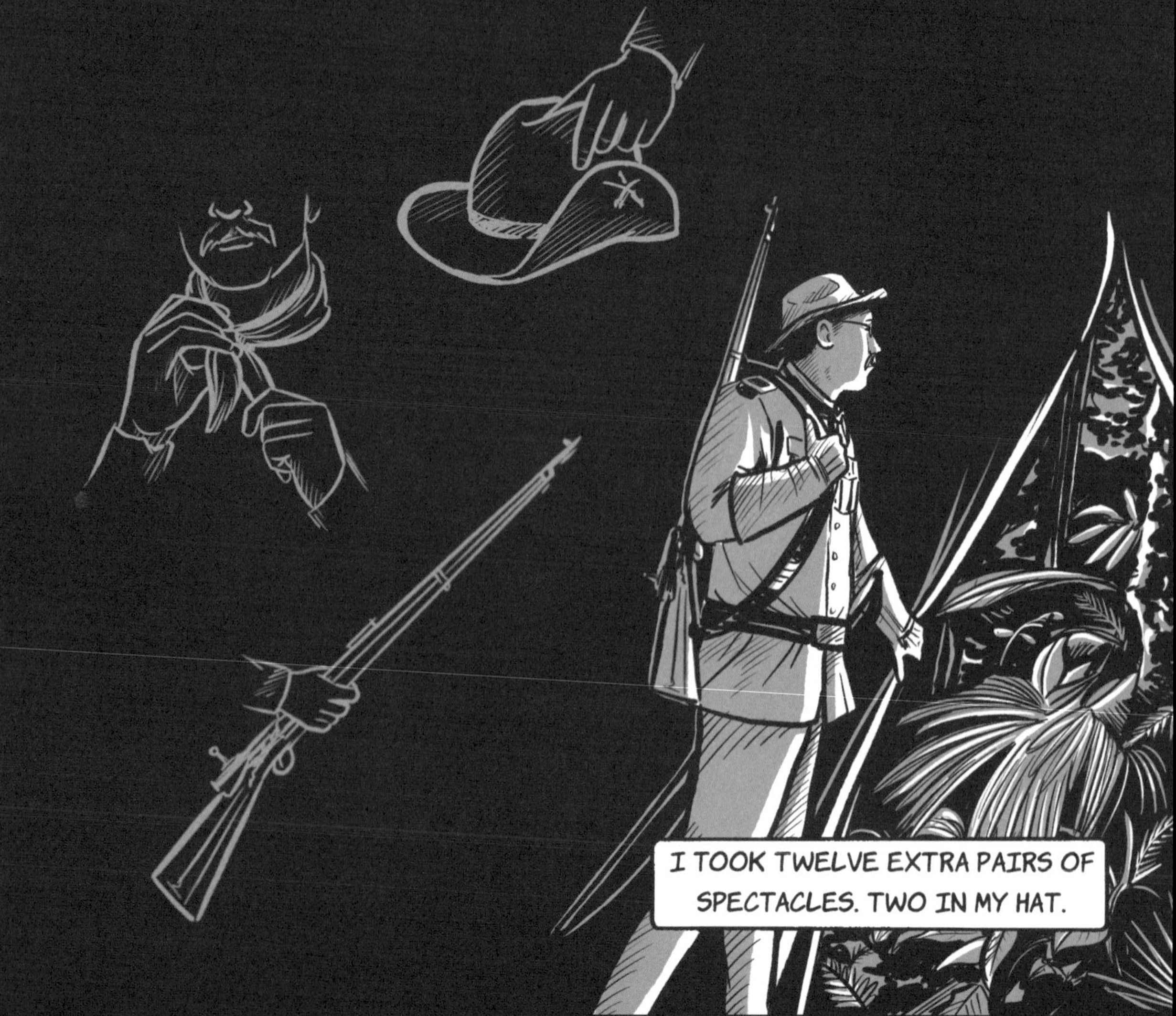
I TOOK TWELVE EXTRA PAIRS OF SPECTACLES. TWO IN MY HAT.

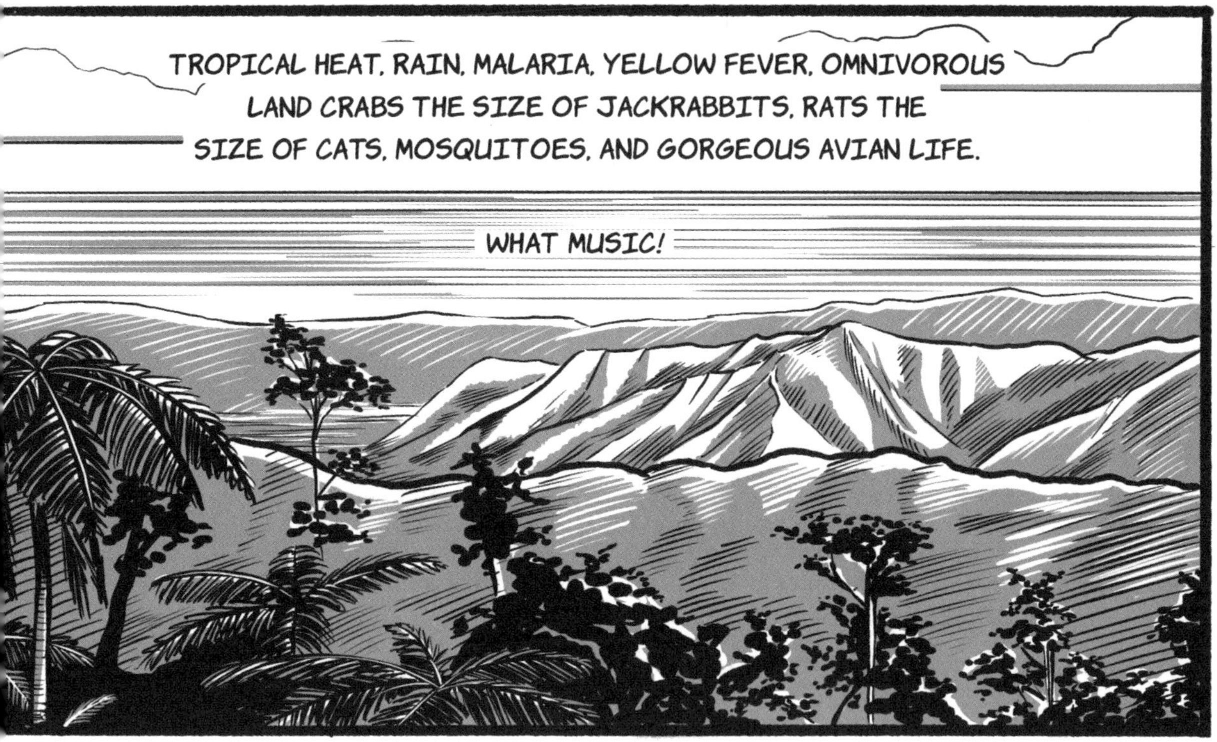
TROPICAL HEAT. RAIN. MALARIA. YELLOW FEVER. OMNIVOROUS LAND CRABS THE SIZE OF JACKRABBITS. RATS THE SIZE OF CATS. MOSQUITOES. AND GORGEOUS AVIAN LIFE.
WHAT MUSIC!

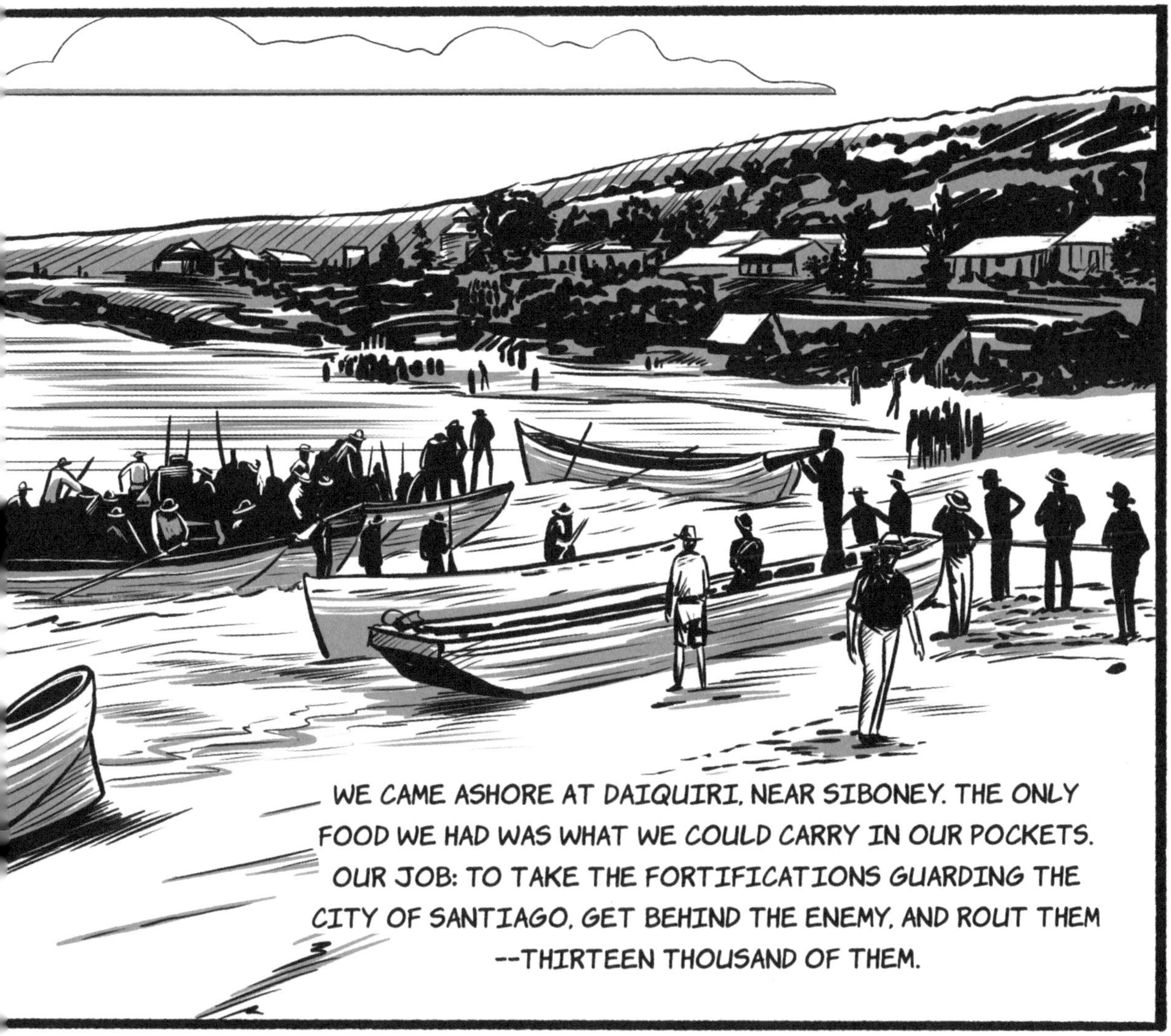
WE CAME ASHORE AT DAIQUIRI, NEAR SIBONEY. THE ONLY FOOD WE HAD WAS WHAT WE COULD CARRY IN OUR POCKETS. OUR JOB: TO TAKE THE FORTIFICATIONS GUARDING THE CITY OF SANTIAGO, GET BEHIND THE ENEMY, AND ROUT THEM --THIRTEEN THOUSAND OF THEM.

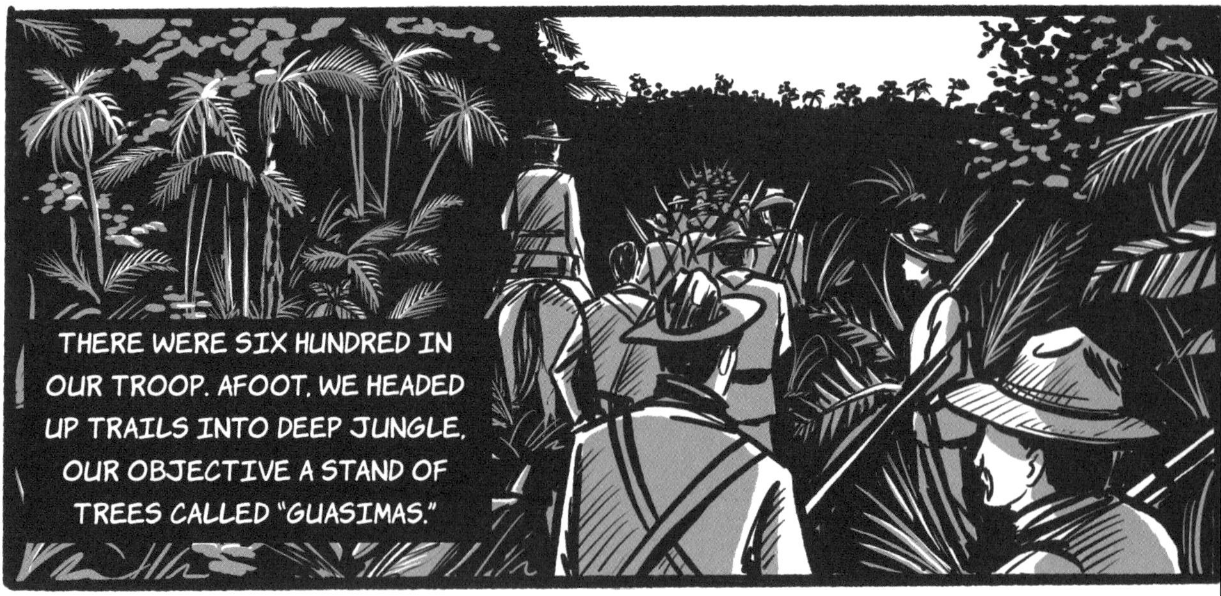
THERE WERE SIX HUNDRED IN OUR TROOP. AFOOT, WE HEADED UP TRAILS INTO DEEP JUNGLE, OUR OBJECTIVE A STAND OF TREES CALLED "GUASIMAS."

AND ABOVE, A HILL, ON A STRING OF HILLS CALLED SAN JUAN HEIGHTS, WHICH STOOD BEFORE SANTIAGO.

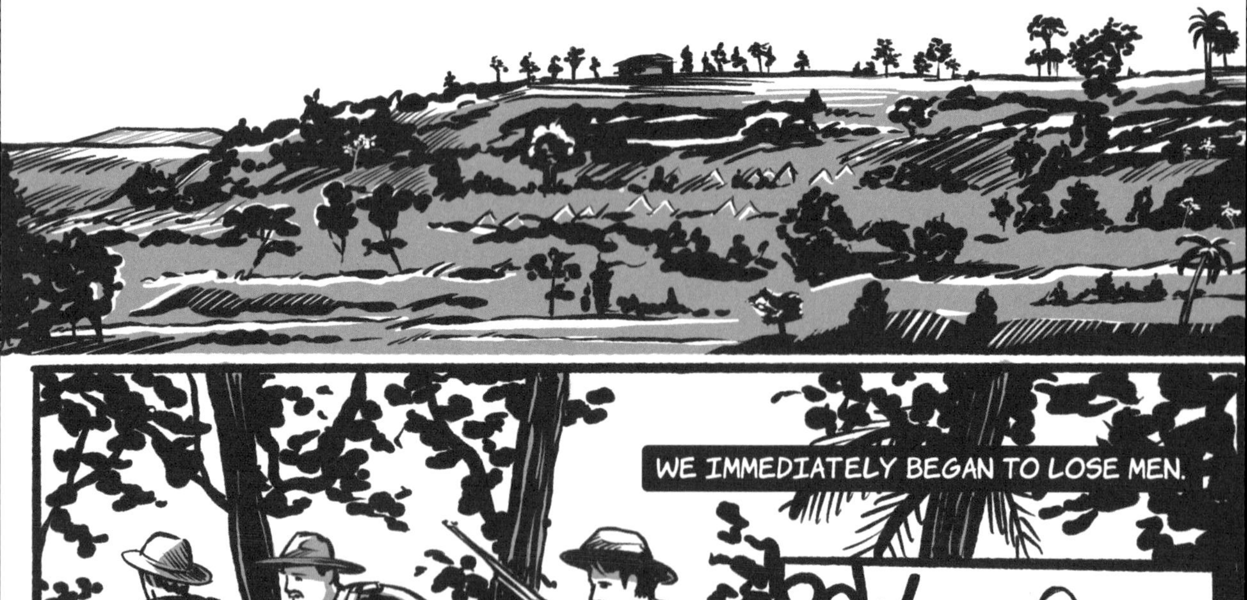

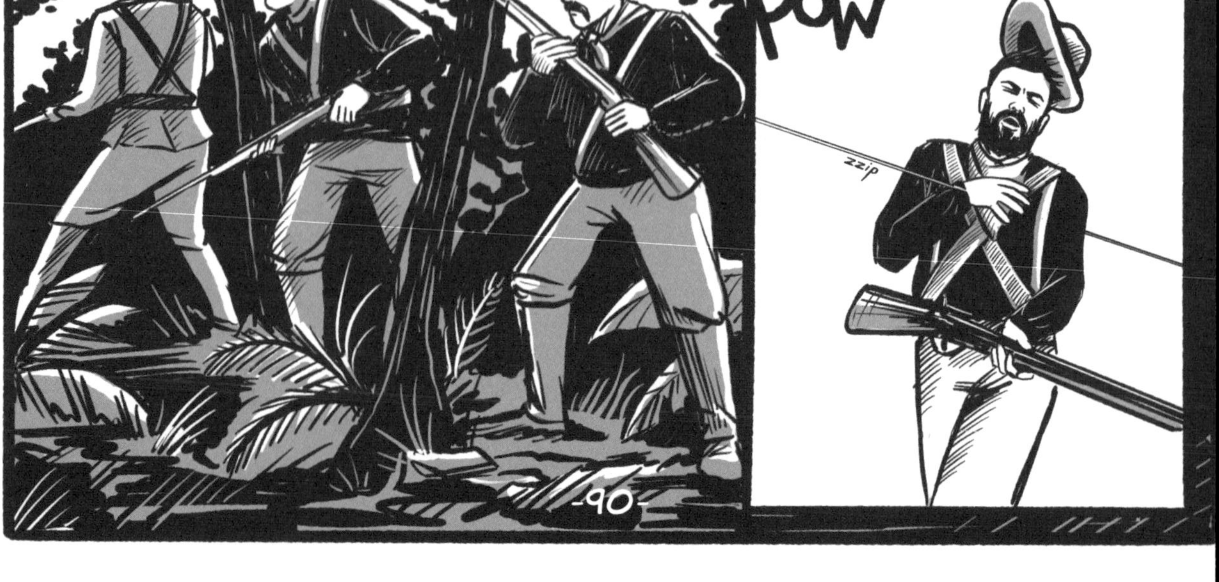
WE IMMEDIATELY BEGAN TO LOSE MEN.
POW
zzip

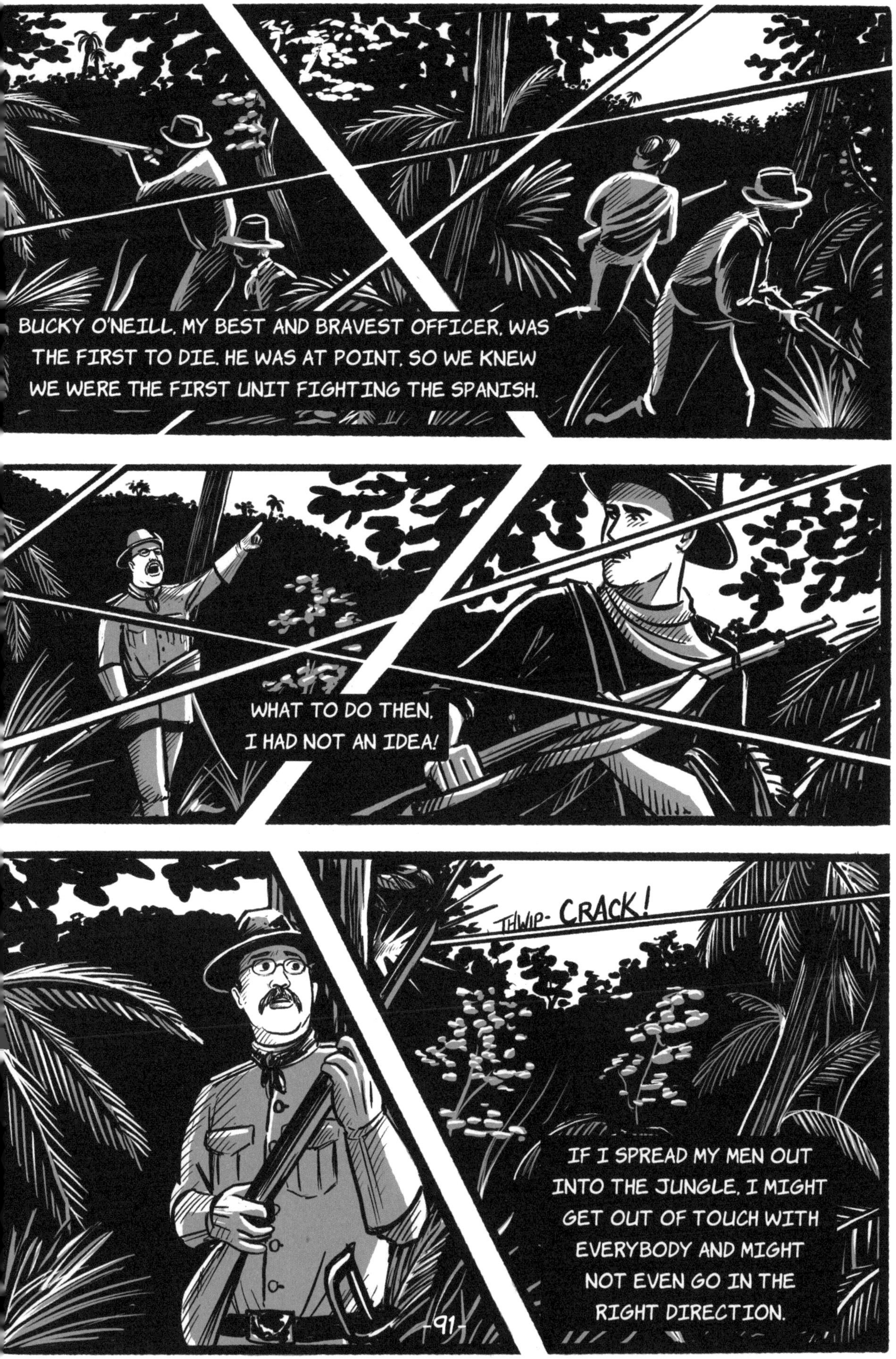
BUCKY O'NEILL, MY BEST AND BRAVEST OFFICER, WAS THE FIRST TO DIE. HE WAS AT POINT, SO WE KNEW WE WERE THE FIRST UNIT FIGHTING THE SPANISH.
WHAT TO DO THEN, I HAD NOT AN IDEA!
THWIP- CRACK!
IF I SPREAD MY MEN OUT INTO THE JUNGLE, I MIGHT GET OUT OF TOUCH WITH EVERYBODY AND MIGHT NOT EVEN GO IN THE RIGHT DIRECTION.

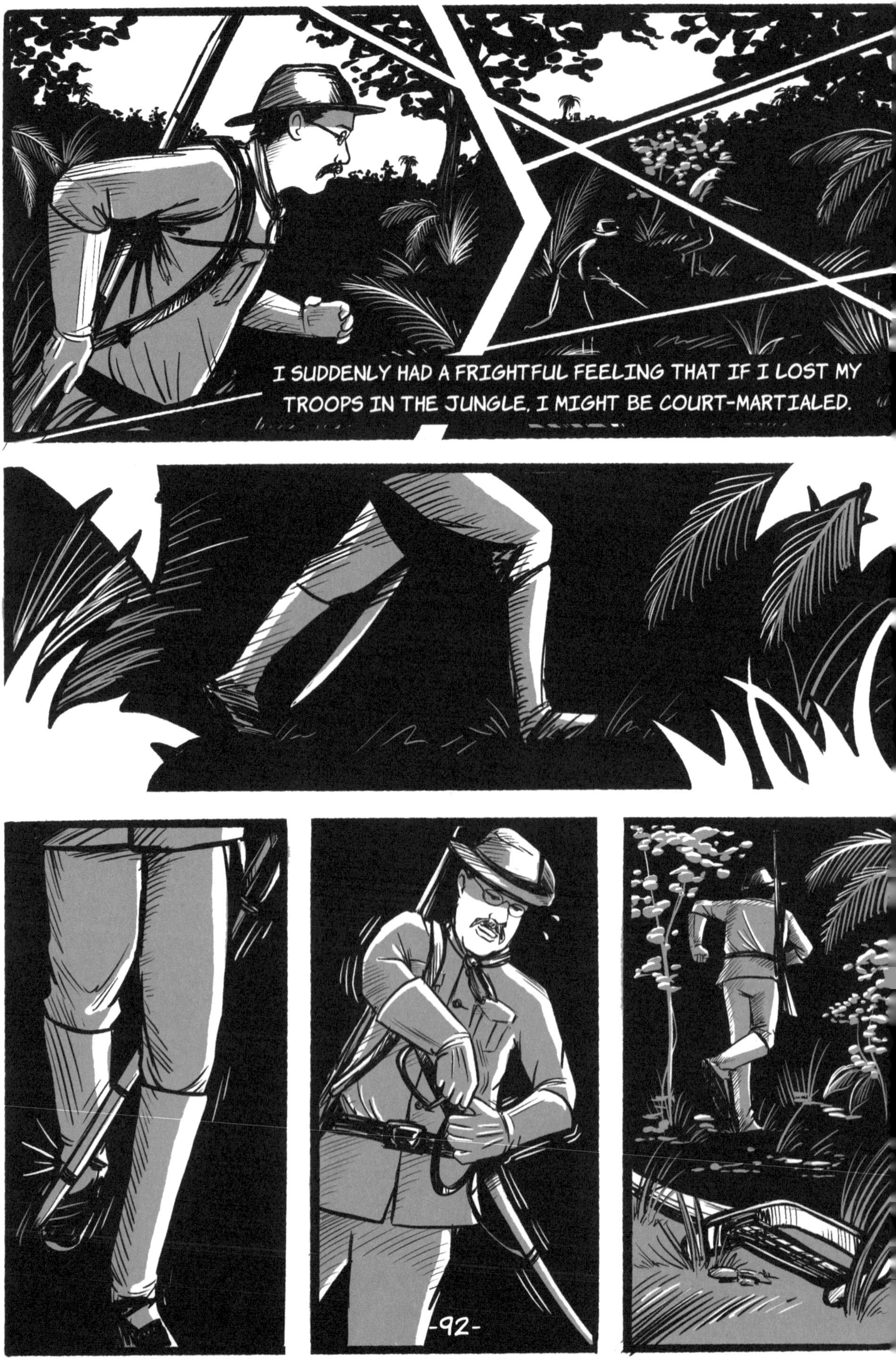
I SUDDENLY HAD A FRIGHTFUL FEELING THAT IF I LOST MY TROOPS IN THE JUNGLE, I MIGHT BE COURT-MARTIALED.

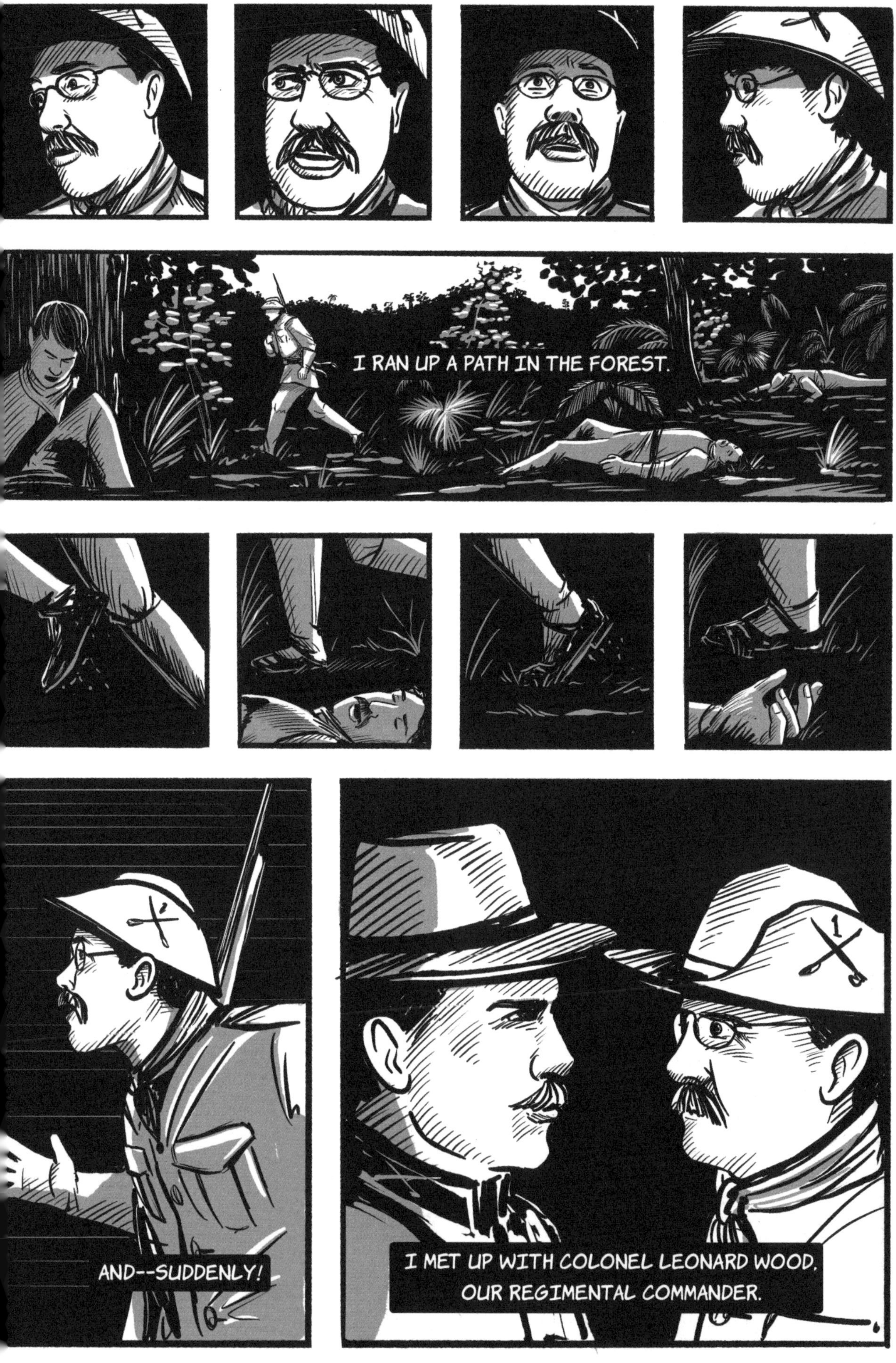
I RAN UP A PATH IN THE FOREST.
AND--SUDDENLY!
I MET UP WITH COLONEL LEONARD WOOD, OUR REGIMENTAL COMMANDER.

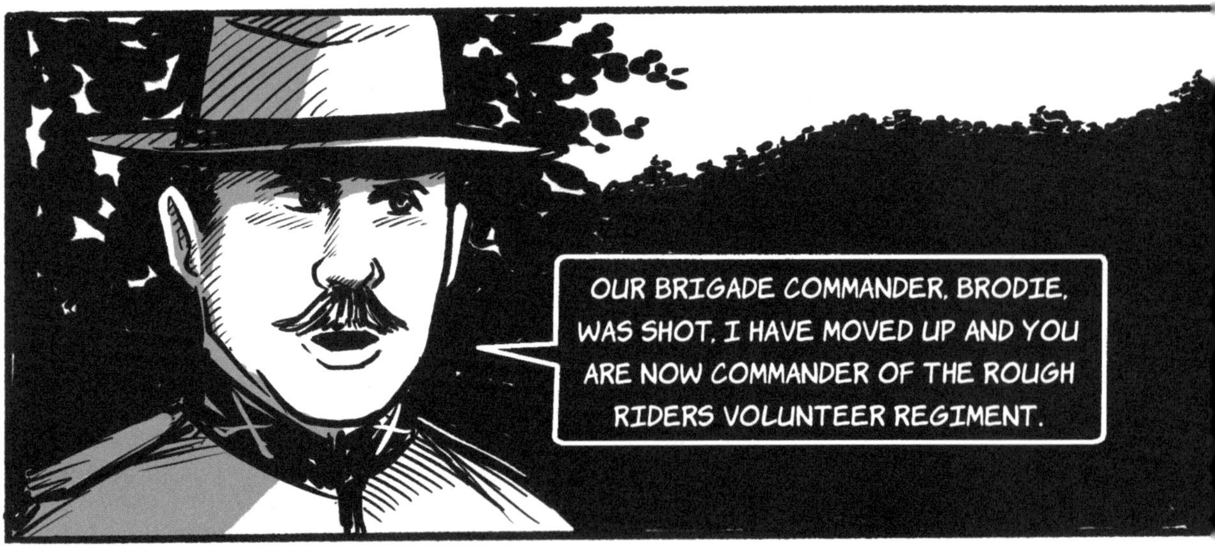
OUR BRIGADE COMMANDER, BRODIE, WAS SHOT. I HAVE MOVED UP AND YOU ARE NOW COMMANDER OF THE ROUGH RIDERS VOLUNTEER REGIMENT.

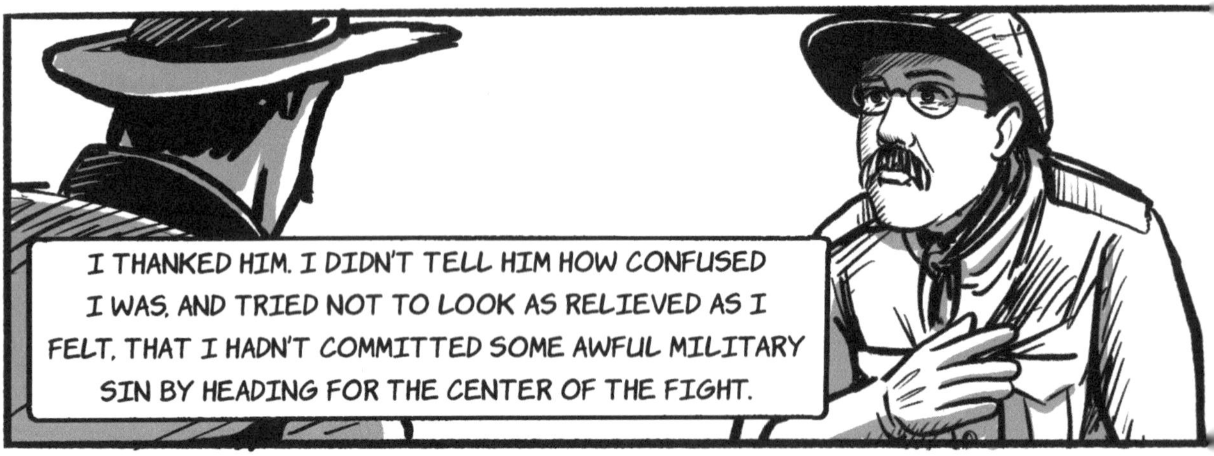
I THANKED HIM. I DIDN'T TELL HIM HOW CONFUSED I WAS, AND TRIED NOT TO LOOK AS RELIEVED AS I FELT, THAT I HADN'T COMMITTED SOME AWFUL MILITARY SIN BY HEADING FOR THE CENTER OF THE FIGHT.

WE SPENT THE NIGHT HELPING THE WOUNDED, BURYING THE DEAD, AND TRYING TO FIND FOOD AMID CONTINUOUS ARTILLERY BARRAGES FROM BOTH SIDES.

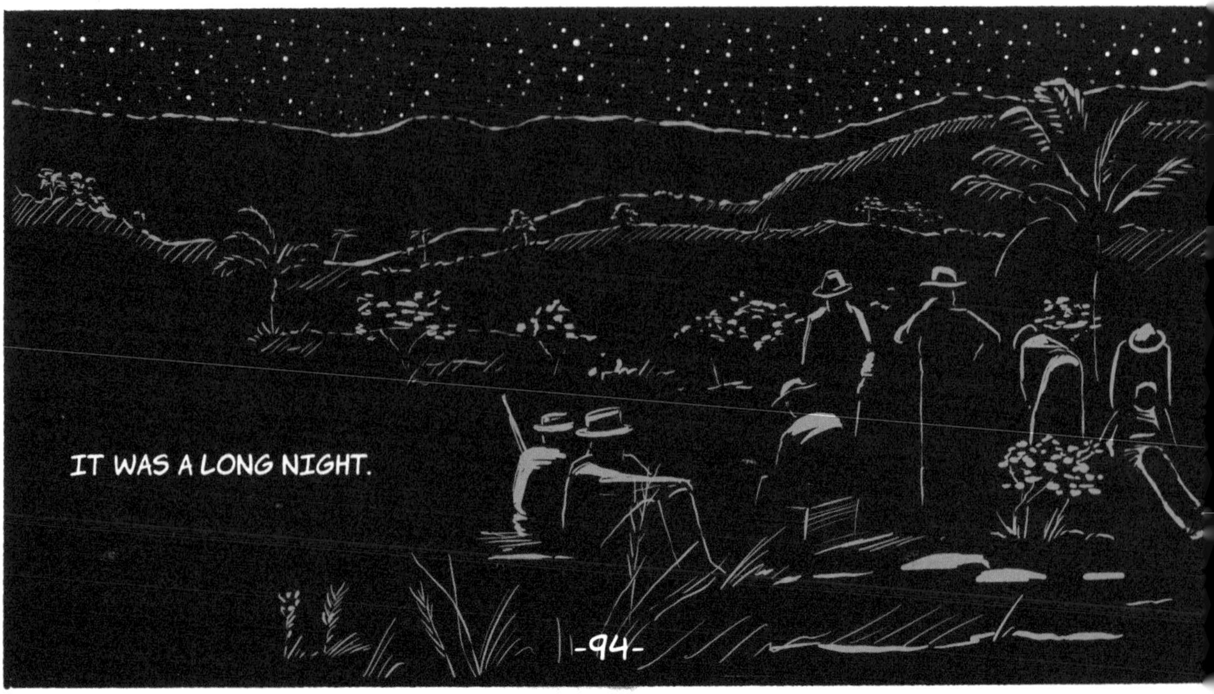
IT WAS A LONG NIGHT.

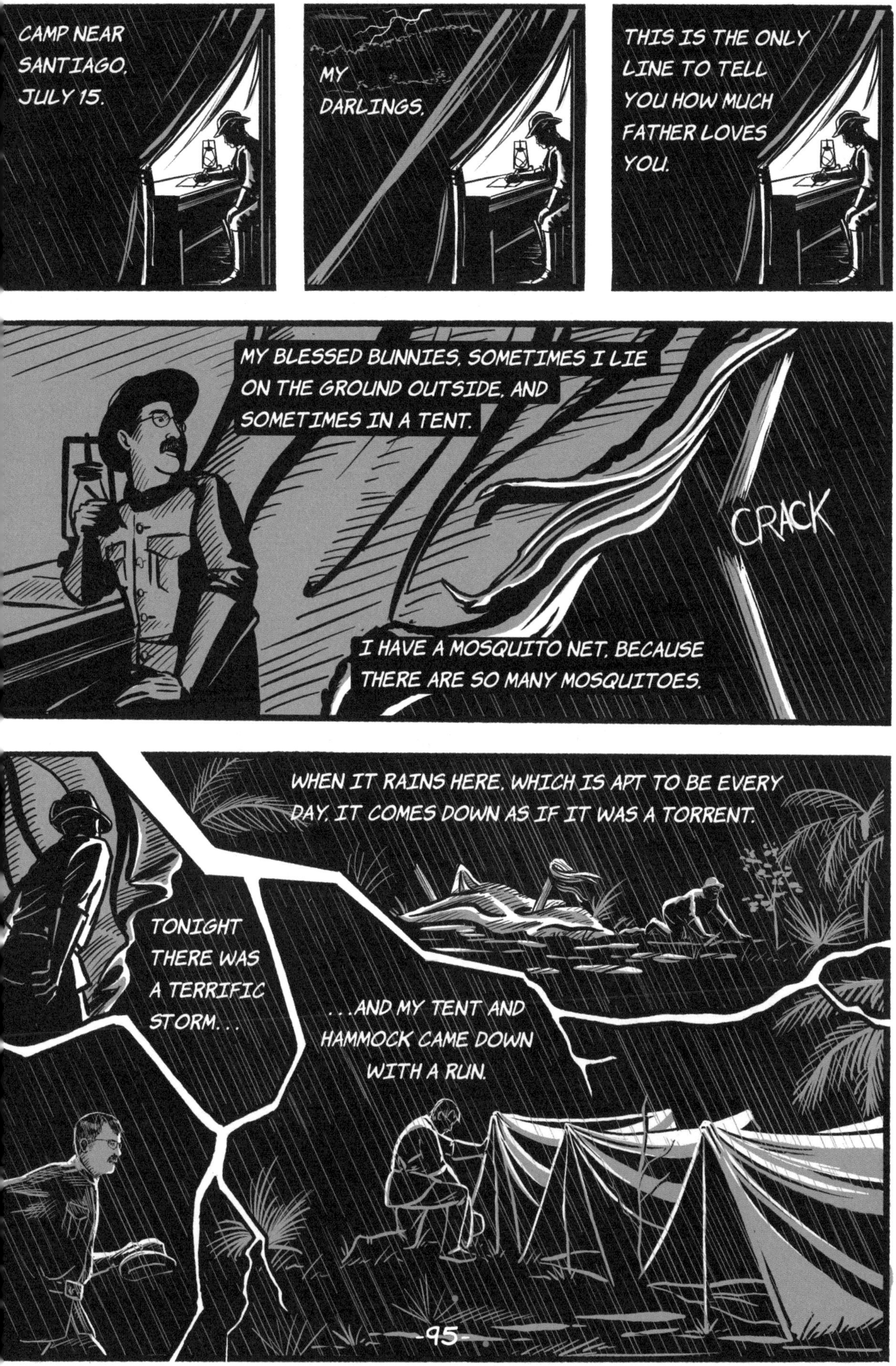
CAMP NEAR SANTIAGO, JULY 15.
MY DARLINGS,
THIS IS THE ONLY LINE TO TELL YOU HOW MUCH FATHER LOVES YOU.
MY BLESSED BUNNIES, SOMETIMES I LIE ON THE GROUND OUTSIDE, AND SOMETIMES IN A TENT.
CRACK
I HAVE A MOSQUITO NET, BECAUSE THERE ARE SO MANY MOSQUITOES.
WHEN IT RAINS HERE, WHICH IS APT TO BE EVERY DAY, IT COMES DOWN AS IF IT WAS A TORRENT.
TONIGHT THERE WAS A TERRIFIC STORM...
...AND MY TENT AND HAMMOCK CAME DOWN WITH A RUN.

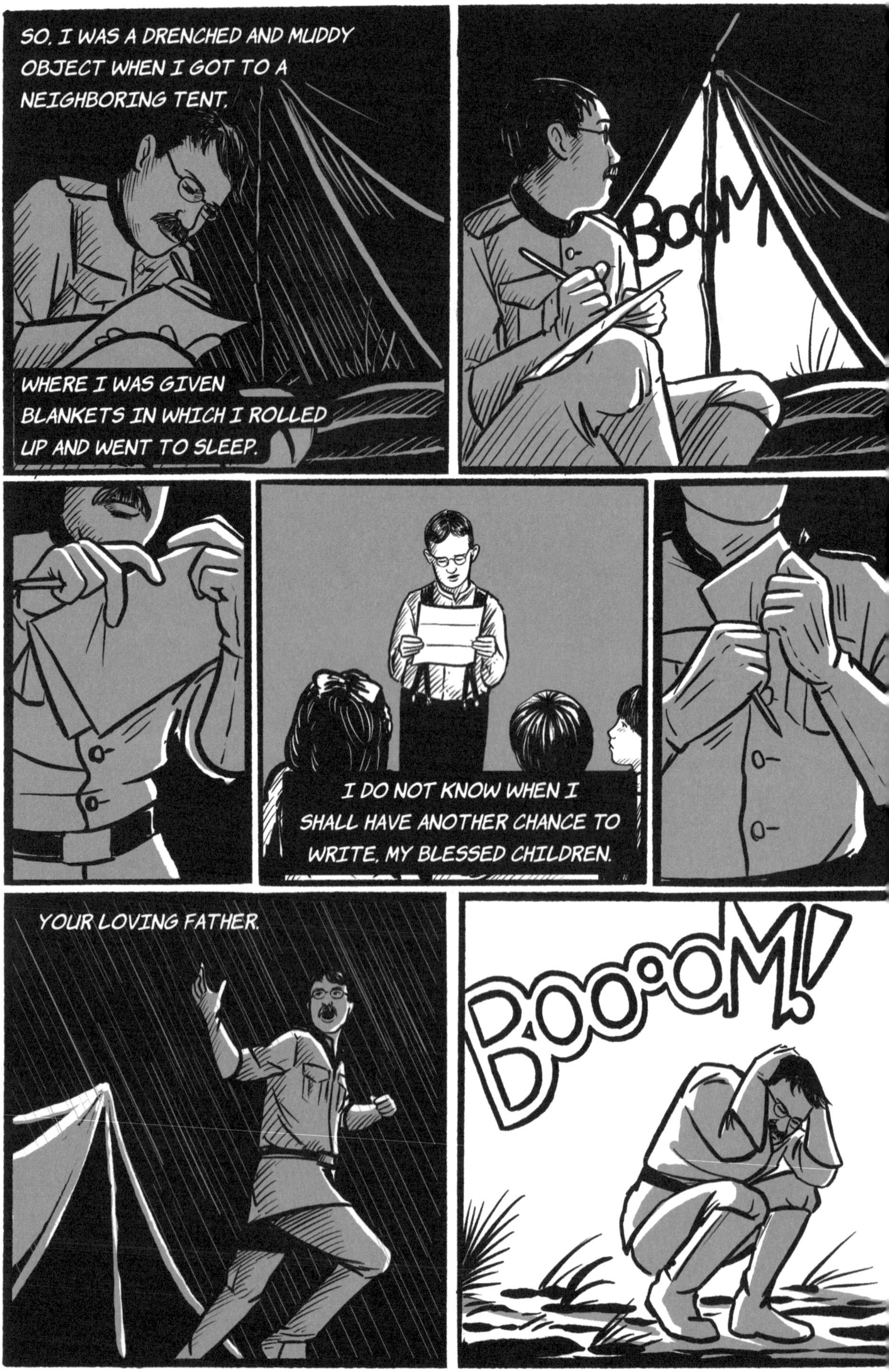

SO, I WAS A DRENCHED AND MUDDY OBJECT WHEN I GOT TO A NEIGHBORING TENT.
WHERE I WAS GIVEN BLANKETS IN WHICH I ROLLED UP AND WENT TO SLEEP.
BOOM
I DO NOT KNOW WHEN I SHALL HAVE ANOTHER CHANCE TO WRITE, MY BLESSED CHILDREN.
YOUR LOVING FATHER.
BOOOOM!

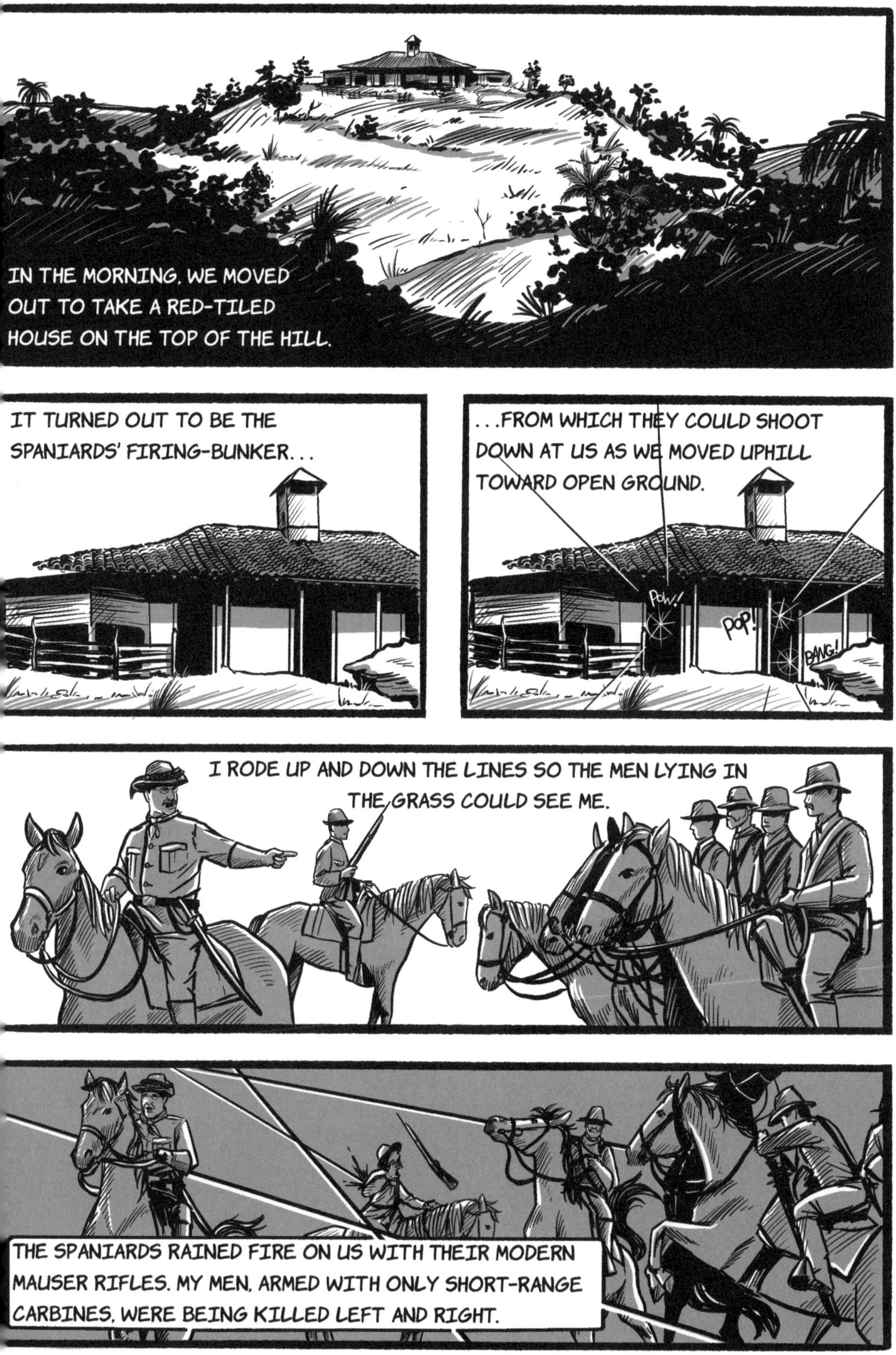
IN THE MORNING, WE MOVED OUT TO TAKE A RED-TILED HOUSE ON THE TOP OF THE HILL.
IT TURNED OUT TO BE THE SPANIARDS' FIRING-BUNKER...
...FROM WHICH THEY COULD SHOOT DOWN AT US AS WE MOVED UPHILL TOWARD OPEN GROUND.
POW!
POP!
BANG!
I RODE UP AND DOWN THE LINES SO THE MEN LYING IN THE GRASS COULD SEE ME.
THE SPANIARDS RAINED FIRE ON US WITH THEIR MODERN MAUSER RIFLES. MY MEN, ARMED WITH ONLY SHORT-RANGE CARBINES, WERE BEING KILLED LEFT AND RIGHT.

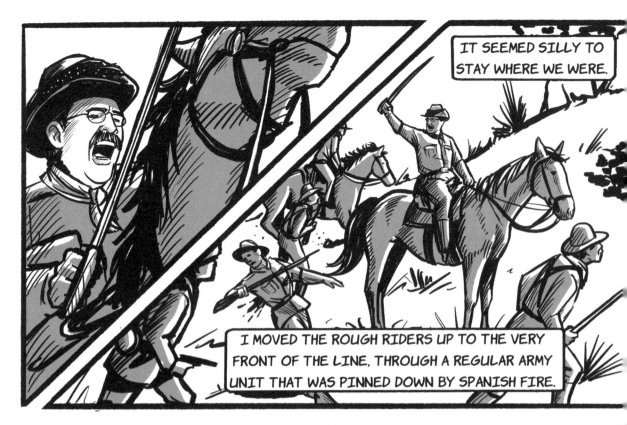

IT SEEMED SILLY TO STAY WHERE WE WERE.

I MOVED THE ROUGH RIDERS UP TO THE VERY FRONT OF THE LINE, THROUGH A REGULAR ARMY UNIT THAT WAS PINNED DOWN BY SPANISH FIRE.

WHY WON'T YOU CHARGE?

WE HAVE NO ORDERS!

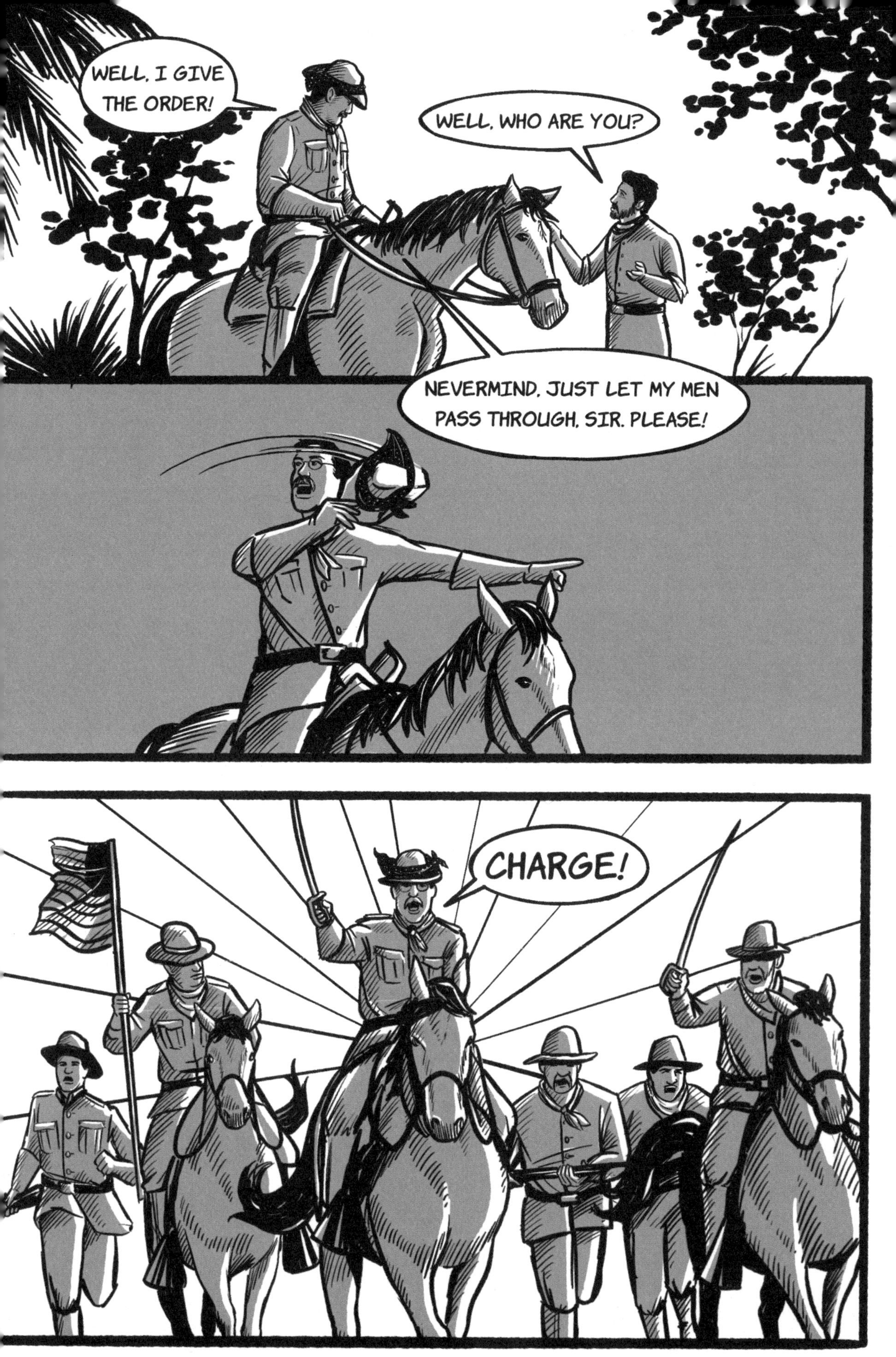
WELL, I GIVE THE ORDER!
WELL, WHO ARE YOU?
NEVERMIND. JUST LET MY MEN PASS THROUGH, SIR. PLEASE!
CHARGE!

THE BATTLE OF SAN JUAN
BY RICHARD HARDING DAVIS

THE problems which presented them selves to the commanding General of the Santiago expedition might be ... as follows ...

might retard the advance of the army upon it, and, finally, to take Santiago by assault, or by siege.

The selection of a landing-place for the army was one much discussed, and, possibly, Siboney and Baiquiri were as suitable purpose as any of the others might ... but when we recollect the original purpose of the expedition they seem ... the seat of the ... the original reason ... was a

THE HEARST CORRESPONDENT, RICHARD HARDING DAVIS, WAS WITH US, AND HE THEN DESCRIBED THE TAKING OF SAN JUAN HILL FOR HIS NEWSPAPER.

They had no glittering bayonets. They were not massed in regular array. The few men in advance crept up a steep sunny hill, the top of which roared and flashed with flame.

The men held their guns pressed against their breasts and moved forward with difficulty, as though they were wading waist high in water. It was much more wonderful than any swinging charge could have been.

They walked to greet death at every step, many sinking suddenly, pitching forward and disappearing in the high grass.

But the others waded on, stubbornly, forming a thin blue line that kept creeping higher and higher up the hill, inevitable as the rising tide.

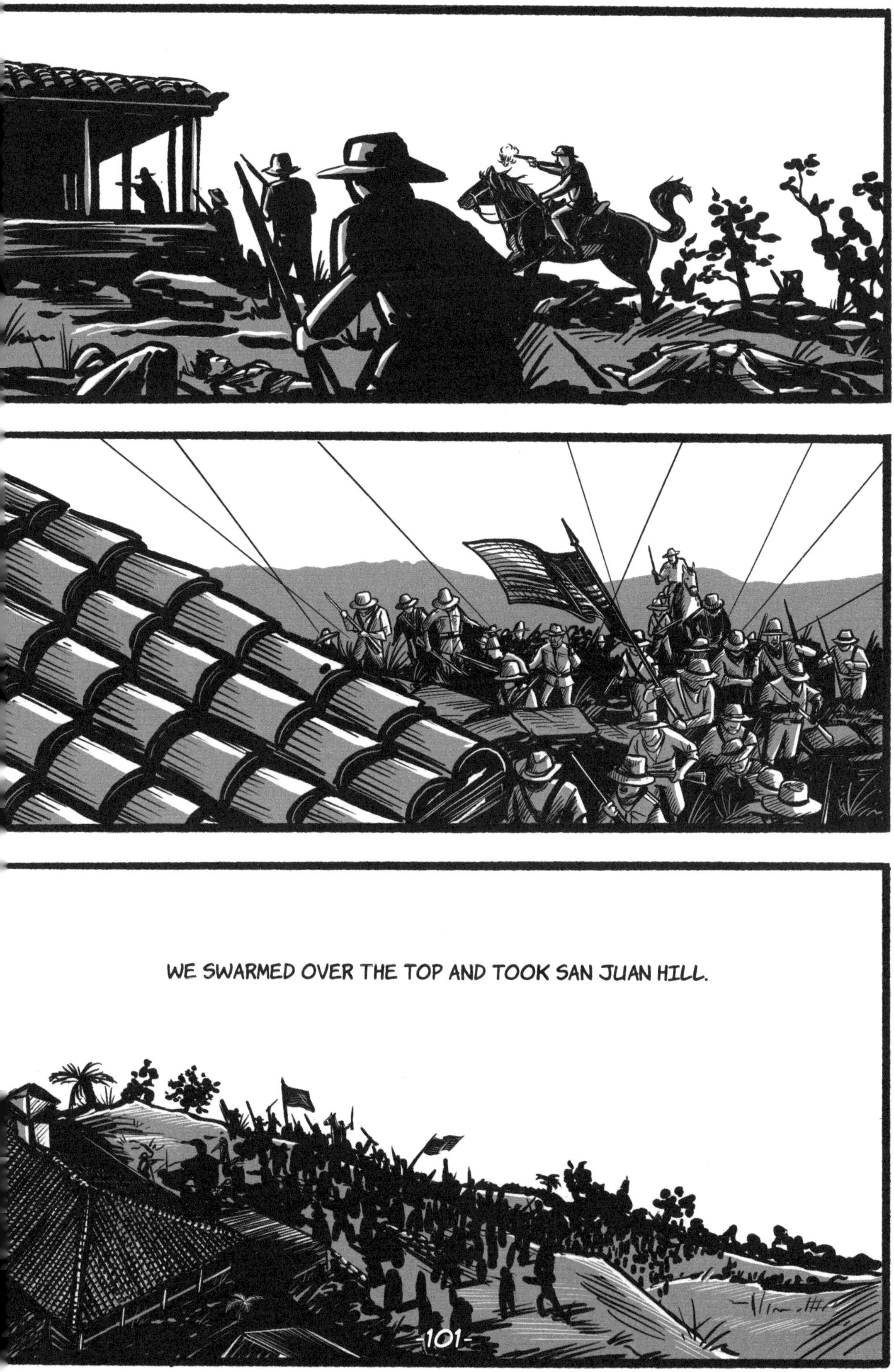
WE SWARMED OVER THE TOP AND TOOK SAN JUAN HILL.

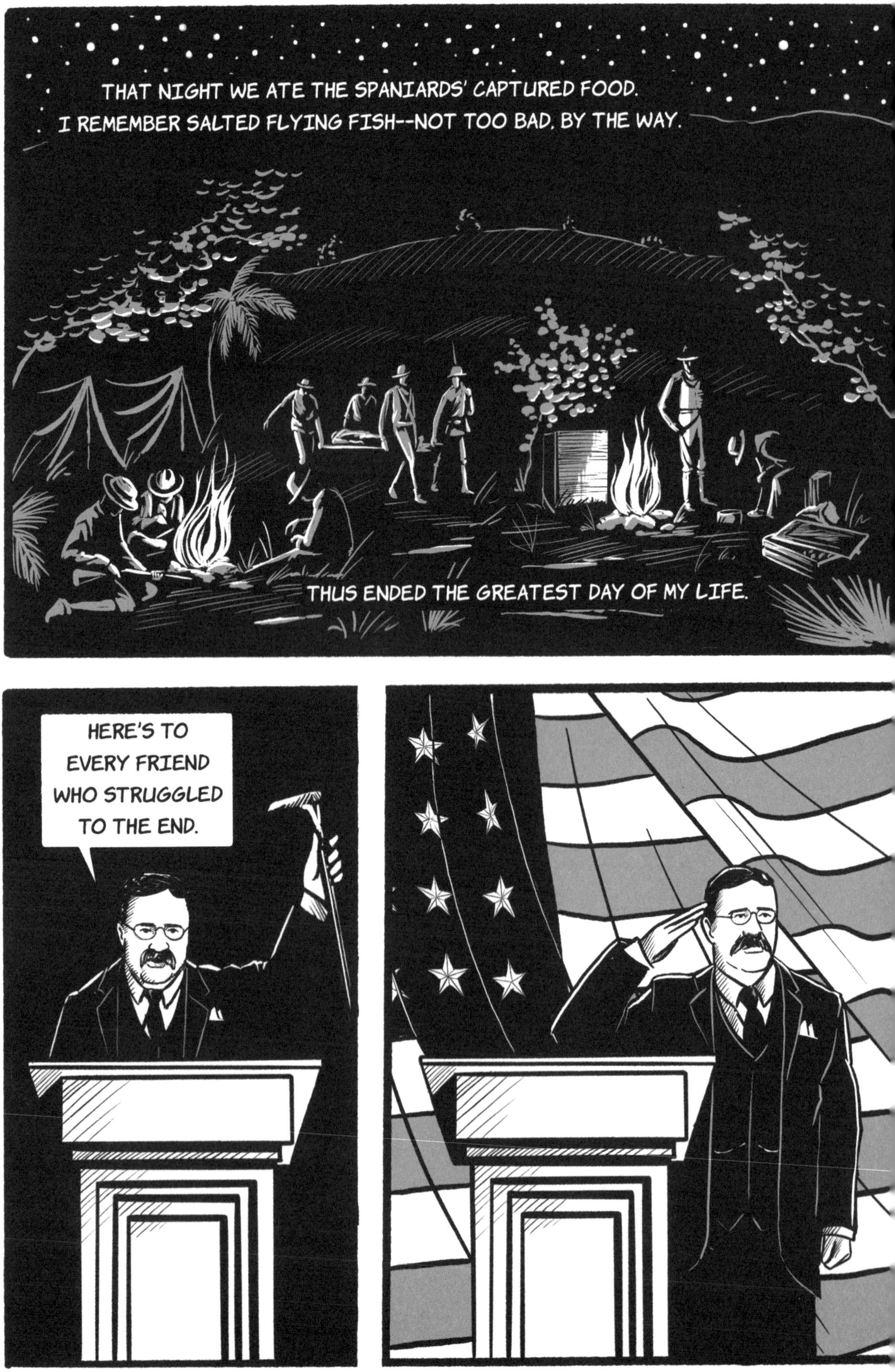
THAT NIGHT WE ATE THE SPANIARDS' CAPTURED FOOD.
I REMEMBER SALTED FLYING FISH--NOT TOO BAD, BY THE WAY.
THUS ENDED THE GREATEST DAY OF MY LIFE.
HERE'S TO EVERY FRIEND WHO STRUGGLED TO THE END.

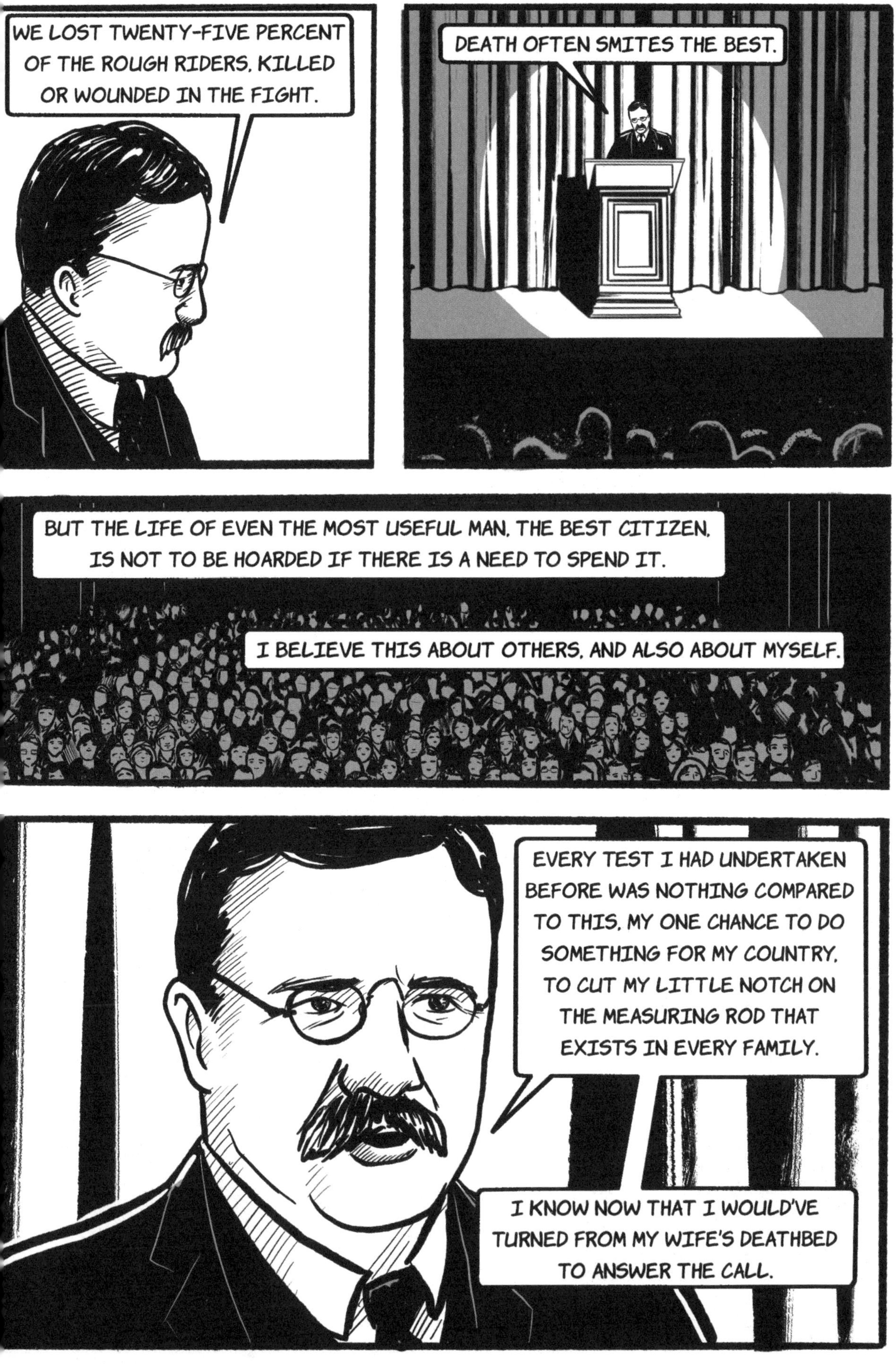
WE LOST TWENTY-FIVE PERCENT OF THE ROUGH RIDERS, KILLED OR WOUNDED IN THE FIGHT.
DEATH OFTEN SMITES THE BEST.
BUT THE LIFE OF EVEN THE MOST USEFUL MAN, THE BEST CITIZEN, IS NOT TO BE HOARDED IF THERE IS A NEED TO SPEND IT.
I BELIEVE THIS ABOUT OTHERS, AND ALSO ABOUT MYSELF.
EVERY TEST I HAD UNDERTAKEN BEFORE WAS NOTHING COMPARED TO THIS, MY ONE CHANCE TO DO SOMETHING FOR MY COUNTRY, TO CUT MY LITTLE NOTCH ON THE MEASURING ROD THAT EXISTS IN EVERY FAMILY.
I KNOW NOW THAT I WOULD'VE TURNED FROM MY WIFE'S DEATHBED TO ANSWER THE CALL.

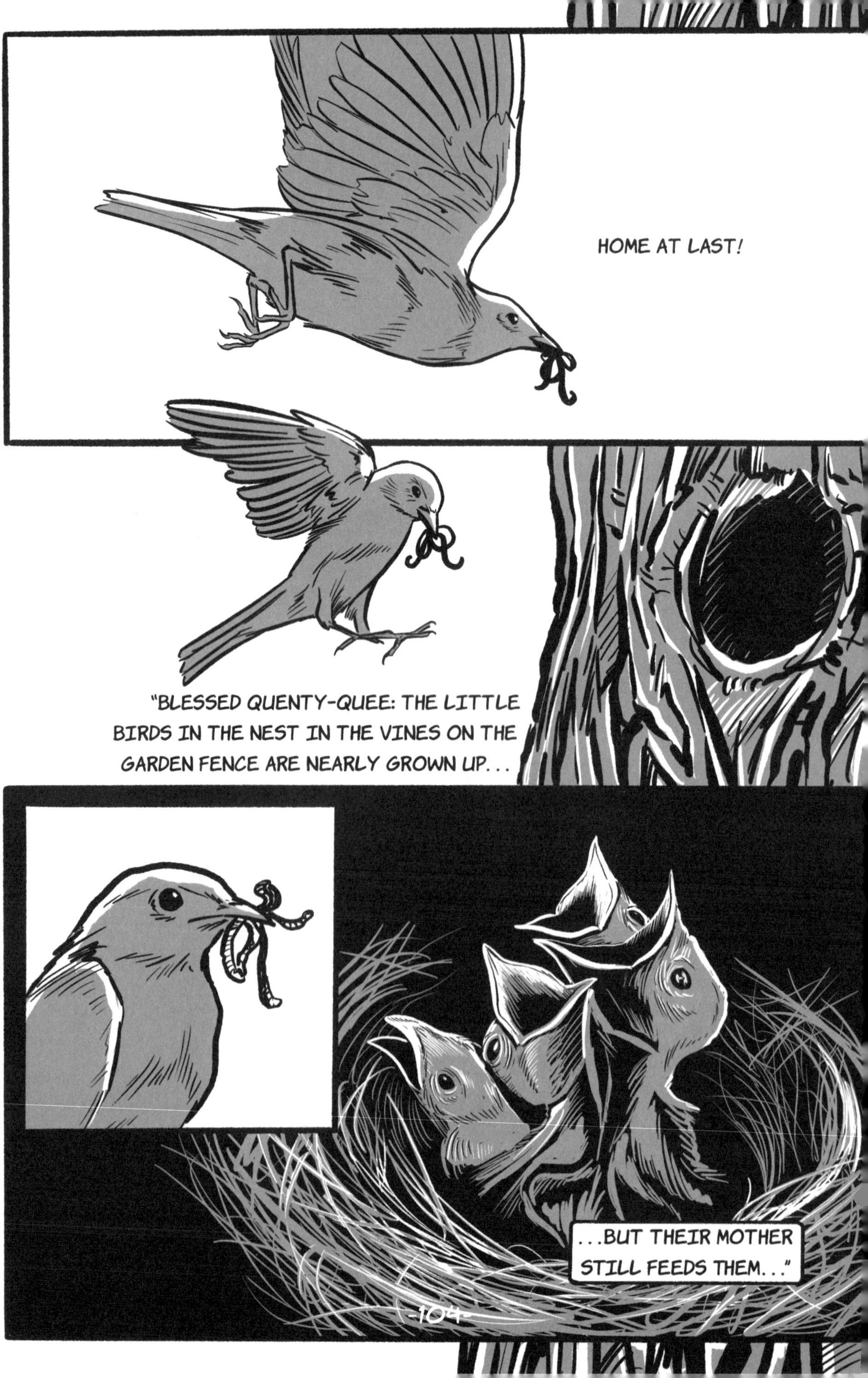
HOME AT LAST!
"BLESSED QUENTY-QUEE: THE LITTLE BIRDS IN THE NEST IN THE VINES ON THE GARDEN FENCE ARE NEARLY GROWN UP...
...BUT THEIR MOTHER STILL FEEDS THEM..."

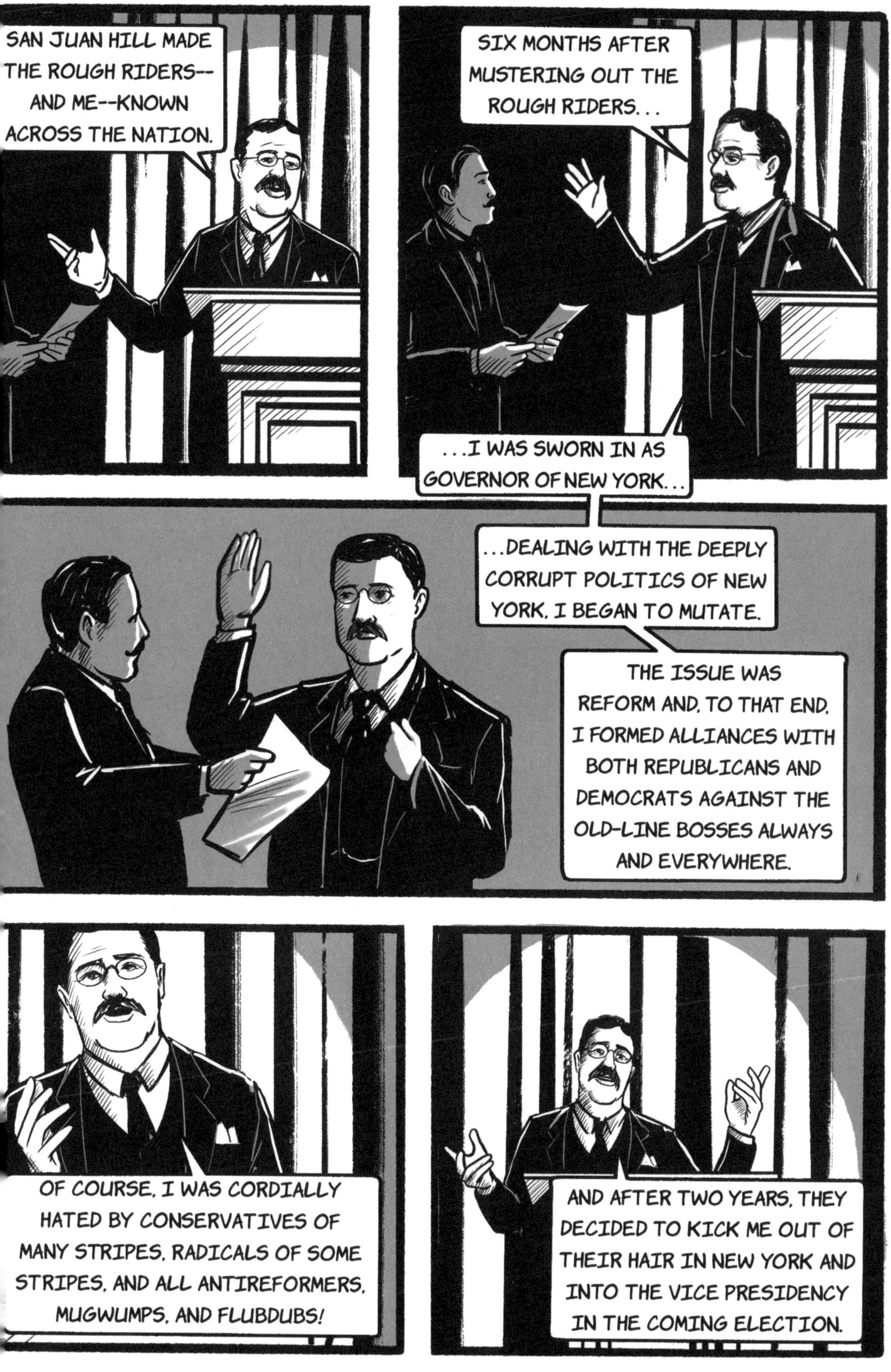

SAN JUAN HILL MADE THE ROUGH RIDERS--AND ME--KNOWN ACROSS THE NATION.
SIX MONTHS AFTER MUSTERING OUT THE ROUGH RIDERS...
...I WAS SWORN IN AS GOVERNOR OF NEW YORK...
...DEALING WITH THE DEEPLY CORRUPT POLITICS OF NEW YORK, I BEGAN TO MUTATE.
THE ISSUE WAS REFORM AND, TO THAT END, I FORMED ALLIANCES WITH BOTH REPUBLICANS AND DEMOCRATS AGAINST THE OLD-LINE BOSSES ALWAYS AND EVERYWHERE.
OF COURSE, I WAS CORDIALLY HATED BY CONSERVATIVES OF MANY STRIPES, RADICALS OF SOME STRIPES, AND ALL ANTIREFORMERS, MUGWUMPS, AND FLUBDUBS!
AND AFTER TWO YEARS, THEY DECIDED TO KICK ME OUT OF THEIR HAIR IN NEW YORK AND INTO THE VICE PRESIDENCY IN THE COMING ELECTION.

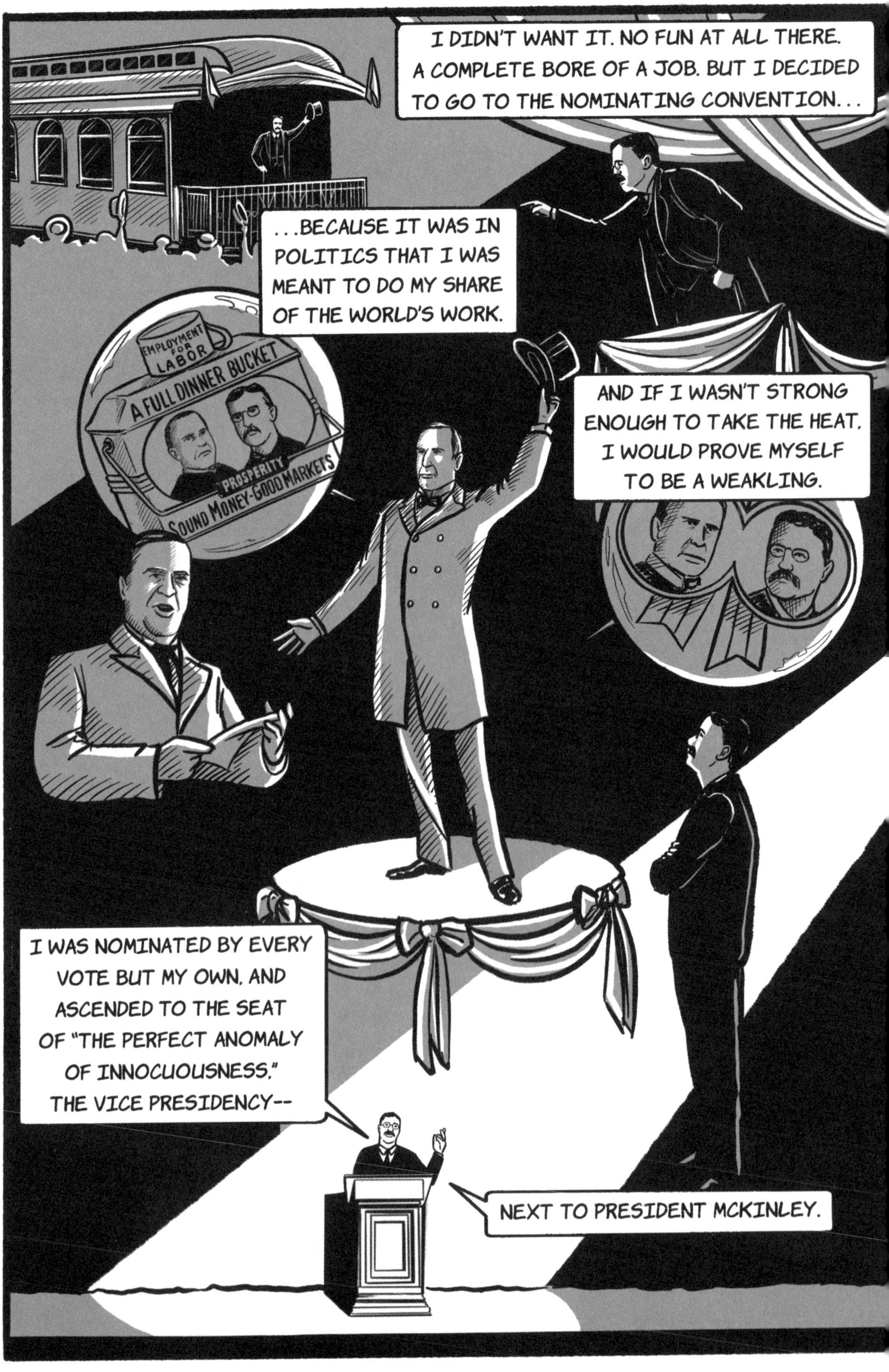
I DIDN'T WANT IT. NO FUN AT ALL THERE. A COMPLETE BORE OF A JOB. BUT I DECIDED TO GO TO THE NOMINATING CONVENTION...
...BECAUSE IT WAS IN POLITICS THAT I WAS MEANT TO DO MY SHARE OF THE WORLD'S WORK.
EMPLOYMENT FOR LABOR
A FULL DINNER BUCKET
PROSPERITY
SOUND MONEY-GOOD MARKETS
AND IF I WASN'T STRONG ENOUGH TO TAKE THE HEAT, I WOULD PROVE MYSELF TO BE A WEAKLING.
I WAS NOMINATED BY EVERY VOTE BUT MY OWN, AND ASCENDED TO THE SEAT OF "THE PERFECT ANOMALY OF INNOCUOUSNESS," THE VICE PRESIDENCY--
NEXT TO PRESIDENT MCKINLEY.

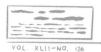

BUFFALO EVE

VOL. XLII—NO. 126.   BUFFALO, N. Y., FRIDAY,

EXTRA!   EXTRA!

PRESIDENT M'KINLEY SHOT!

Two Bullets Sent Into Body
By a Stranger
Pan-Americ

He Sank Down and Was at
Once Taken to the Ex-
position Hospital.

Pan-American Grounds
—4:15 P. M.--Bulle
sident McKi
shot at
Music.
He
hospi

STEEL MEN'S
LAST OFF

BIG SHAKE-UP OF
POLICE OFFICERS.

Capt. Michael Regan Transferred to
1 Station and Capt. John
Taylor to No. 3.

NK KILLEEN SENT
TO NO. 13 AT BLACK ROCK.

nd Transferred to No. 4--In-
s Martin and Donovan Change
Places--Two Precinct Detec-
tives Shifted.

SHERIFF
LONDON TOWN,

EXCIT

alted Official of the

SIX MONTHS AFTER THE ELECTION, PRESIDENT MCKINLEY WAS SHOT DEAD BY AN ANARCHIST, AND I BECAME THE PRESIDENT OF THE UNITED STATES.

THE YOUNGEST IN HISTORY. I WAS 42.

FOUR YEARS YOUNGER THAN MY FATHER WHEN HE DIED.

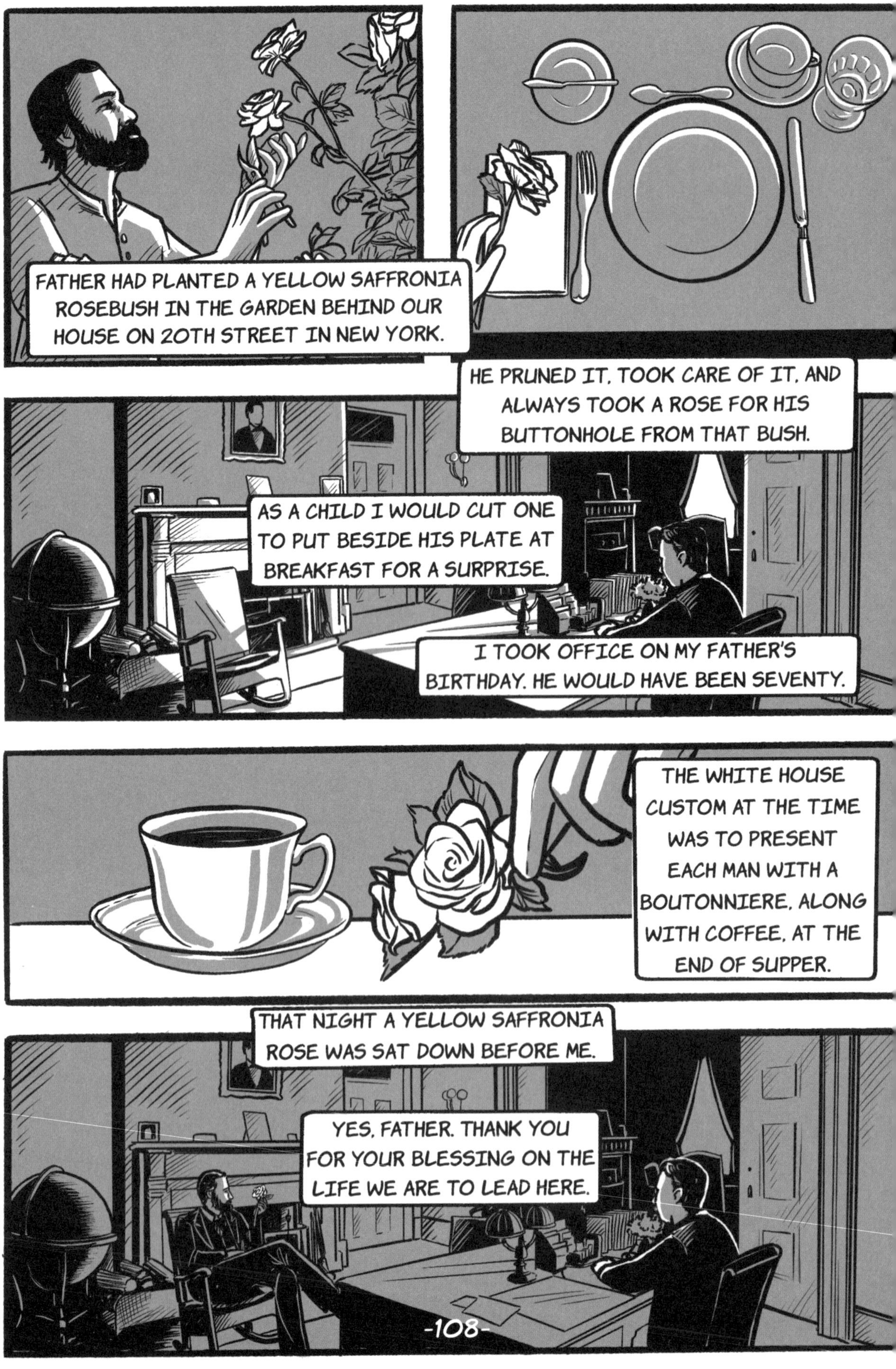
FATHER HAD PLANTED A YELLOW SAFFRONIA ROSEBUSH IN THE GARDEN BEHIND OUR HOUSE ON 20TH STREET IN NEW YORK.
HE PRUNED IT, TOOK CARE OF IT, AND ALWAYS TOOK A ROSE FOR HIS BUTTONHOLE FROM THAT BUSH.
AS A CHILD I WOULD CUT ONE TO PUT BESIDE HIS PLATE AT BREAKFAST FOR A SURPRISE.
I TOOK OFFICE ON MY FATHER'S BIRTHDAY. HE WOULD HAVE BEEN SEVENTY.
THE WHITE HOUSE CUSTOM AT THE TIME WAS TO PRESENT EACH MAN WITH A BOUTONNIERE, ALONG WITH COFFEE, AT THE END OF SUPPER.
THAT NIGHT A YELLOW SAFFRONIA ROSE WAS SAT DOWN BEFORE ME.
YES, FATHER. THANK YOU FOR YOUR BLESSING ON THE LIFE WE ARE TO LEAD HERE.

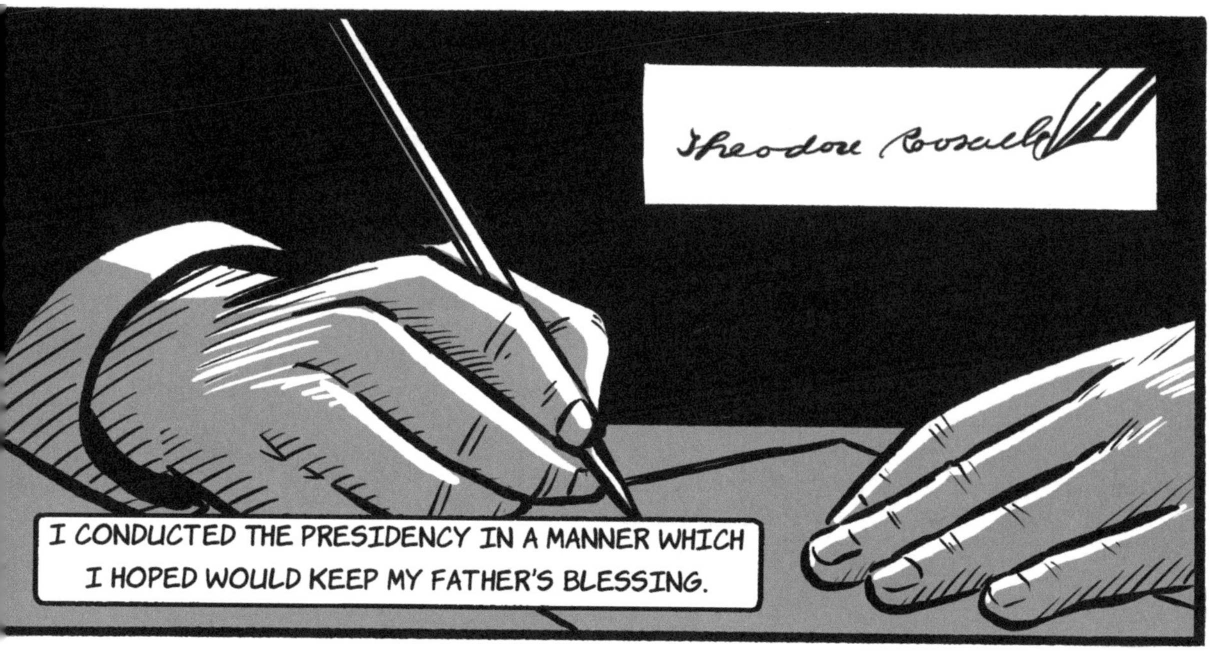
Theodore Roosevelt
I CONDUCTED THE PRESIDENCY IN A MANNER WHICH I HOPED WOULD KEEP MY FATHER'S BLESSING.

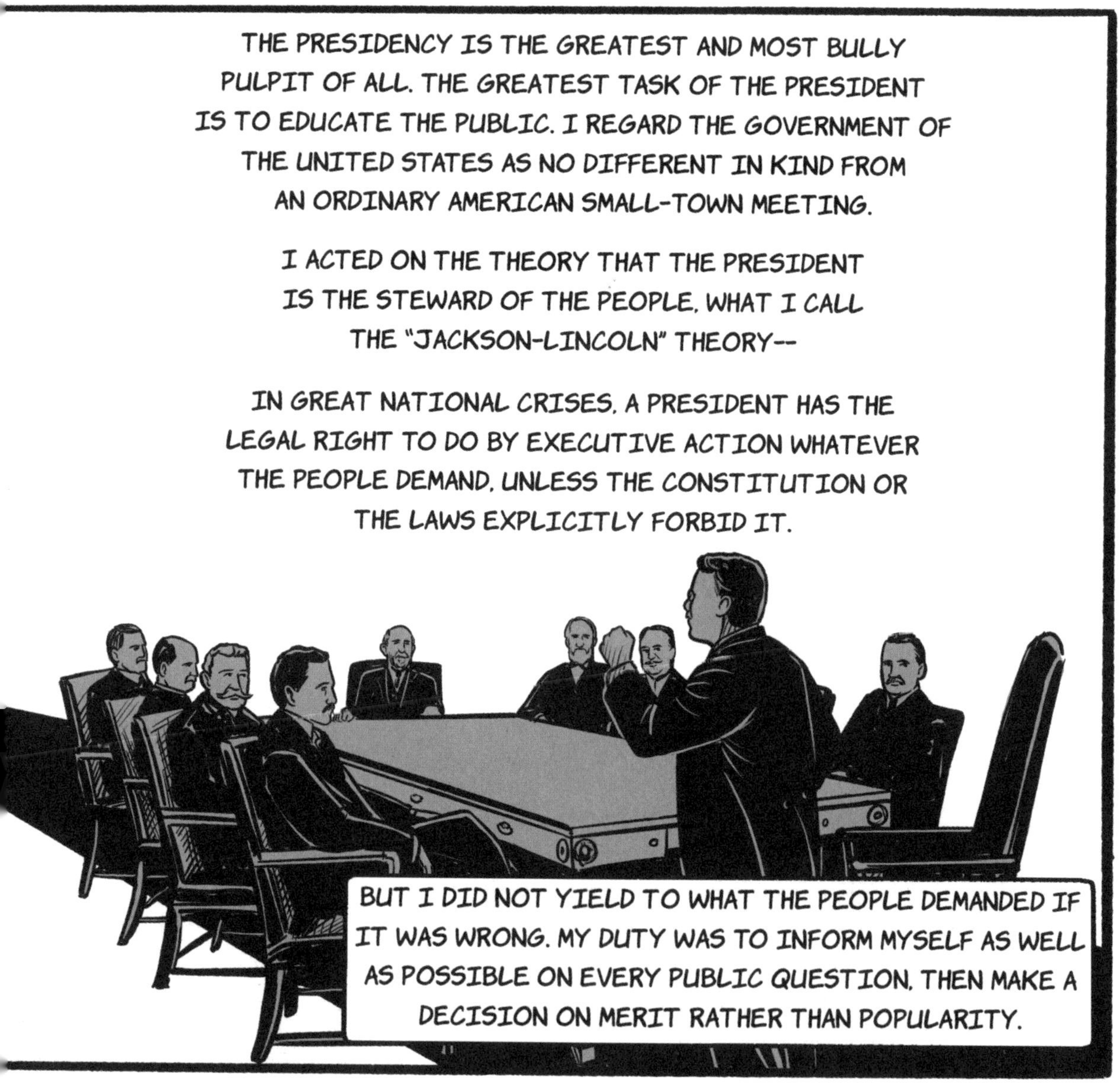
THE PRESIDENCY IS THE GREATEST AND MOST BULLY PULPIT OF ALL. THE GREATEST TASK OF THE PRESIDENT IS TO EDUCATE THE PUBLIC. I REGARD THE GOVERNMENT OF THE UNITED STATES AS NO DIFFERENT IN KIND FROM AN ORDINARY AMERICAN SMALL-TOWN MEETING.
I ACTED ON THE THEORY THAT THE PRESIDENT IS THE STEWARD OF THE PEOPLE, WHAT I CALL THE "JACKSON-LINCOLN" THEORY--
IN GREAT NATIONAL CRISES, A PRESIDENT HAS THE LEGAL RIGHT TO DO BY EXECUTIVE ACTION WHATEVER THE PEOPLE DEMAND, UNLESS THE CONSTITUTION OR THE LAWS EXPLICITLY FORBID IT.
BUT I DID NOT YIELD TO WHAT THE PEOPLE DEMANDED IF IT WAS WRONG. MY DUTY WAS TO INFORM MYSELF AS WELL AS POSSIBLE ON EVERY PUBLIC QUESTION, THEN MAKE A DECISION ON MERIT RATHER THAN POPULARITY.

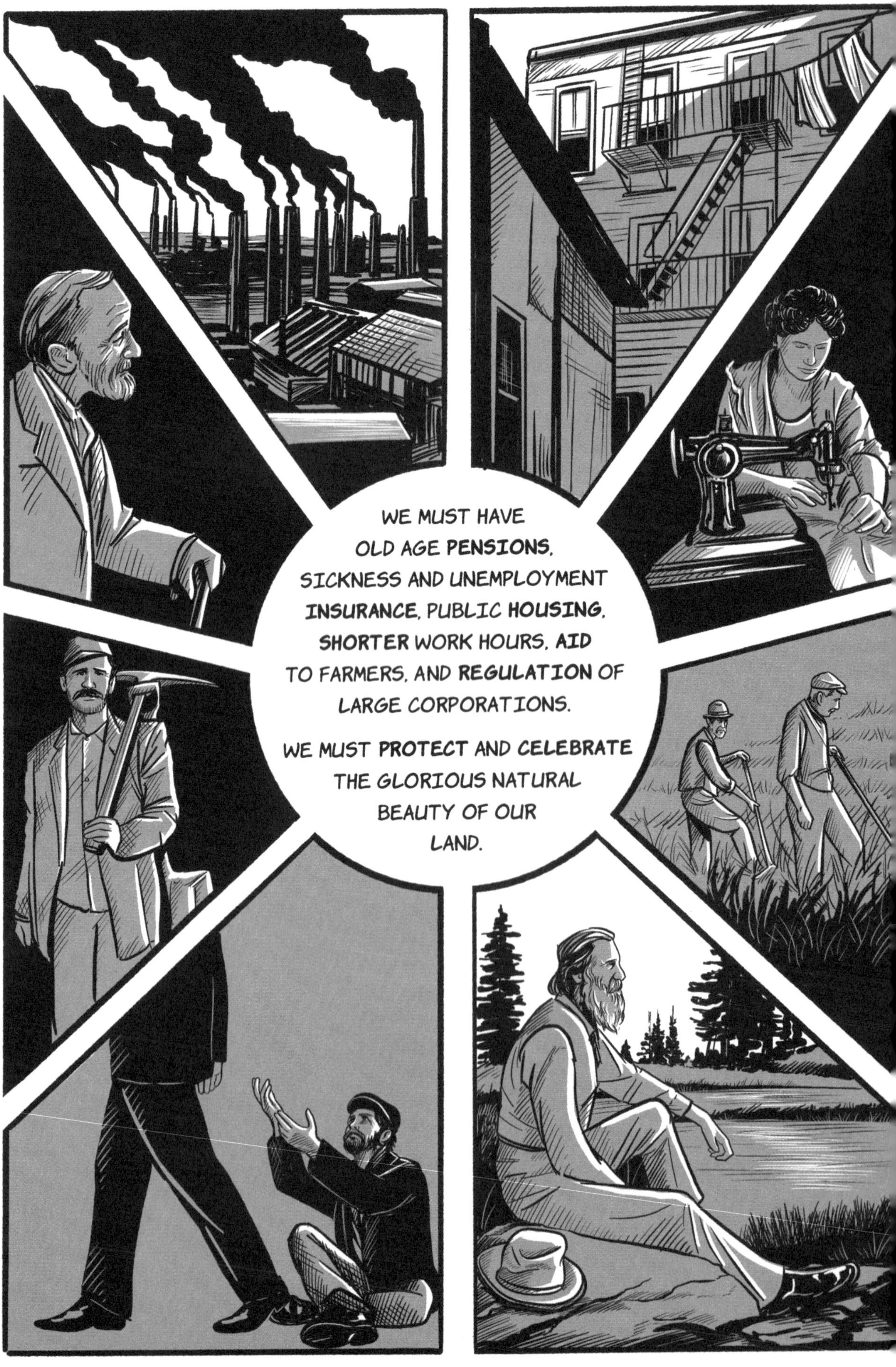
WE MUST HAVE
OLD AGE PENSIONS,
SICKNESS AND UNEMPLOYMENT
INSURANCE, PUBLIC HOUSING,
SHORTER WORK HOURS, AID
TO FARMERS, AND REGULATION OF
LARGE CORPORATIONS.
WE MUST PROTECT AND CELEBRATE
THE GLORIOUS NATURAL
BEAUTY OF OUR
LAND.

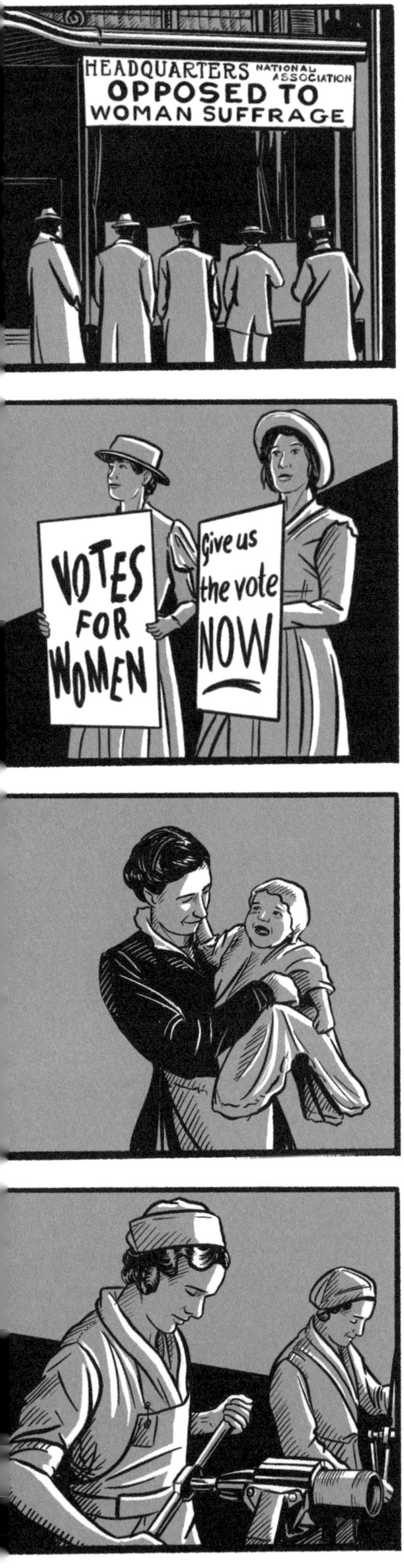
HEADQUARTERS NATIONAL ASSOCIATION
OPPOSED TO
WOMAN SUFFRAGE
VOTES FOR WOMEN
Give us the vote NOW

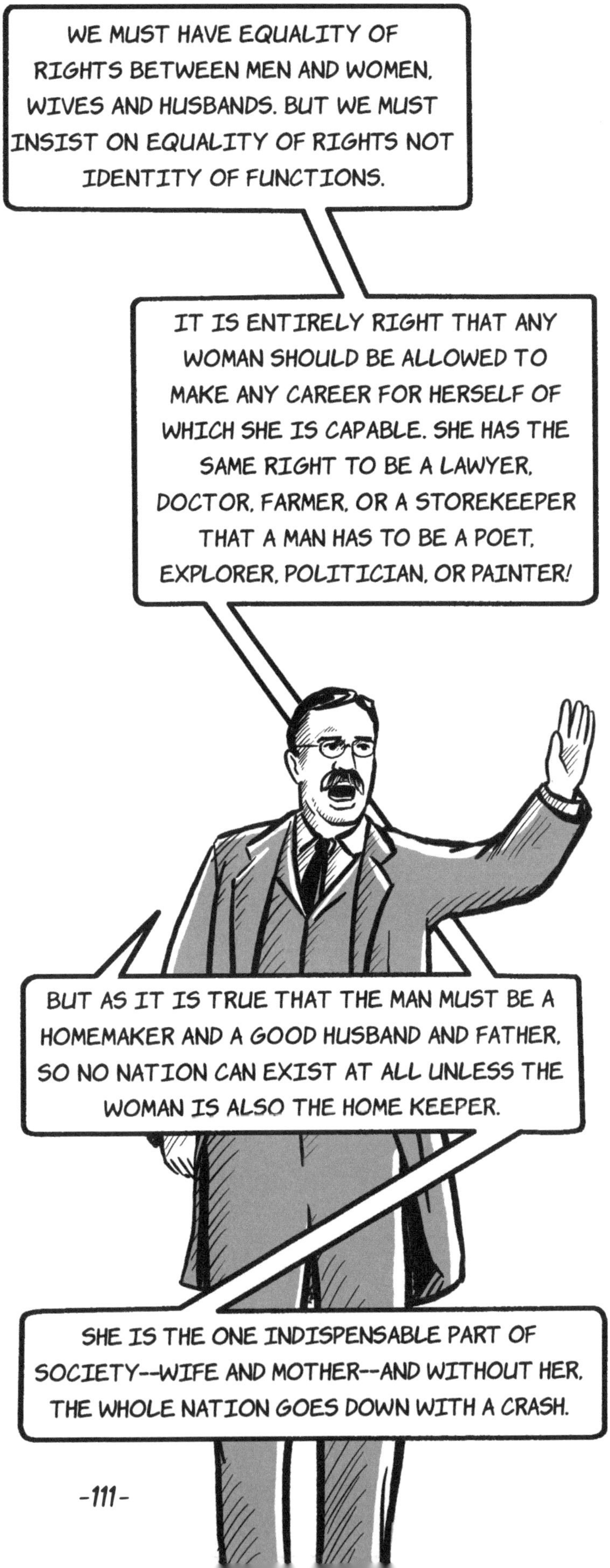
WE MUST HAVE EQUALITY OF RIGHTS BETWEEN MEN AND WOMEN, WIVES AND HUSBANDS. BUT WE MUST INSIST ON EQUALITY OF RIGHTS NOT IDENTITY OF FUNCTIONS.
IT IS ENTIRELY RIGHT THAT ANY WOMAN SHOULD BE ALLOWED TO MAKE ANY CAREER FOR HERSELF OF WHICH SHE IS CAPABLE. SHE HAS THE SAME RIGHT TO BE A LAWYER, DOCTOR, FARMER, OR A STOREKEEPER THAT A MAN HAS TO BE A POET, EXPLORER, POLITICIAN, OR PAINTER!
BUT AS IT IS TRUE THAT THE MAN MUST BE A HOMEMAKER AND A GOOD HUSBAND AND FATHER, SO NO NATION CAN EXIST AT ALL UNLESS THE WOMAN IS ALSO THE HOME KEEPER.
SHE IS THE ONE INDISPENSABLE PART OF SOCIETY--WIFE AND MOTHER--AND WITHOUT HER, THE WHOLE NATION GOES DOWN WITH A CRASH.

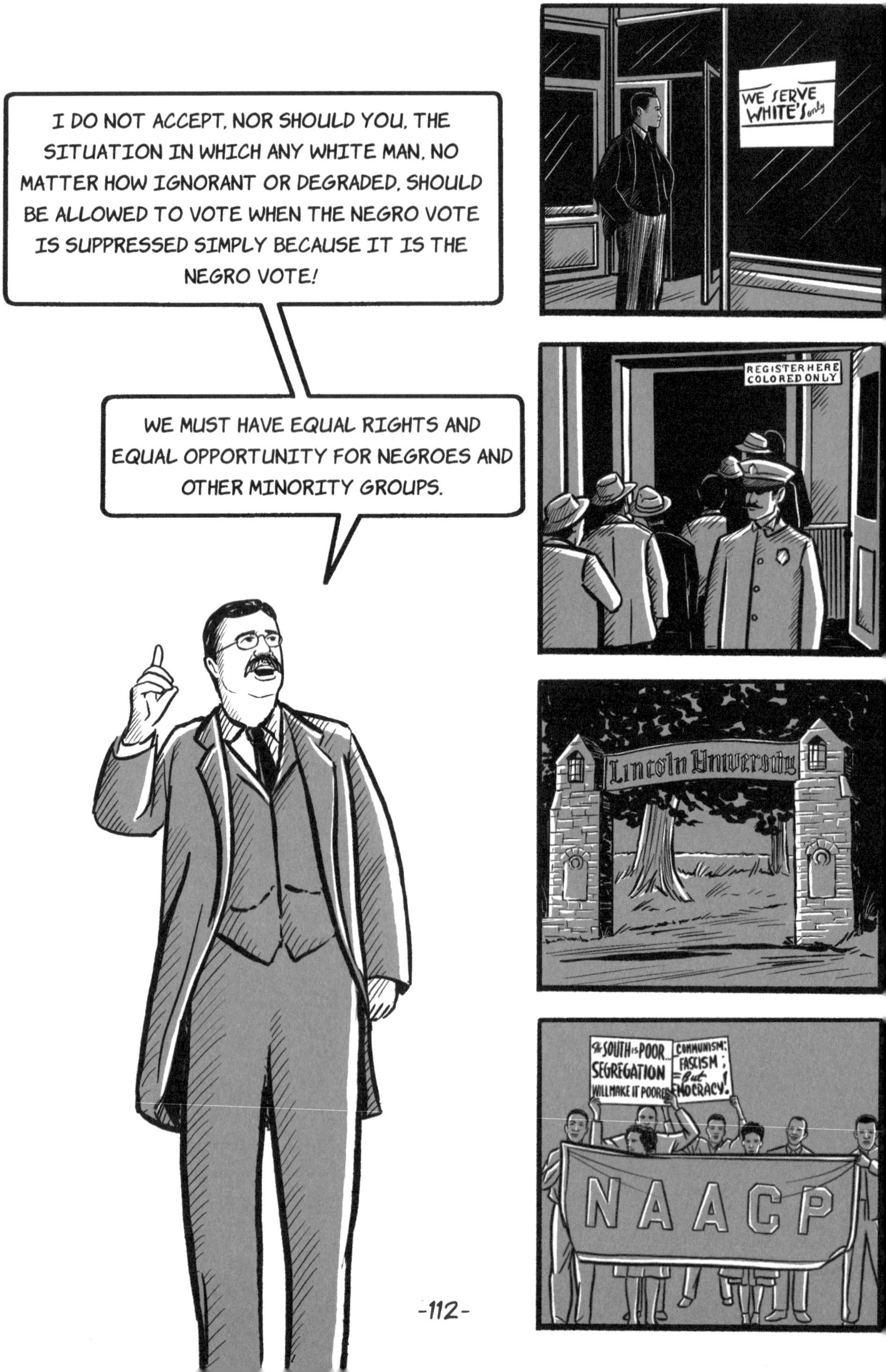
I DO NOT ACCEPT, NOR SHOULD YOU, THE SITUATION IN WHICH ANY WHITE MAN, NO MATTER HOW IGNORANT OR DEGRADED, SHOULD BE ALLOWED TO VOTE WHEN THE NEGRO VOTE IS SUPPRESSED SIMPLY BECAUSE IT IS THE NEGRO VOTE!
WE MUST HAVE EQUAL RIGHTS AND EQUAL OPPORTUNITY FOR NEGROES AND OTHER MINORITY GROUPS.
WE SERVE WHITE'S only
REGISTER HERE COLORED ONLY
Lincoln University
The SOUTH is POOR... SEGREGATION WILL MAKE IT POORER
COMMUNISM; FASCISM; But MOCRACY!
NAACP

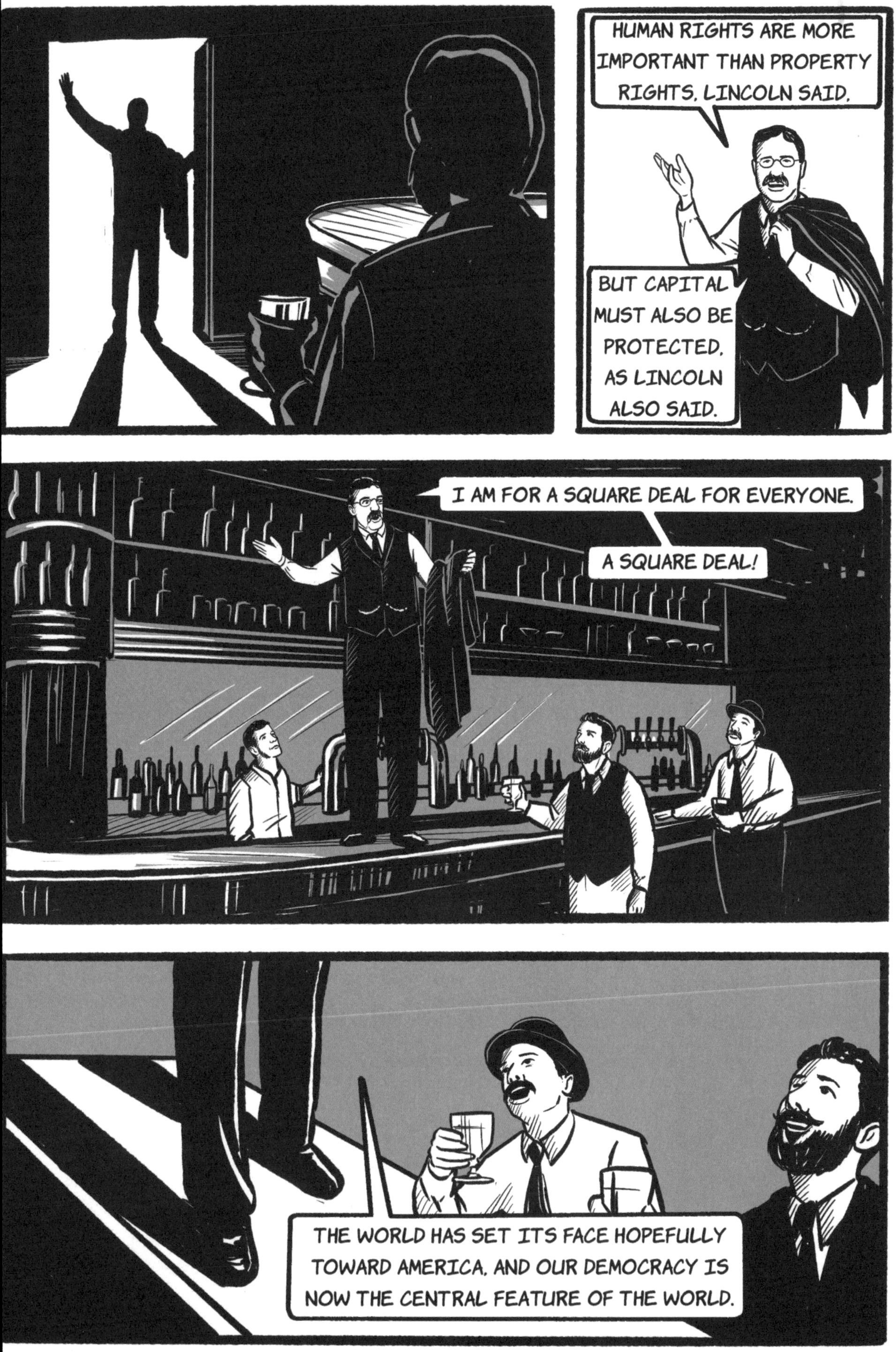
HUMAN RIGHTS ARE MORE IMPORTANT THAN PROPERTY RIGHTS, LINCOLN SAID.
BUT CAPITAL MUST ALSO BE PROTECTED, AS LINCOLN ALSO SAID.
I AM FOR A SQUARE DEAL FOR EVERYONE.
A SQUARE DEAL!
THE WORLD HAS SET ITS FACE HOPEFULLY TOWARD AMERICA, AND OUR DEMOCRACY IS NOW THE CENTRAL FEATURE OF THE WORLD.

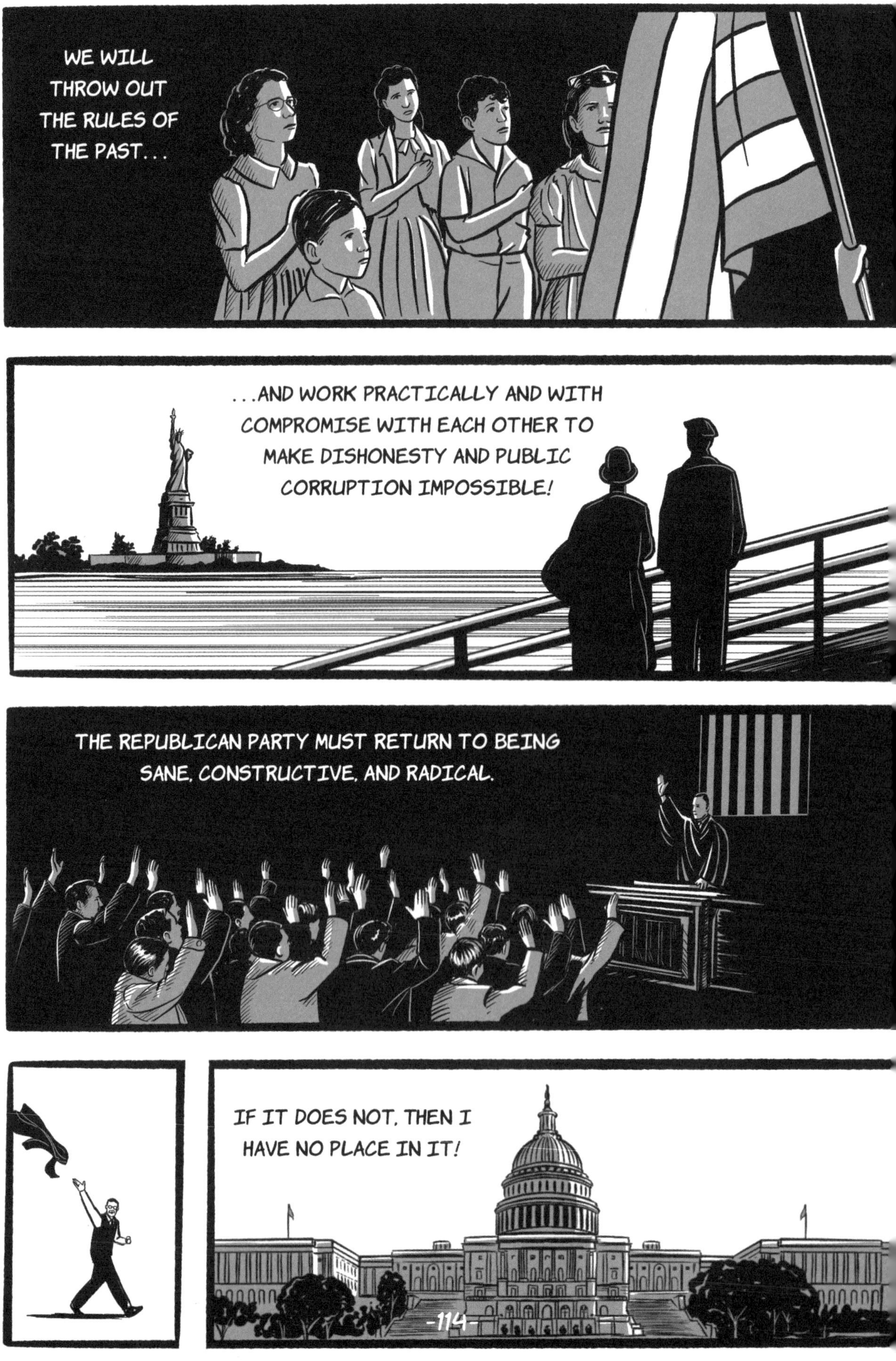
WE WILL THROW OUT THE RULES OF THE PAST...
...AND WORK PRACTICALLY AND WITH COMPROMISE WITH EACH OTHER TO MAKE DISHONESTY AND PUBLIC CORRUPTION IMPOSSIBLE!
THE REPUBLICAN PARTY MUST RETURN TO BEING SANE, CONSTRUCTIVE, AND RADICAL.
IF IT DOES NOT, THEN I HAVE NO PLACE IN IT!

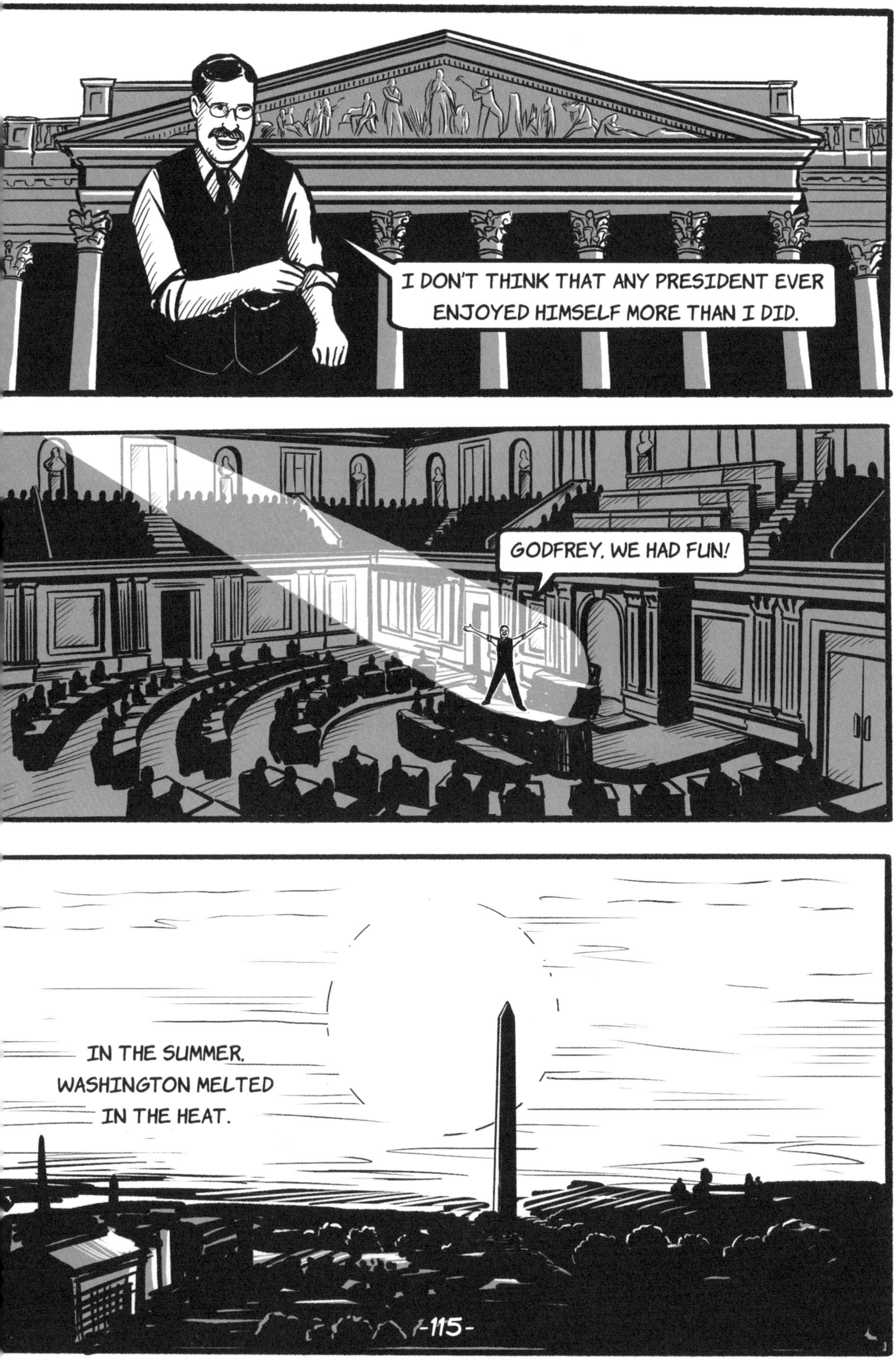
I DON'T THINK THAT ANY PRESIDENT EVER ENJOYED HIMSELF MORE THAN I DID.
GODFREY, WE HAD FUN!
IN THE SUMMER, WASHINGTON MELTED IN THE HEAT.

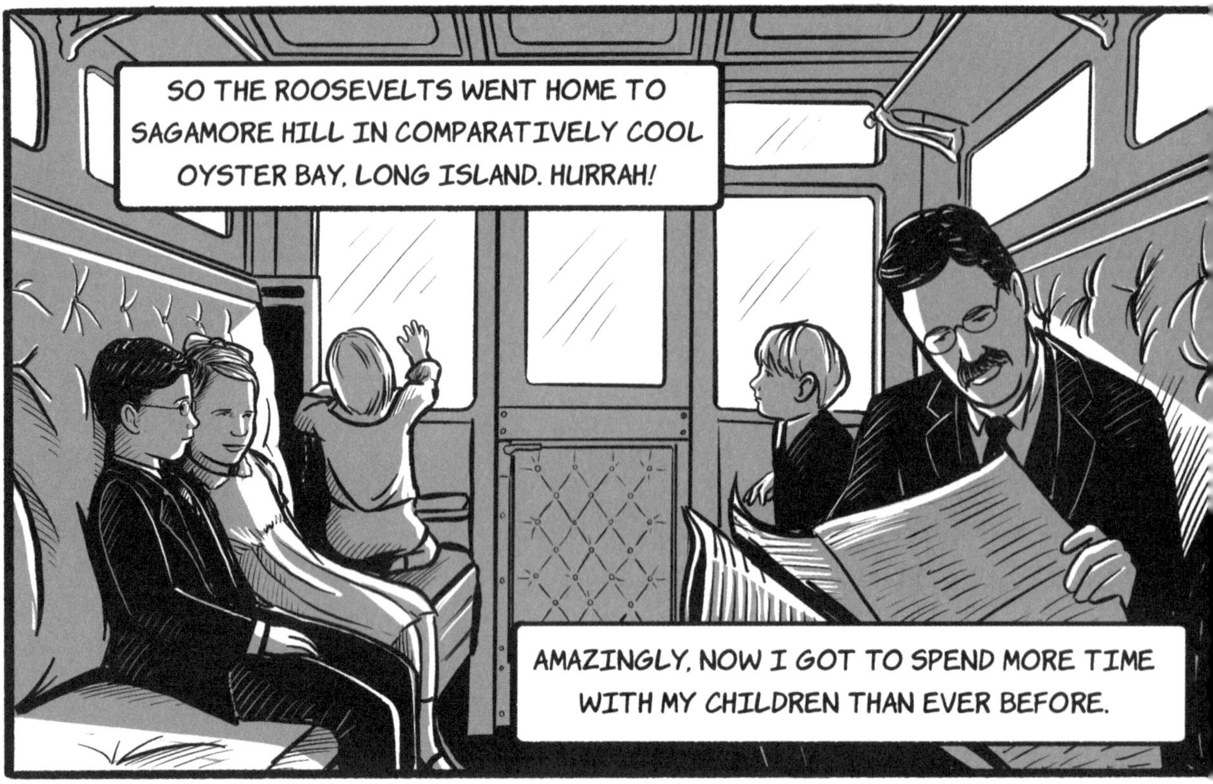
SO THE ROOSEVELTS WENT HOME TO SAGAMORE HILL IN COMPARATIVELY COOL OYSTER BAY, LONG ISLAND. HURRAH!
AMAZINGLY, NOW I GOT TO SPEND MORE TIME WITH MY CHILDREN THAN EVER BEFORE.

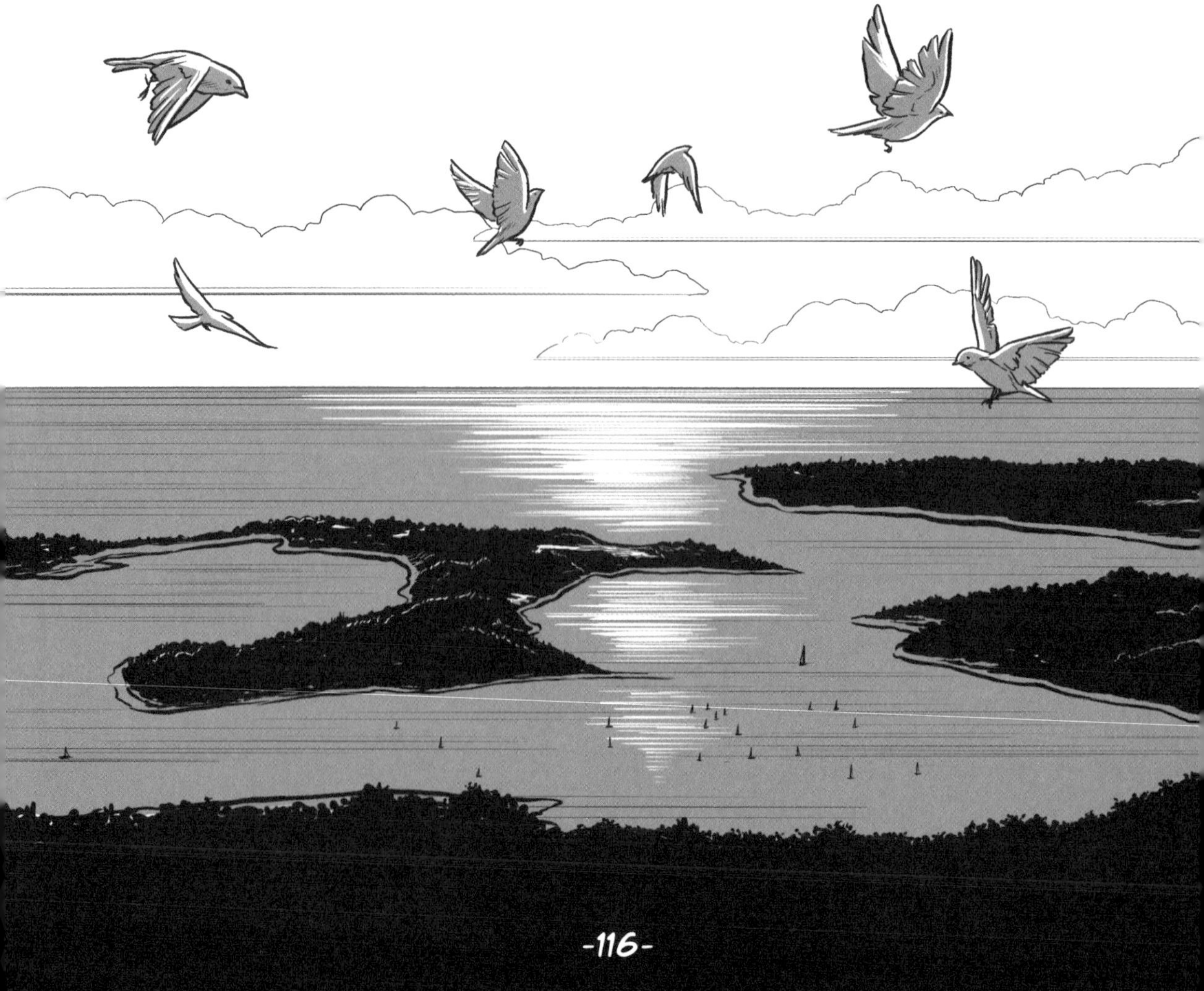

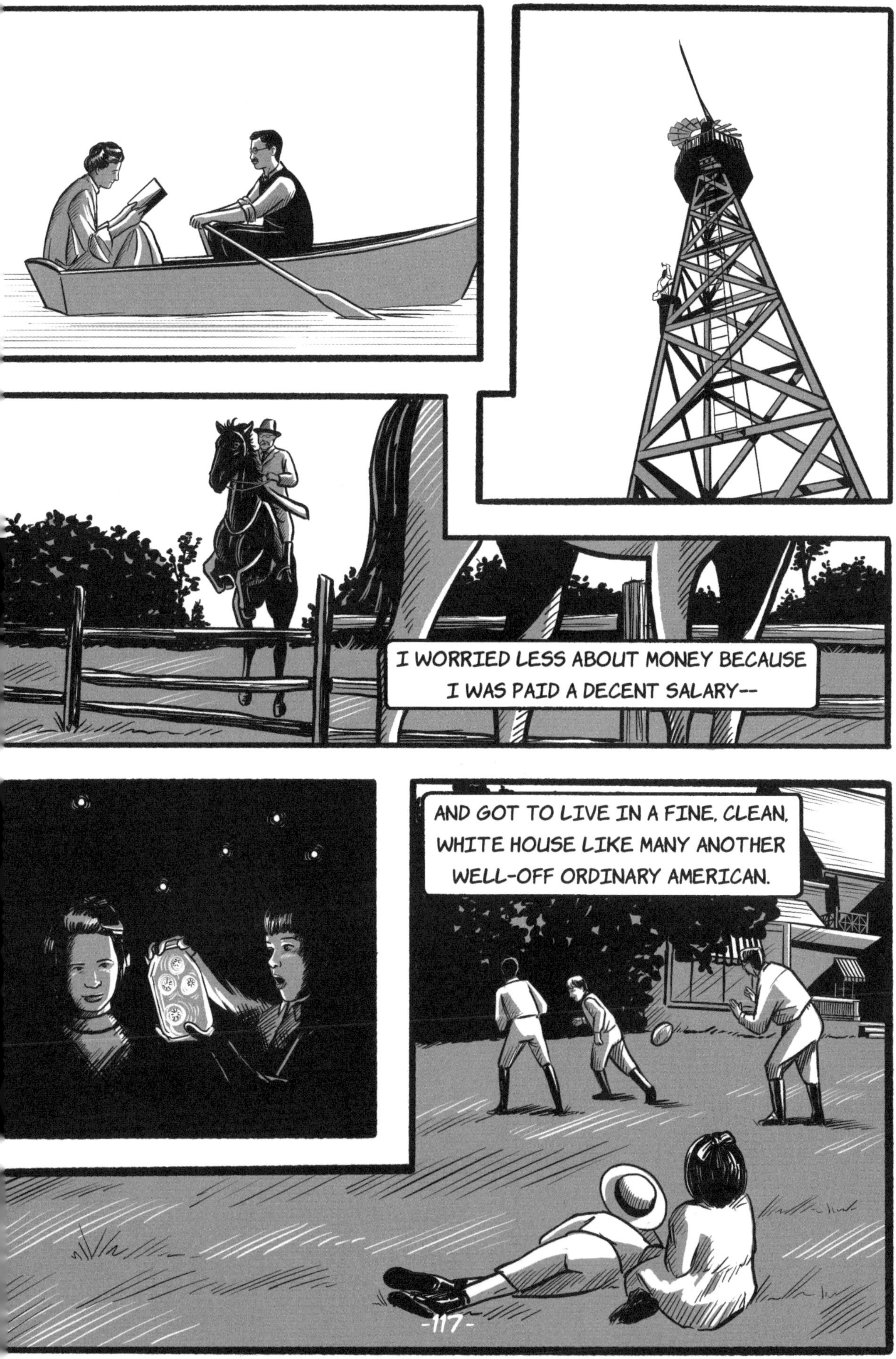
I WORRIED LESS ABOUT MONEY BECAUSE I WAS PAID A DECENT SALARY--
AND GOT TO LIVE IN A FINE, CLEAN, WHITE HOUSE LIKE MANY ANOTHER WELL-OFF ORDINARY AMERICAN.

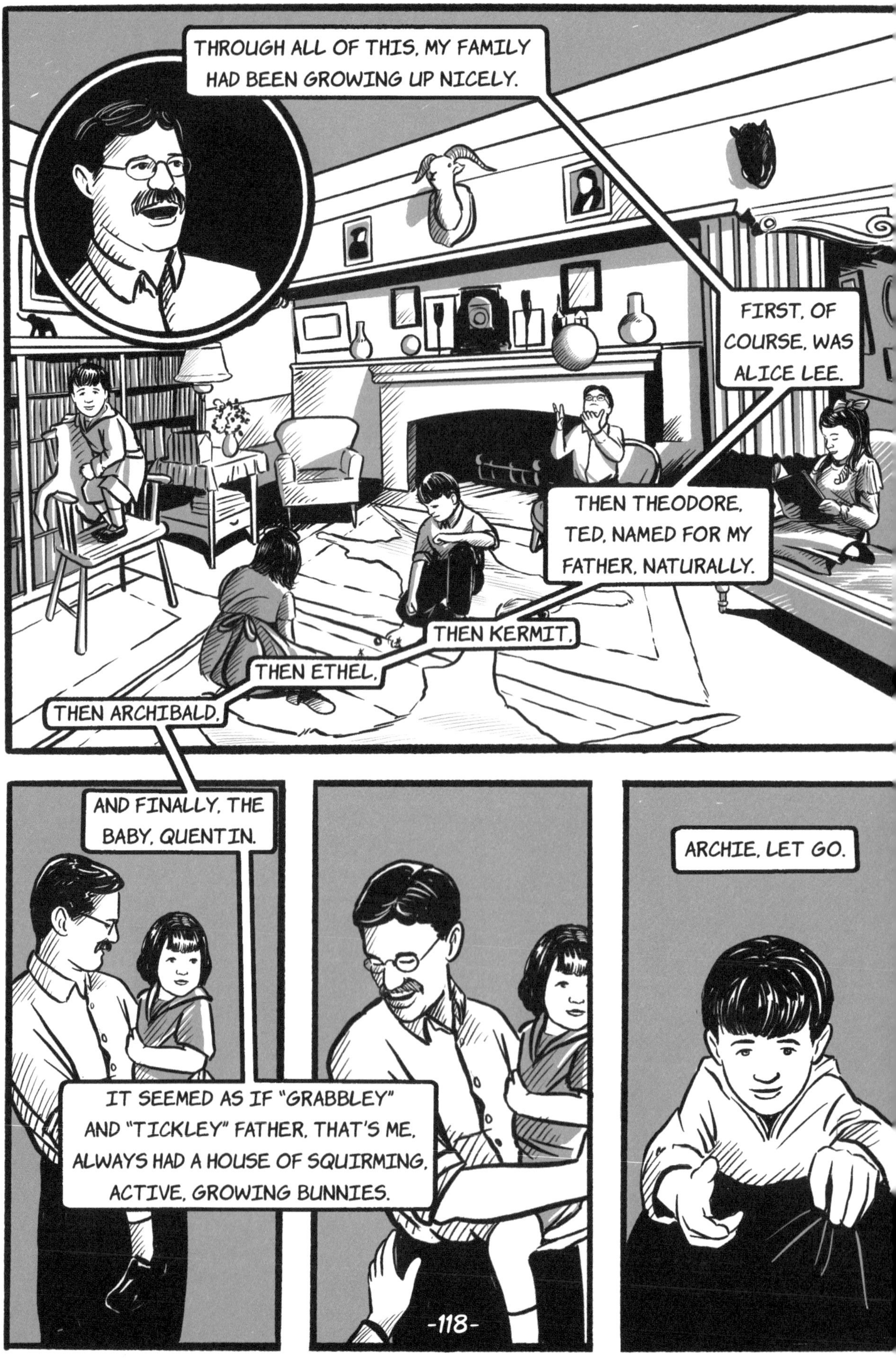
THROUGH ALL OF THIS, MY FAMILY HAD BEEN GROWING UP NICELY.
FIRST, OF COURSE, WAS ALICE LEE.
THEN THEODORE, TED, NAMED FOR MY FATHER, NATURALLY.
THEN KERMIT,
THEN ETHEL,
THEN ARCHIBALD,
AND FINALLY, THE BABY, QUENTIN.
IT SEEMED AS IF "GRABBLEY" AND "TICKLEY" FATHER, THAT'S ME, ALWAYS HAD A HOUSE OF SQUIRMING, ACTIVE, GROWING BUNNIES.
ARCHIE, LET GO.

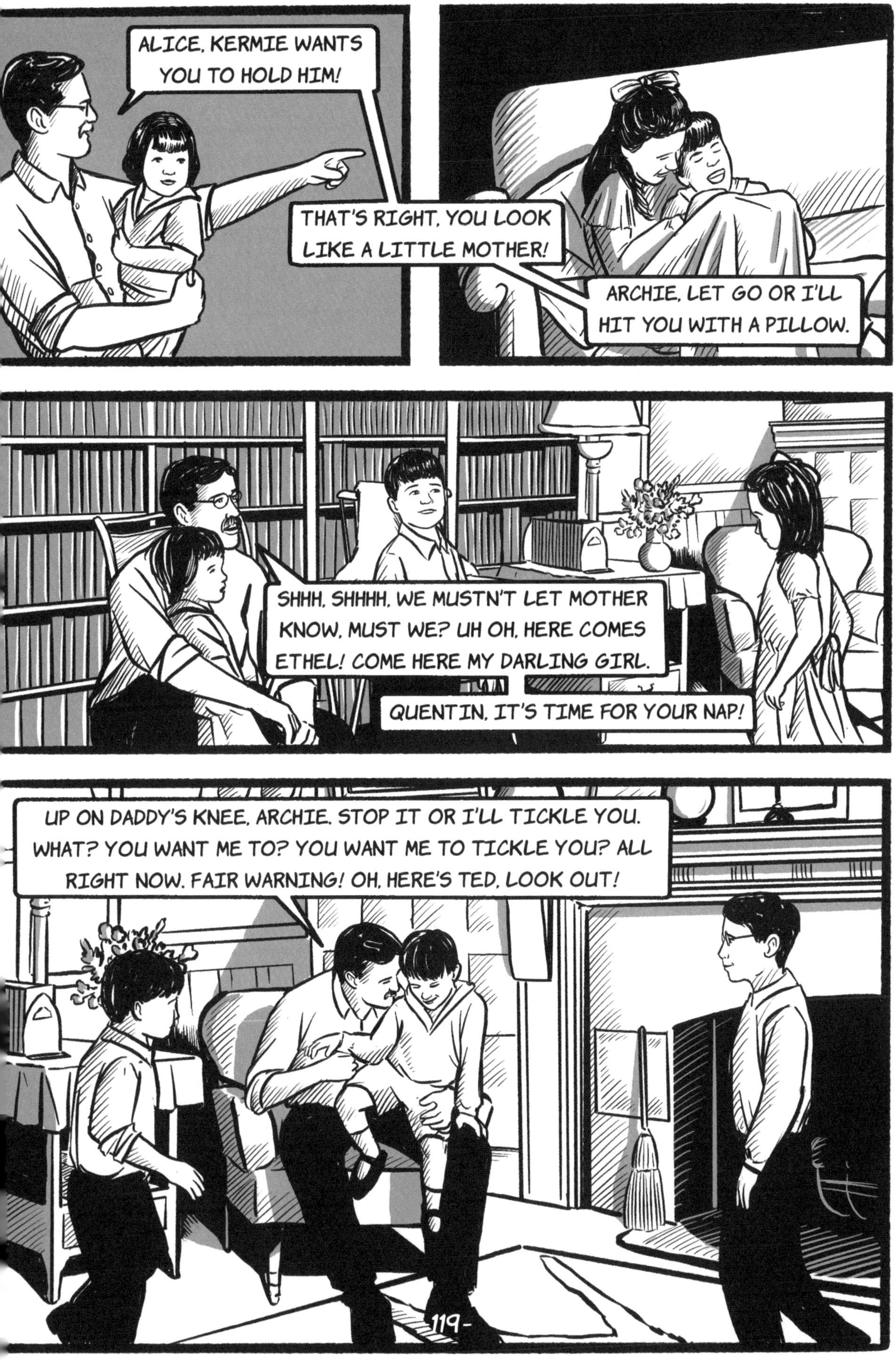
ALICE, KERMIE WANTS YOU TO HOLD HIM!
THAT'S RIGHT, YOU LOOK LIKE A LITTLE MOTHER!
ARCHIE, LET GO OR I'LL HIT YOU WITH A PILLOW.
SHHH, SHHHH, WE MUSTN'T LET MOTHER KNOW, MUST WE? UH OH, HERE COMES ETHEL! COME HERE MY DARLING GIRL.
QUENTIN, IT'S TIME FOR YOUR NAP!
UP ON DADDY'S KNEE, ARCHIE. STOP IT OR I'LL TICKLE YOU. WHAT? YOU WANT ME TO? YOU WANT ME TO TICKLE YOU? ALL RIGHT NOW. FAIR WARNING! OH, HERE'S TED, LOOK OUT!

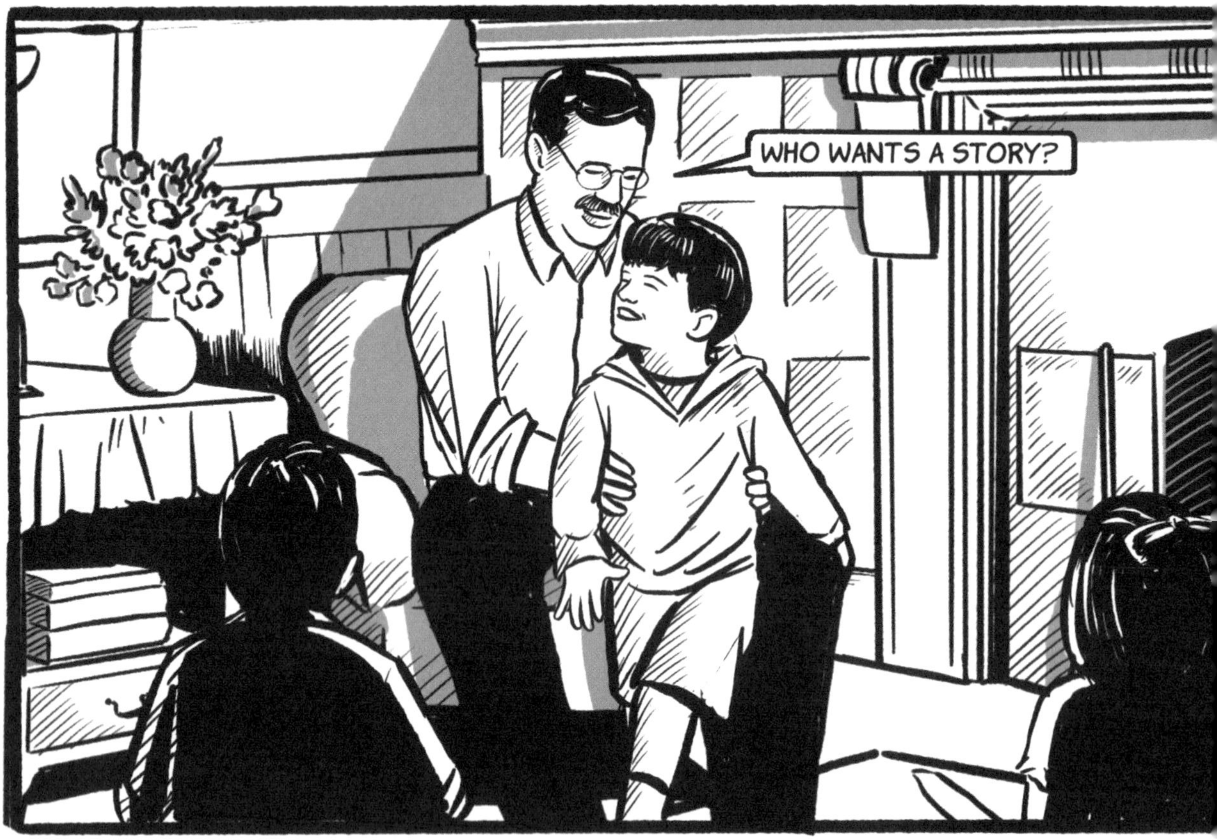
WHO WANTS A STORY?

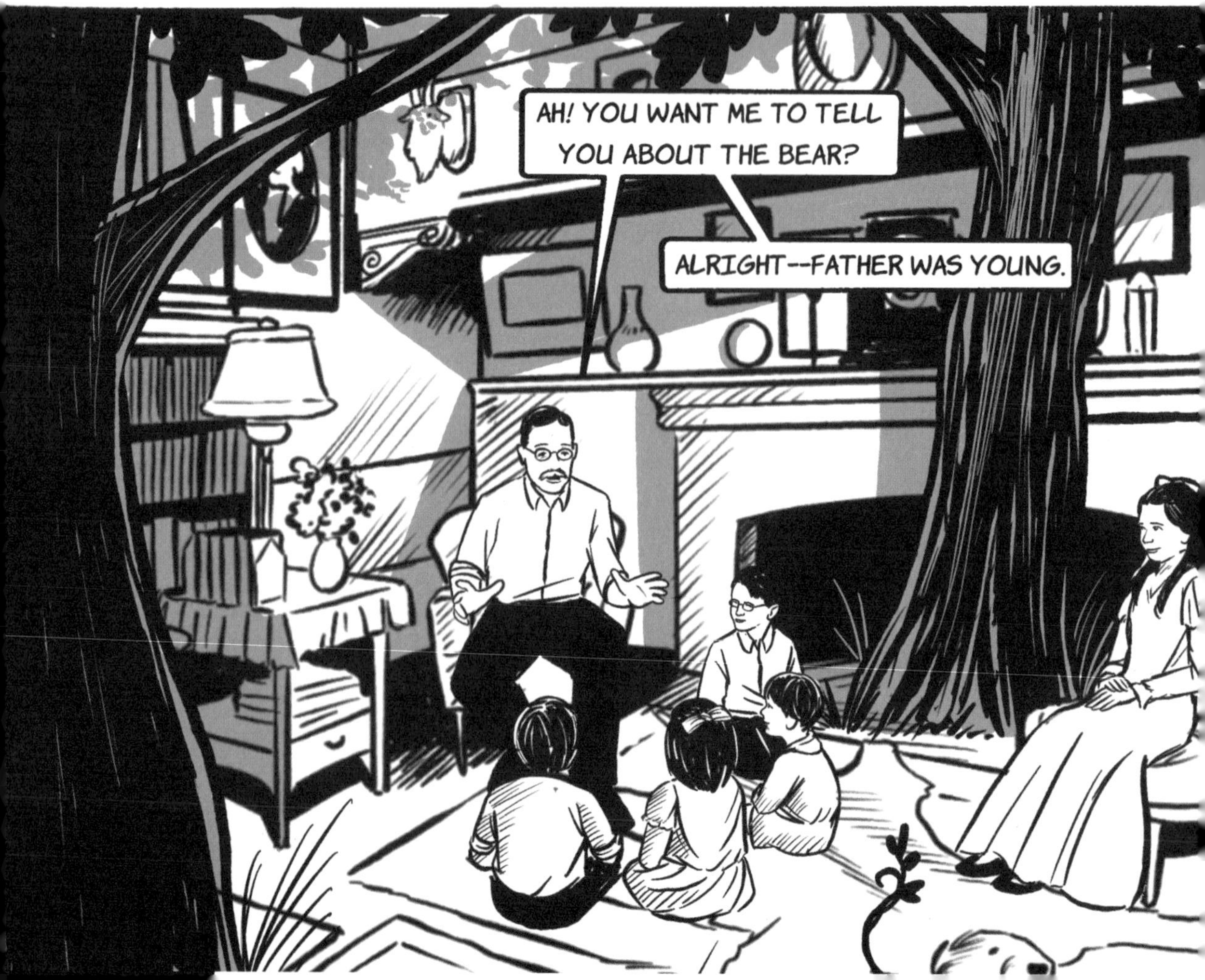
AH! YOU WANT ME TO TELL YOU ABOUT THE BEAR?
ALRIGHT--FATHER WAS YOUNG.

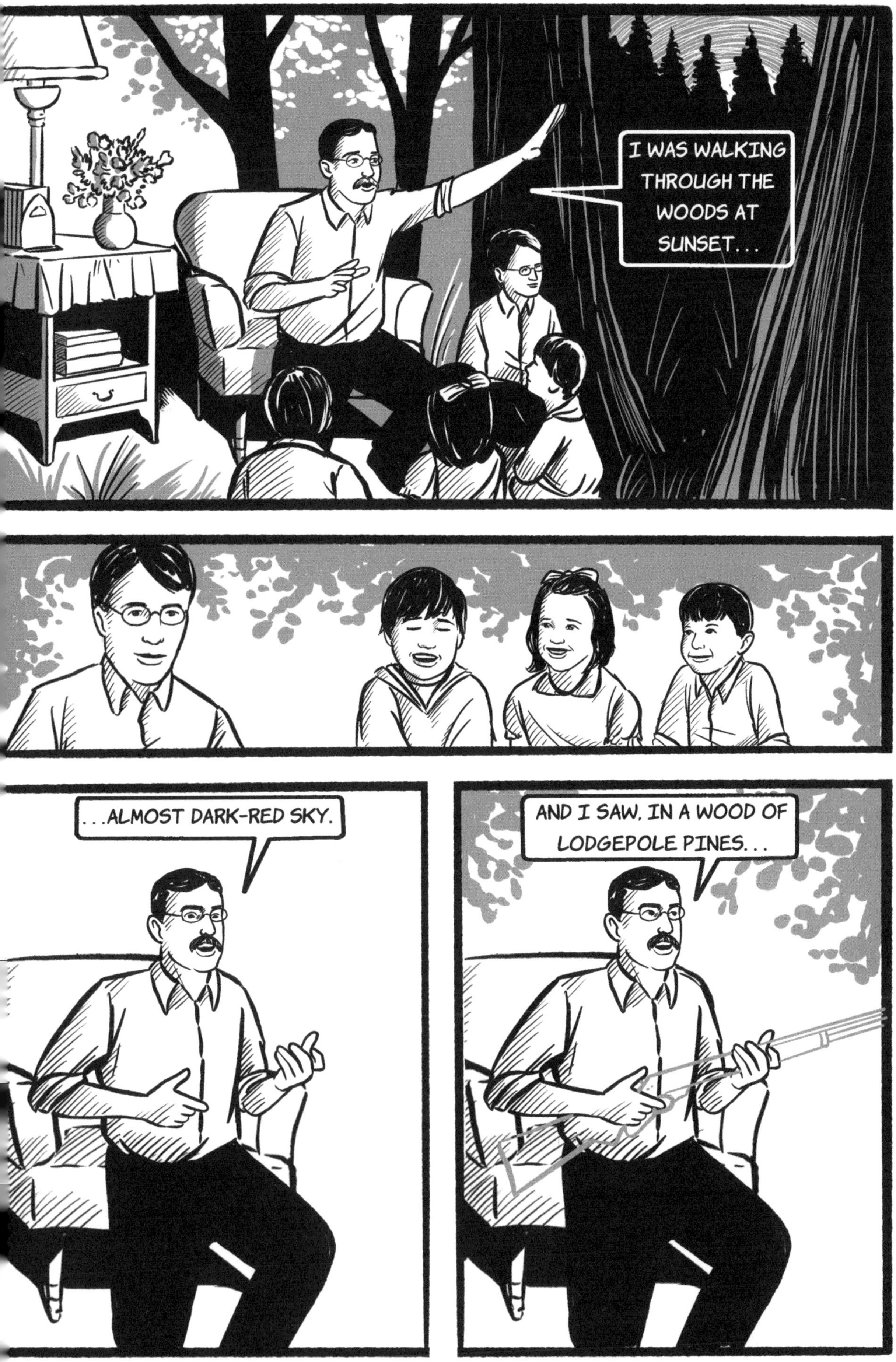
I WAS WALKING THROUGH THE WOODS AT SUNSET...
...ALMOST DARK-RED SKY.
AND I SAW, IN A WOOD OF LODGEPOLE PINES...

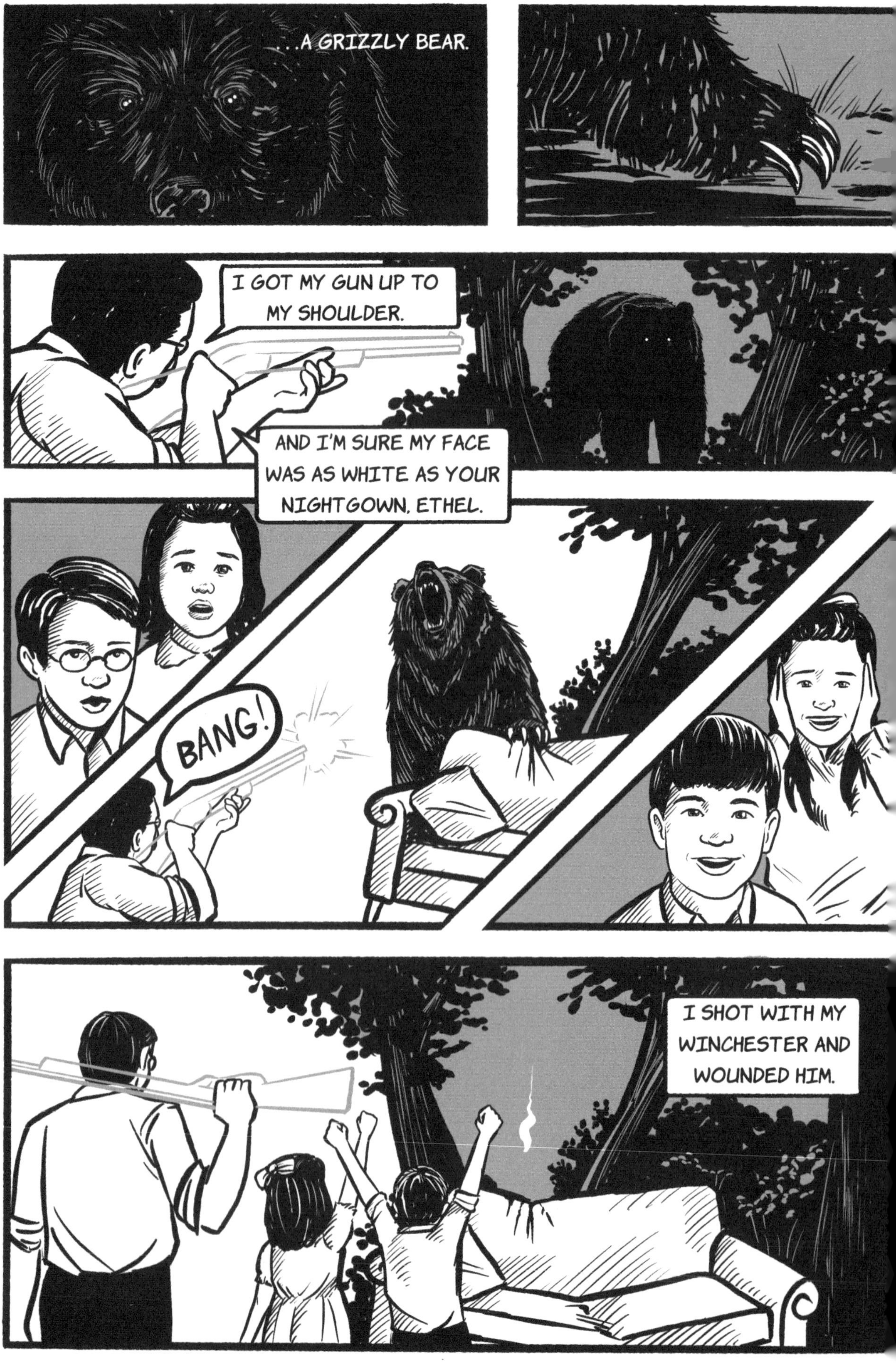
. . .A GRIZZLY BEAR.
I GOT MY GUN UP TO MY SHOULDER.
AND I'M SURE MY FACE WAS AS WHITE AS YOUR NIGHTGOWN, ETHEL.
BANG!
I SHOT WITH MY WINCHESTER AND WOUNDED HIM.

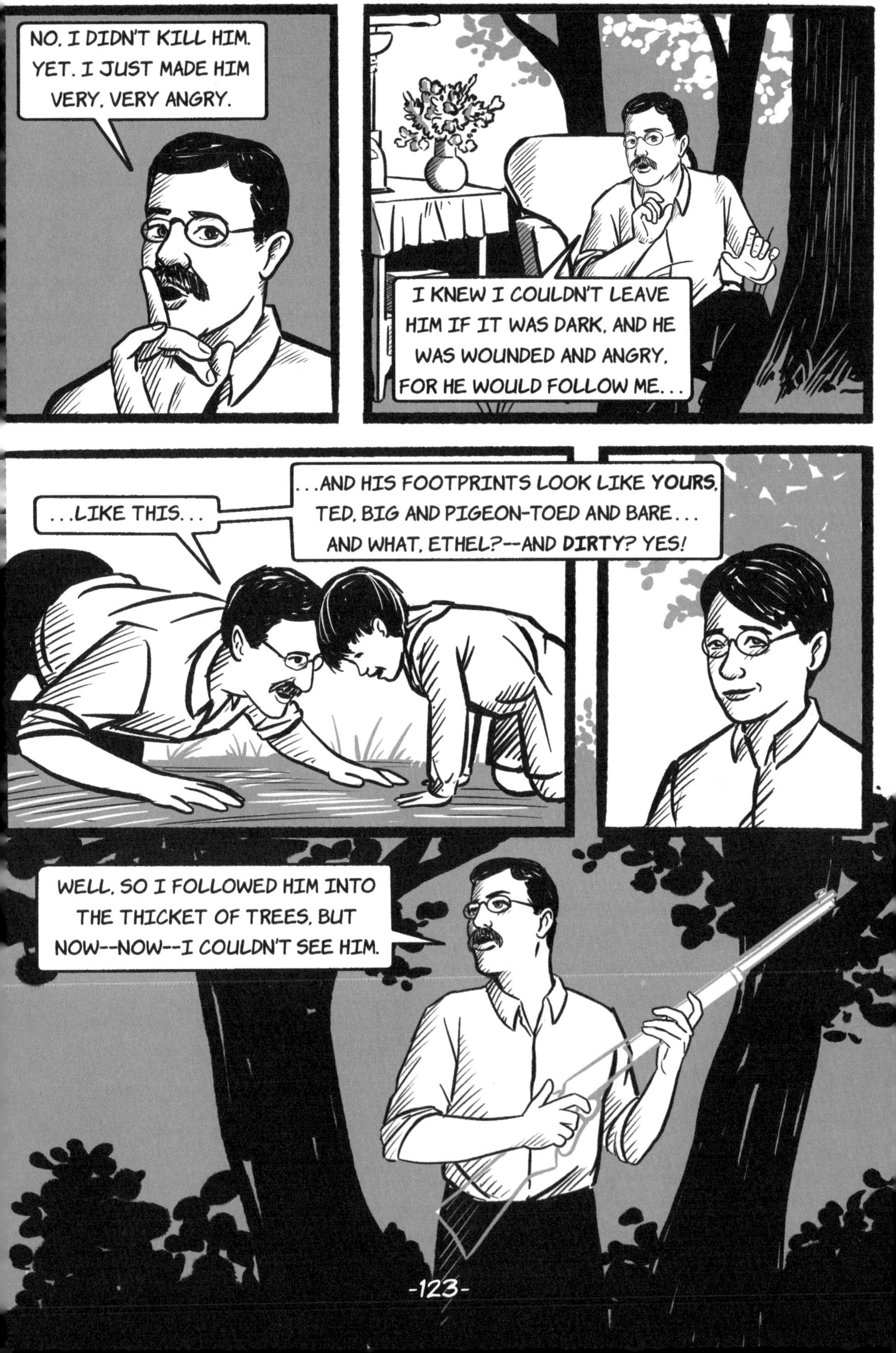
NO, I DIDN'T KILL HIM. YET. I JUST MADE HIM VERY, VERY ANGRY.
I KNEW I COULDN'T LEAVE HIM IF IT WAS DARK, AND HE WAS WOUNDED AND ANGRY, FOR HE WOULD FOLLOW ME...
...LIKE THIS...
...AND HIS FOOTPRINTS LOOK LIKE **YOURS**, TED, BIG AND PIGEON-TOED AND BARE... AND WHAT, ETHEL?--AND **DIRTY**? YES!
WELL, SO I FOLLOWED HIM INTO THE THICKET OF TREES, BUT NOW--NOW--I COULDN'T SEE HIM.

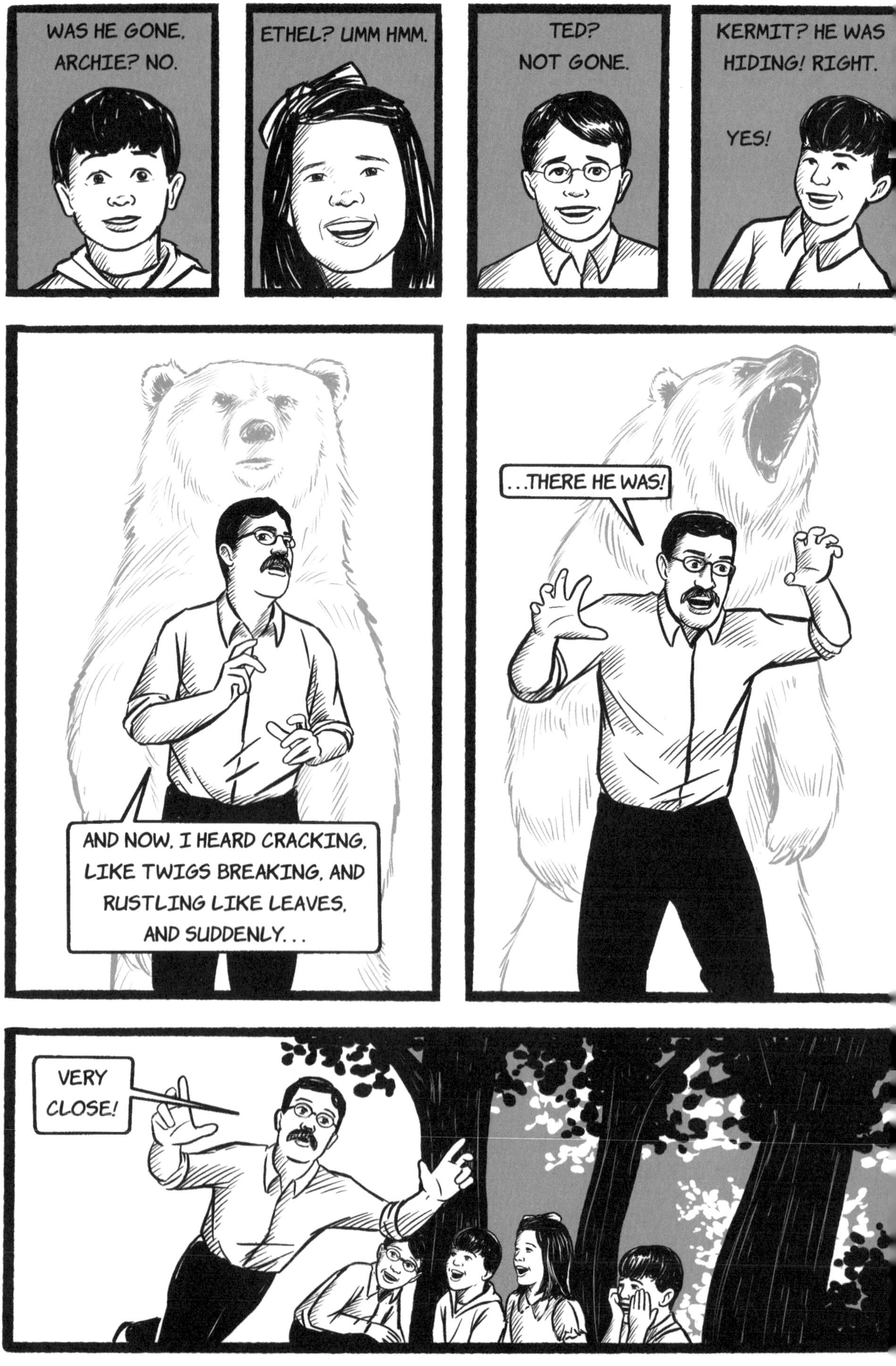
WAS HE GONE. ARCHIE? NO.
ETHEL? UMM HMM.
TED? NOT GONE.
KERMIT? HE WAS HIDING! RIGHT.
YES!
AND NOW, I HEARD CRACKING, LIKE TWIGS BREAKING, AND RUSTLING LIKE LEAVES, AND SUDDENLY...
...THERE HE WAS!
VERY CLOSE!

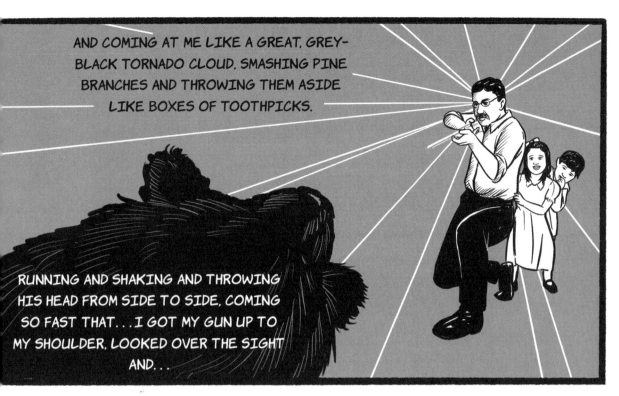

AND COMING AT ME LIKE A GREAT, GREY-BLACK TORNADO CLOUD, SMASHING PINE BRANCHES AND THROWING THEM ASIDE LIKE BOXES OF TOOTHPICKS.

RUNNING AND SHAKING AND THROWING HIS HEAD FROM SIDE TO SIDE, COMING SO FAST THAT... I GOT MY GUN UP TO MY SHOULDER, LOOKED OVER THE SIGHT AND...

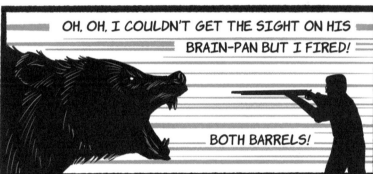

OH, OH, I COULDN'T GET THE SIGHT ON HIS BRAIN-PAN BUT I FIRED!

BOTH BARRELS!

BANG

AND I JUMPED TO ONE SIDE --RIGHT, KERMIT! TO GET OUT OF THE SMOKE! AND THERE HE WAS!

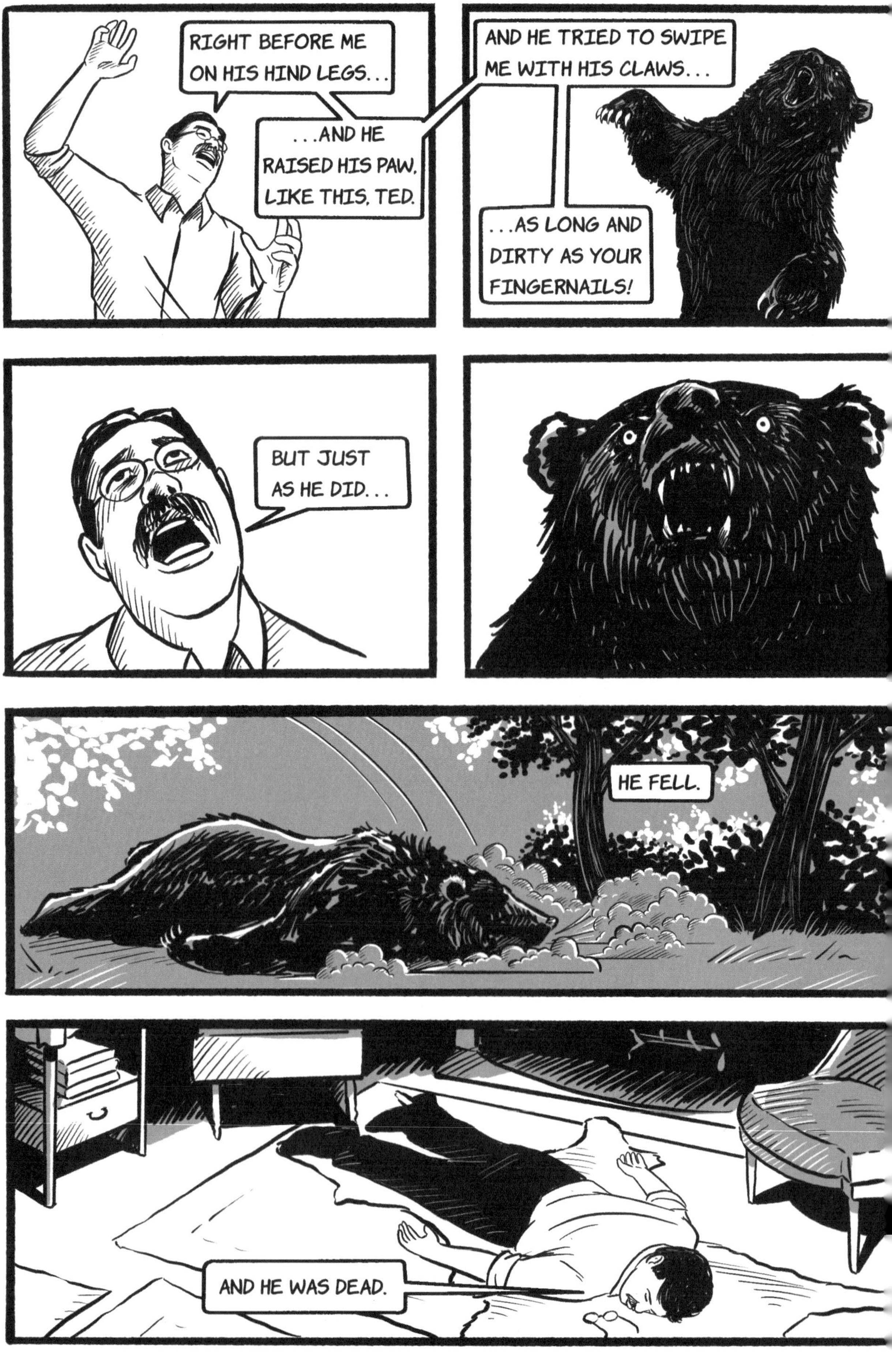
RIGHT BEFORE ME ON HIS HIND LEGS...
...AND HE RAISED HIS PAW, LIKE THIS, TED.
AND HE TRIED TO SWIPE ME WITH HIS CLAWS...
...AS LONG AND DIRTY AS YOUR FINGERNAILS!
BUT JUST AS HE DID...
HE FELL.
AND HE WAS DEAD.

OH, ETHEL, DON'T CRY. ARCHIE, DON'T CRY.
PAPA'S NOT DEAD. THE BEAR WAS DEAD --TED, DON'T LAUGH--
AND PAPA HAD TO SKIN HIM. . .
. . .AND TIE THE WET SLIMY SKIN ON TO THE BACK OF A LITTLE PONY THAT DIDN'T LIKE IT ONE BIT, AND IT KEPT ON SLITHERING OUT LIKE GREASY, BLOODY GUTS AND--
--KERMIT, DON'T UPCHUCK! ETHEL! NO! DON'T GET SICK! SHHH!
WAAAAAAAAAAHHHHH!!!!!
UH OH. YOU'VE WAKED QUENTIN.
MOTHER'S GOING TO BE VERY ANGRY AT ALL OF YOU. TIME FOR HIDE AND SEEK!

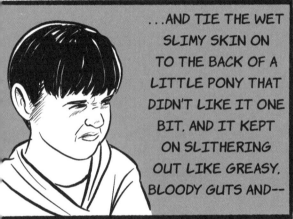

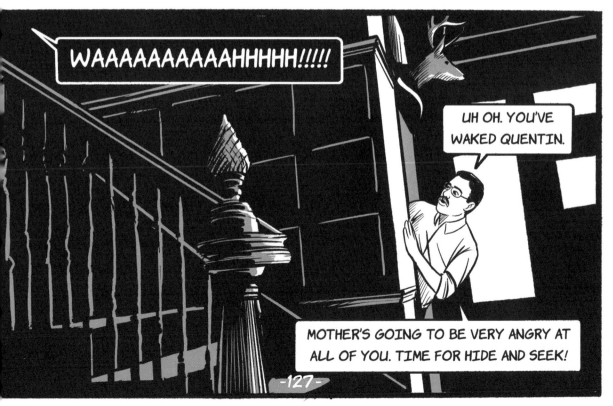

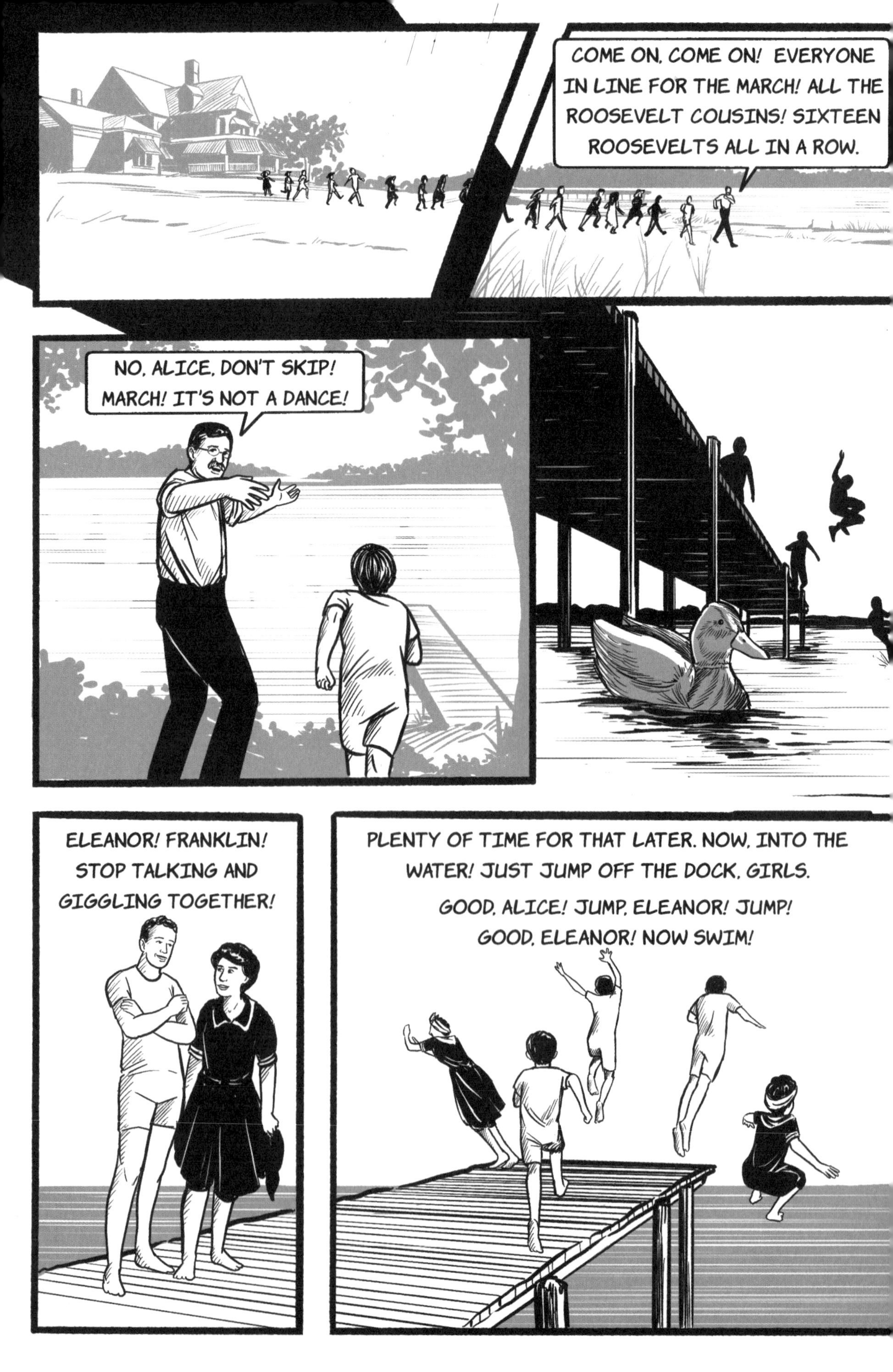
COME ON, COME ON! EVERYONE IN LINE FOR THE MARCH! ALL THE ROOSEVELT COUSINS! SIXTEEN ROOSEVELTS ALL IN A ROW.
NO, ALICE, DON'T SKIP! MARCH! IT'S NOT A DANCE!
ELEANOR! FRANKLIN! STOP TALKING AND GIGGLING TOGETHER!
PLENTY OF TIME FOR THAT LATER. NOW, INTO THE WATER! JUST JUMP OFF THE DOCK, GIRLS.
GOOD, ALICE! JUMP, ELEANOR! JUMP! GOOD, ELEANOR! NOW SWIM!

YOU CAN'T? ELEANOR, YOU CAN'T SWIM?

UH OH, HERE I COME!

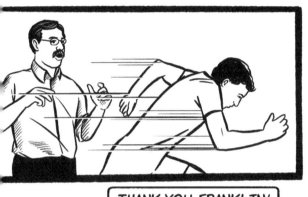

THANK YOU, FRANKLIN!

YES, YES, HOLD HER ABOVE THE WATER!

FRANKLIN IS QUITE A STRONG YOUNG MAN WITH A STRONG MIND, IN SPITE OF HIS FLUBDUB FATHER, WHO'S MERELY RICH, THAT'S ALL, RICH AND WHO OPPOSED ME ON THE COAL STRIKE SETTLEMENT!

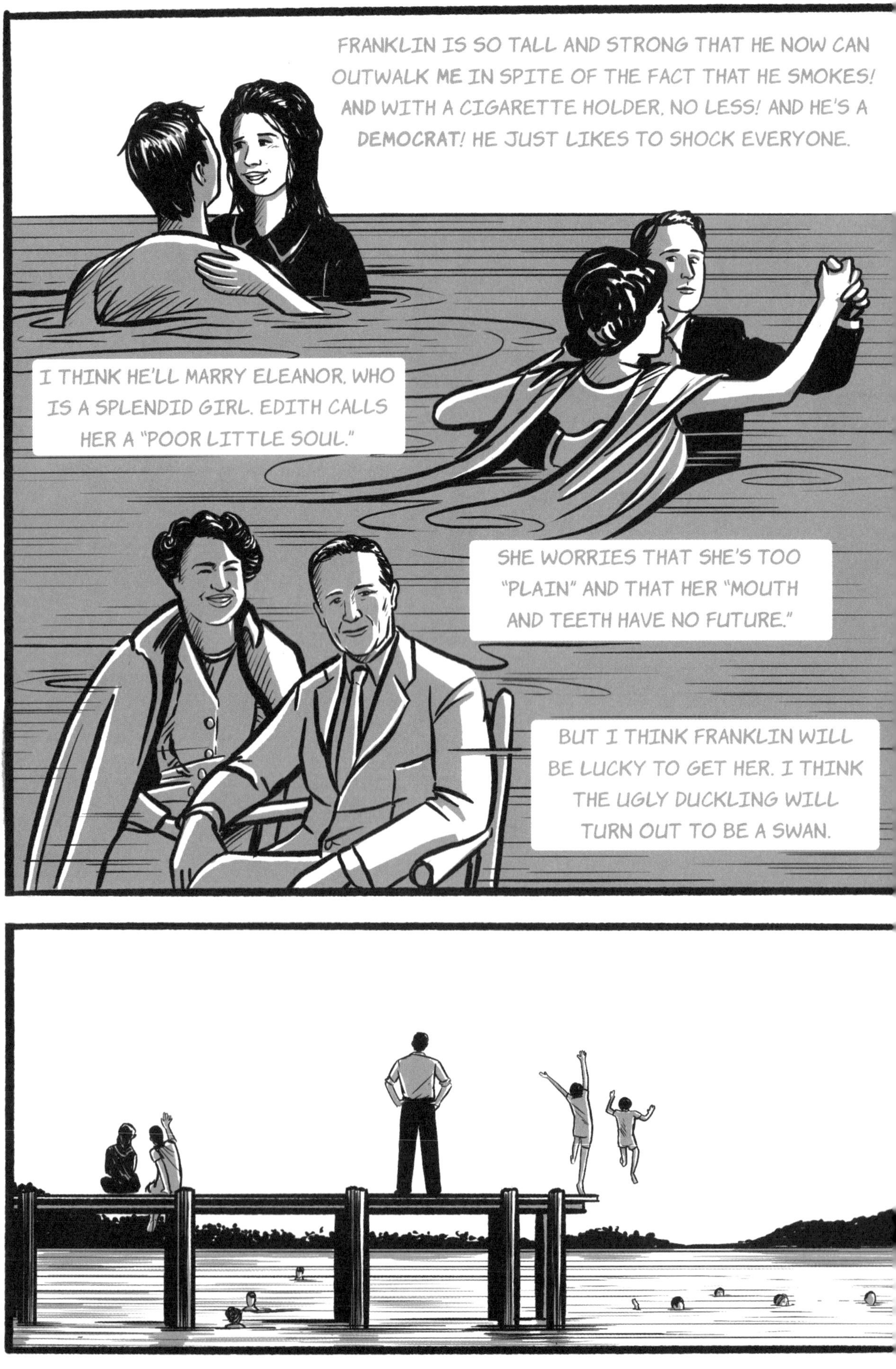
FRANKLIN IS SO TALL AND STRONG THAT HE NOW CAN OUTWALK ME IN SPITE OF THE FACT THAT HE SMOKES! AND WITH A CIGARETTE HOLDER, NO LESS! AND HE'S A DEMOCRAT! HE JUST LIKES TO SHOCK EVERYONE.
I THINK HE'LL MARRY ELEANOR, WHO IS A SPLENDID GIRL. EDITH CALLS HER A "POOR LITTLE SOUL."
SHE WORRIES THAT SHE'S TOO "PLAIN" AND THAT HER "MOUTH AND TEETH HAVE NO FUTURE."
BUT I THINK FRANKLIN WILL BE LUCKY TO GET HER. I THINK THE UGLY DUCKLING WILL TURN OUT TO BE A SWAN.

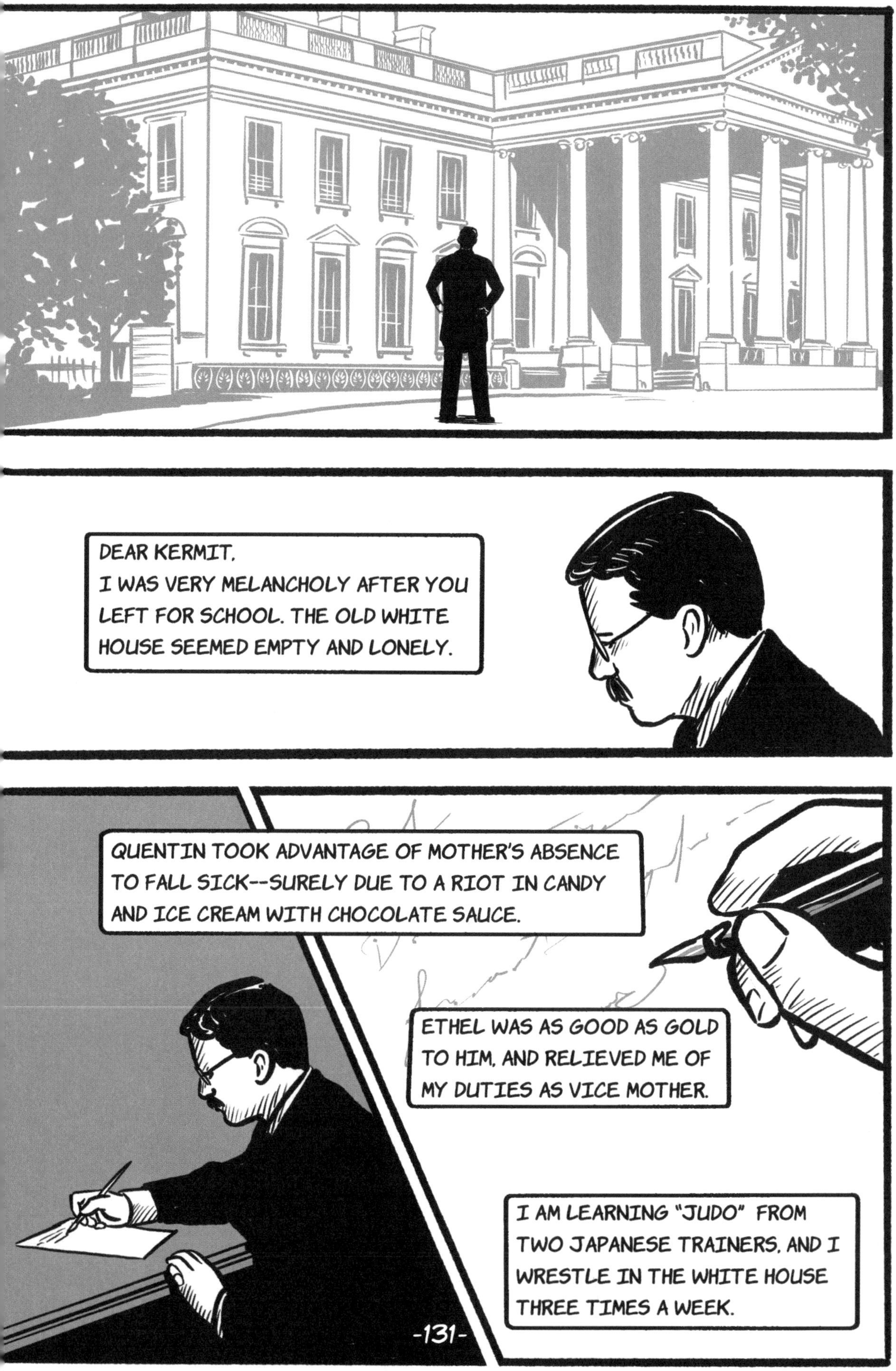
DEAR KERMIT,
I WAS VERY MELANCHOLY AFTER YOU LEFT FOR SCHOOL. THE OLD WHITE HOUSE SEEMED EMPTY AND LONELY.
QUENTIN TOOK ADVANTAGE OF MOTHER'S ABSENCE TO FALL SICK--SURELY DUE TO A RIOT IN CANDY AND ICE CREAM WITH CHOCOLATE SAUCE.
ETHEL WAS AS GOOD AS GOLD TO HIM, AND RELIEVED ME OF MY DUTIES AS VICE MOTHER.
I AM LEARNING "JUDO" FROM TWO JAPANESE TRAINERS, AND I WRESTLE IN THE WHITE HOUSE THREE TIMES A WEEK.

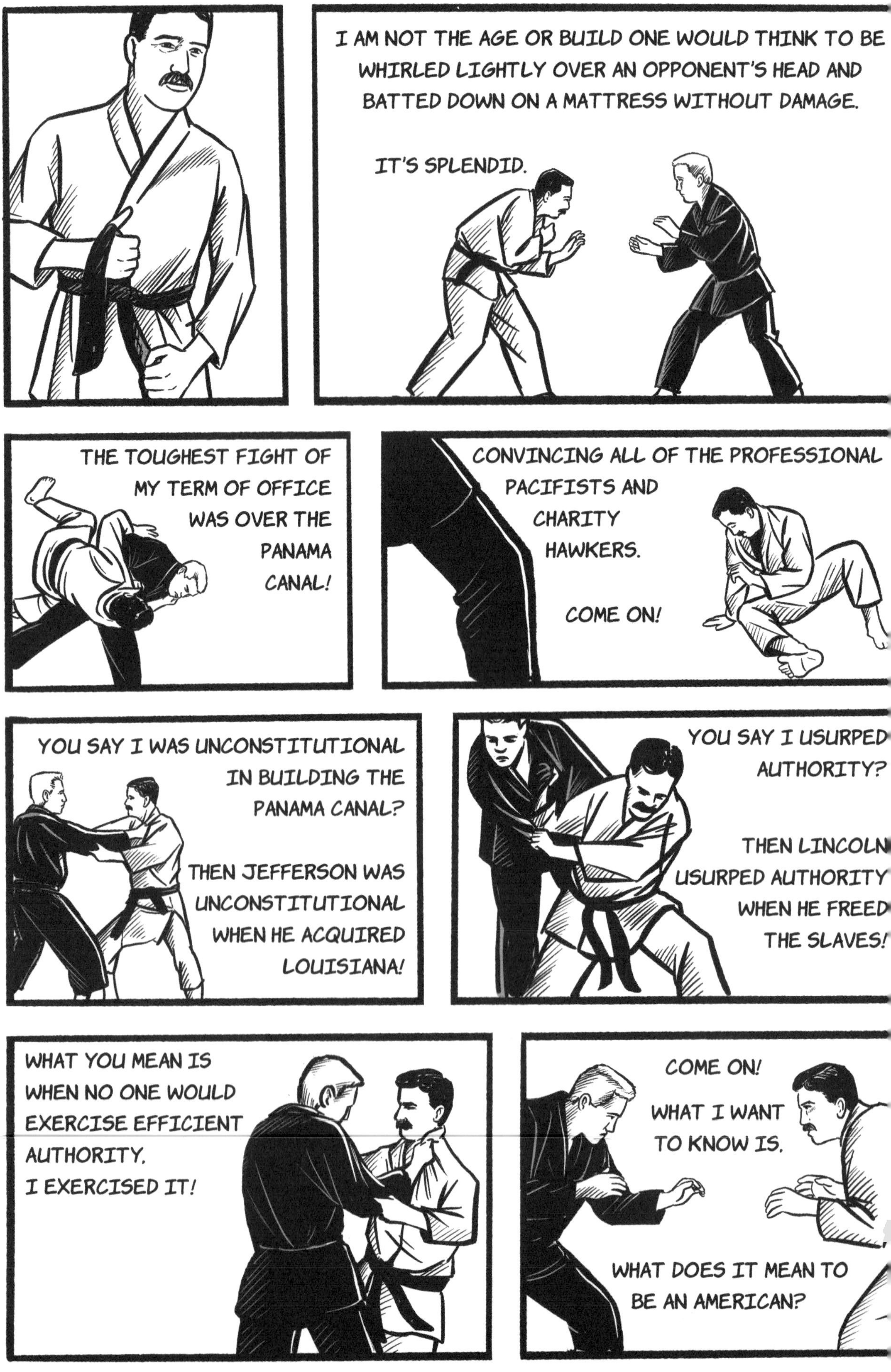
I AM NOT THE AGE OR BUILD ONE WOULD THINK TO BE WHIRLED LIGHTLY OVER AN OPPONENT'S HEAD AND BATTED DOWN ON A MATTRESS WITHOUT DAMAGE.
IT'S SPLENDID.
THE TOUGHEST FIGHT OF MY TERM OF OFFICE WAS OVER THE PANAMA CANAL!
CONVINCING ALL OF THE PROFESSIONAL PACIFISTS AND CHARITY HAWKERS.
COME ON!
YOU SAY I WAS UNCONSTITUTIONAL IN BUILDING THE PANAMA CANAL?
THEN JEFFERSON WAS UNCONSTITUTIONAL WHEN HE ACQUIRED LOUISIANA!
YOU SAY I USURPED AUTHORITY?
THEN LINCOLN USURPED AUTHORITY WHEN HE FREED THE SLAVES!
WHAT YOU MEAN IS WHEN NO ONE WOULD EXERCISE EFFICIENT AUTHORITY.
I EXERCISED IT!
COME ON!
WHAT I WANT TO KNOW IS.
WHAT DOES IT MEAN TO BE AN AMERICAN?

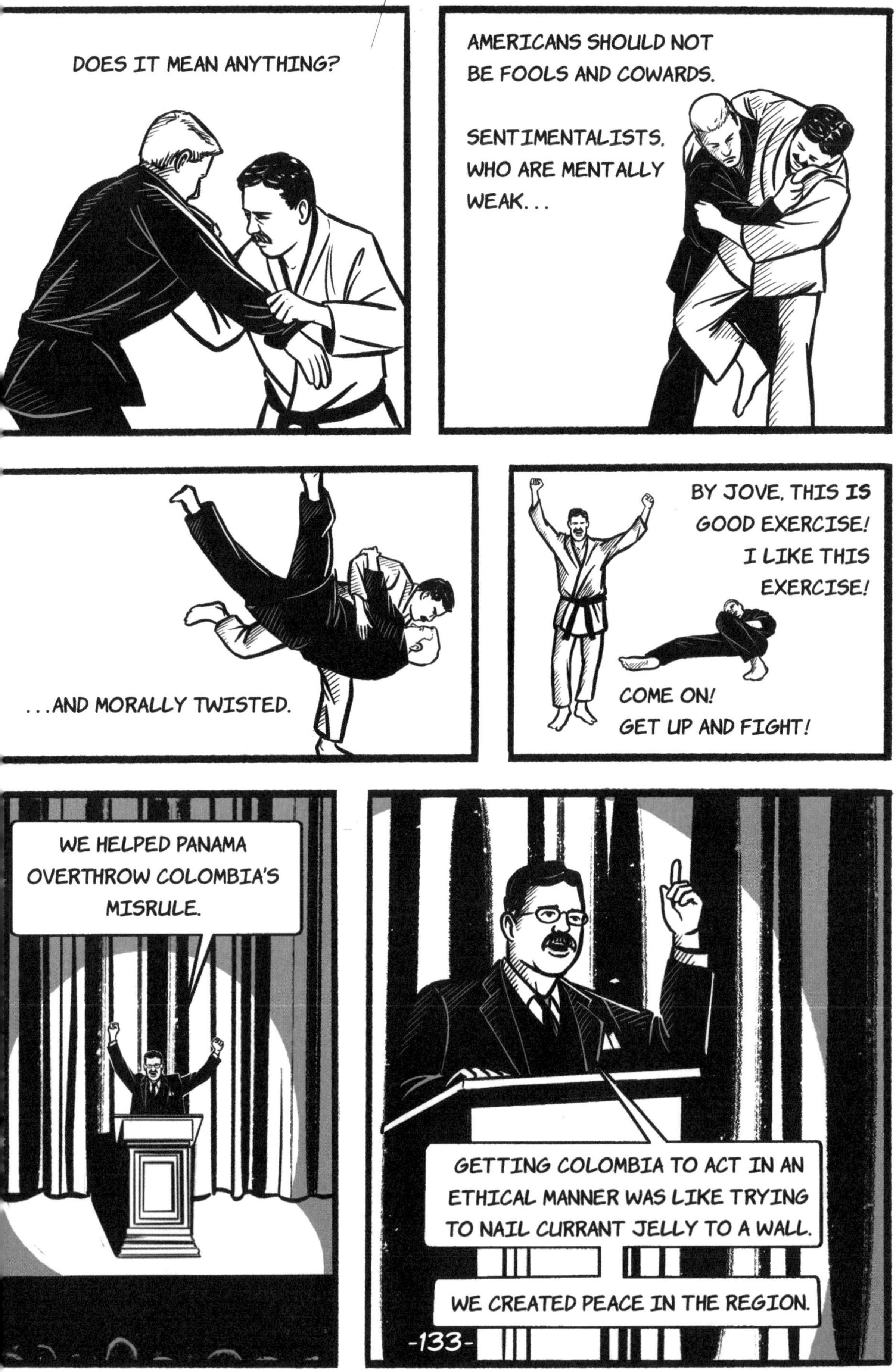
DOES IT MEAN ANYTHING?
AMERICANS SHOULD NOT BE FOOLS AND COWARDS.
SENTIMENTALISTS, WHO ARE MENTALLY WEAK...
...AND MORALLY TWISTED.
BY JOVE, THIS IS GOOD EXERCISE! I LIKE THIS EXERCISE!
COME ON! GET UP AND FIGHT!
WE HELPED PANAMA OVERTHROW COLOMBIA'S MISRULE.
GETTING COLOMBIA TO ACT IN AN ETHICAL MANNER WAS LIKE TRYING TO NAIL CURRANT JELLY TO A WALL.
WE CREATED PEACE IN THE REGION.

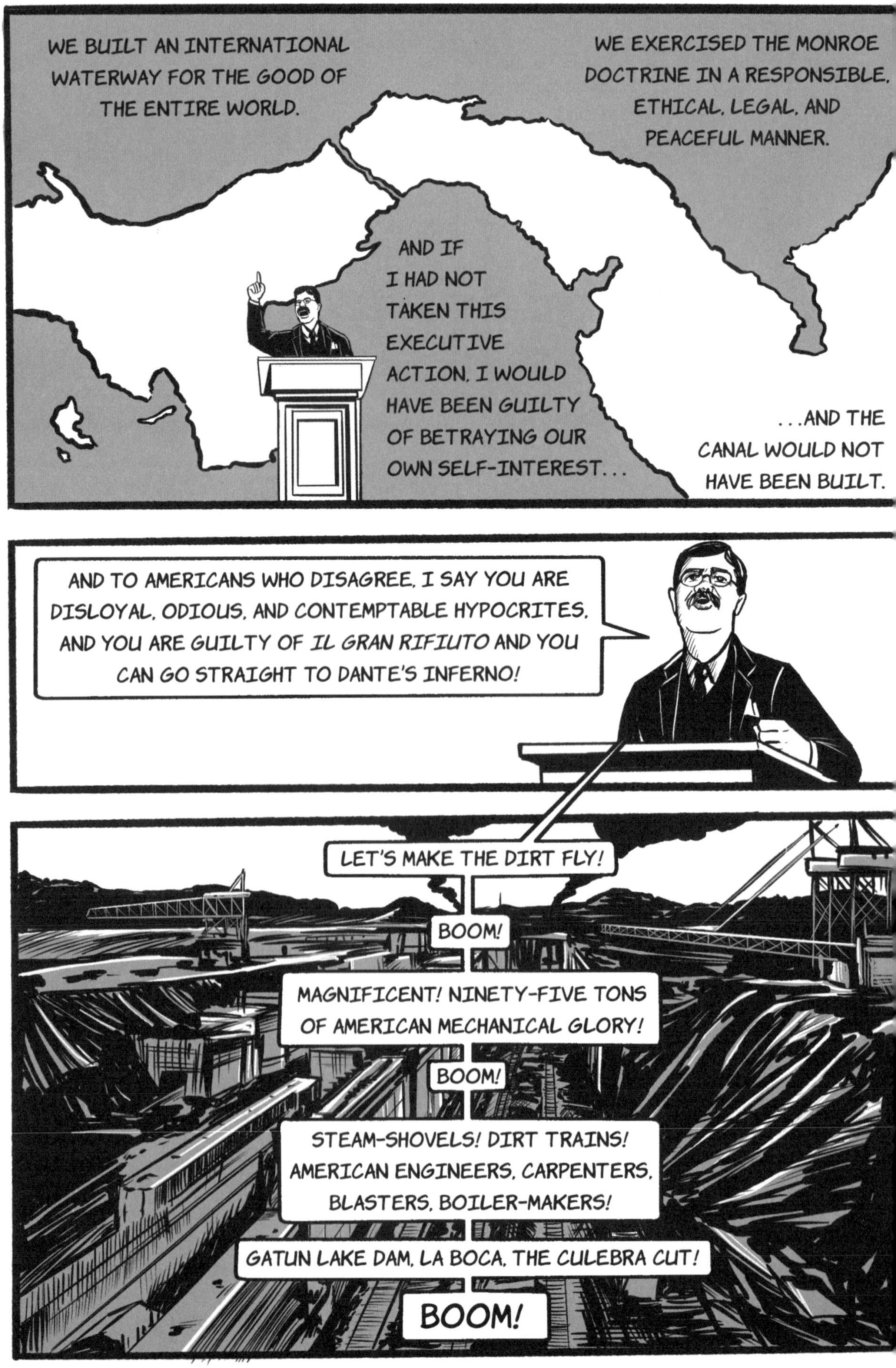
WE BUILT AN INTERNATIONAL WATERWAY FOR THE GOOD OF THE ENTIRE WORLD.
WE EXERCISED THE MONROE DOCTRINE IN A RESPONSIBLE, ETHICAL, LEGAL, AND PEACEFUL MANNER.
AND IF I HAD NOT TAKEN THIS EXECUTIVE ACTION, I WOULD HAVE BEEN GUILTY OF BETRAYING OUR OWN SELF-INTEREST...
...AND THE CANAL WOULD NOT HAVE BEEN BUILT.
AND TO AMERICANS WHO DISAGREE, I SAY YOU ARE DISLOYAL, ODIOUS, AND CONTEMPTABLE HYPOCRITES, AND YOU ARE GUILTY OF *IL GRAN RIFIUTO* AND YOU CAN GO STRAIGHT TO DANTE'S INFERNO!
LET'S MAKE THE DIRT FLY!
BOOM!
MAGNIFICENT! NINETY-FIVE TONS OF AMERICAN MECHANICAL GLORY!
BOOM!
STEAM-SHOVELS! DIRT TRAINS! AMERICAN ENGINEERS, CARPENTERS, BLASTERS, BOILER-MAKERS!
GATUN LAKE DAM, LA BOCA, THE CULEBRA CUT!
BOOM!

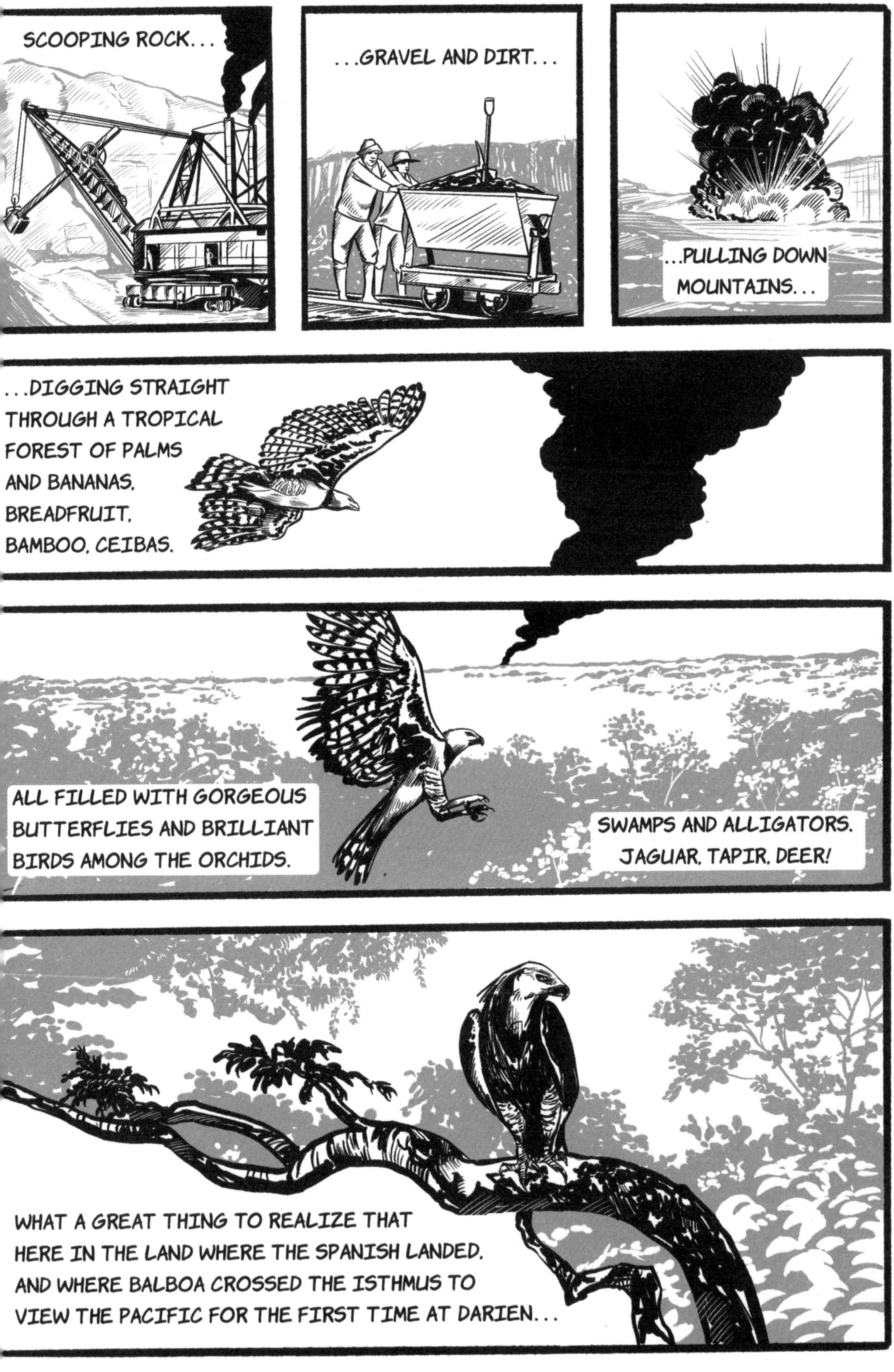
SCOOPING ROCK...
...GRAVEL AND DIRT...
...PULLING DOWN MOUNTAINS...
...DIGGING STRAIGHT THROUGH A TROPICAL FOREST OF PALMS AND BANANAS, BREADFRUIT, BAMBOO, CEIBAS.
ALL FILLED WITH GORGEOUS BUTTERFLIES AND BRILLIANT BIRDS AMONG THE ORCHIDS.
SWAMPS AND ALLIGATORS. JAGUAR, TAPIR, DEER!
WHAT A GREAT THING TO REALIZE THAT HERE IN THE LAND WHERE THE SPANISH LANDED, AND WHERE BALBOA CROSSED THE ISTHMUS TO VIEW THE PACIFIC FOR THE FIRST TIME AT DARIEN...

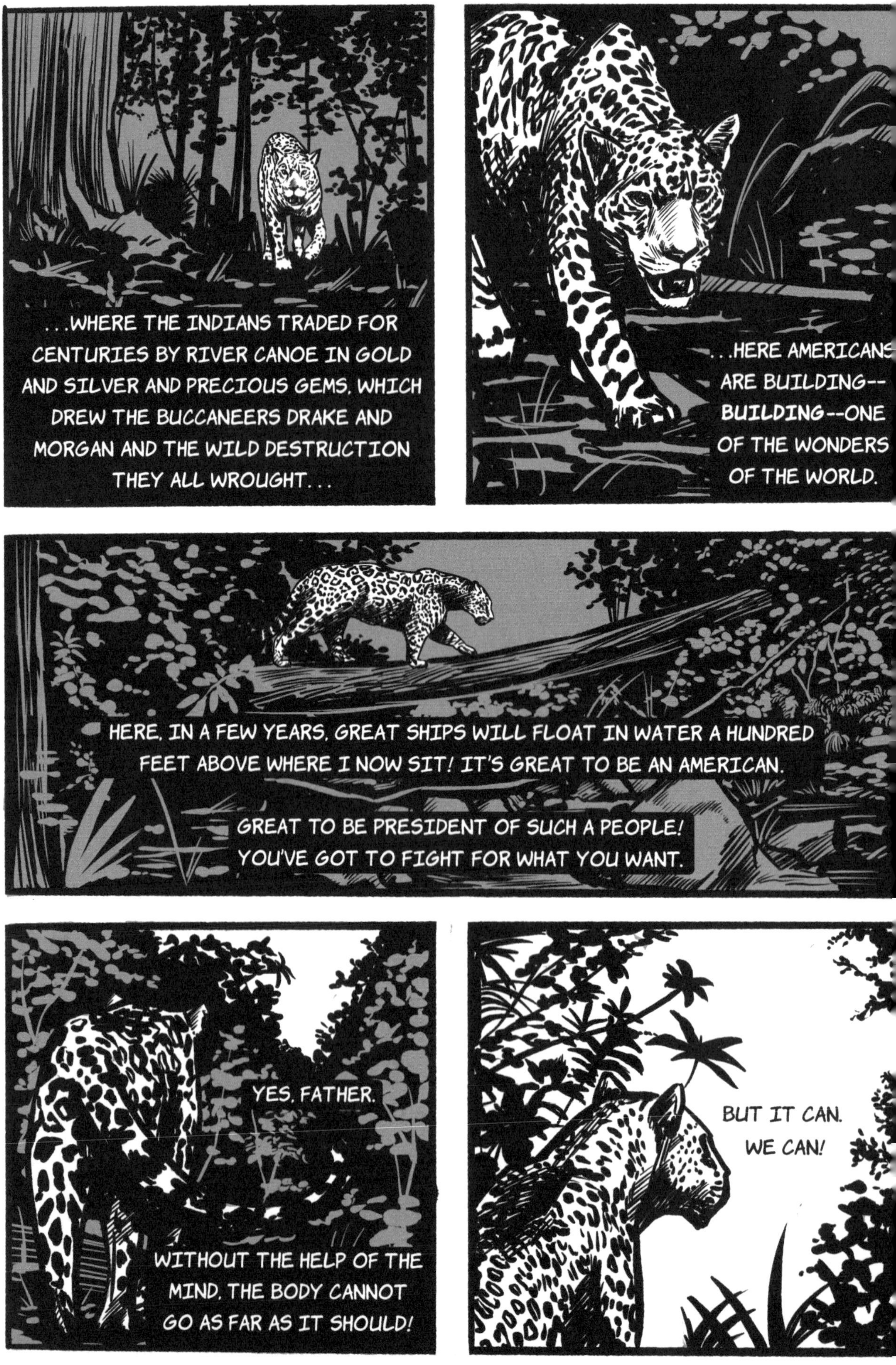
...WHERE THE INDIANS TRADED FOR CENTURIES BY RIVER CANOE IN GOLD AND SILVER AND PRECIOUS GEMS, WHICH DREW THE BUCCANEERS DRAKE AND MORGAN AND THE WILD DESTRUCTION THEY ALL WROUGHT...
...HERE AMERICANS ARE BUILDING-- BUILDING--ONE OF THE WONDERS OF THE WORLD.
HERE, IN A FEW YEARS, GREAT SHIPS WILL FLOAT IN WATER A HUNDRED FEET ABOVE WHERE I NOW SIT! IT'S GREAT TO BE AN AMERICAN.
GREAT TO BE PRESIDENT OF SUCH A PEOPLE! YOU'VE GOT TO FIGHT FOR WHAT YOU WANT.
YES, FATHER.
WITHOUT THE HELP OF THE MIND, THE BODY CANNOT GO AS FAR AS IT SHOULD!
BUT IT CAN. WE CAN!

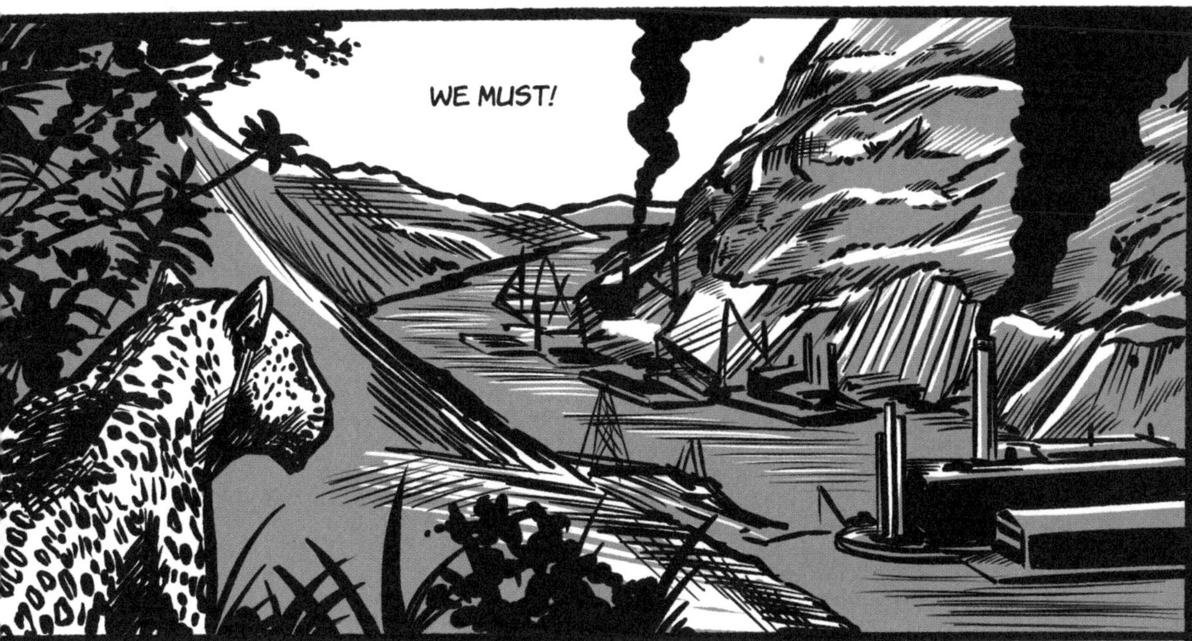
WE MUST!

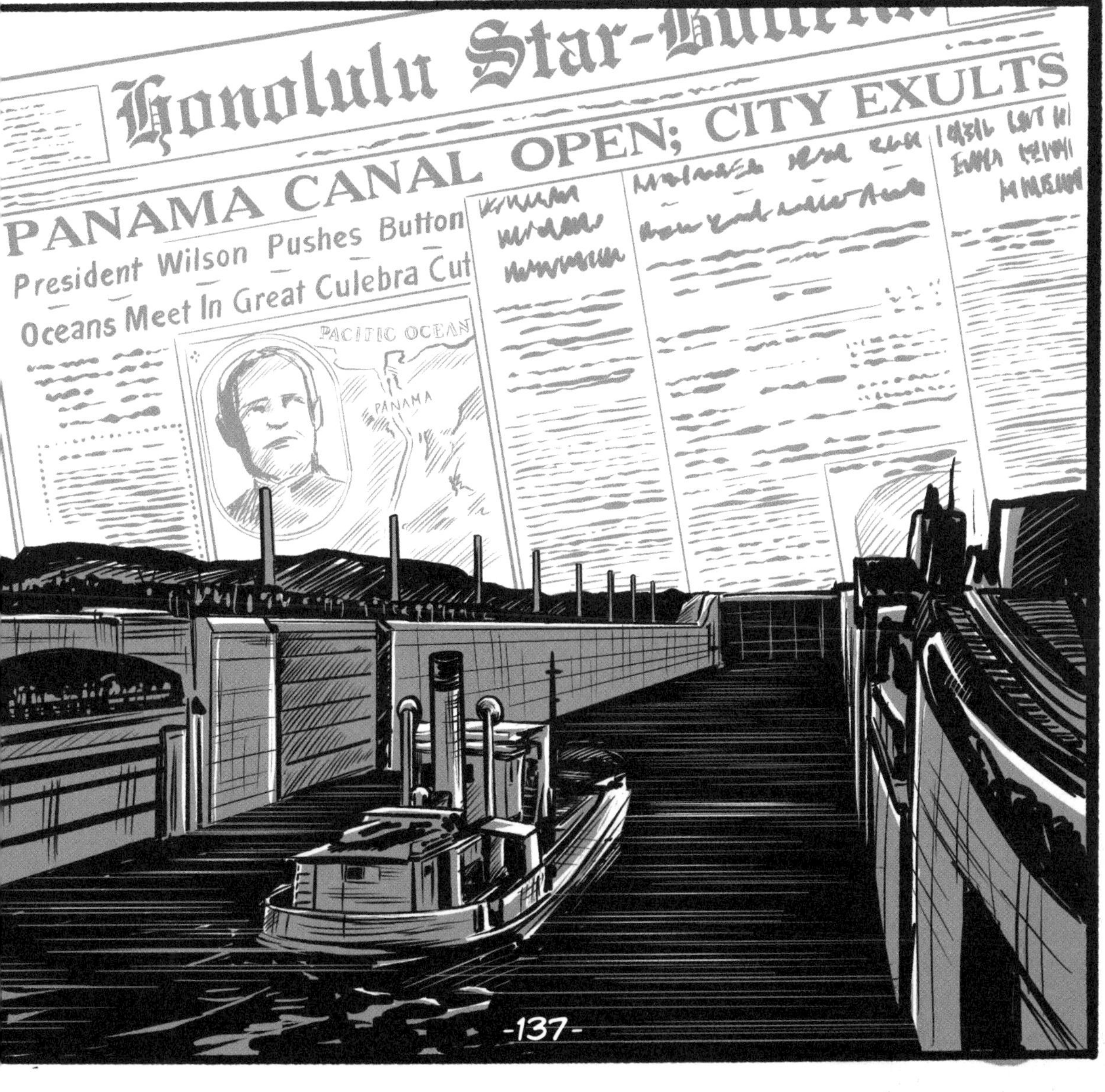
Honolulu Star-
PANAMA CANAL OPEN; CITY EXULTS
President Wilson Pushes Button
Oceans Meet In Great Culebra Cut
PACIFIC OCEAN
PANAMA

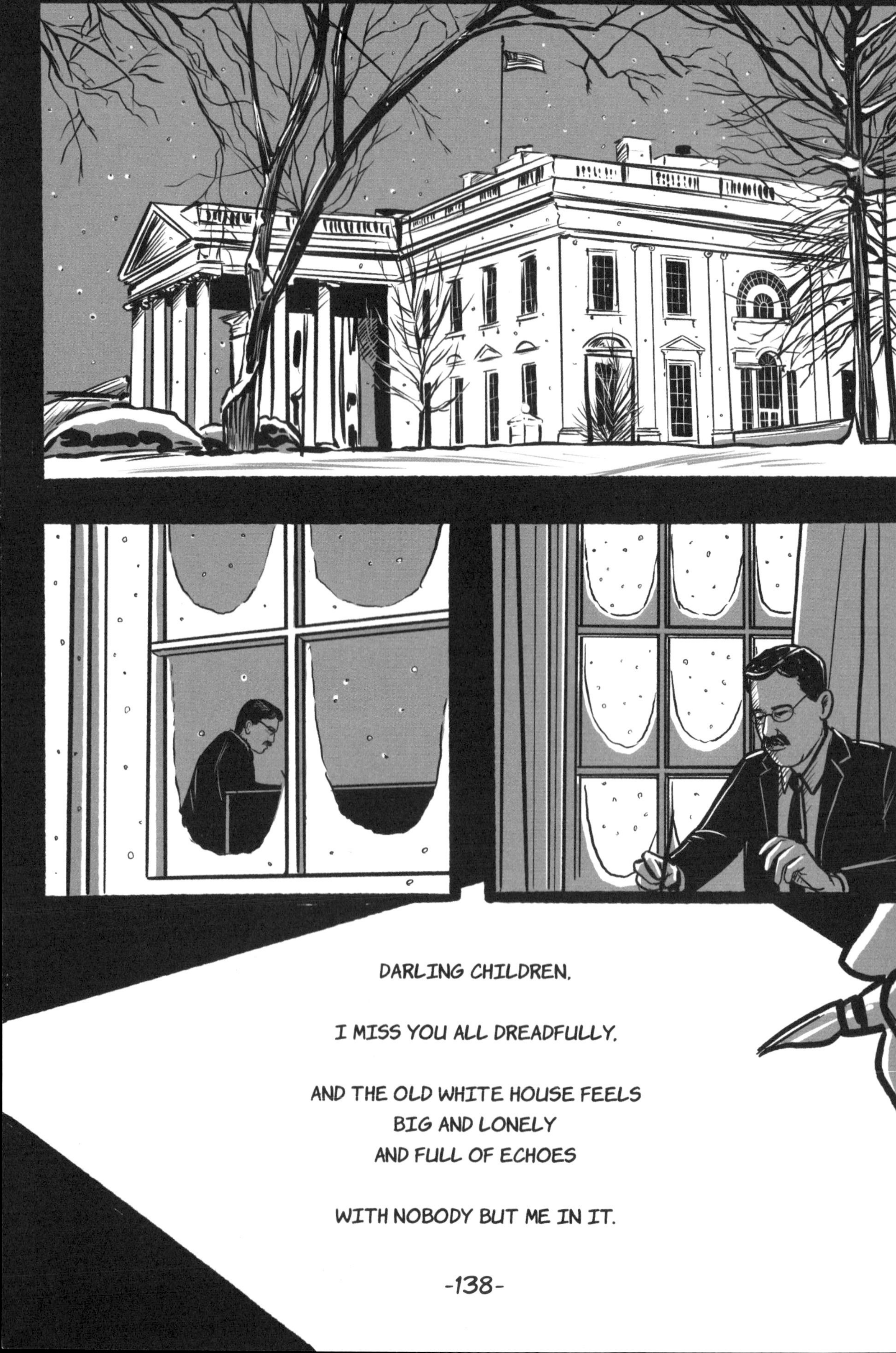
DARLING CHILDREN,
I MISS YOU ALL DREADFULLY,
AND THE OLD WHITE HOUSE FEELS BIG AND LONELY AND FULL OF ECHOES
WITH NOBODY BUT ME IN IT.

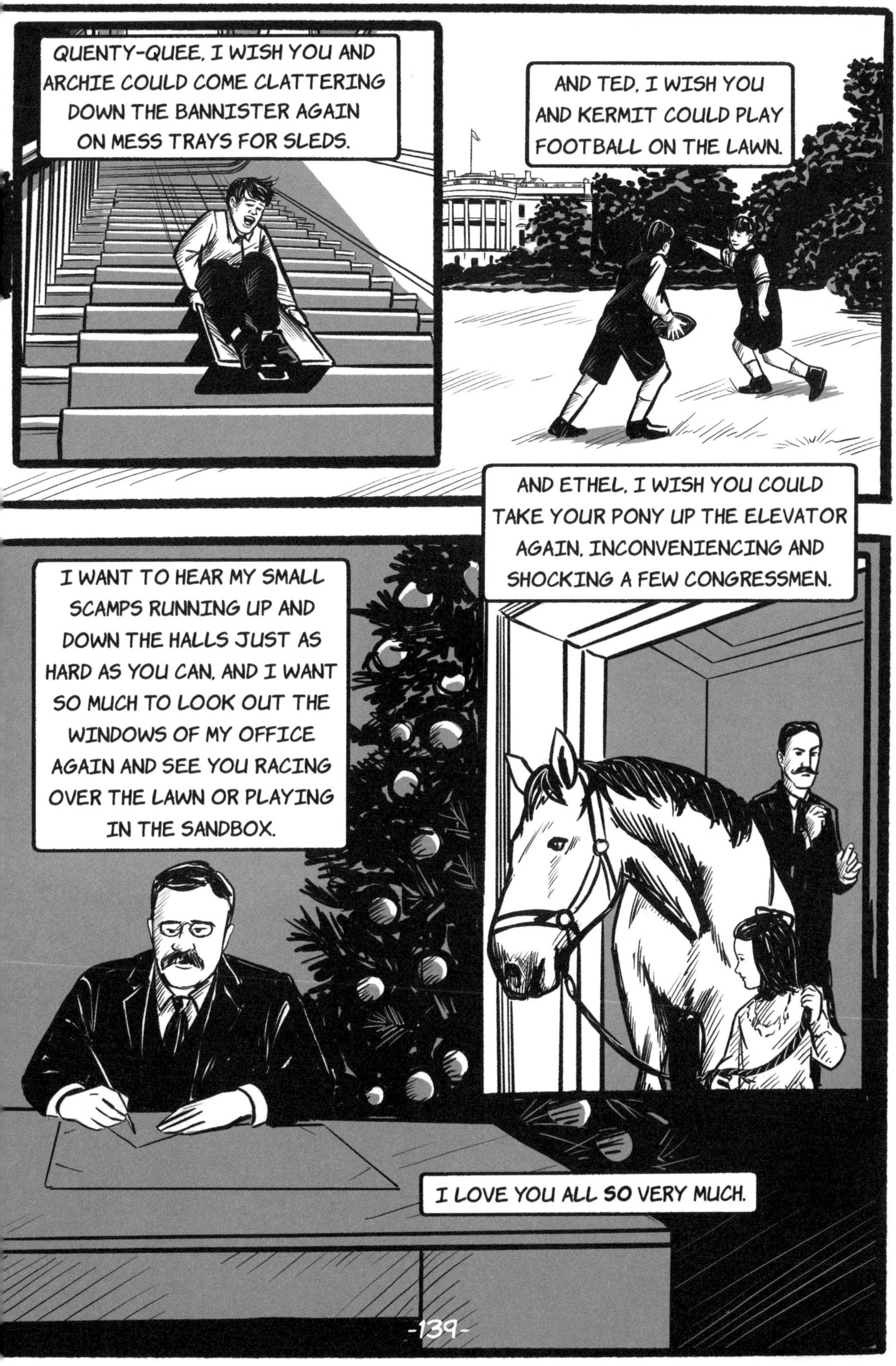
QUENTY-QUEE, I WISH YOU AND ARCHIE COULD COME CLATTERING DOWN THE BANNISTER AGAIN ON MESS TRAYS FOR SLEDS.
AND TED, I WISH YOU AND KERMIT COULD PLAY FOOTBALL ON THE LAWN.
AND ETHEL, I WISH YOU COULD TAKE YOUR PONY UP THE ELEVATOR AGAIN, INCONVENIENCING AND SHOCKING A FEW CONGRESSMEN.
I WANT TO HEAR MY SMALL SCAMPS RUNNING UP AND DOWN THE HALLS JUST AS HARD AS YOU CAN, AND I WANT SO MUCH TO LOOK OUT THE WINDOWS OF MY OFFICE AGAIN AND SEE YOU RACING OVER THE LAWN OR PLAYING IN THE SANDBOX.
I LOVE YOU ALL SO VERY MUCH.

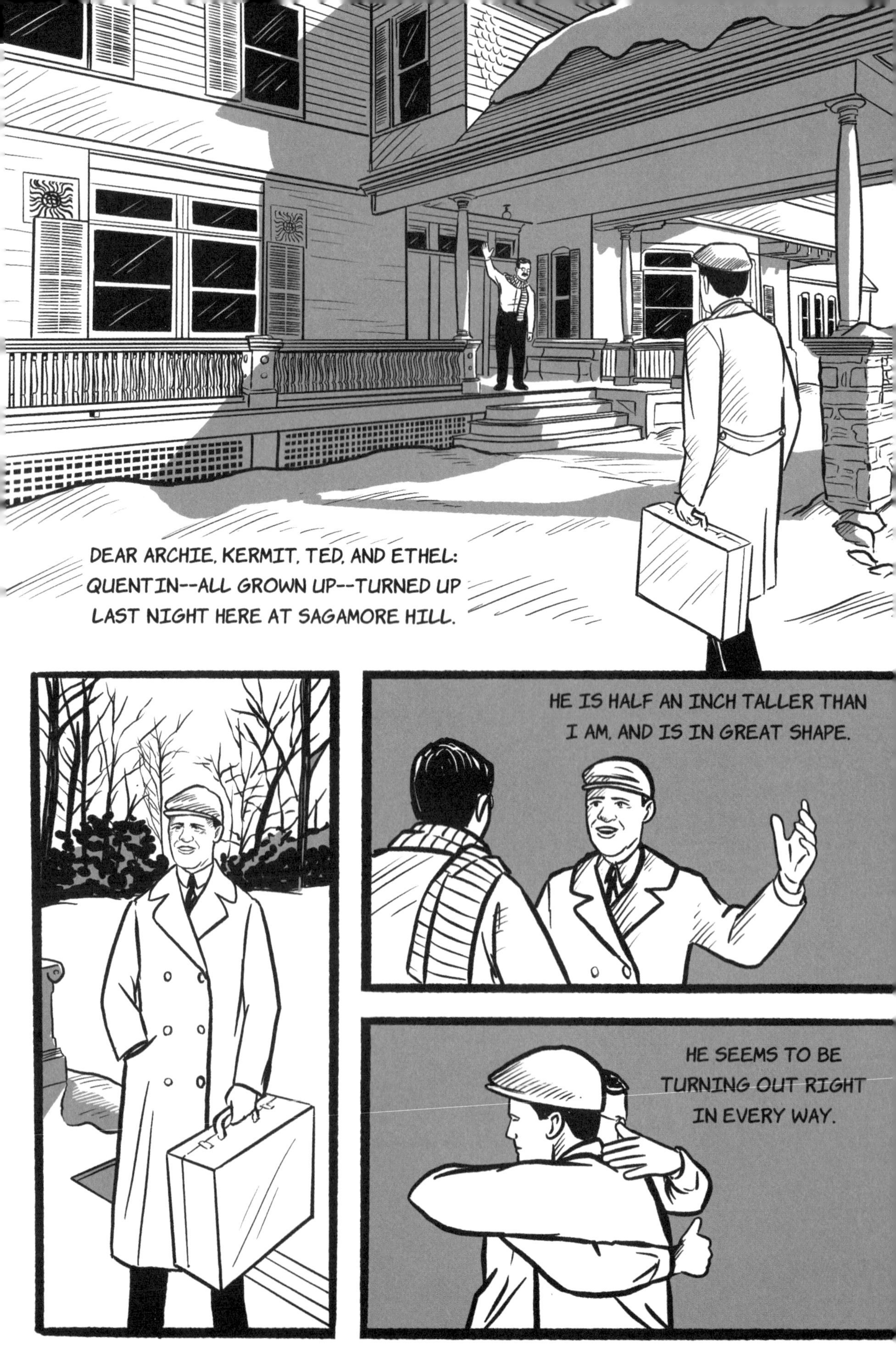
DEAR ARCHIE, KERMIT, TED, AND ETHEL: QUENTIN--ALL GROWN UP--TURNED UP LAST NIGHT HERE AT SAGAMORE HILL.
HE IS HALF AN INCH TALLER THAN I AM, AND IS IN GREAT SHAPE.
HE SEEMS TO BE TURNING OUT RIGHT IN EVERY WAY.

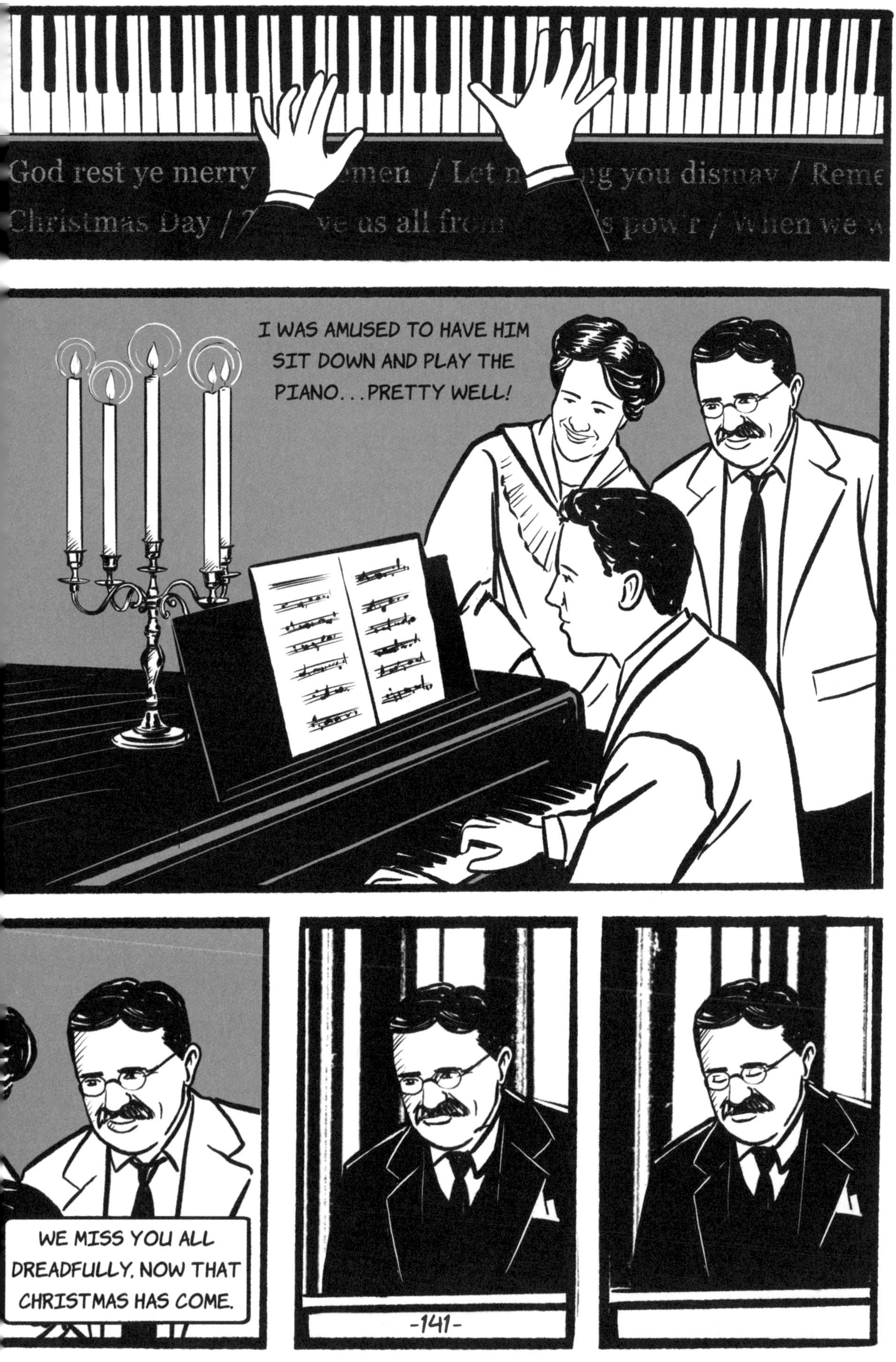
God rest ye merry emen / Let n ng you dismay / Reme
Christmas Day / ve us all from s pow'r / When we w
I WAS AMUSED TO HAVE HIM SIT DOWN AND PLAY THE PIANO. . .PRETTY WELL!
WE MISS YOU ALL DREADFULLY, NOW THAT CHRISTMAS HAS COME.

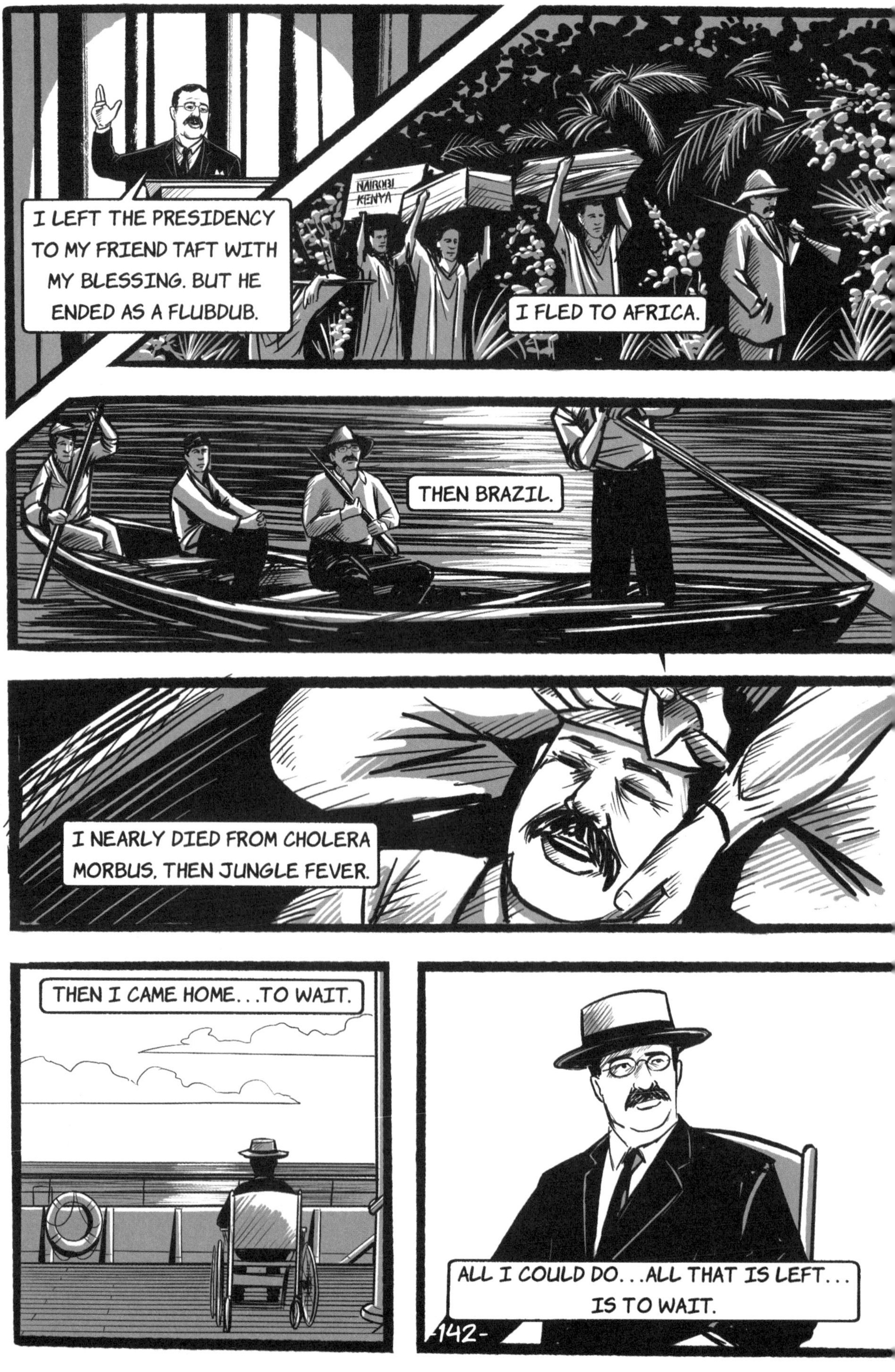
I LEFT THE PRESIDENCY TO MY FRIEND TAFT WITH MY BLESSING. BUT HE ENDED AS A FLUBDUB.
NAIROBI KENYA
I FLED TO AFRICA.
THEN BRAZIL.
I NEARLY DIED FROM CHOLERA MORBUS. THEN JUNGLE FEVER.
THEN I CAME HOME...TO WAIT.
ALL I COULD DO...ALL THAT IS LEFT... IS TO WAIT.

I RAN FOR PRESIDENT AGAIN, AND FAILED.

GOT SHOT BY AN ANARCHIST IN THE PROCESS.

TOOK A BULLET IN MY CHEST. "OLD FOUR-EYES" SAVED MY LIFE.

AND THIS. WORDS! WORDS MATTER!

GAVE MY SPEECH ANYWAY AND THEN I WENT TO THE HOSPITAL.

SO LET ME FINISH WHAT I'VE COME HERE TO SAY TONIGHT.

FRIENDS, I SHALL ASK YOU TO BE AS QUIET AS POSSIBLE. I DON'T KNOW WHETHER YOU FULLY UNDERSTAND THAT I HAVE JUST BEEN SHOT; BUT IT TAKES MORE THAN THAT TO KILL A BULL. FORTUNATELY I HAD MY YOU SEE I WAS GOING LONG SPEECH, AND THERE IS A BULLET—THERE IS WHERE THE BULLET WENT THROUGH—AND IT PROBABLY SAVED ME FROM IT GOING INTO MY HEART. THE BULLET IS IN ME NOW, SO THAT I CAN NOT MAKE A VERY LONG SPEECH, BUT I WILL TRY MY BEST.

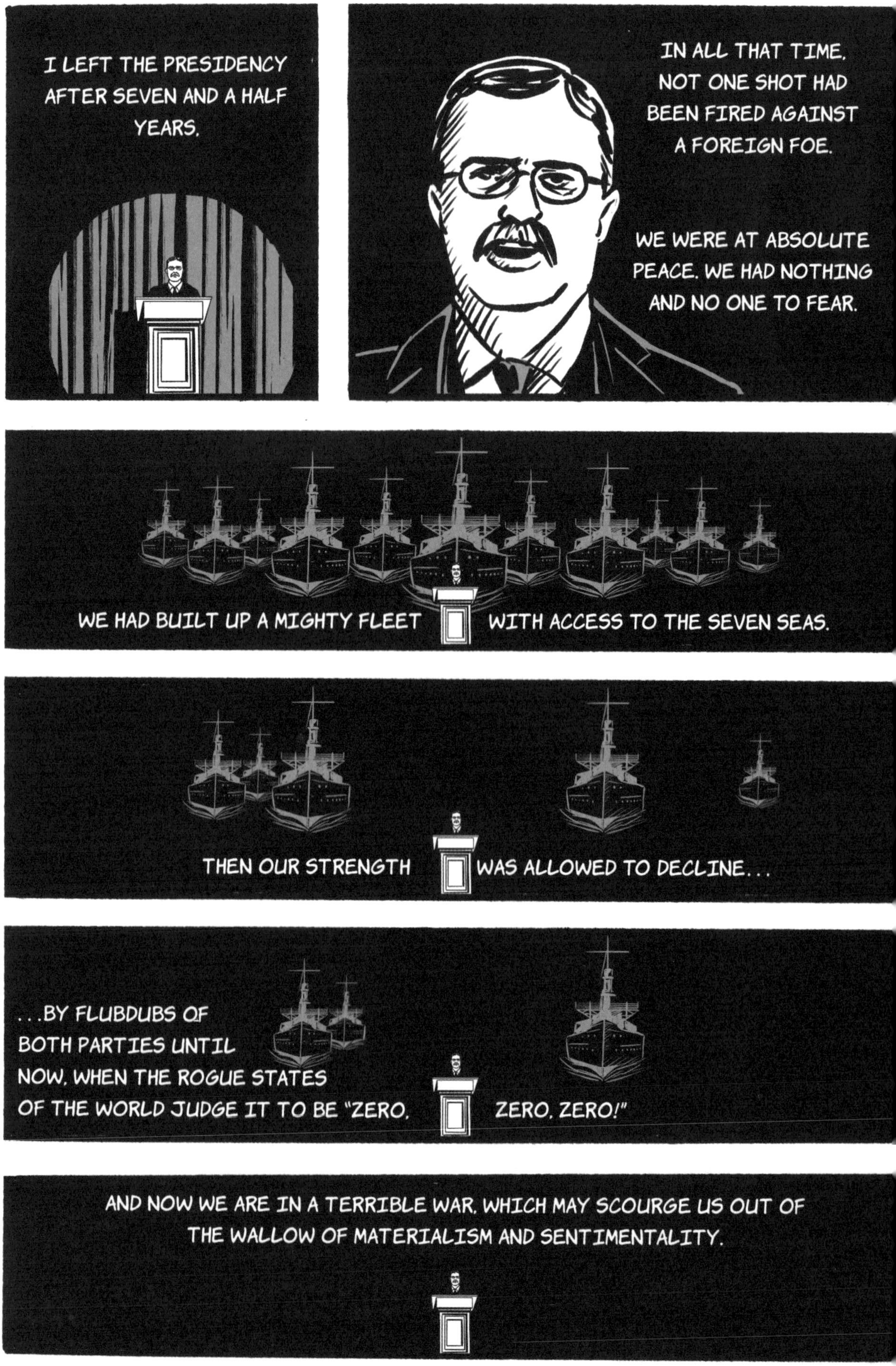
I LEFT THE PRESIDENCY AFTER SEVEN AND A HALF YEARS.
IN ALL THAT TIME, NOT ONE SHOT HAD BEEN FIRED AGAINST A FOREIGN FOE.
WE WERE AT ABSOLUTE PEACE. WE HAD NOTHING AND NO ONE TO FEAR.
WE HAD BUILT UP A MIGHTY FLEET
WITH ACCESS TO THE SEVEN SEAS.
THEN OUR STRENGTH
WAS ALLOWED TO DECLINE...
...BY FLUBDUBS OF BOTH PARTIES UNTIL NOW, WHEN THE ROGUE STATES OF THE WORLD JUDGE IT TO BE "ZERO,
ZERO, ZERO!"
AND NOW WE ARE IN A TERRIBLE WAR, WHICH MAY SCOURGE US OUT OF THE WALLOW OF MATERIALISM AND SENTIMENTALITY.

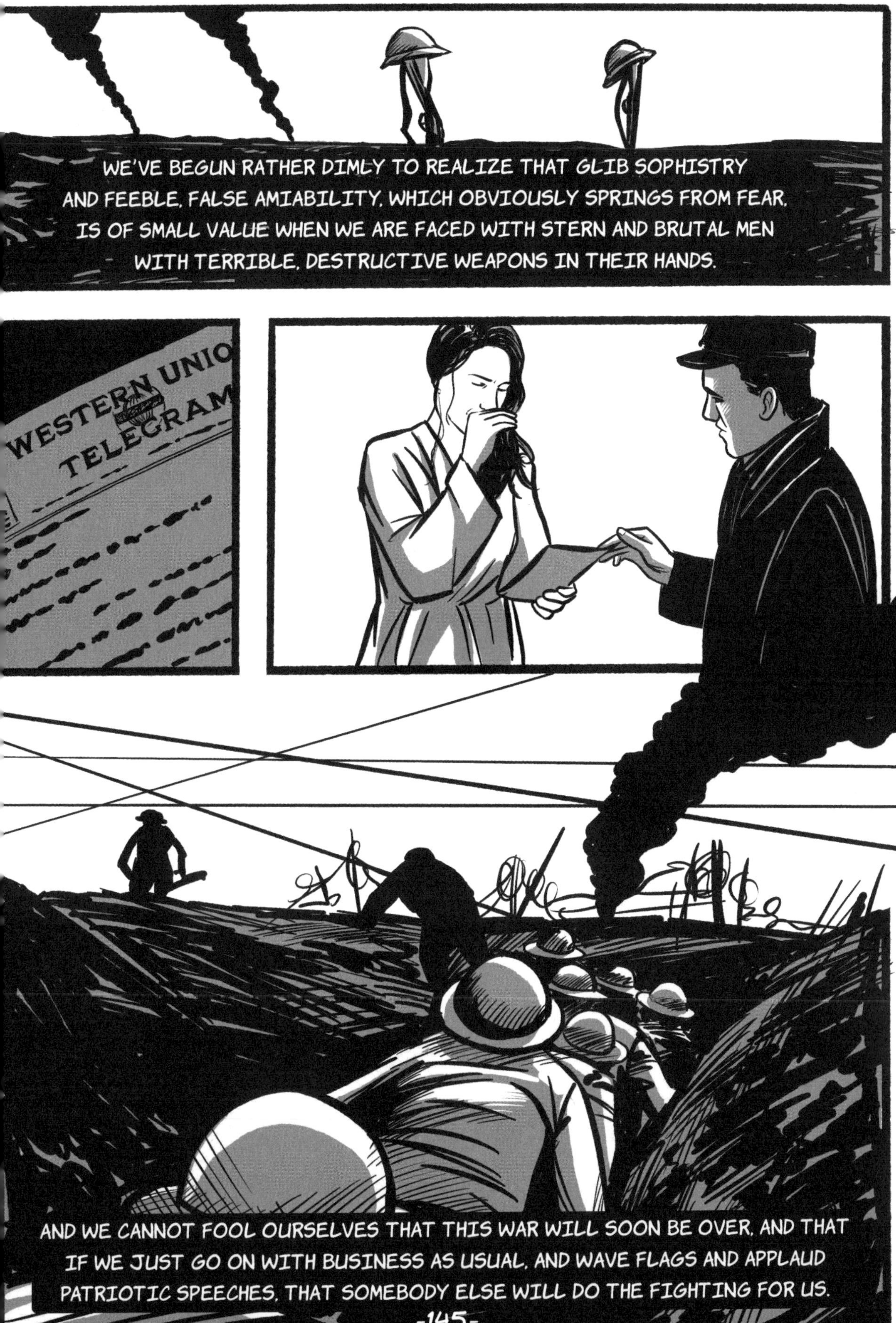
WE'VE BEGUN RATHER DIMLY TO REALIZE THAT GLIB SOPHISTRY AND FEEBLE, FALSE AMIABILITY, WHICH OBVIOUSLY SPRINGS FROM FEAR, IS OF SMALL VALUE WHEN WE ARE FACED WITH STERN AND BRUTAL MEN WITH TERRIBLE, DESTRUCTIVE WEAPONS IN THEIR HANDS.
WESTERN UNIO
TELEGRAM
AND WE CANNOT FOOL OURSELVES THAT THIS WAR WILL SOON BE OVER, AND THAT IF WE JUST GO ON WITH BUSINESS AS USUAL, AND WAVE FLAGS AND APPLAUD PATRIOTIC SPEECHES, THAT SOMEBODY ELSE WILL DO THE FIGHTING FOR US.

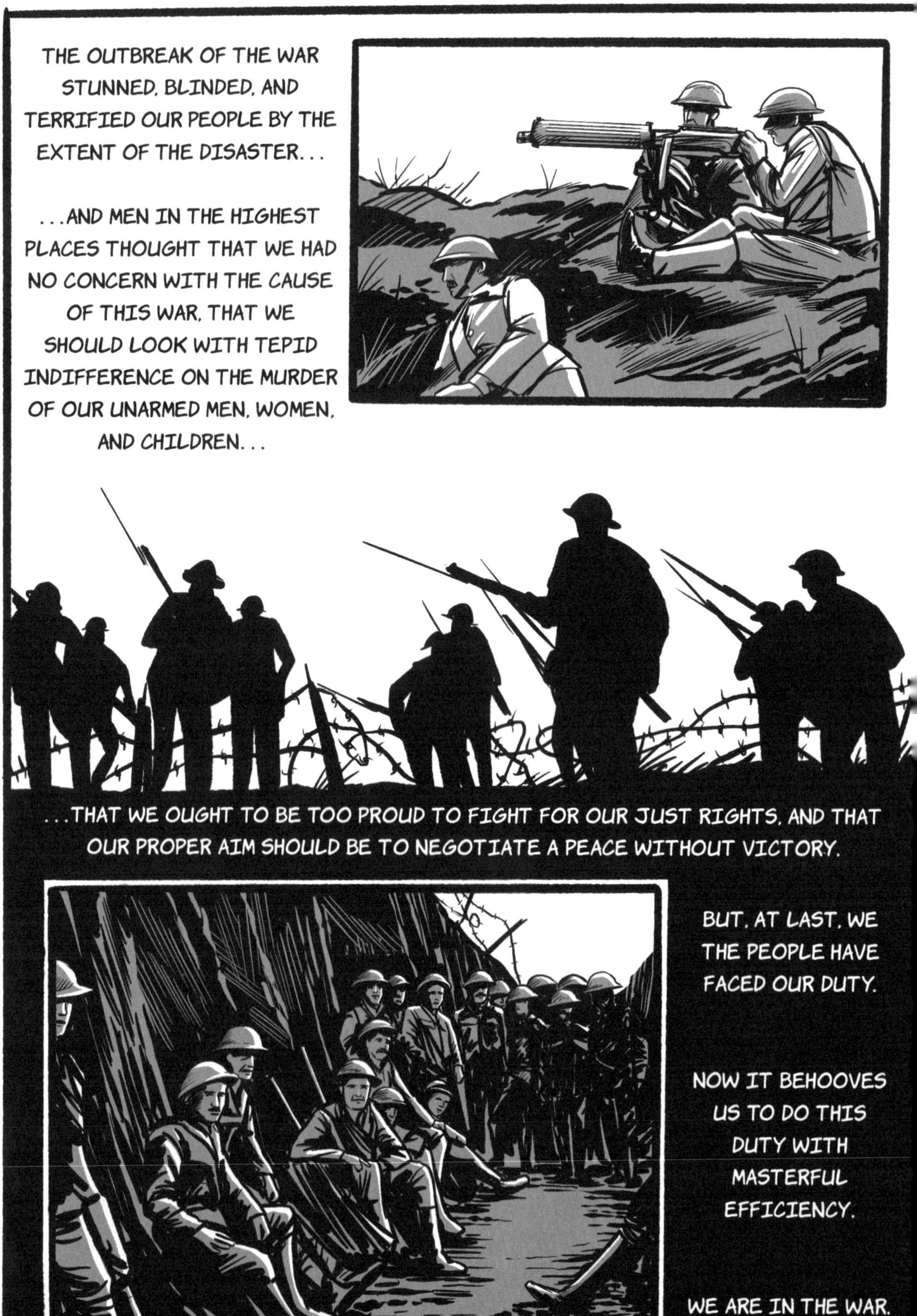
THE OUTBREAK OF THE WAR STUNNED, BLINDED, AND TERRIFIED OUR PEOPLE BY THE EXTENT OF THE DISASTER...
...AND MEN IN THE HIGHEST PLACES THOUGHT THAT WE HAD NO CONCERN WITH THE CAUSE OF THIS WAR, THAT WE SHOULD LOOK WITH TEPID INDIFFERENCE ON THE MURDER OF OUR UNARMED MEN, WOMEN, AND CHILDREN...
...THAT WE OUGHT TO BE TOO PROUD TO FIGHT FOR OUR JUST RIGHTS, AND THAT OUR PROPER AIM SHOULD BE TO NEGOTIATE A PEACE WITHOUT VICTORY.
BUT, AT LAST, WE THE PEOPLE HAVE FACED OUR DUTY.
NOW IT BEHOOVES US TO DO THIS DUTY WITH MASTERFUL EFFICIENCY.
WE ARE IN THE WAR.

WE HAVE SENT OUR HUSBANDS, BROTHERS, AND SONS OVERSEAS TO SPILL THEIR BLOOD LIKE WATER UNDER THE FLAG.

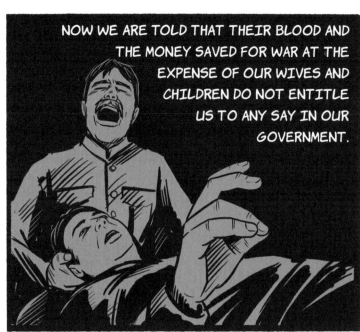

NOW WE ARE TOLD THAT THEIR BLOOD AND THE MONEY SAVED FOR WAR AT THE EXPENSE OF OUR WIVES AND CHILDREN DO NOT ENTITLE US TO ANY SAY IN OUR GOVERNMENT.

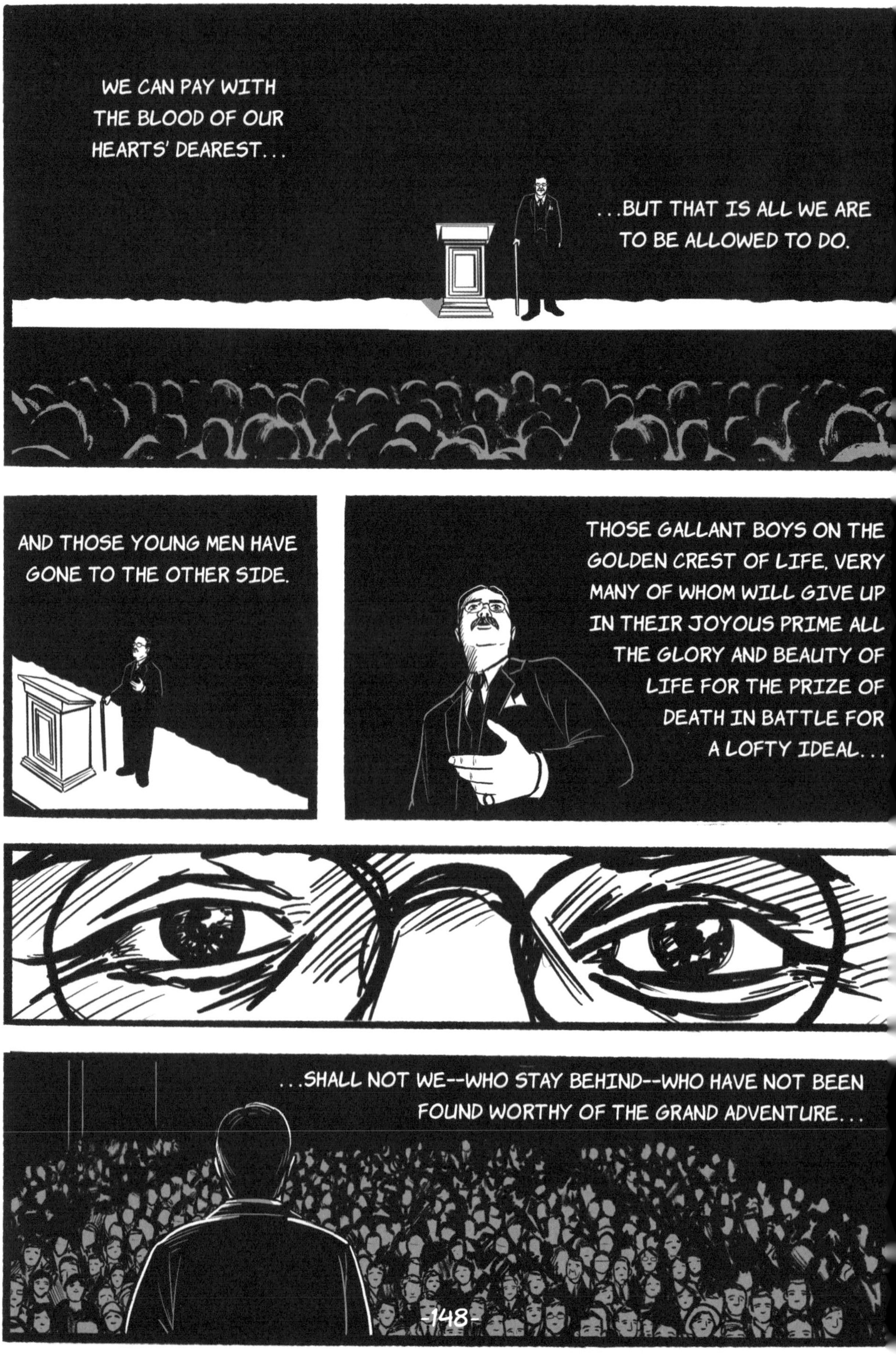
WE CAN PAY WITH THE BLOOD OF OUR HEARTS' DEAREST...
...BUT THAT IS ALL WE ARE TO BE ALLOWED TO DO.
AND THOSE YOUNG MEN HAVE GONE TO THE OTHER SIDE.
THOSE GALLANT BOYS ON THE GOLDEN CREST OF LIFE, VERY MANY OF WHOM WILL GIVE UP IN THEIR JOYOUS PRIME ALL THE GLORY AND BEAUTY OF LIFE FOR THE PRIZE OF DEATH IN BATTLE FOR A LOFTY IDEAL...
...SHALL NOT WE--WHO STAY BEHIND--WHO HAVE NOT BEEN FOUND WORTHY OF THE GRAND ADVENTURE...

...SHALL NOT WE MAKE CERTAIN THAT WHEN THOSE WHO LIVE COME HOME, THEY SHALL COME HOME TO A NATION THAT FOR THEM, FOR THE WOMEN WHO SENT THEM INTO BATTLE...

...AND FOR THE CHILDREN WHO ARE TO COME AFTER THEM, WILL BE A NATION THEY CAN BE PROUD TO HAVE FOUGHT FOR, OR TO HAVE DIED FOR?

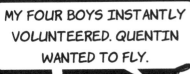

MY FOUR BOYS INSTANTLY VOLUNTEERED. QUENTIN WANTED TO FLY.

AT FIRST THEY WOULDN'T TAKE HIM BECAUSE HIS EYES ARE ...LIKE MINE...WEAK.

BUT HE GOT IN.

THEN HE SAID TO HIS BROTHERS, "I SUPPOSE WE MUST NOW PRACTICE WHAT FATHER PREACHES."

WHAT SHALL I SAY TO YOU, MY DEAR QUINIKENS?

ARE WE OLD MEN, WHOSE LIVES ARE BEHIND US, WRONG TO MAKE WAR THROUGH OUR DEAR CHILDREN?

I WOULD GLADLY GIVE MY LIFE.

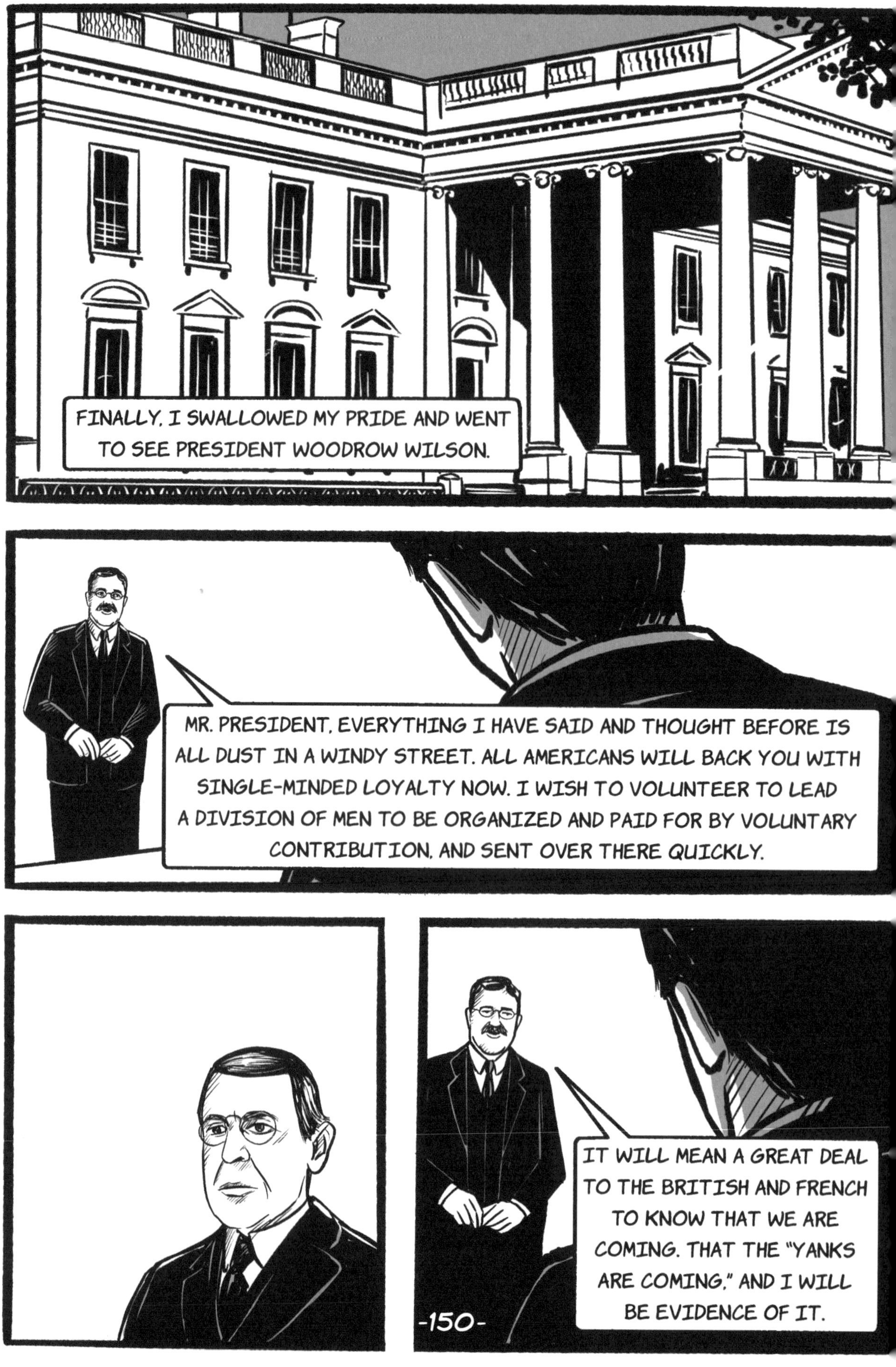
FINALLY, I SWALLOWED MY PRIDE AND WENT TO SEE PRESIDENT WOODROW WILSON.
MR. PRESIDENT, EVERYTHING I HAVE SAID AND THOUGHT BEFORE IS ALL DUST IN A WINDY STREET. ALL AMERICANS WILL BACK YOU WITH SINGLE-MINDED LOYALTY NOW. I WISH TO VOLUNTEER TO LEAD A DIVISION OF MEN TO BE ORGANIZED AND PAID FOR BY VOLUNTARY CONTRIBUTION, AND SENT OVER THERE QUICKLY.
IT WILL MEAN A GREAT DEAL TO THE BRITISH AND FRENCH TO KNOW THAT WE ARE COMING. THAT THE "YANKS ARE COMING," AND I WILL BE EVIDENCE OF IT.

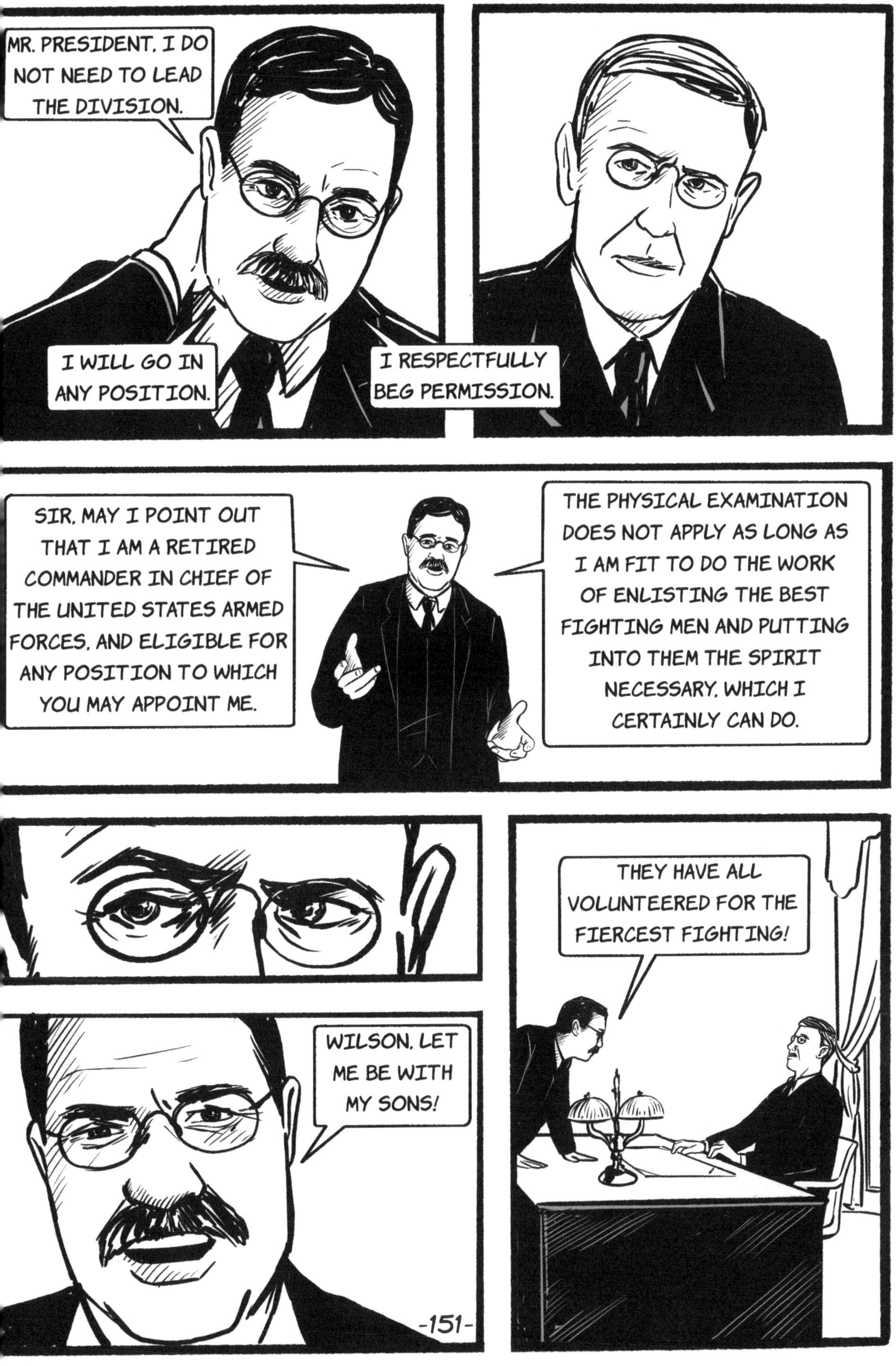
MR. PRESIDENT, I DO NOT NEED TO LEAD THE DIVISION.
I WILL GO IN ANY POSITION.
I RESPECTFULLY BEG PERMISSION.
SIR, MAY I POINT OUT THAT I AM A RETIRED COMMANDER IN CHIEF OF THE UNITED STATES ARMED FORCES, AND ELIGIBLE FOR ANY POSITION TO WHICH YOU MAY APPOINT ME.
THE PHYSICAL EXAMINATION DOES NOT APPLY AS LONG AS I AM FIT TO DO THE WORK OF ENLISTING THE BEST FIGHTING MEN AND PUTTING INTO THEM THE SPIRIT NECESSARY, WHICH I CERTAINLY CAN DO.
WILSON, LET ME BE WITH MY SONS!
THEY HAVE ALL VOLUNTEERED FOR THE FIERCEST FIGHTING!

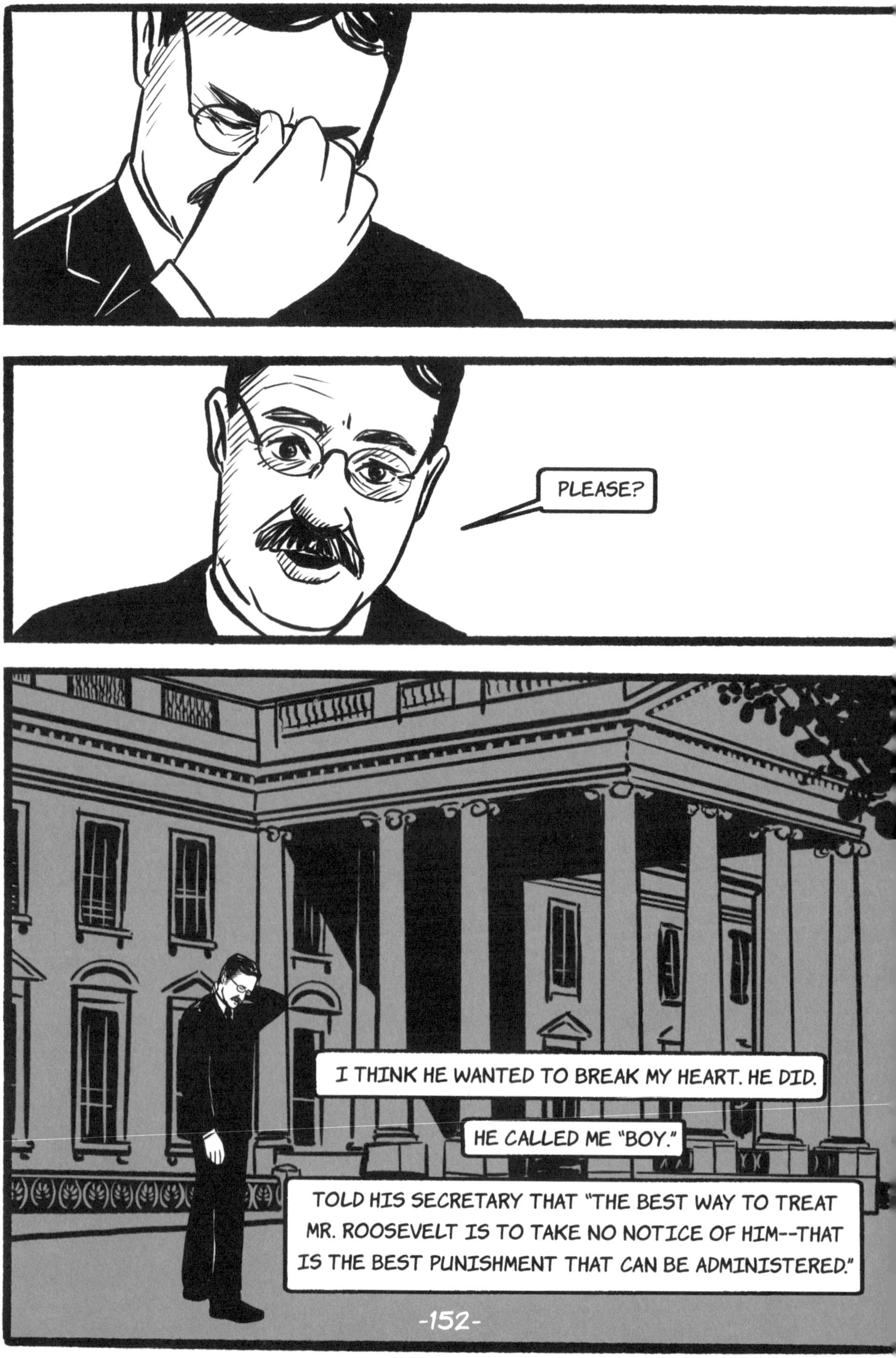
PLEASE?
I THINK HE WANTED TO BREAK MY HEART. HE DID.
HE CALLED ME "BOY."
TOLD HIS SECRETARY THAT "THE BEST WAY TO TREAT MR. ROOSEVELT IS TO TAKE NO NOTICE OF HIM--THAT IS THE BEST PUNISHMENT THAT CAN BE ADMINISTERED."

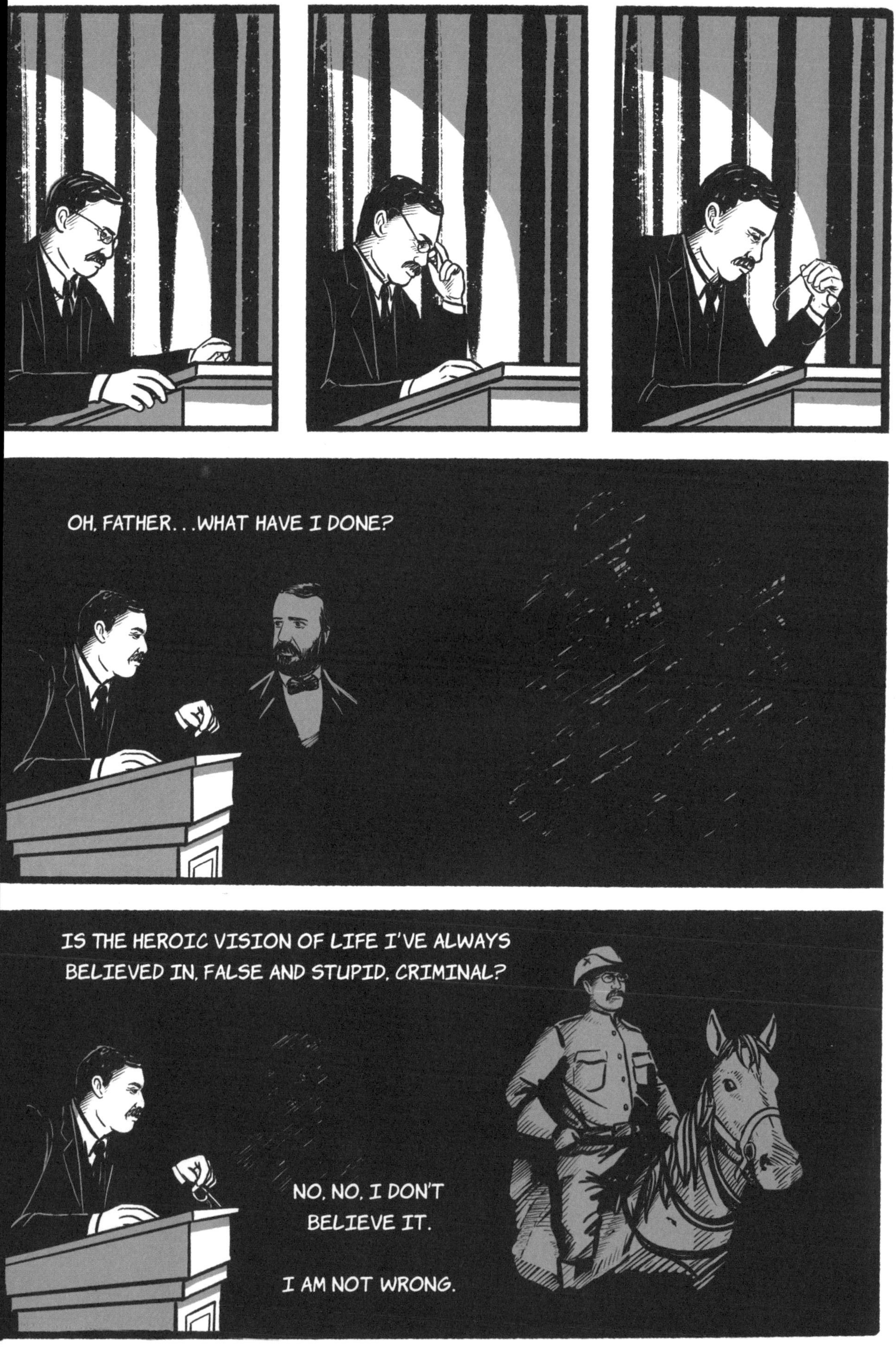
OH, FATHER. . .WHAT HAVE I DONE?
IS THE HEROIC VISION OF LIFE I'VE ALWAYS BELIEVED IN, FALSE AND STUPID, CRIMINAL?
NO, NO, I DON'T BELIEVE IT.
I AM NOT WRONG.

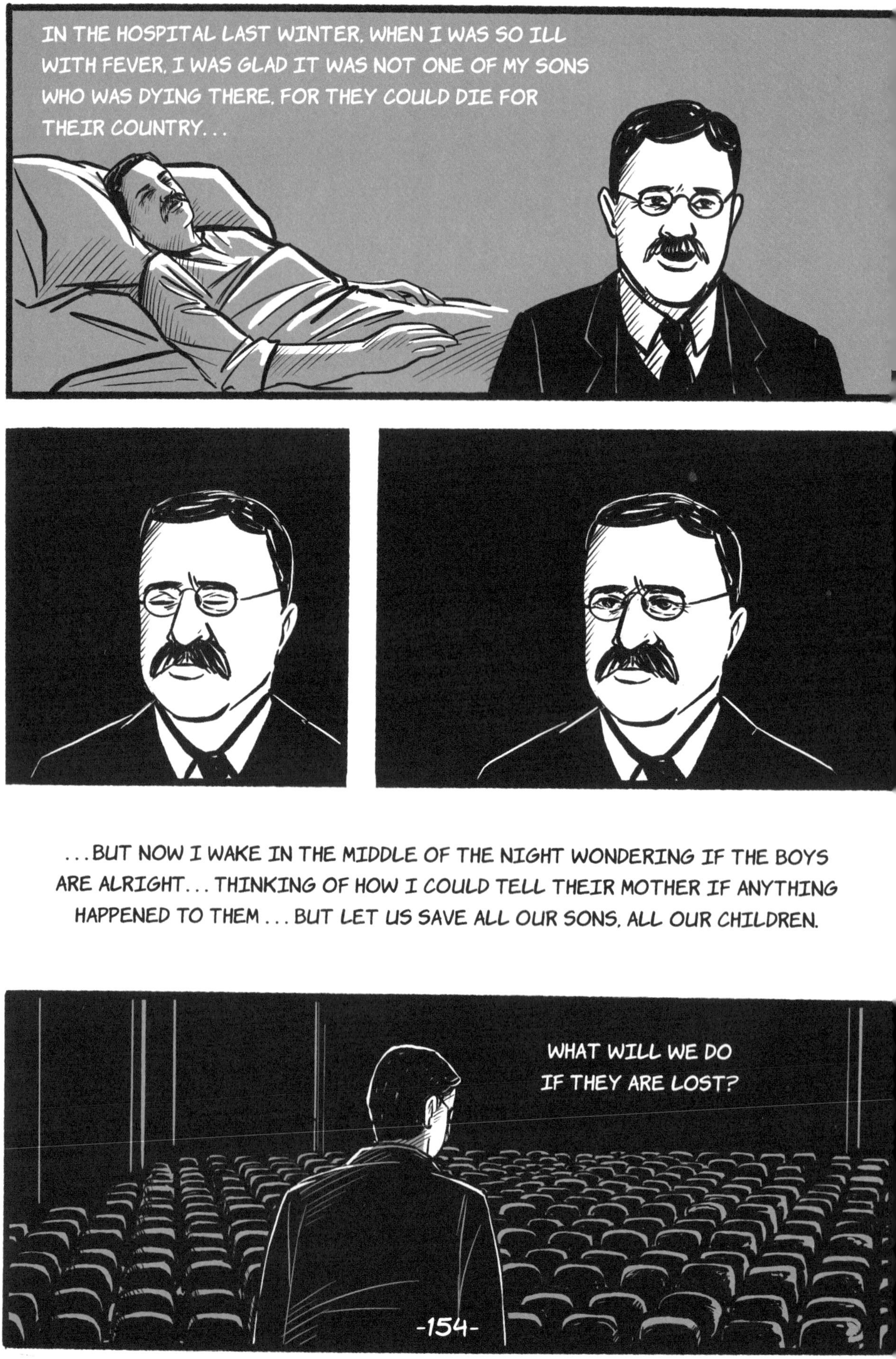
IN THE HOSPITAL LAST WINTER, WHEN I WAS SO ILL WITH FEVER, I WAS GLAD IT WAS NOT ONE OF MY SONS WHO WAS DYING THERE, FOR THEY COULD DIE FOR THEIR COUNTRY...
...BUT NOW I WAKE IN THE MIDDLE OF THE NIGHT WONDERING IF THE BOYS ARE ALRIGHT... THINKING OF HOW I COULD TELL THEIR MOTHER IF ANYTHING HAPPENED TO THEM ... BUT LET US SAVE ALL OUR SONS, ALL OUR CHILDREN.
WHAT WILL WE DO IF THEY ARE LOST?

TED...
WOUNDED AND GASSED...
THE DISTINGUISHED SERVICE CROSS AND THE SILVER STAR.

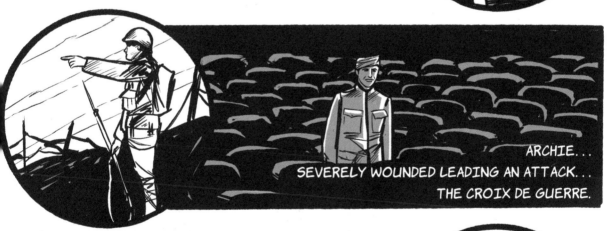

ARCHIE...
SEVERELY WOUNDED LEADING AN ATTACK...
THE CROIX DE GUERRE.

KERMIT...
IN THE MIDDLE EAST WITH THE BRITISH ARMY. FINALLY
GETTING INTO FRANCE, AND INTO THE THICK OF IT.

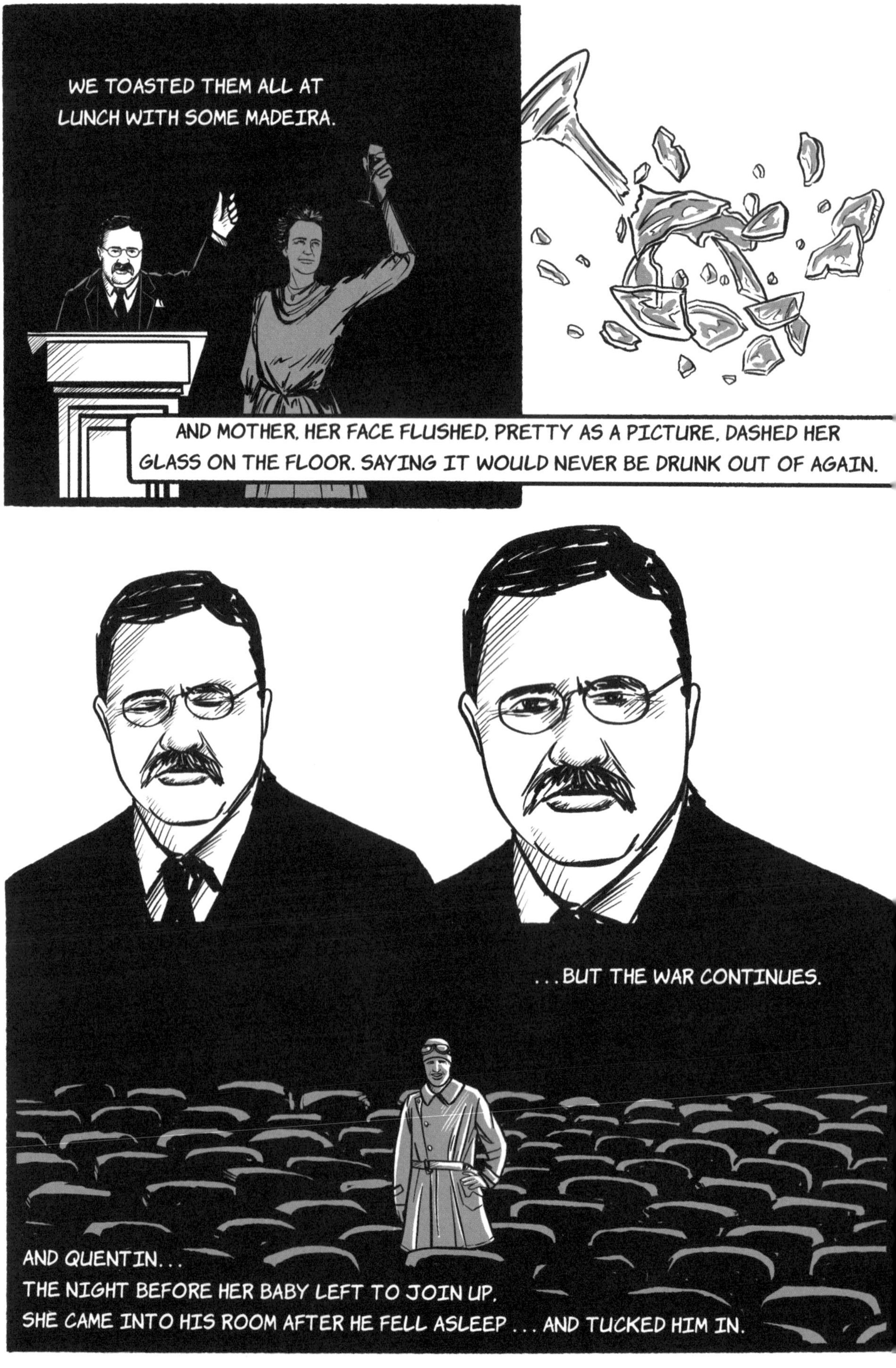
WE TOASTED THEM ALL AT LUNCH WITH SOME MADEIRA.
AND MOTHER, HER FACE FLUSHED, PRETTY AS A PICTURE, DASHED HER GLASS ON THE FLOOR, SAYING IT WOULD NEVER BE DRUNK OUT OF AGAIN.
. . . BUT THE WAR CONTINUES.
AND QUENTIN. . .
THE NIGHT BEFORE HER BABY LEFT TO JOIN UP,
SHE CAME INTO HIS ROOM AFTER HE FELL ASLEEP . . . AND TUCKED HIM IN.

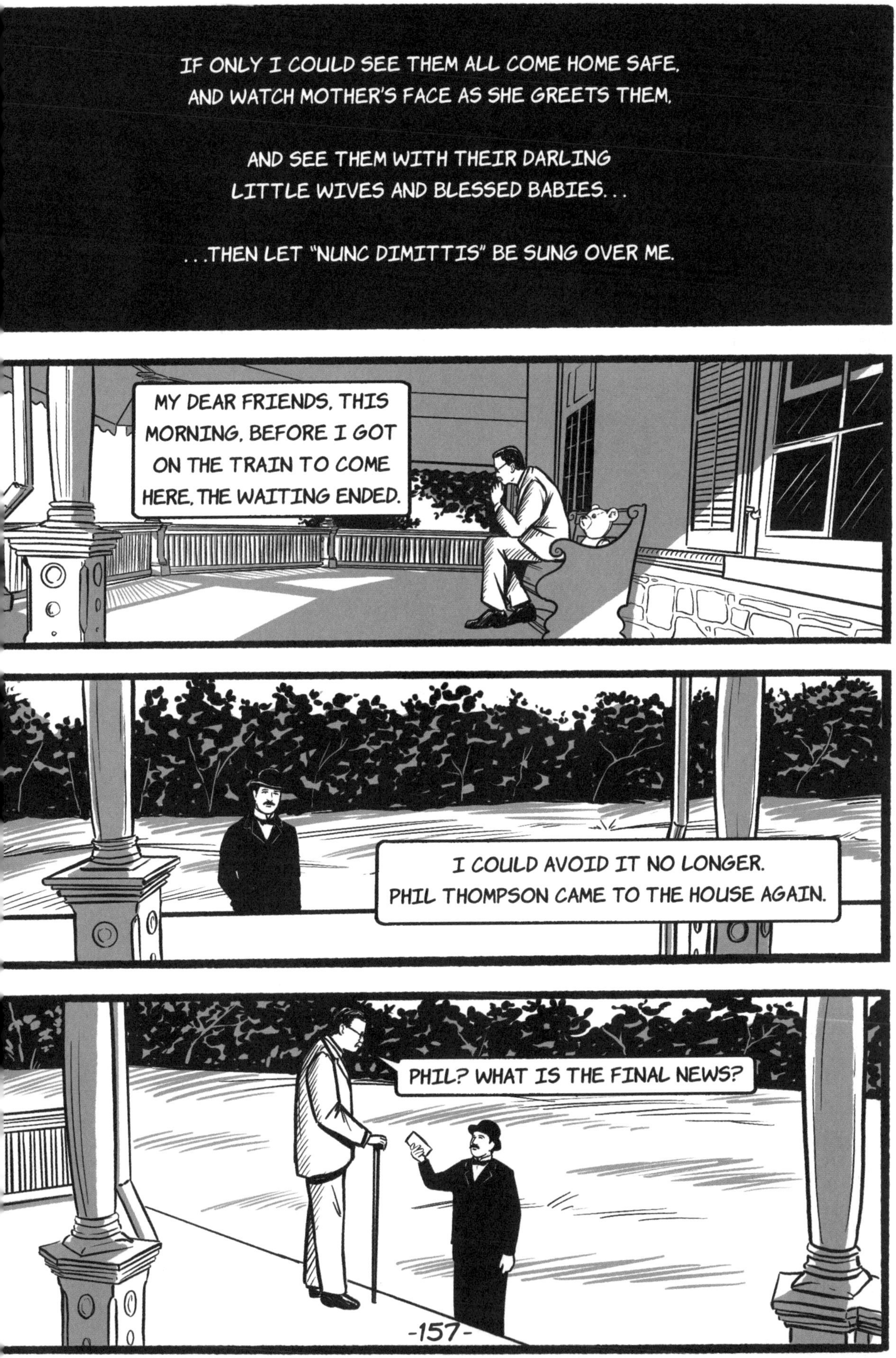
IF ONLY I COULD SEE THEM ALL COME HOME SAFE,
AND WATCH MOTHER'S FACE AS SHE GREETS THEM,
AND SEE THEM WITH THEIR DARLING
LITTLE WIVES AND BLESSED BABIES. . .
. . .THEN LET "NUNC DIMITTIS" BE SUNG OVER ME.
MY DEAR FRIENDS, THIS MORNING, BEFORE I GOT ON THE TRAIN TO COME HERE, THE WAITING ENDED.
I COULD AVOID IT NO LONGER.
PHIL THOMPSON CAME TO THE HOUSE AGAIN.
PHIL? WHAT IS THE FINAL NEWS?

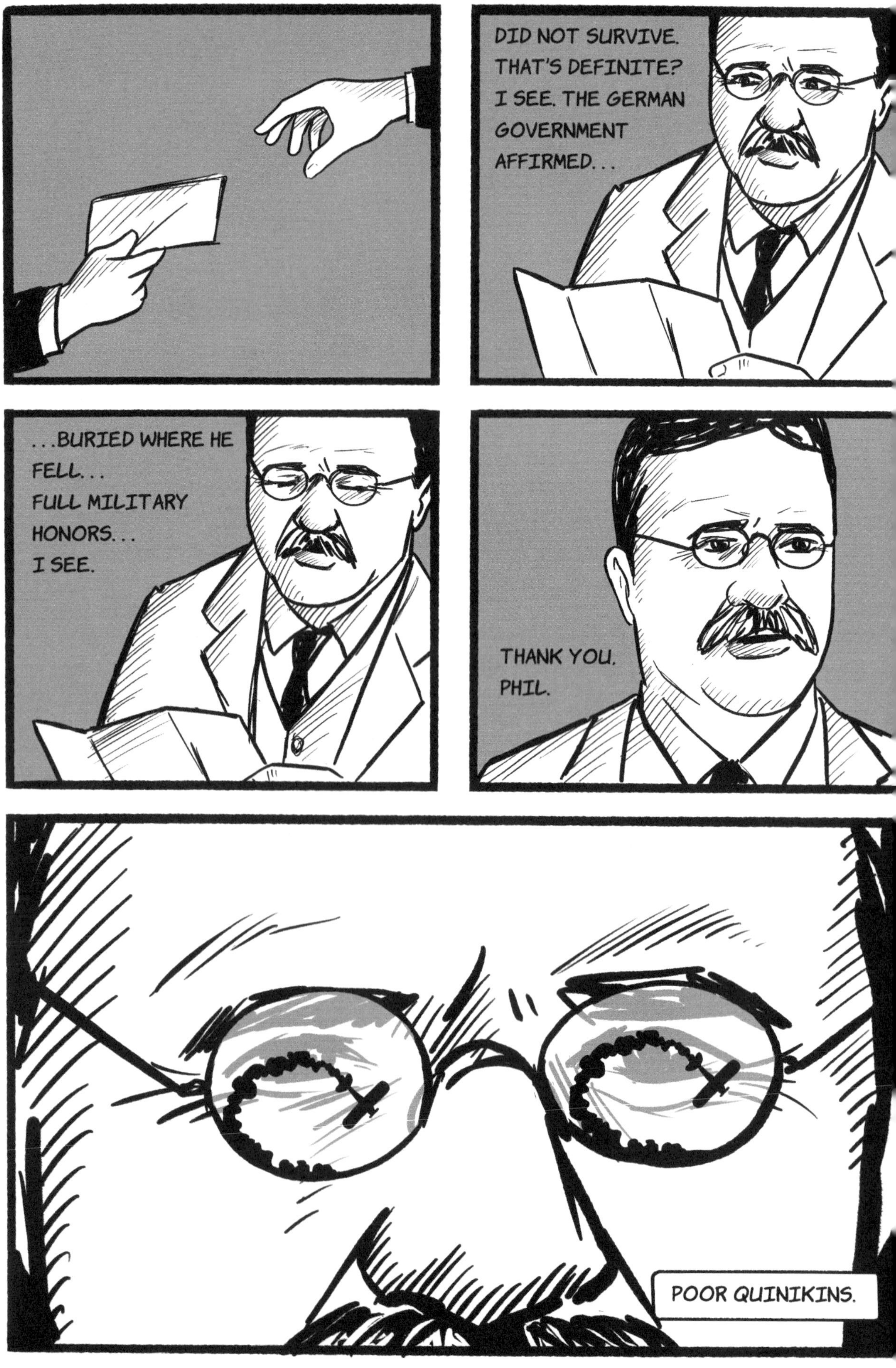
DID NOT SURVIVE. THAT'S DEFINITE? I SEE. THE GERMAN GOVERNMENT AFFIRMED. . .
. . .BURIED WHERE HE FELL. . .
FULL MILITARY HONORS. . .
I SEE.
THANK YOU, PHIL.
POOR QUINIKINS.

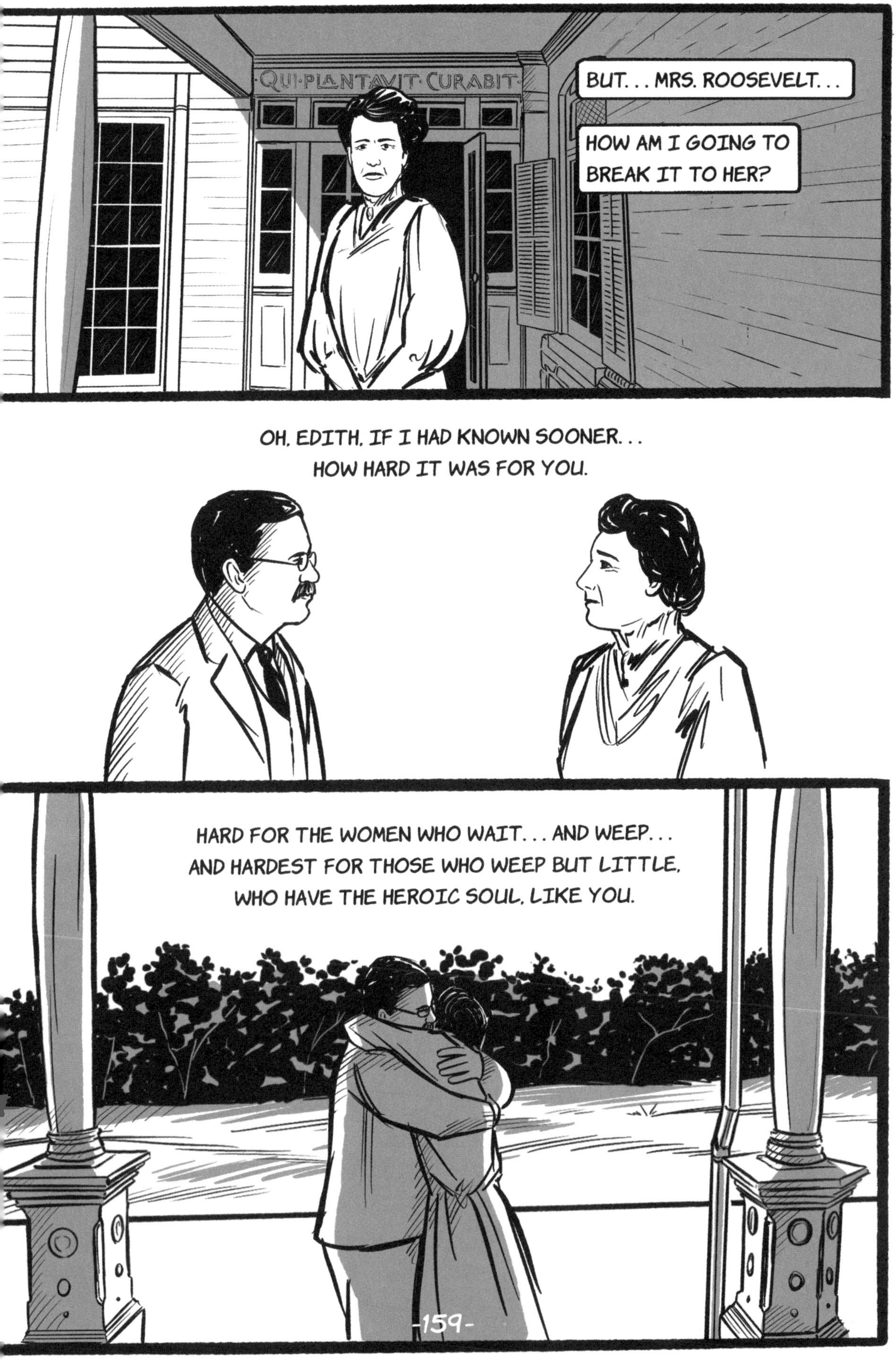
QUI·PLANTAVIT·CURABIT
BUT. . . MRS. ROOSEVELT. . .
HOW AM I GOING TO BREAK IT TO HER?
OH, EDITH, IF I HAD KNOWN SOONER. . . HOW HARD IT WAS FOR YOU.
HARD FOR THE WOMEN WHO WAIT. . . AND WEEP. . . AND HARDEST FOR THOSE WHO WEEP BUT LITTLE, WHO HAVE THE HEROIC SOUL, LIKE YOU.

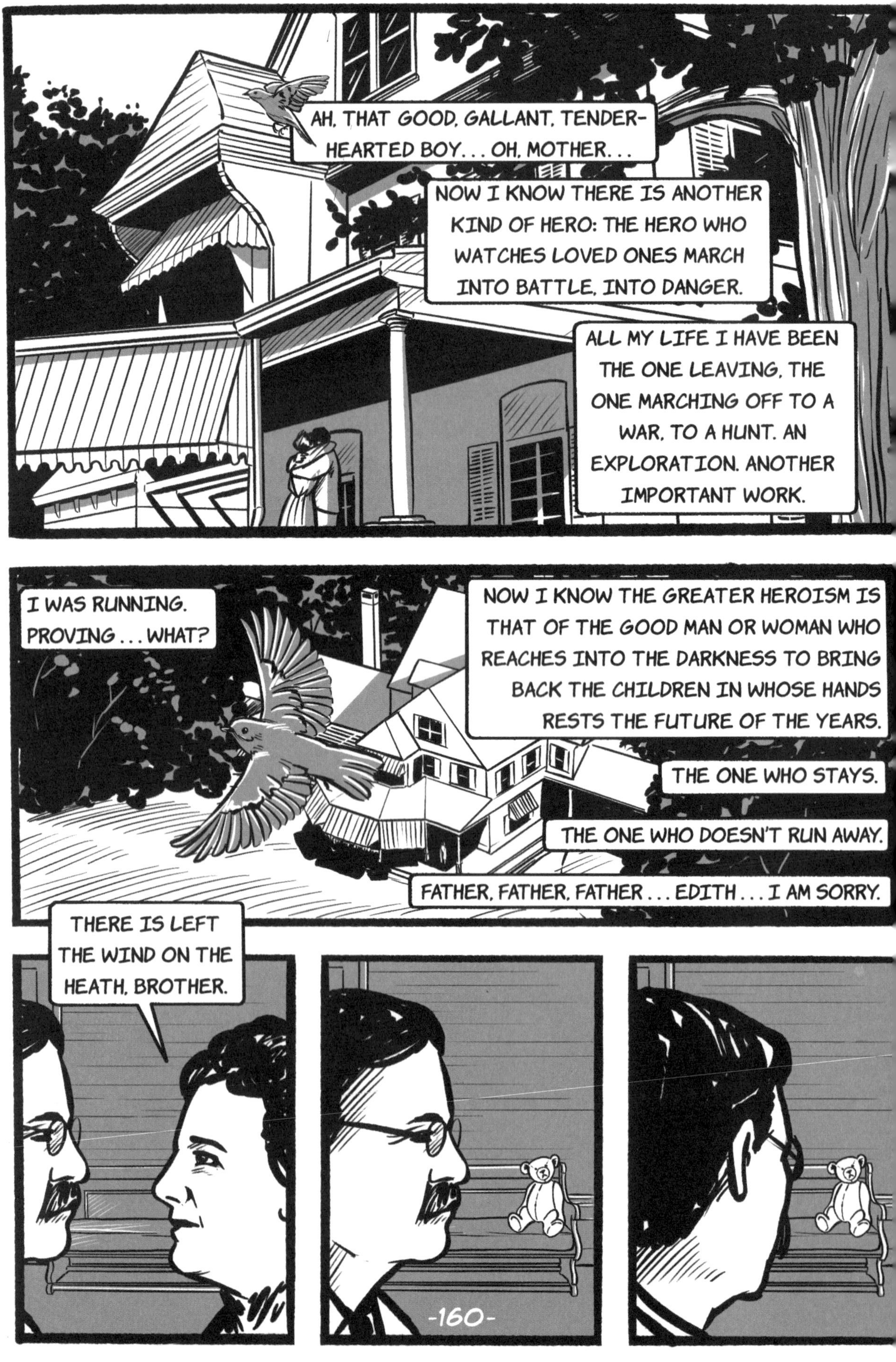
AH, THAT GOOD, GALLANT, TENDER-HEARTED BOY... OH, MOTHER...
NOW I KNOW THERE IS ANOTHER KIND OF HERO: THE HERO WHO WATCHES LOVED ONES MARCH INTO BATTLE, INTO DANGER.
ALL MY LIFE I HAVE BEEN THE ONE LEAVING, THE ONE MARCHING OFF TO A WAR, TO A HUNT. AN EXPLORATION. ANOTHER IMPORTANT WORK.
I WAS RUNNING. PROVING... WHAT?
NOW I KNOW THE GREATER HEROISM IS THAT OF THE GOOD MAN OR WOMAN WHO REACHES INTO THE DARKNESS TO BRING BACK THE CHILDREN IN WHOSE HANDS RESTS THE FUTURE OF THE YEARS.
THE ONE WHO STAYS.
THE ONE WHO DOESN'T RUN AWAY.
FATHER, FATHER, FATHER... EDITH... I AM SORRY.
THERE IS LEFT THE WIND ON THE HEATH, BROTHER.

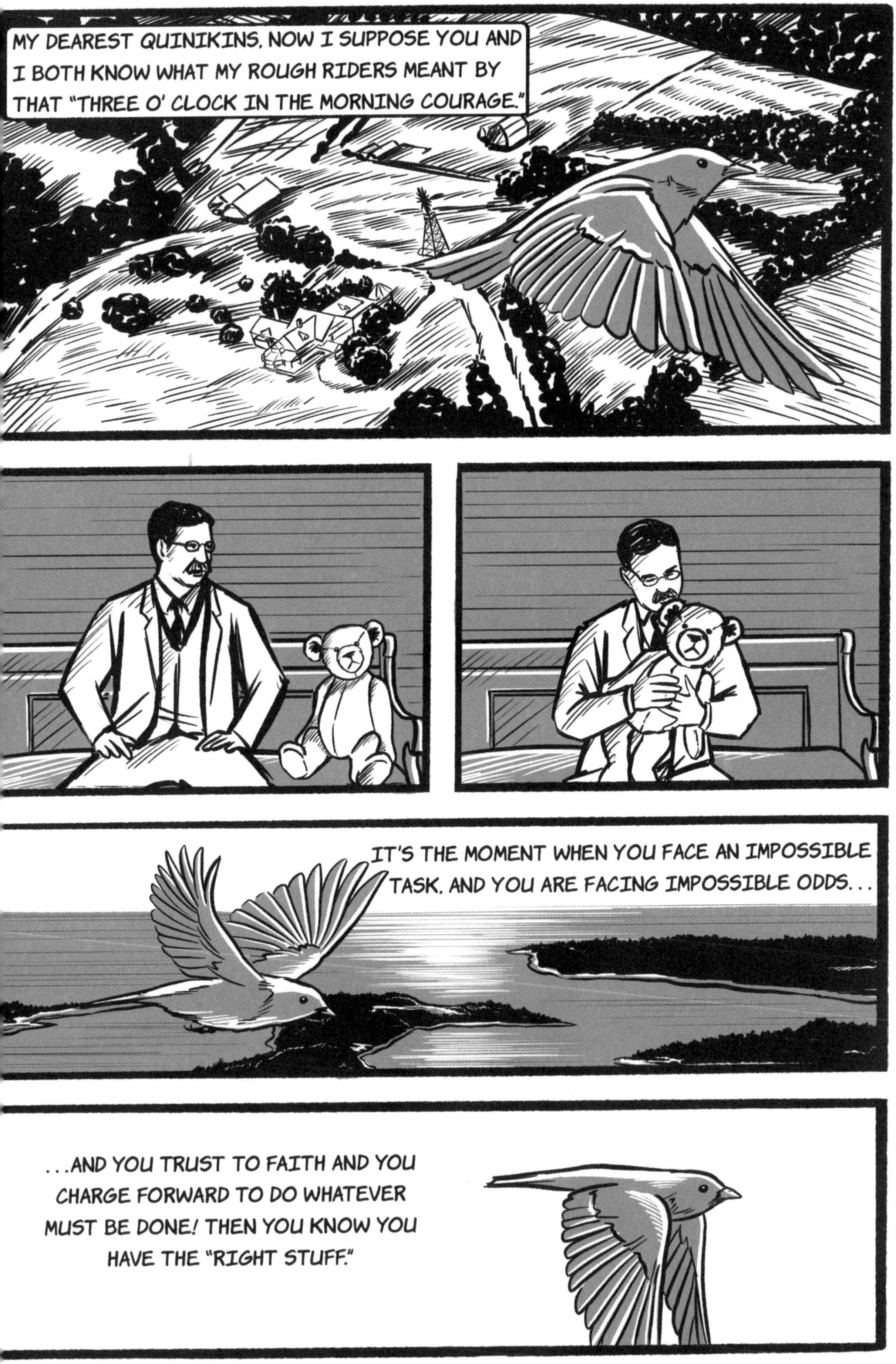
MY DEAREST QUINIKINS, NOW I SUPPOSE YOU AND I BOTH KNOW WHAT MY ROUGH RIDERS MEANT BY THAT "THREE O' CLOCK IN THE MORNING COURAGE."
IT'S THE MOMENT WHEN YOU FACE AN IMPOSSIBLE TASK, AND YOU ARE FACING IMPOSSIBLE ODDS. . .
. . .AND YOU TRUST TO FAITH AND YOU CHARGE FORWARD TO DO WHATEVER MUST BE DONE! THEN YOU KNOW YOU HAVE THE "RIGHT STUFF."

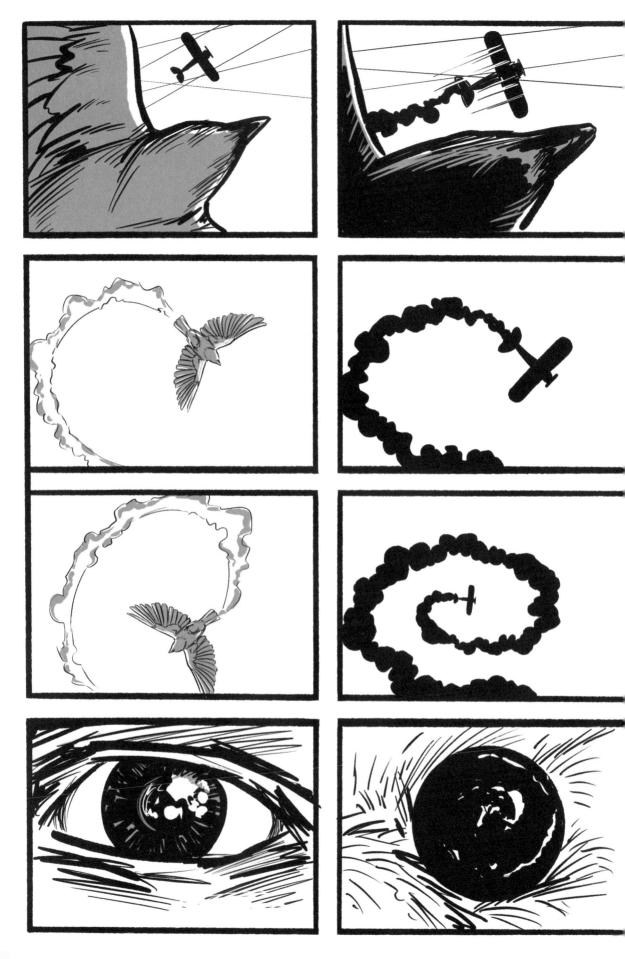

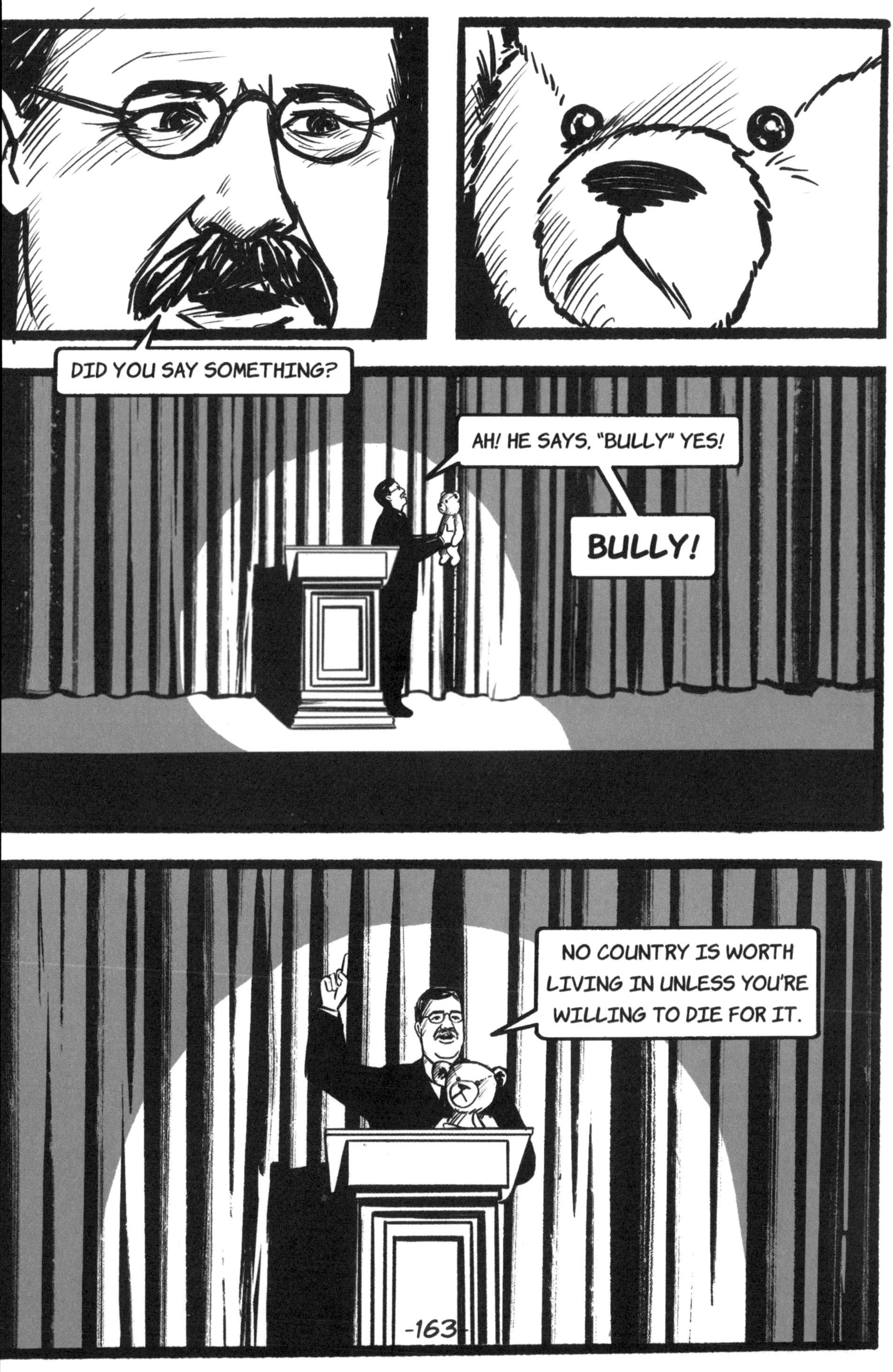
DID YOU SAY SOMETHING?
AH! HE SAYS, "BULLY" YES!
BULLY!
NO COUNTRY IS WORTH LIVING IN UNLESS YOU'RE WILLING TO DIE FOR IT.

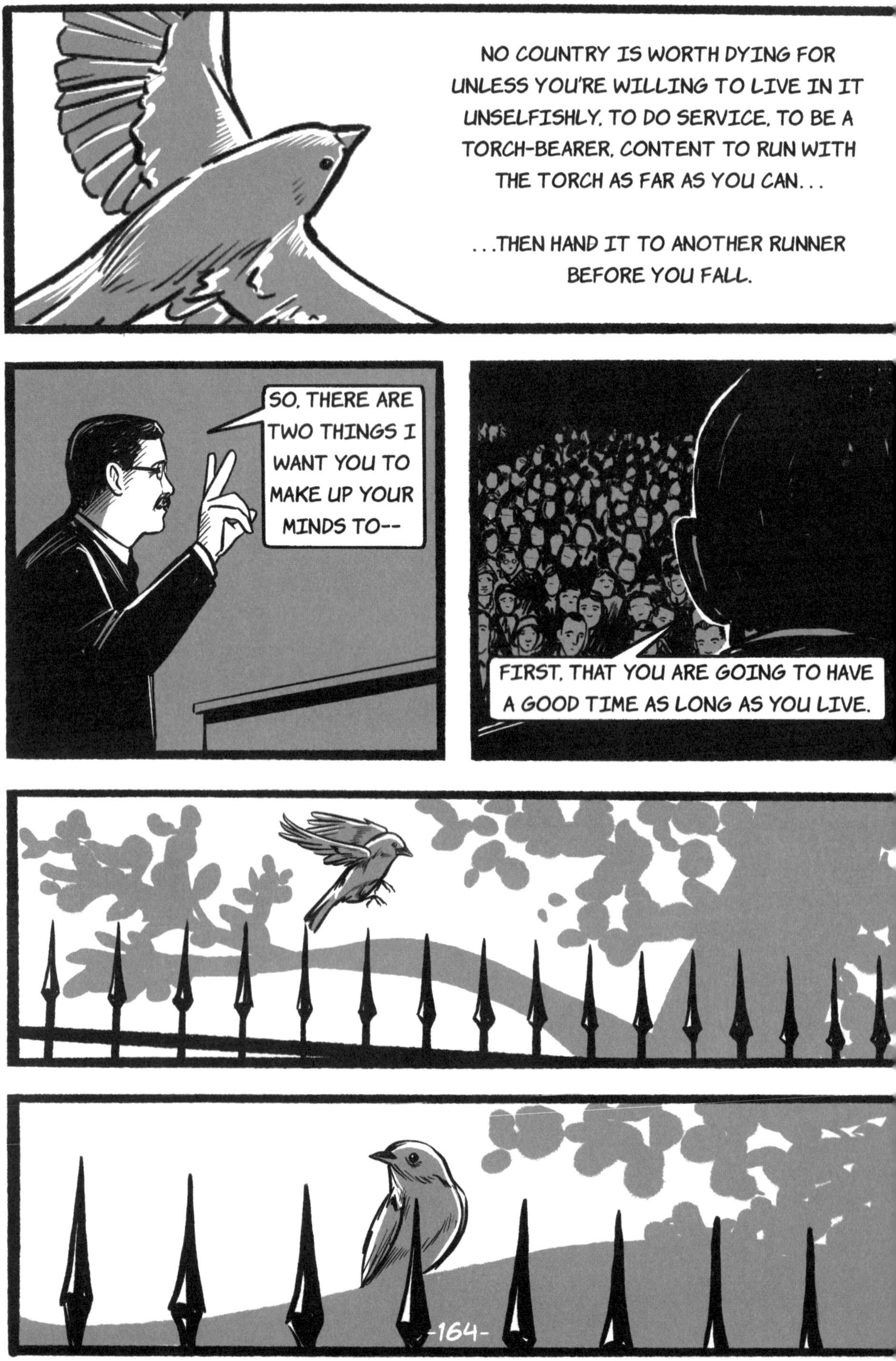
NO COUNTRY IS WORTH DYING FOR UNLESS YOU'RE WILLING TO LIVE IN IT UNSELFISHLY, TO DO SERVICE, TO BE A TORCH-BEARER, CONTENT TO RUN WITH THE TORCH AS FAR AS YOU CAN...
...THEN HAND IT TO ANOTHER RUNNER BEFORE YOU FALL.
SO, THERE ARE TWO THINGS I WANT YOU TO MAKE UP YOUR MINDS TO--
FIRST, THAT YOU ARE GOING TO HAVE A GOOD TIME AS LONG AS YOU LIVE.

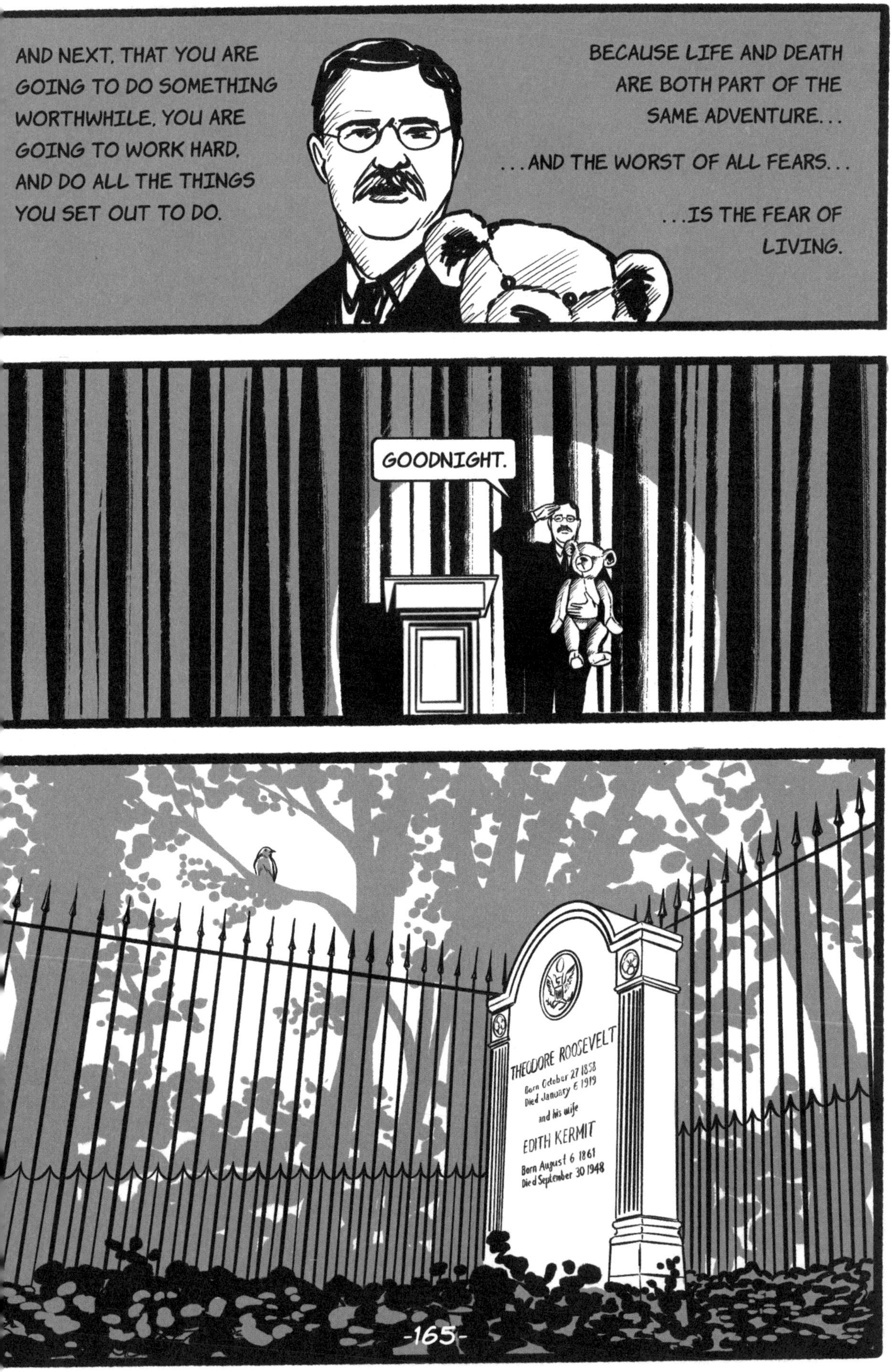
AND NEXT, THAT YOU ARE GOING TO DO SOMETHING WORTHWHILE. YOU ARE GOING TO WORK HARD, AND DO ALL THE THINGS YOU SET OUT TO DO.
BECAUSE LIFE AND DEATH ARE BOTH PART OF THE SAME ADVENTURE...
...AND THE WORST OF ALL FEARS...
...IS THE FEAR OF LIVING.
GOODNIGHT.
THEODORE ROOSEVELT
Born October 27 1858
Died January 6 1919
and his wife
EDITH KERMIT
Born August 6 1861
Died September 30 1948

AMERICA, AMERICA
GOD SHED HIS GRACE ON THEE
'TIL SELFISH GAIN NO LONGER STAIN
THE BANNER OF THE FREE

OH BEAUTIFUL, FOR PATRIOT DREAM
THAT SEES BEYOND THE YEARS
YOUR ALABASTER CITIES GLEAM
UNDIMMED BY HUMAN TEARS

AMERICA, AMERICA
GOD SHED HIS GRACE ON THEE
AND CROWN THY GOOD WITH BROTHERHOOD
FROM SEA TO SHINING SEA

THE END

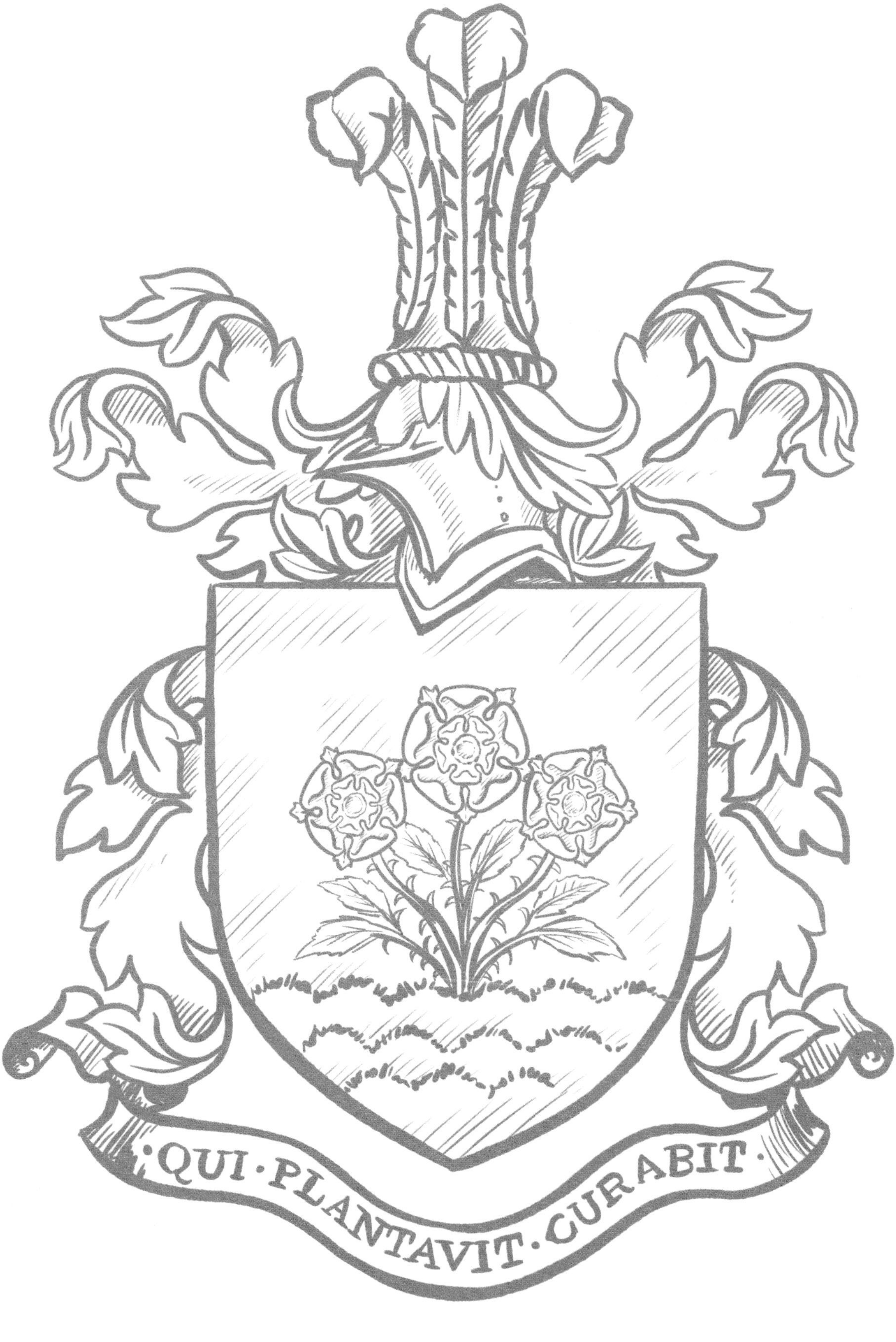
·QUI·PLANTAVIT·CURABIT·

ABOUT THE CREATORS

LAURENCE LUCKINBILL is a renowned actor, playwright, and director who has worked in television, film, and theater for decades. Well known as Spock's brother Sybok in *Star Trek V: The Final Frontier*, Laurence is an Emmy winning, Tony Award–nominated actor who has toured the country in acclaimed solo plays depicting the lives of Lyndon Johnson, Clarence Darrow, Teddy Roosevelt, and Ernest Hemingway. He has five children and lives in California with his wife, Lucie Arnaz.

ERYCK TAIT is a Brooklyn-based illustrator and designer. He works primarily in storyboarding and concept art for advertising as well as freelance illustration and fabrication. He resides in Bushwick with his wife, three cats, and one terrible dog.

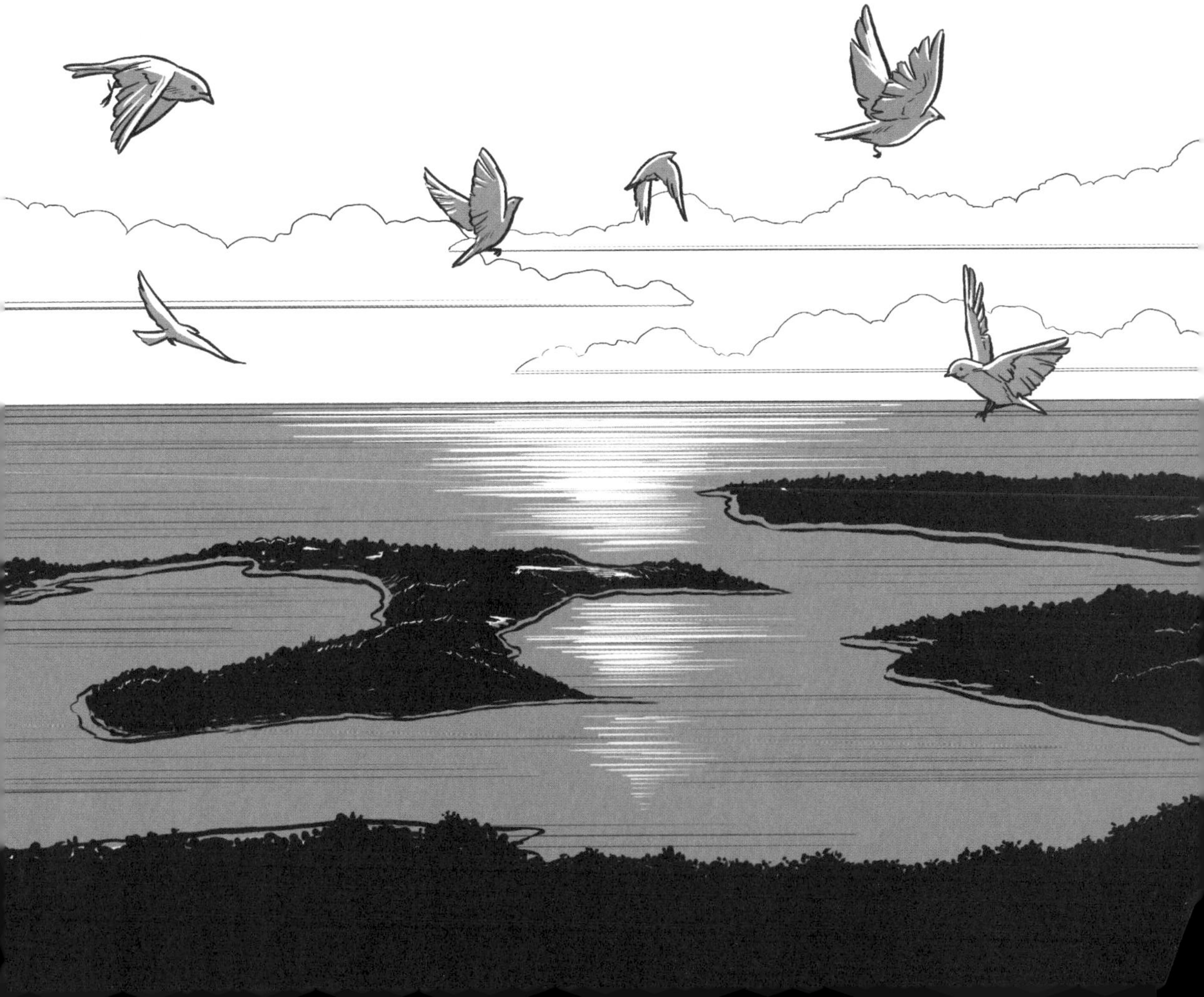